U-Boats
in the
Bahamas

Brick Tower Press
Habent Sua Fata Libelli

Brick Tower Press

Manhanset House
Dering Harbor, New York 11965-0342
Tel: 212-427-7139
bricktower@aol.com • www.BrickTowerPress.com

Library of Congress Cataloging-in-Publication Data
Wiberg, Eric
U-Boats in the Bahamas
ISBN 978-1-899694-62-4

1. Military History : World War II 2. Naval—German U-Boats 3.
Caribbean

First Printing, July 2016

U-Boats in the Bahamas

Eric Wiberg

For my wife, Alexandra, and son, Felix, with gratitude for their forbearance of a five-year obsession with U-boats. And for my father S. Anders Wiberg, for loaning me *The U-Boat War in the Caribbean* in my teens, and he and my mother for their interest, support, and education.

In memory of
Olaus Edvin Gamst Johansen

buried Cross Harbor, Abaco, Bahamas March 10th, 1942
&
David Parson

buried Anderson Settlement, Acklins, Bahamas, August 2nd, 1942
Though their graves are grown over, they are not forgotten.

By the same author:

- *Tanker Disasters*

- *Round the World in the Wrong Season*

- *Juvenilia*

- *Published Writing*

Contents

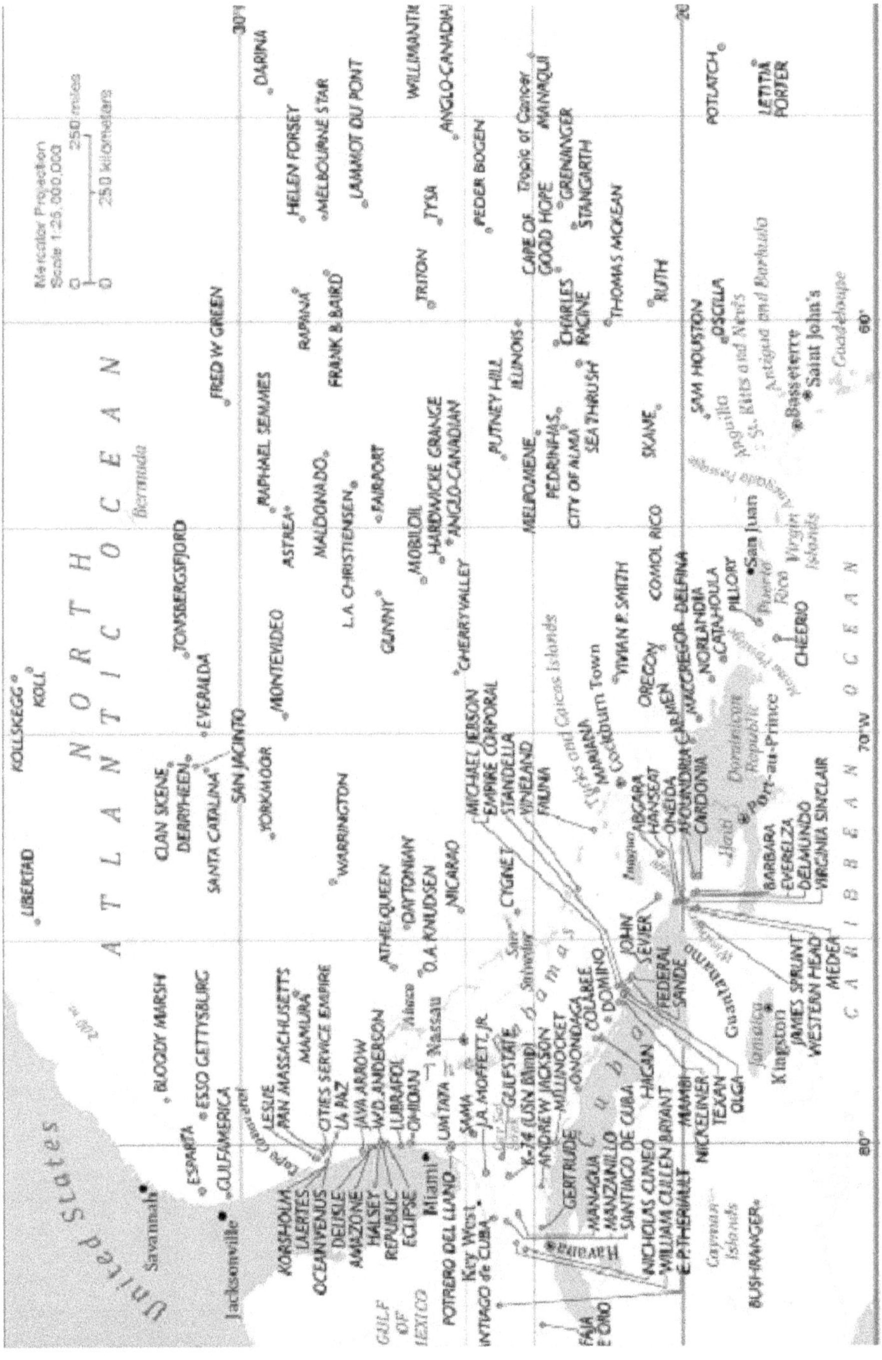

Mercator Projection
Scale 1:25,000,000

250 miles

250 kilometers

NORTH ATLANTIC OCEAN

CARIBBEAN OCEAN

GULF OF MEXICO

United States

Cuba

Bermuda

Turks and Caicos Islands

Virgin Islands

Puerto Rico

Haiti

Dominican Republic

Jamaica

Guadeloupe

Savannah

Jacksonville

Miami

Key West

Nassau

Havana

Cockburn Town

Port-au-Prince

San Juan

Saint John's

Basseterre

Tropic of Cancer

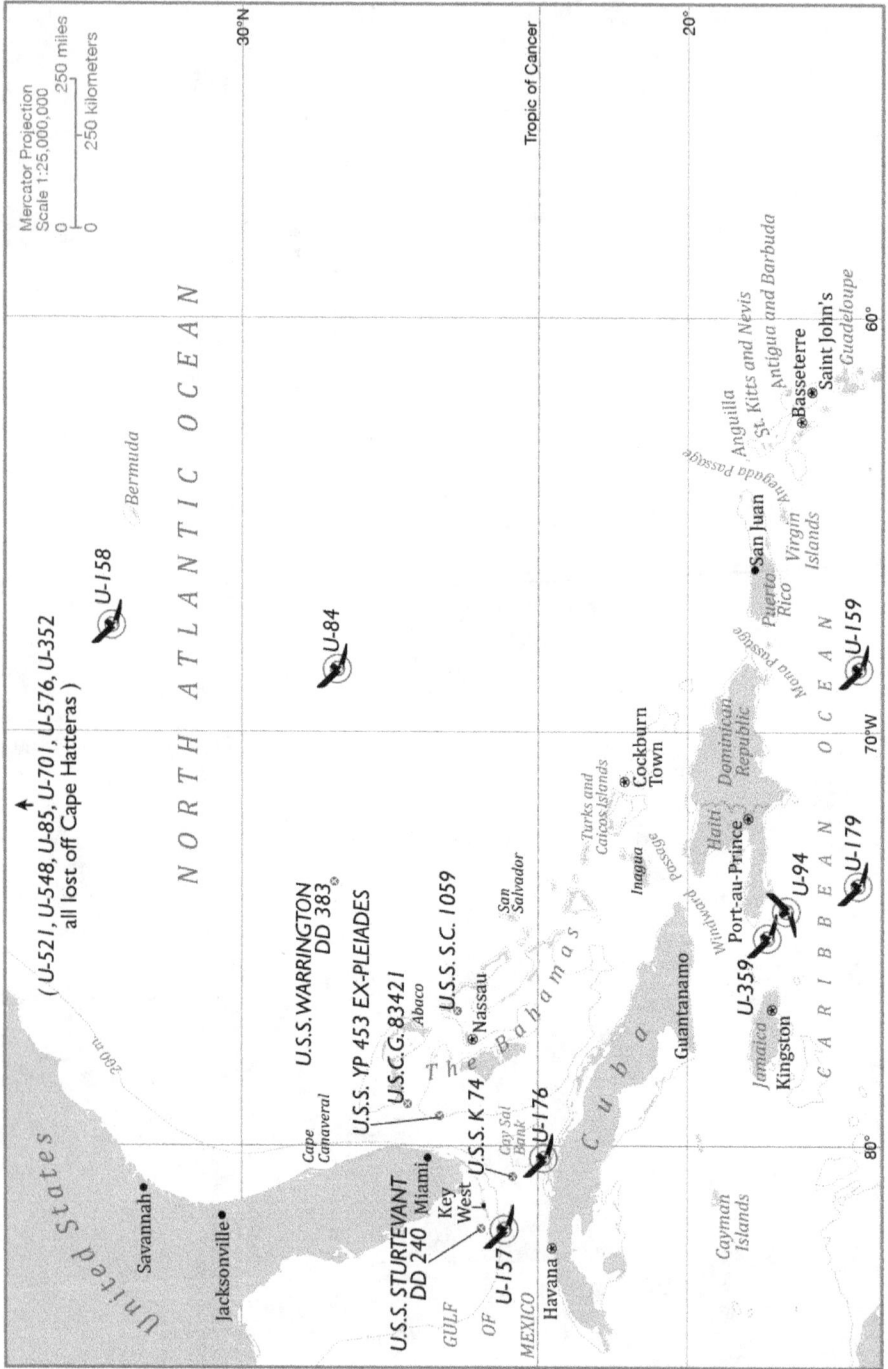

Mercator Projection
Scale 1:25,000,000
0 _____ 250 miles
0 _____ 250 kilometers

30°N

20°

Tropic of Cancer

Bermuda

N O R T H   A T L A N T I C   O C E A N

U-158

U-84

60°

Anguilla
St. Kitts and Nevis
Antigua and Barbuda
●Basseterre
Saint John's
Guadeloupe

San Juan●
Puerto
Rico
Virgin
Islands

Anegada Passage

U-159

Mona Passage

(U-521, U-548, U-85, U-701, U-576, U-352
all lost off Cape Hatteras)

70°W

Cockburn
Town

*Turks and
Caicos Islands*

*San
Salvador*

Dominican
Republic

Haiti

Port-au-Prince ●

U-94

U-179

Inagua

Passage Bosout

T h e   B a h a m a s

Windward Passage

U-359

C A R I B B E A N   O C E A N

U.S.S. WARRINGTON
DD 383

Abaco

U.S.S. YP 453 EX-PLEIADES

U.S.C.G. 83421

U.S.S. S.C. 1059

●Nassau

Guantanamo

Jamaica
Kingston ●

Cape
Canaveral

Savannah●

Jacksonville●

U n i t e d   S t a t e s

200 m

U.S.S. K 74 ●

Cay Sal
Bank

U-176

C u b a

U.S.S. STURTEVANT
DD 240 Miami●
West ●
Key

U-157

GULF

OF

MEXICO

Havana ●

*Cayman
Islands*

80°

PREFACE

The morning of Saturday 7th August 1943 began clear and calm, with good visibility from the bluff on which the town of Clarence Town, Long Island, Bahamas is perched. During the summer when school was not in session young Ancil Rudolph Pratt was able to take his father's horses out to pasture in the morning. He and his friends Wellington Smith, Kipling Simms, Jeffrey Strachan and Isaac Taylor liked to take the horses to the coast southeast of Clarence Town and enjoy playing on the seashore while the horses ate fresh grass.

Pratt remembers that it was a clear sunny day and the boys had made it to the bluffs around mid day when they all saw something so unusual that they remembered it to their dying days, and confirmed it by looking at photos later. They were several miles southeast of town on the bluffs. A boat of some sort emerged from the water about two miles out to sea. They could clearly see the "sail" or conning tower, but not any people on deck or on board. The craft was moving slowly and leaving a wake behind it. The boys could clearly see machinery on deck.

A semi-submerged U-Boat, such as Pratt would have seen U-732, without the men on deck.
Source: U-Boot im der Karibik, *Archive of Peter Tamn*

Judging from the comparative distance between telephone poles strung along the coast, which are spaced roughly 200 feet apart, they estimated the length of the vessel to be about 200 feet. After ten to fifteen minutes the submarine submerged, though a kind of radio mast was still visible. The sun was over their heads at midday, the submarine headed from left to right away from land, towards the southeast. The boy's backs were to the high bushes and trees. They watched the mast cutting through the water and heading away.

Asked whether he had witnessed a submarine in Bahamian waters during World War II, Mr. Pratt, a former insurance salesman in Nassau for 25 years who runs a shop in Clarence Town and is a well-respected member of the community, replied "it couldn't be nothing else." It also could not have been any other day – Sunday the boys would have been in Church and in weekdays engaged in either school or church. "This is not no story," he says, "I'm telling you I saw it with my own eyes."

Type VIIC German submarine, or U-boat, at the German Naval memorial, Laboe; 220 feet long.
Source: wikipedia.org/wiki/German_Type_VII_submarine

The channel off Long Island was used by eight German and Italian submarines in World War II: the Italian submarine *Finzi* and the German U-boats U-84, U-108, U-129, U-185, U-508, U-732, and U-751. U-84 had transited the Crooked Island Channel east of Long Island on the 10th of July 1942, and the British Admiralty reported a submarine spotted on the 22nd of July, which might also have been U-129 under Hans-Ludwig Witt, however the sub was described heading southeast (same direction as U-84) and Witt was heading back to Europe.

Neither can be verified with certainty, though possibly the sighting of U-84 was made on an earlier date by fisherman and reported on the 22nd when they returned. The source of the sighting was "Hardbargain South Side Long Island course South East." Hard Bargain was a largely abandoned salt harvesting community, also just south of Clarence Town Long Island. Given the certainty of it being a Saturday in early August 1943, it was much easier to verify the sighting by young Pratt and his friends.

Ancil Rudolph Pratt in his store in Clarence Town Long Island, early 2013. Born 11 April, 1934, he witnessed U-732 under Carlsen passing Clarence Town Long Island on 7 August 1943.
Source: Kevin James photograph, with permission of Mr. Pratt

On Saturday the 7th of August 1942 *Oberleutnant zur See* Claus-Peter Carlsen, aged 23, was conning his submarine, U-732 back to Brest, France. He was on the 58th day of an 83-day patrol during which he attacked Allied ships three times and was counter-attacked more often, first by two US Kingfisher reconnaissance airplanes, and another time driven away from a convoy by two American destroyers. On the afternoon of Friday the 6th of July U-732 put the north coast of Cuba

astern and passed west of Great Inagua in the southern Bahamas. At 10
pm local time on the 6th Carlsen noted his intention in the sub's log
book, or KTB, that he intended to take a winding course through
Crooked Island Passage as part of his return voyage.

By 2 am on Saturday U-732 was able to take a visual bearing on
Castle Island Light at the southern tip or Acklins Island. He noted that
the light was "shining peacefully and is very good for position-fixing." At
5:30 am the submarine submerged, having ventilated and charged its
batteries on the surface. By submerging it made itself less vulnerable to
detection and attack by enemy aircraft and ships, however their transit
of the winding passage was only about halfway completed. They would
need to verify their position before they were through. At 10 am they
were southeast of the coast of Long Island, and by early afternoon were
only seven or eight miles from land. If the submarine was on the surface
it would have been visible from an elevation ashore with 12-mile
visibility on a clear day.

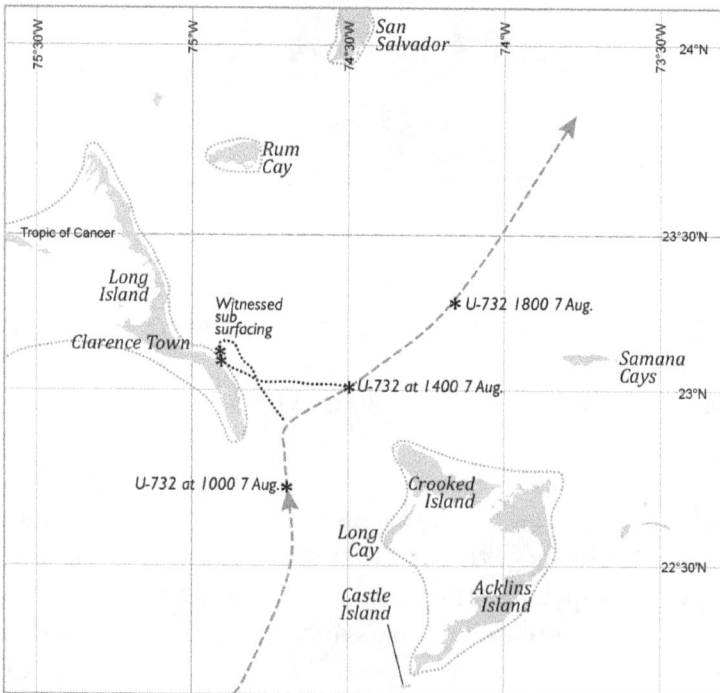

During the hours between 2 pm (it might have been noon depending on the time difference between Germany and the Bahamas), and 4 pm, when the sub was next reported east of Clarence Town, Carlsen did not record anything, whether he surfaced or not was not noted. Certainly the sub could achieve four times its submerged speed of about three knots, allowing it to cover substantially more ground. It is also possible that before crossing the wide Atlantic Carlsen wanted to visually verify his position, particularly to line up a safe passage between Samana Cay to the south and Rum Cay and San Salvador to the north. In particular there are two large, Spanish-colonial-style churches on the bluffs east of Clarence Town which would have served as reliable beacons enabling a captain to confirm their exact position.

*St. Paul's Anglican Church, Clarence Town Long Island Bahamas,
taken from the steeple of
St. Peter's Roman Catholic Church, with a view out to sea eastwards.
Source: home.comcast.net/~srweiss/bahamas05/roadtrip.html*

Whether Carlsen took the calculated risk of surfacing southeast of and out of sight of Clarence Town proper will not be known with certitude. He demonstrated in writing a propensity to approach landmarks and verify his position as recently as passing Castle Island Light some 12 hours before. The evidence suggests that five pairs of eyes witnessed the submarine indeed surfacing for a short time before heading east to break free of the shallow Bahamas and head back for Europe, where U-732 arrived on the last day of the same month. If so it would be the only verifiable incidence of a living witness having seen a German submarine patrolling in the region – one Saturday morning out of some 1,500 other days where the enemy prowled the watery region around the islands over the course of more than two and a half years.

Claus-Peter Carlsen, Commander of U-732.
Source: uboat.net/men/commanders/163.html

FOREWORD

Global conflicts first appeared in the 18th century after European nations, prompted by commercial, imperialistic, avaricious and sometimes religious motivations, had established out-posts and colonies around the world. The first world war began in 1739 with what the English felt would be a tidy little conflict in the Caribbean and Spanish colonies in Central and South America. With the excuse of avenging the Spanish mistreatment of an English merchant captain during which the Spanish summarily separated him from his right ear, the British launched the War of Jenkin's Ear. Their goal was to break the Spanish monopoly on trade with their colonies in the new world.

Things did not go as planned, the war in the Caribbean was a debacle for the British and Commodore Anson's eight-ship squadron that was intended to attack the Spanish on the West Coast of South America was decimated with only one of the eight ships able to carry the war around the world and return to England. When France joined Spain in the fight against the British, the tidy little War of Jenkin's Ear morphed into a global conflict known as the War of Austrian Succession. When the peace was hammered out for that world war, a fortress on an island on the Gulf of St. Lawrence was exchanged for Madras on the Bay of Bengal and the treaty included provisions impacting the British and Spanish islands in and around the Caribbean.

Exactly 200 years later, in 1939, another war began between European nations that would sweep around the world and penetrate all corners of the globe – the Aleutian Islands, the Channel Islands, the innumerable islands of the South Pacific and, yes, the islands in and around the Caribbean. In *U-boats in the Bahamas and Turks and Caicos*, Eric Wiberg gives us the first detailed, meticulously researched and documented glimpse of that "theater of war". Until the United States entered the war, the waters along the East Coasts of both North and

South America were protected by the Pan American Neutrality Zone and were "off-limits" to Axis warships.

Since the Bahamas and the Caribbean Islands were within this zone, there was a delay in the war's intrusion there. Other than the arrival in the Bahamas in October of 1940 of two sailors whose ship had been sunk 3,000 miles away and who travelled for 70 days to reach the Bahamas, those pleasant islands escaped the visible impact until the "invasion" of the U-boats. Despite the fact that these activities took place in a literal backwater of the war, the losses were felt just as deeply as those in the frontlines and the successes were just as sweet. Importantly, this book tells one more key part of the big story and is one more piece in the giant puzzle of the history of World War II. Its value for historians cannot be underestimated.

Throughout the stories of the attacks by German and Italian submarines on Allied shipping in the water around the Bahamas and the Turks and Caicos, several consistent themes emerge in Wiberg's thorough accounts. Prime among them is the heroism of the merchant mariners who time and again put themselves in danger as they performed the critical task of moving supplies, military and civilian, which were vital to ultimate victory. We see a Norwegian captain abandoning his stricken ship, yet courageously re-boarding her three times in attempts to save her.

We read of numerous instances of sailors having their ships shot out from under them and then continuously going back to sea and having additional ships torpedoed and sunk. We can also recognize what we know today as Post Traumatic Stress Disorder (PTSD), which was seldom recognized 75 years ago. We read the tale of a mariner who, after surviving three sinkings, is termed unfit for further duty at sea, takes a job ashore and is unable to talk of his experiences for the rest of his life.

Another consistent theme is the kindness and generosity of people ashore when distressed sailors reached land. Wiberg pays proper credit to the controversial Duchess of Windsor, whose husband was the wartime governor of the Bahamas. She readily took on her role as the leader of the Red Cross in the islands and personally greeted and saw to the well-being of many of the stranded sailors. Just as she carried out this official duty, this book relates the heartening tales of everyday

Bahamians, often poor and on outlying islands, who generously provided for these desperate castaways.

So often books about war are rife with man's inhumanity toward man. In this book, to be certain, lives are lost in the midst of the attacks or in their aftermaths, but there is also a consistent presence of gallantry. After the brutality of an attack, the submarines, German and Italian, moved among the crowded lifeboats gathering information to record their triumphs, but also asking if those in the boats needed assistance and providing information to help the survivors reach the nearest land. Wiberg also acknowledges the heroism of the Axis submariners as he recounts not only their victories but also their deaths as many of the subs were eventually tracked down and sunk.

Eric Wiberg has made a significant contribution to the bibliography of World War II history. His meticulous research allows us to relate to our heroes, even one with the colorful name of Capt. Bowleg. We follow them from the tense life aboard ship in a war zone, through the chaos of attack and sinking, and the ordeal of reaching safety. We know them as real people and we also know their attackers as real people. We also see the generosity of the people of the Bahamas.

History isn't great events, it is the continuum of many small events carried out by real people. U-Boats in the Bahamas and Turks and Caicos gives us an intimate glimpse of those events and, importantly, those people.

J. Revell Carr
Santa Fe, NM

INTRODUCTION

There were 112 German and Italian submarine patrols to and around the Bahamas and Turks and Caicos Islands during World War II. Of those, 54 submarines sank 130 Allied merchant ships. This is the story of a select 10 of those ships, and the 327 men who, in the effort to survive their sinking, made their way ashore and actually set foot on Bahamian and Turks and Caican sand. The book does not attempt to answer the larger questions – the why – of what happened. It seeks to depict, on the most human and personal level, what happened to those men and the people who welcomed them ashore. The perspective is not from 30,000 feet, but rather it aims to depict the action from arm's length. This is not an academic work, its purpose is to simply record and depict what actually happened, not argue any thesis. Because of censorship and the fact that most original documents are not kept in the Bahamas but overseas, little has generally been published about World War II in the Bahamas and Turks and Caicos, allowing fact to be supplanted by rumor.

The primary reason for writing this book is simple: a book covering the sinking of Allied ships by Axis submarines in the Bahamas in World War II has never been written. The closest analysis was Gaylord Kelshall's *The U-Boat War in the Caribbean*, whose focus was activity south of the Greater Antilles (Cuba, Hispaniola, Puerto Rico), and the US Gulf Coast. This study adds over 75 vessels to Mr. Kelshall's seminal work from the mid 1980's. U-boat attacks in the waters off Cape Hatteras have been treated extensively in *Operation Drumbeat* by Michael Gannon as well as *Torpedo Junction* by Homer Hickham and Gary Gentile's *The Fuhrer's U-Boats in American Waters*. Activities in the US Gulf Coast were covered by *Torpedoes in the Gulf* by Melanie Wiggins. The focus of this book is the sinking of merchant marine ships north of the Greater Antilles as far as Bermuda and East Florida out to Anegada and a bit beyond. Each sentence is meant to give the reader something new, and ever word is meant to be supported by fact.

SUMMARY OF AXIS ACTIVITIES

In early March 1942, the German Type IXC submarine U-128 under *Kapitanlieutnant* Ulrich Heyse came deliberately around Elbow Cay light, off Hope Town Abaco, heading south to the entrance to the Northeast Providence channel in pursuit of his prey, the Norwegian tanker *O. A. Knudsen*. Heyse wasn't the first U-Boat commander entering the greater Bahamas area looking for glory, nor would he be the last. In fact at least three U-boats preceded him. During the same week, Heyse and his crew shared the waters of the Bahamas with both German and Italian submarines. At the peak, on the 1st of July 1942, there were 12 submarines in the region: U-84, U-94, U-134, U-153, U-154, U-203, U-332, U-505 (now on exhibit in Chicago), U-507, U-571, and the Italian submarines *Finzi* and *Morosini*.

Over a three-year period, from 1942 to 1944, 88 Axis commanders would try their luck in the greater Bahamas area (defined as a line extending eastwards from Bermuda to Anegada). Seventeen of the submarines would not return to base. This is their story, chronologically outlined, to give the reader a sense of the depth of the invasion of these waters. It is the tale of 112 submarine incursions, by different skippers and in different boats with the same mission in mind: destroy as many Allied vessels – from schooners to tankers – in as short a period as possible and then return safely to base in France, Germany or Norway.

Between 21 January 1942 and 8 September 1944 there were 1,403 patrol days sailed in the region. Thirteen skippers made two missions into the area: Hans-Ludwig Witt, Günther Krech, Reinhardt "Teddy" Suhren, Hans-Georg "Fritz" Poske, Peter "Ali" Cremer, Albrecht Achilles, Friedrich-Wilhelm Wissman, Walther Kölle, Horst Uphoff, Günther Müller-Stöckheim, Ludwig Foster, Ugo Giudice and Günther Pfeffer. No skipper made three or more patrols to the region, though individual submarines made as many as four patrols into the area.

*Günther Müller-Stöckheim with his colleague
Carl Emmermann during a mid-ocean rendezvous between U-67 and
U-172 in mid-June 1942, in the Caribbean Sea.
Source: U- Boot- Krieg in der Karibik 1942-1945,
Gaylord Kelshall, U-Boat Museum, Cuxhaven*

A number of submarines made repeated patrols under different commanders. In fact, 16 submarines came back twice. Fourteen of those subs were German and two were Italian. One German submarine, U-518, made three patrols in the area. Only two, U-154 and U-129, came back a record four times. The Germans recorded every torpedo fired, and their records were captured by the Allies following the war. As a result, in most instances copies of the actual logs of each attack are available, on a reconstructed basis when the sub was sunk on the patrol.

As with anything, quantity of patrols does not equate to quality. An Italian submarine, the *Enrico Tazzoli*, made only one patrol there, but in the space of 10 days it attacked six ships, topping records of other boats which made repeated voyages to the same waters. The top five most successful commanders by tonnage sunk were Bauer, Witt, Suhren, Markworth and di Cossato, each with over 30,000 gross registered tons to their credit. The top eight submarines were U-126 with eight attacks on Allied ships, *Enrico Tazzoli*, U-129 and U-564 with six each, U-123 with five, and U-504, U-333, U-66 and the *Morosini* with four ships hit.

Submarines which patrolled to the Bahamas area in early 1942 had a much better chance of success than those on later voyages. This is due to the fact that during the early phase of the war for the United

States, their flank was largely unprotected. For a crucial time at the outset of 1942 the Allies were blind to the German signals intelligence: they could not read their daily fleet dispositions, as they were too well encoded. The Allies during this time were also unprepared: they did not have anti-submarine ships and planes, kept the coasts and lighthouses lit, and were not yet escorting in convoys slow and vulnerable merchant ships. By 1943 and 1944, Axis subs may have been able to spend more time in the region with refueling provided in mid-Atlantic and innovations such as the schnorkel, but they were harried almost around the clock by the Allies and had much more limited target selection.

These 112 patrols travelled into the area from various ports in France and Germany. Some of them went past Key West into the Gulf of Mexico or through the Windward or Mona passages into the Caribbean proper. It took a sub a week on average from first entering the region to transiting through the Bahama Islands. They utilized a number of chokepoints: the Northeast Providence Channel, the Old Bahama Channel, the Caicos Passage, the Crooked Island Passage, or the Straits of Florida. Because the Bahamas sit on a 10,000-square-mile shallow plateau, subs could simply wait at the channels like dogs around a dining table.

A submarine might enter and leave the region several times during a single patrol. Including both inward and outward transits, subs crossed the line between Bermuda and Anegada 170 times in either direction, 56 entered or left between Bermuda and Savannah, Georgia, 45 by utilizing the Windward Passage between Cuba and Haiti. Thirty patrols utilized the Anegada Passage which forms the northeast corner of the Caribbean Sea. Thirty sailed between Key West and Havana, and 26 used the Mona Passage between Puerto Rico and the Dominican Republic. Once inside the zone, at least 20 subs transited the Old Bahama Channel. Thirty-one used the Caicos Passage, 10 used the Crooked Island Passage, and a dozen the Northeast or Northwest Providence channels. Twenty-six used the Gulf Stream in the Straits of Florida.

Some submarines simply nipped the fringe of the zone by entering or exiting the Caribbean via the Anegada Passage, or circling Bermuda. Altogether each sub averaged 14 days in the area, including inward and outward voyages. The longest patrol in the region was 60

days, by Friedrich Markworth in U-66. The shortest was a single day, by
Mohr in U-124.

Johann Mohr of U-124, in a photograph taken during patrol.
Source: U-Boat Museum, Cuxhaven, from U-Boot im der Karibik

The 88 skippers who attacked the Bahamas area were an elite of
their corps. Forty six, or over half, were awarded the highest decoration
in the German Navy – the Knights Cross. A further 11 of them obtained
even higher decorations. Together they sank, in aggregate, 989 Allied
ships in the course of the war (most of them well beyond the Bahamas),
weighing a total of 4,998,476 tons of merchant shipping (Gross
Registered Tons– the weight of the ship itself, not including cargo). This
is an average of 10 ships and 50,000 tons per skipper. In the Bahamas
area specifically, the average was 6,670 tons and 1.5 ships per skipper,
per patrol.

    With respect to tonnage, one U-boat skipper mused that he
worked for the largest metal scrapping effort of the war, as their mission
was to demolish as much enemy tonnage as possible. Often, the carrying
capacity of a ship well exceeded its weight. So, when one factors in the
cost, time, material and infrastructure required to replace the tonnage,
the damage to the Allied war effort is exponentially much beyond nearly
five million tons of ships lost. This was particularly the case when one
considers that the United States was able to contribute the least to the
war effort, in early 1942, before Liberty Ships and naval craft could be
rolled off the slips in a matter of weeks if not days.

On the technical side, it is informative to know what model of submarine was most utilized in these attacks. The Germans used two designs in the Bahamas campaign – the Type IX model, accounting for over half, or 64 of the missions, and the Type VII in which 40 patrols were undertaken. The subs were Type IXC, VIIC, IXC/40, VIIB, IXB, and VIID. The Italians used four submarines of the Calvi Class, one Oceanico, and one Marcello class.

As weapons, the U-boats themselves need to be understood in the context of the men who manned them. The fact that most U-Boat commanders were killed on their very first patrol speaks of the extreme riskiness of this activity, despite the many months of training and preparation which the Germans invested in each commander. During the overall war from 1939 to 1945, the Germans trained 1,418 commanders who served aboard 1,156 submarines which entered service. Of these, 538 skippers lost their lives in the line of duty – in a service which suffered 66 percent attrition, the highest of any service on either side during the war fought by and against Germany.

A total of 863 submarines – or 10 times those that served near the Bahamas – saw action (the balance were used as training boats or were lost before they could engage the Allies). Any boat which made it to the Bahamas was by definition a front line boat in one of the elite flotillas. Most of them – 43, or over a third – sailed for the 2nd Flotilla based in Lorient in the Bay of Biscay. Twenty-one others set off from the 10th Flotilla's based in the same French port. Fourteen were in the 1st Flotilla based in Brest, six from the 9th Flotilla also in Brest, 10 were from the 3rd Flotilla in La Pallice, seven from the 7th Flotilla in Saint Nazaire, three from the 6th Flotilla in the same port. Seven patrols were represented by the Italian and German joint venture Betasom (standing for Beta for Bordeaux and Som for Somergibili, which means submarines in Italian). These were based in Bordeaux, France.

There were more than 112 departures for the region (a number of subs were sunk enroute), but only 95 successful return voyages. Seventeen subs, or roughly 15% were sunk after reaching the Bahamas area. Although the overwhelming majority of patrols set off from French ports, eight began in Kiel, Germany. These were mostly outbound boats which returned to the French ports, using a patrol to the Bahamas as a re-positioning voyage.

Three patrols had unusual endings – one submarine was damaged and interned in El Ferrol Spain, another returned to Flensburg, Germany, and a third to Kristiansand, Norway, which has been overrun by the Germans in April 1940 (though a fleet of roughly a thousand Norwegian ships managed to escape and was in the hands of "free" Norwegians). There were a total of nine ports in four countries – overwhelmingly France, Germany, Norway and Spain. It is interesting to note how vitally important the fall of France was to the German invasion of the Caribbean area, and how much less important the impressive coastline of Norway was to this particular effort. Had ports in Portugal, Spain or North Africa – or those in the Azores and Madeira Islands been available to the Germans, the results might have been more devastating. The decision of nations such as Mexico, Cuba, Uruguay, and crucially Brazil to abandon their neutrality and support the Allied war effort was due mostly to the German U-boat armed attacks on those nations' ships – a classic case of Germans shooting themselves in the foot.

The 1,156 aforementioned submarines sank 2,779 Allied merchant and 148 naval war ships totaling 14,119,413 tons and damaged perhaps nearly as many tons of shipping. Of these submarines, 630, or more than half, were lost at sea, 603 were lost as a result of Allied activities – attacks from the air or from enemy ships, depth charges, ramming, etc. In addition, 81 were sunk by mines or from the air in their home bases. Of the 1,418 commanders, nine died in accidents (such as mistiming a jump from the conning tower – a fate suffered by Mützelburg); four in suicides (including Carlo Fecia di Cossato of the *Enrico Tazzoli*); and a handful were court martialed and shot; shot by accident by sentry (Wolfgang Luth); or killed while a prisoner of war (one skipper ran into the camp barbed wire fully expecting to be shot – he was). One amongst them – Teddy Suhren – was awarded the Knight's Cross with Oak Leaves, Swords and Diamonds – an honor bestowed upon only 26 other members of the entire German military.

The commanders who attacked the Bahamas area earned their elite status and accolades – many of them awarded via radio while they were still on patrol for feats accomplished in the region – by the cold mathematics of the tonnage sunk. They sank Allied tonnage and remained alive – they killed more than they were killed. On average each skipper tallied 10 ships sunk – more than that if you include those ships damaged and returned to service. Submarines in enemy territory, like the Bahamas, rarely had the luxury of lingering to ensure the complete loss of each ship sunk, particularly in convoy actions where counter-attack was all but assured.

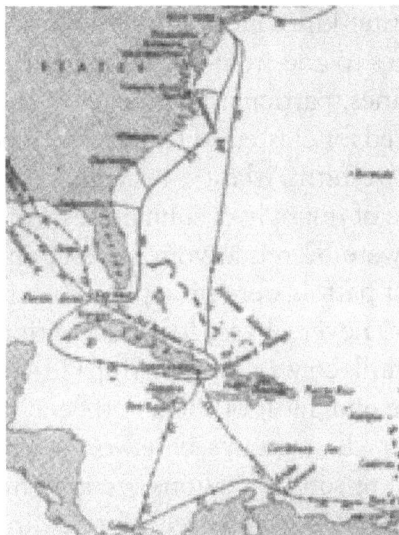

US convoy routes implemented from late May 1942 onwards showing transits around Bahamas.
Source: Samuel Eliot Morison,
History of the United States Navy in World War II

Considering that each submarine patrol lasted on average two months or more, a total 15% loss ratio for the operation was fairly low. This is why the German attacks on the Caribbean in general - and Bahamas in particular - were considered successful investments by the Germans. Of the 130 Allied ships struck by German or Italian submarines in the area, only four subs were lost in the area immediately adjacent to the Bahamas, as opposed to boats lost in transit to and from Europe, or in the Caribbean. Not one submarine was lost in Bahamian territorial waters throughout the entire war. The closest were off Cay Sal Bank and the Saint Nicholas Channel bordering Cuba, the Windward Passage, and in the Bermuda or Cape Hatteras areas.

Submarines were lost near the coasts of eight different countries. Two of them were sunk off the US, one off Key West and the other off New Orleans. Three were lost off Haiti, two off Bermuda, and two off Panama. One each was sunk off Cuba and the Dominican Republic.

Four were attacked and sunk in the Bay of Biscay and two off the Azores Islands whilst on return voyages. After the Allies instituted round-the-clock hunter-killer groups from aircraft carriers in the mid-Atlantic, the passages to and from the Bahamas became more perilous to the Axis submarines, particularly after the Allies targeted resupply submarines and waited for clusters of U-boats to appear. By comparison, Axis patrols in the western Atlantic became, relatively speaking, less dangerous. The issue of resupply of submarines while on patrol is easily overlooked. There were 82 rendezvous or resupply meetings meaning that on average most patrols were resupplied somehow.

Re-supply was never an easy logistical option. At the outset, the so-called *milchkuh* (milk cow, or mother-ship) U-boats were not readily available, and by the end, most of them had been targeted and sunk by the Allies in hunter-killer groups based on aircraft carriers in mid-Atlantic. Thus, most re-supply missions occurred from the latter part of 1942 to the end of 1943. The core of refueling was done by six submarines specifically designed for the task. U-459 took care of 18 submarines in the central Atlantic as they travelled either to or from the Bahamas. U-463 refueled nine subs, and U-462 supplied six. U-460 and U-461 provided fuel for seven vessels and U-488 for a further five. The Italians were, at least at first, the most active at rendezvousing with each other. The *Morosini* resupplied its colleagues twice, as did the *Finzi*. The *Giuliani* did so once, as did the *Da Vinci*.

Among the other reasons for rondezvous, some were just to exchange intelligence, parts, injured crew, or news. The Japanese submarine I-29, for example, met with U-518, which was on its way to the Bahamas. Two submarines received fuel during stops in Spain en route back to base. U-117 managed to provide fuel for three of her fellow submarines. Other submarines also interrupted their patrols to provide fuel or help to others in need. Most of the subs provided only a single exchange with other submarines on an *ad-hoc* basis. At least one of them escorted a damaged submarine back to base across the treacherous Bay of Biscay.

Lest the life of a U-boat commander seem overly grim, it is to be noted that at the time of writing, in mid-2015, no fewer than 13 of the commanders were still alive, including Reinhard Hardegen, the first one to enter the area in January 1942. Herbert Schulze, Wilhelm Schutze, Hans-Heinrich Giessler, Friedrich Markworth, Max Wintermeyer, Friedrich-Wilhelm Wissman, Rupprecht Stock, Richard Becker, Kurt Petersen, Hans-Jurgen Lauterbach-Emden, Claus-Peter Carlsen, and Günther Reeder were all alive. At this time, Hardegen was 101 years of age. Herbert A. Werner, author of *Iron Coffins*, was living in Florida until 2012 and strenuously denied that U-boat crew would have landed in the Bahamas, saying that doing so would have only provided unnecessary risk to all on board.

The demographic make-up of the commanders can be depicted by their relative ages. The oldest skipper to attack the region was Karl Neitzel at age 41, the youngest Hans-Werner Offermann and Claus-Peter Carlsen – both were 23 years of age at the time and were still alive. The average age of all skippers attacking the region was 28 years.

More than half, or 57 of the officers achieved the rank of *Kapitanleutnant*, 26 others that of *Korvettenkapitan*. A further thirteen were *Oberleutnant zur Zee*, and eight were *Fregattenkapitan*. The Italians had a different ranking system aside from Frigate Captain, though they shared in receiving German awards such as the Knights Cross for having served under *GrossAdmiral* Karl Dönitz. Three of the Italians were given the rank of *Capitano di Corvetta* and *Capitano di Fregata*. One was a *Tenente di Vascello*.

The 87 U-Boat commanders were members of long-range front line attack flotillas that led their boats on long patrols, sometimes reliant on refuel and resupply mid-way. The skippers were not only highly decorated and ranked at the highest levels, but they also returned home unscathed at a higher ratio than many of their compatriots. The kill-rate of submarines by Allied forces was comparatively low, particularly in the opening months which witnessed the most intense Axis attacks during which virtually no subs were sunk March-August 1942.

The period during which most Allied sinkings occurred was during the months when Axis submarine activity was at its highest and Allied defenses at their weakest. In March 1942, 21 vessels were lost; in April, there were 14; then in May, a further 23. In June a record 25 ships were sunk. By July the number was reduced to 11 and in August, 12 were sunk. During this six-month period, the Allies lost a total of 106 ships in the greater Bahamas region alone.

Most months saw only a small handful of submarines enter the Bahamas region, many of them in transit to other areas such as the Caribbean and US Gulf region. However, the March to August 1942 period, saw a spike of activity in conjunction with Operation *Neuland*, the wave of U-boats sent to the New World - following the immensely successful attacks of Operation Drumbeat in January 1942. In March 1942, six subs entered the area, mostly from the Cape Hatteras region, but in April this figure more than doubled to 15 incursions. Ten more followed in May, 16 in June, a dozen in July and 13 in August. After September 1942, aside from a spike in July 1943, when seven submarines entered the region, the numbers were low - zero to three patrols, per month. As a corollary, the greatest concentration of patrol days in the region again was in the period March to August 1942, reaching a high of 230 days in May. The peak was achieved in July, 1942, with 270 patrol days in the region that month. By October of the same year there were none.

This Axis tactic of intense attacks followed by periods of absence, was designed in part to throw – and keep – the Allied defenders off balance and in suspense. Arguably it was effective. Aside from simply sinking Allied tonnage, the U-boat offensive could be considered a success if it just bled valuable resources from the Allies towards a comparatively unimportant theatre of the overall war. In conclusion, it is clear that the U-boat skippers performed their missions admirably well in difficult circumstances, as they probed the Caribbean and the Gulf of Mexico in tandem with their Bahamas-related exploits. They sank more than they were sunk – they did their jobs.

PART I:

U-BOAT ACTIVITY 21 JANUARY TO 5 MARCH 1942:

From the outset of war to when the O. A. *Knudsen* was sunk on March 5th 1942 there were 10 ships attacked by German and Italian submarines inside the area bounded by Havana, Savannah, Bermuda and Anegada or just eastwards of that line. The first ship sunk in the region by any submarine in either world war was the US tanker *Pan Massachusetts*. It was destroyed by *Kapitanleutnant* Ulrich Heyse in U-128 on the 19th of February. He followed by sinking the *Cities Services Empire*, a US freighter, off Cape Canaveral three days later. Heyse was not the first Axis sub into the region. U-123 under the leader of the Operation Drumbeat boats, Reinhard Hardegen had dipped southwest of Bermuda on the 21st and 22nd of January. He was followed by *Kapitanluetnant* Günther Müller-Stöckheim in U-67 who simply ducked into the Anegada passage on the 11th of February. U-129 under Asmus Nicolai "Nico" Clausen, probed the eastern area on the 13th of February without sinking anything there.

On Valentines Day U-504 under *Korvettenkapitan* Hans-Georg Freidrich Poske, known as "Fritz" entered the area southeast of Bermuda westbound towards Florida. On the 22nd of February he sank the American freighter *Republic* off Florida, and four days later sent the Dutch gasoline tanker *Mamura* to the bottom. Sadly all 49 of the officers and crew, many of them Chinese, were drowned. On the same day, also northeast of Abaco, he sank the US ship *W. D. Anderson*. After rounding the north end of Grand Bahama and a probe of the coast of Florida near Cape Canaveral U-504 returned the way it had come, exiting the area south of Bermuda on 18 March.

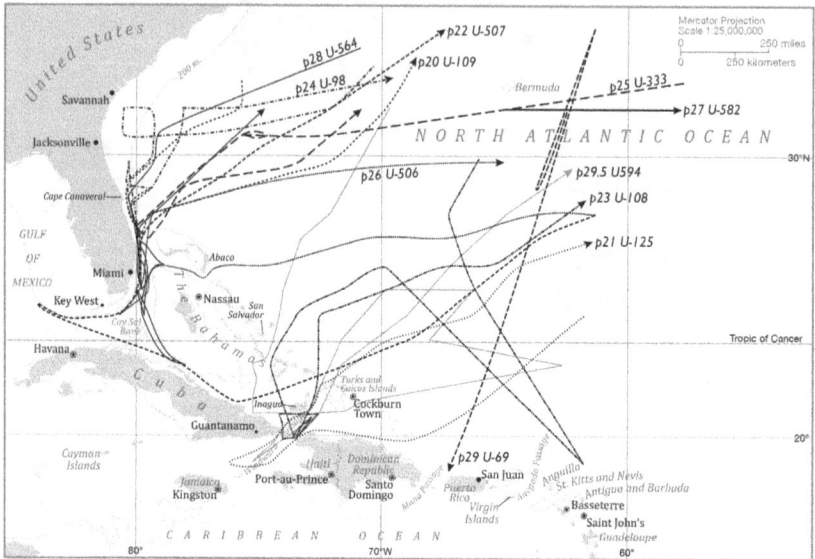

Next came U-156 under Werner Hartenstein on his way from the Mona Passage back to France on the 25ᵗʰ of February. Hartenstein and his crew were fresh from a bombardment of the Allied refineries in Aruba, where the barrel of his main deck gun had exploded and been sawn off. He sank the British ship *Macgregor* north of Puerto Rico and the Dominican Republic on the 27ᵗʰ of February and followed this the next day by attacking the *Oregon*, a US freighter, killing six. On the 3ʳᵈ of March Carlo Fecia di Cossato aboard the Italian submarine *Enrico Tazzoli* chased the British tanker *Rapana*, however the ship escaped.

On the 4ᵗʰ of March there was a report in the *New York Times* about campers witnessing a shelling attack on Mona Light, Mona Island, in the passage of that name on the 3ʳᵈ of March, however whoever attacked the island, it was not a German or Italian submarine, as none were in close proximity at the time, and none of them reported making such an attack. Probably this was an Allied vessel or aircraft having target practice without knowing that people were on the little-visited island at the time, and the incident has been withheld from the military records.

Meanwhile to the northeast U-126 under *Kapitanleutnant* Ernst Bauer sank the Norwegian ship *Gunny* on the 2nd of March, followed three days later by the *Mariana* just east of Mayaguana. Again – all the 36 officers and men were killed, though the ship sank a mere 27 miles upwind of the southern Bahamas, and several were seen alive by Bauer. Bauer continued a lengthy patrol in which he encircled the Bahamas, from the Windward Passage to off Key West, through the Northwest and Northeast Providence channels past Nassau, and then back northeast, exiting south of Bermuda on the 19th of March.

ULRICH HEYSE & U-128

It will be instructive to depict the life of a German submarine, or U-boat. On that basis U-128 was chosen as a demonstrative vessel, not only because its patrol east of Abaco resulted in the day-long attack on the O. A. *Knudsen,* and the burial of Seaman Olaus Johansen on Abaco, but because the boat's crew was captured almost in entirety and interrogated at length. The resulting 63-page report by the Office of Naval Intelligence (ONI) covers her war career – everything from manufacture to manning.

U-128 was first and foremost a fighting machine designed to sink as many Allied ships in its lifetime as quickly and efficiently as possible. Accommodations were made for sufficient men on board (between 48 and 56 men) to accomplish this. By all accounts accommodation on German submarines was far inferior in creature comforts than those of their American counterparts. U-128 was one of 54 Type IXC boats commissioned, and was built at the Deschimag AG Wesser shipyard at on the Wesser River in Bremen. Part of a series starting with U-125, other clusters of boat numbers in the same series were the ones starting with the famous U-161, U-171, U-501 and U-507, all of which were to prove active in the Bahamas area. IXCs got their name because they improved on the IXB type by adding 43 tons of fuel storage space and expanding the range to 13,400 nautical miles at 10 knots. They also had mine-carrying and mine-laying capacity, though this was never utilized by U-128. If so configured, subs in the series could carry 44 TMA or 66 TMB mines.

A German U-boat under way with officers and some crew manning the conning tower.
Source: William Gordonson, U-Boat Tactics of World War II

U-128 was ordered on the 7th of August 1939 and its keel was laid down on the 10th of July the following year. It was launched on the 20th of February, 1941 after roughly seven months of construction, and commissioned under the watchful eye of its first commander, *Kapitanleutnant* Ulrich Heyse, on the 12th of May 1941. He was to serve aboard her until the 28th of February 1943. The submarine was only ever assigned to the 2nd Flotilla, whose nickname was Saltzwedel, after a WWI commander, first as a training boat in the Baltic from its commissioning to 30 November 1941, then, after the fall of France, as a front boat in the same flotilla in France. Founded in 1936 and flying under the insignia of a submarine intertwined in an upright letter Z, the Second Flotilla (*Unterseebootsflotille*) was a combat flotilla which moved from Kiel to Wilhelmshaven to Lorient France from May 1941 onwards.

The Flotilla Commander at the relevant time was
Kovettenkapitan Victor Schütze, a holder of the prestigious Knights Cross.
Fegattenkapitan Ernst Kals, another Knights Cross holder, assumed
command from January 1943 to October 1944. There were a total of 91
U-boats of many types assigned to the 2nd Flotilla in the course of its
history, ranging in numbers from U-25 to U-1228. On the fall of France
in August 1944 the last U-boats left Lorient for Norway and the 2nd
Flotilla as it was ceased to exist.

What did the U-boat look like? To most it would have seemed
sleek, fearsome, and fast. It would have been painted a wartime grey,
with a pointed bow, gradually sloping forward deck which contained a
large cannon, and ended at the base of a conning tower. Some subs had
dragon-like metal teeth fixed to the bow and slanting back whose
purpose was to cut wires of submarine booms laid out by the Allies to
protect harbors. Others had aerial radio cables connecting the bow and
stern with the conning tower.

Since most U-boats did not have either radar or prior
intelligence on Allied ship and naval movements, they relied heavily
on the radio to receive intelligence on the movements of Allied convoys
and other Axis submarines, and to transmit reports of successes in the
field as well as requests for assistance and advice. It was not unusual for
a U-boat which required more fuel, torpedoes, or technical or medical
assistance to have a compatriot submarine vectored to it in order to assist
– without bases in enemy territory they relied upon each other and on
the centralized headquarters, called BdU (*Befehlshaber der Unterseeboote*,
for supreme commander U-boats), lead by Großadmiral Karl Dönitz,
based for most of the war in Chateau de Pignerolles at Saint-
Barthélemy-d'Anjou, France.

The conning tower looked like an upturned jar planted roughly
midway down the length of the submarine. Through this all personnel
entered and exited the interior, or pressure hull of the submarine, and
on it they obtained some protection from the wind, waves, ice and
breaking seas. The crew did have emergency hatches forward and aft
from which to escape, and there were torpedo-loading chambers forward
as well. The conning tower held the periscopes, which enabled the
commander to see above the surface without the submarine being seen,

as well as guns, mounted binoculars, firing sites, and air intakes for the diesel engines and ventilation system.

In terms of decorations on the conning tower, U-128 had more than most. Submarines, like their crew, were assigned flotillas and received recognition (pennants showing tonnage in numbers of each new merchant or naval victim flown from the wire says or radio antennas during and after patrols. Here is a list from the ONI report on U-128's insignia:

1   "White Horse. On both sides of the conning tower. It stemmed from the adoption of U-128 by the Organization Todt, which had a song about a white horse.
2   Coat of arms of the city of Ulm. Ulm was the city which had adopted U-128 and which had entertained some of her crew between the fifth and sixth patrols.
3   Olympic Rings.
4   Gray U-boat with streak of lightning across it. This is the flotilla device."

We learn from the ONI report that "As *Kapitänleutnant* Heyse was a friend of Todt, U-128 had been adopted by the O.T. [Organization Todt]. The crew had the privilege of visiting the pleasant rest home of the organization in the castle of Pongalec (phonetic spelling). This castle is five stories in height and is reported to be situated about 18 miles southeast of Hennebont. It is built on a level clearing in the forest and is said not to be camouflaged. The crew of U-128 had their farewell party here before sailing on their last cruise." Survivors of U-128 also spoke of "some fifty girls from the Paris office of the Organization Todt... " welcoming them ashore from patrols, and of being hosted in Paris and Germany by members of the organization.

U-128 was a Type IXC boat – and thus serves as a prototype of the vast majority of the submarines, called in German *unterseeboot* for "under sea boat," which were either Type IX, IXC or IXC/40. Though called a 750-ton boat (referring to its weight out of the water), this model displaced a total of 1,540 tons of water – 1,232 submerged and

1,120 on the surface. The length overall was 251.84 feet, and the length of the pressure hull, or cocoon around which the rest of the submarine was built, was 192.75 feet. The boat was 22.18 feet wide at its widest, and the pressure hull was 14.44 feet wide. The draft was 15.42 feet from the waterline, meaning that the sub needed at least 15-and-a-half feet of water between the sea floor and the sea surface to be able to move forward safely. This ruled out a lot of the shallow, reef-strewn banks of the Bahamas to a German submarine. From the waterline to its highest point above water the sub was 30.84 feet – this is called the air draft.

These U-boats achieved far greater speed and range on the surface – 13,450 nautical miles (a nautical mile being roughly 1.18 statute miles), at a cruising speed of 18.3 knots (or nautical miles per hour). The submerged cruising speed was only 7.3 knots. The power in horsepower under its oxygen-draft diesel engines (on the surface) was 4,400 horsepower, and submerged, on its quieter electric motors, 1,000 horsepower. This was provided by two Siemens motors of 500 h.p. each. The diesels were manufactured by M.A.N. and were of nine cylinders, and four cycles of 2,200 h.p. each. The nickname for the port diesel was HH or "Haw" and for the starboard Hott, or "Gee."

The engines kept the batteries – critical equipment – continually charged to the point that an emergency dive was always possible on the available charge. The batteries were lead-acid type with a capacity of 12,500 ampere-hours. They constantly needed to be recharged and the boat ventilated to prevent chlorine buildup which could debilitate or kill the crew (after the sub was sunk, U-128's Chief Engineer, though rescued, subsequently died of chlorine poisoning, as did other senior members of the engineering team). While cruising at its most economical rate, to and from a patrol area, the sub utilized both diesel and electric power to achieve six to seven knots. One diesel engine turned at 250 rotations per minute (r.p.m.), and one electric motor churned at 150 r.p.m.. These engines turned two propeller shafts, one on either side of the centerline. In order to escape being seen by enemy ships or from the air by enemy aircraft, or depth-charge bombs dropped by either, the submarines were capable of submerging 755 feet, though in extremes even this boundary might be pushed (over its life the U-128 is not believed to have dived beyond 660 feet).

In terms of armament the submarine was capable of carrying 22 torpedoes, generally broken down by 15 electric and seven air torpedoes. There were a total of six torpedo tubes – four forward (two each on either side of the bow) and two on the stern; one on either side. Though the stern-firing torpedoes were utilized in convoy actions, on solo encounters on the high seas they were generally reserved for firing a *coup-de-grace* shot to finish off an already damaged victim, when time and safety from enemy aircraft permitted. Since a submarine commander usually fired a spread of three to four torpedoes at a target, the average expenditure of U-128 on its first dozen or so victims was four torpedoes per sinking. The First Watch Officer (1WO, or second in command) generally fired the torpedoes when surfaced, and the commander, from periscope depth when submerged. Some 1WO's, like Teddy Suhren, gained recognition and awards for skill at torpedo attacks before becoming a commander.

The submarine's deck armament consisted of a 105-millimeter (4.1-inch) gun mounted forward of the conning tower, meaning that each shell was over four inches in diameter. The incendiary shells could be over three feet in length and weigh over 110 pounds. They had to be relayed by hand up from a locker below in the submarine, except for an emergency supply kept in a small locker embedded in the conning tower. Other gunnery on board the submarine consisted of a 37-millimeter (1.5-inch-diameter) anti-aircraft gun aft on the conning tower, as well as another 20-millimeter anti-aircraft cannon located aft on the bridge platform. This was supplemented by four C-38 machine guns also on the bridge, which could be mounted and un-mounted as the need arose (in other words the submarine would not submerge with them in place except in cases of emergency). When time permitted the deck guns were greased periodically and caps inserted in the barrels before each submersion, and they were aligned with the hull to reduce drag.

Kapitanleutnant Ulrich Heyse was born in Berlin-Friedenau on the 27th of September in 1906 and thus aged 34 at the time of U-128's commissioning, and 35 when he patrolled the Bahamas (he would survive the war and live to 1970 and the age of 64). A member of the Crew of 1933, he sank 12 ships for 83,639 tons over his career, which is the same tally for U-128 since he was one of only two commanders of the sub and the only one to confirm sinking enemy ships on her. (His successor, Hermann Steinert was seen as much more hesitant and was, according to survivors, much less liked than Heyse).

Survivors of U-128 who had served under him described Heyse to their captors thus: "He was popular with his crew; on occasion he would sit down with the kitchen detail, whip out his pocket knife and while peeling potatoes would talk about and discuss with crew members any subject which interested them. He also would now and then have several glasses of beer with his crew, when on shore. No doubt, his leadership contributed to the success of U-128 while under his command; most prisoners expressed their belief that U-128 would not have met with its fate on May 17, 1943, had Heyse been its commander. ...prior to his entry into the German Navy, had served on merchant ships."

"To this background many of his men attribute the sympathetic attitude of Heyse toward crew members of torpedoed ships. Foodstuff, cigarettes, and even rum, if necessary, were supplied, and in more than one instance Heyse explained that he was sorry that his duty compelled him to sink their ships. While in the navy, Heyse had served as executive officer on a destroyer and had made a cruise as commander pupil in another U-boat."

Ulrich Heyse of U-128
Source: uboat.net

After learning that the *O.A. Knudsen* had been built in Germany Heyse remarked that her builders must have "accounted for her slow sinking." Ulrich Heyse rose from *Offiziersanwärter* in 1933 to *Korvettenkapitän* on 1 April 1943. Having served in the merchant marine, he then went to the surface fleet of the Kreigsmarine, serving on the destroyer *Theodor Riedel*. During 1939 – 1940 Heyse undertook 12 patrols on the *Riedel* before transferring to U-boats in July. His first U-boat was U-37, which he led on one short (non-offensive) patrol as *Kommandantenschüler* (commander-in-training). Over his career he served 311 war patrol days over five war patrols, all of them in U-128.

In 1940 Heyse was awarded the Iron Cross 2nd Class, and on the day he returned from the Bahamas patrol this was increased to 1st Class. The same day (March 24, 1942) he also received the U-Boat War Badge of 1939. Roughly half a year later, based on a reported tonnage of 98,000 tons (actually it was 83,639 which is not as much of an exaggeration as some other skippers'), he received the Knights Cross of the Iron Cross, one of the highest awards of the German military, making him a Knight of the Wehrmacht. To give an idea of the rarity of this award, he was only the 143rd recipient in the Kriegsmarine and the 78th in the U-boat arm at the time he received it, in recognition of "extreme battlefield bravery or successful military leadership."

In March 1943, a year after his return from the Bahamas, and after two patrols to Brazil, Heyse moved ashore to become an instructor in U-boat learning divisions called *Unterseebootslehrdivision*. Two years later, in March of 1945 he rose to command the 32nd (training) Flotilla. The war would end within two months and Heyse would survive it.

The executive officer of U-128 from commissioning to her Bahamas patrol was *Oberleutnant* Helmut Kurrer, who graduated in the Crew of 1935. He was born on 16 February 1916 and was thus ten years junior to Heyse and turned 26 during the patrol (three days before the sinking of the *Pan Massachusetts*). He rose through the ranks from Midshipman in 1936 to *Korvettenkapitan* in 1943. On 15th August 1942, less than five months after returning from the Bahamas patrol, Kurrer was promoted to commander of U-189. Within a year he and the crew would be lost south of Greenland's Cape Farewell on 23rd April, 1943, a mere 21 days into the submarine's first patrol. He received no decorations during his career, which seems odd since Rolf Bahn, who was Second Watch Officer beneath him, was awarded the U-Boat War Badge 1939 on arrival back from U-128's patrol to the Bahamas.

The Second Watch Officer, or third in command, on the Bahamas patrol, Bahn succeeded Kurrer to the 1WO or First Watch Officer role on the third patrol. Bahn was born on 6 March 1918 in Rustringen – he celebrated his 24th birthday the day after the sinking of the O. A. *Knudsen*. Starting as an *Offizieranwarter* in 1935 (he was a member of the Crew of 1936), Bahn rose to command two submarines, U-1235 and U-876 at the end of the war. However neither submarine went on a war patrol, and perhaps as a result Bahn survived the war. In September 1942 he earned the Iron Cross 1st Class, and in August 1943 Bahn was promoted to *Kapitänleutnant*. He is believed to be alive at the time of this writing,

The names of every crew member during U-128's patrol to the Bahamas in March 1942 are not known, and crew changed at least incrementally after each patrol, due to attrition, rotation, and promotion, as well as the need to mingle greenhorns with more experienced crew. However a full list of the crew, which consisted of 54 persons, when it was sunk off Brazil on May 17, 1943 was compiled by the ONI. The crew was composed of four officers, three midshipmen, 16 petty officers, and 31 enlisted men. This list can be seen as representative of what the crew composition would have been like on the patrol to the Bahamas.

There were two lieutenants in their mid-20s, an Engineering Lieutenant, three Midshipmen, a Reserve Ensign, two Boatswain's mates (Bosun, or petty officer), six Machinists or Machinist's Mates, two Radiomen, one Coxswain, a Torpedoman's mate, 12 Firemen (engine room crew) and 12 Seamen (deck crew). The junior ratings ranged in age from 18 to 26.

A summary of the early career of U-128 before its Bahamas patrol is germane to illustrate the typical life of a German submarine. Two months before the boat's commissioning most deck and engineering officers arrived to closely follow the final fitting out of their charge. Seamen and torpedo ratings followed closer to the take-over date. Two days after commissioning, on the 14th of May 1941, the submarine transited the Kaiser Wilhelm Canal to Kiel, where it passed its tests for U-boat Acceptance command in roughly three weeks. Once accepted

U-128 moved to Warnemeunde for torpedo practice, then Stettin for a final overhaul, taking about a month. The crew was allowed ten day's leave during this period. In early July 1941 U-128 under Heyse sailed for Oslo for diving tests, however it struck an uncharted rock and was seriously damaged, ripping open its bottom and damaging the starboard torpedo caps. After 25 of the crew were taken of by the light cruiser *Nurnburg* and the boat was towed off the rock by the depot ship *Odin*, the sub received emergency repairs in Horten, Norway. Historian Clay Blair Jr. notes that Heyse, "...a one-time merchant marine officer, was one of the most mature and experienced ship handlers in the submarine force. He survived the court of inquiry and retained command."

Returning to Kiel for repairs, it was decided to undertake the diving tests in the Baltic instead. These took place in Gotenhafen near Danzig and off Hela. By November 1941 the boat moved to Bornholm for silent running tests before returning to Stettin. In Stettin torpedoes and supplies were loaded and then U-128 sailed for Kiel. Her first patrol, to her new base in the 2nd Flotilla in Lorient, began on the day after the Japanese attacked Pearl Harbor, but a day before Hitler declared war on the United States on the 9th of December 1941. On the night of the 9th U-128 arrived in Kristiansand, Norway, where most of the crew were accommodated ashore in a hotel. The following morning the sub was escorted two hours out of the port on its first war patrol. Heading between the Faroes and Shetlands islands, U-128 encountered an Allied trawler at which it fired a torpedo. Suspecting that the trawler was a trap, and failing to hit it with the torpedo, the submarine continued on its course, mostly on the surface, right into the Bay of Biscay.

Just after noon on Christmas Eve, 1941, U-128 arrived in Lorient at 8 am and was escorted by minesweepers to the *Salzwedel Kaserne* (a bulkhead) for four hours, arriving at noon. No Allied aircraft or enemy ships were sighted during the entire 13-day patrol. The US interrogators surmised that "....it may well be assumed that the quick trip was partially due to the desire on everybody's part to celebrate Christmas on land." Between 24 December 1941 and January 8th, 1942 U-128 was supplied and provisioned. Her torpedoes were all offloaded, checked, and re-loaded. A lighter (barge) came along side and pumped diesel oil aboard, and provisions were loaded for an extended patrol to the Americas. On the 8th of January a minesweeper and two patrol boats escorted her into the Bay of Biscay, starting at 11 am. The crossing of the Atlantic was apparently uneventful, probably punctuated by a series of diving drills.

U-128's patrol in the Bahamas region lasted 24 days in sum. Beginning on the 13th of February, the submarine entered the area by crossing a line between Bermuda and Anegada. In fact Heyse came quite close to the southeast coast of Bermuda, possibly using Saint David's Light located there as a navigational "fix," as it is visible for up to 20 nautical miles (given his later experience of being attacked by aircraft from Bermuda, Heyse would do well to give the island a wide berth). On the 14th of February U-128 turned south for a day, then turned back east-southeast, leaving the area briefly on the 15th and performing a kind of patrol line south of Bermuda. On the 15th the boat reversed course and motored due west for the next four days, passing north of Abaco and Grand Bahama and arriving off the coast of Florida near Cape Canaveral on the 18th of February.

On the following day, slightly to the north of Canaveral, U-128 made the first kill of the war off the Florida coast when it sank the US tanker *Pan Massachusetts*. From there the boat headed southeast across the Gulf Stream, finding no targets. It returned to the coast of Florida and three days later sank the *Cities Services Empire*, also off Canaveral. U-128 again headed southeast, to the north of Walker's Cay, before returning to the Florida coast. It patrolled off Florida fruitlessly for a week, from the 22nd of February to the 3rd of March. On the 3rd the submarine made a feint to the northeast towards Bermuda before turning south towards the Northeast Providence Channel, aiming for shipping coming out of the Straits of Florida for Europe. On the 4th it rounded Abaco for its fateful encounter with the *O. A. Knudsen.*

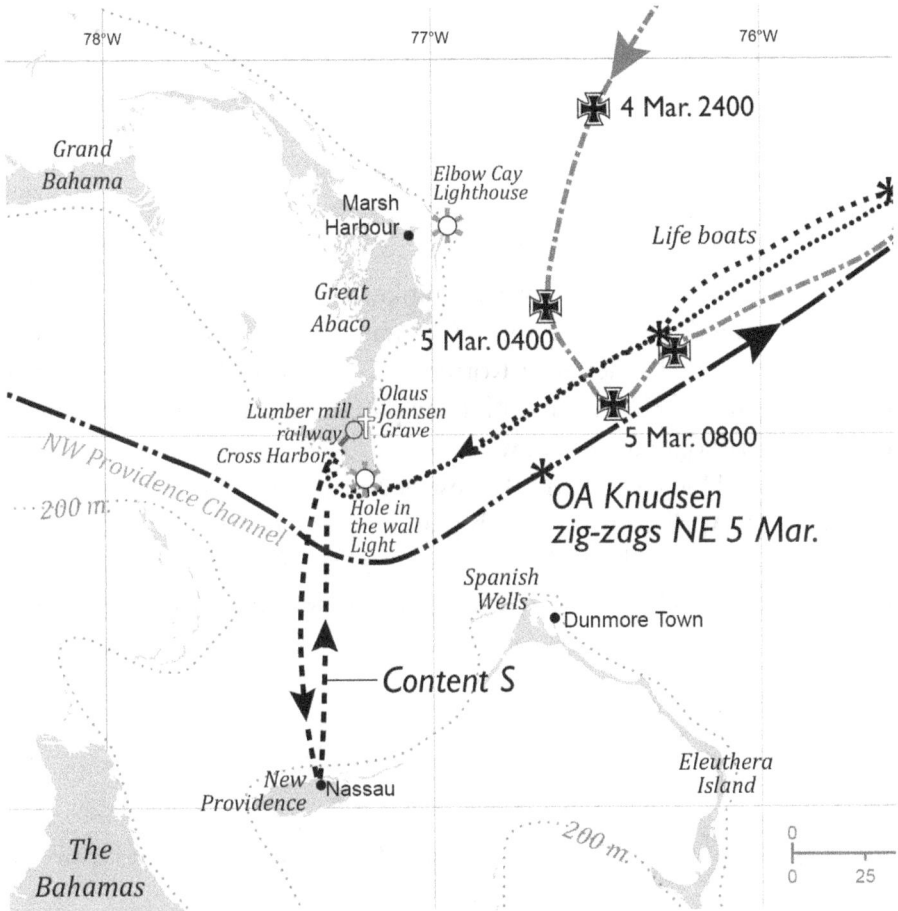

O. A. KNUDSEN

The 11,007-ton Norwegian tanker O. A. *Knudsen* was built by the Deutsche Werft in Hamburg Germany in August 1938. She was commissioned by Unilever of Rotterdam, however, the Knut Knutsen OAS company of Haugesund, Norway purchased the completed ship – the firm is still operating today.

Once Haugesund and the rest of Norway were occupied by Nazi Germany in April 1940, ownership and control of the O. A. *Knudsen* was assumed by the Norwegian Shipping and Trading Mission, (also known as Nortraship) who then put her under charter to the British

Tanker O. A. Knudsen, *like its captain of Haugesund, Norway*
Source: Kristian Olav Bringedal, from an article in Uskedalposten, Side 18, Krigsseglarane frå

Tankers Company of London. There were four tankers with the name O. A. *Knudsen*, and her predecessor had also been attacked by a U-boat, during the First World War. There was another O. A. *Knudsen* launched by Gotaverken of Sweden in January 1951 which was 11,051 gross tons. She sailed until 1960, meaning that from 1907 to 1960 – 53 years – there was almost always an O. A. *Knudsen* sailing the world's seas. The O. A. *Knudsen* of World War II was 508.1 feet in overall length, 60.2 feet wide, and 36.5 feet deep. She could carry 16,150 deadweight tons of liquid cargo. She was powered by a seven cylinder M.A.N. Diesel engine of 4,500 horsepower which propelled the ship at an impressive 13 knots.

O. A. *Knudsen's* Master was Captain Knut Olasen Bringedal, and under him were 39 men, of whom 29 were Norwegians, five were British, three were Estonian, one was Latvian and another was Canadian. The crew subsequently told interviewers that they were a close-knit unit, most of them having been together since the fall of Norway.

Captain Knut O. Bringedal of the O. A. Knudsen
Source: Photo courtesy of Kristian O. Bringedal,
a relative of Capt. Bringedal

Bringedal was born in Kvinnherad, Uskedalen, between Haugesund and Bergen on the west coast of Norway, on the 5th of January 1894 and was 36 at the time. He had joined the O. A. *Knudsen* on the 24th of March 1939 – nearly three years previously – as Mate and risen to Captain. The ship was in Naples, Italy when the men learned of the fall Norway. To escape from Italy, they pumped the cargo tanks full of seawater to act as ballast and made a bold run for Gibraltar and the open Atlantic on the 9th of April. They had almost made it when a French naval patrol boat intercepted them and escorted them to the French North African port of Oran, where they wallowed for about a month, from 12 April to 16 May, 1940.

*Captain Bringedal hosting and a fellow officer (left) an ship's agent (right)
aboard one of his earlier commands.*
Source: Photo courtesy of Kristian Bringedal, nephew of Capt. Bringedal

Finally the ship made her way to Suez and ultimately Melbourne,
Australia, under the ownership of Norwegians and control of the British.
She made two trips to Australia, five more to the British West Indies,
and was on her second trip to England in March of 1942 when attacked
off the Bahamas. Not all of the crew had been on board since 1940.
Messman Barleif Hårstad fled the Nazi occupation by leaving Tromsø
for Svalbard in June 1940. In September 1941 he was evacuated to
England. Waldemar Lund was born in Søgne, on the very southern tip
of Norway, on the 30th of June, 1916. At the age of 25 he and four other
young men decided to escape from Norway in a small open boat to join
the merchant navy in the United Kingdom.

After leaving on the 26th of September 1941, the men
encountered a three-day storm on the Dogger Bank in the North Sea,
and two of them were washed overboard and pulled back in. Since their
little five-mile-an-hour motor failed them, they had to sail much of the
way. The voyage took a total of ten days. On the 6th of October, they
were sighted by a coastal boat off England and taken to shore. They
received marksmanship training in Dumbarton, Scotland.

Following this, Lund sailed to Canada, where he received further
training as a gunner. He met the *O. A. Knudsen* in Halifax following

her voyage from Aruba. The ship had sailed independently laden with petroleum between the 13th and 20th of December, probably utilizing the Windward Passage and Crooked Island Passage through the Bahamas. They arrived in Glasgow on the 10th of January 1942 and stayed until the 23rd – long enough to sign aboard another Norwegian sailor with a story to tell – Olaus Johansen.

Olaus Edvin Gamst Johansen was born on the 24th March 1884 on Måsøy, or Seagull Island, in Finnmark County, in the remote far north of Norway at nearly 71 degrees north. At the outset of war, Olaus went to the even more distant Svalbard archipelago, which stretches as far north as 81 degrees. There he gained employment as a miner. By then he was 55 years old and his wife had died, leaving him to support five children. After a British raid on the island between August 25 and September 3rd 1941, Johansen decided to emigrate to England and escape the Nazi occupation.

Olaus Johansen and his three sons, Norway, late 1930s
Source: Rebecca Mason, great-granddaughter of Olaus Johansen, UK

Johansen arrived in the UK on the 10th of October, 1941. Three months later, on the 12th of January, 1942, he signed aboard the O. A. *Knudsen* in Glasgow. Johansen was able to join the *Knudsen* because of an extraordinary series of coincidences. During Christmas 1941, a 15-

year-old Ordinary Seaman named William George Gill celebrated the
holiday with friends a bit too much. In the words of his son, Michael,
young William missed the ship which was to carry him from Halifax
back to the UK. "This was taken very seriously and he and several other
shipmates got into serious trouble. But boys will be boys....." As luck
would have it, on the 27th of December, Gill was able to sign aboard
the *Knudsen*, where "he and his friend were the only two on the ship
that could speak English." In their effort to join their original ship back
in the UK, Gill signed off in Glasgow on the 13th of January, a day after
Johansen replaced him, making room for the older Norwegian. It was
to prove a fateful crew change. As an Able-Bodied Seaman on an ocean-
going tanker, Johansen was in for the kind of adventurous existence in
tropical climes which would be worlds apart from the confines of a mine
in the Arctic Ocean.

On her final voyage, the O. A. *Knudsen* left the Clyde River,
Glasgow, on the 23rd of January 1942 for Mobile, Alabama. She sailed
in Convoy ON 59 and, after dispersing from the convoy on February
6th, arrived in Mobile on the 17th of February. The tanker left on the
24th of February for Port Arthur, Texas to load a full cargo of kerosene
and gasoline. The loading and characteristics of the cargo were relevant
to her attack and the sequence of explosions later. According to a
diagram drawn by officers, pool engine spirit (gasoline) was loaded in
tanks number one to five in the bow, or front of the ship, and pool
vaporizing oil (kerosene – less flammable) was loaded in tanks number
six to nine, which were further aft. Starting at the bow of the ship, there
was a dry hold on the bow, then the next five rows of tanks were filled
with gasoline, then the following four rows of tanks (forward of the
bridge) were filled with kerosene. The aft section of the ship was
occupied with engine fuel (bunker) tanks, cabins and the bridge. Below
these lay the engine room, and farther aft store rooms with crew quarters
above.

The O. A. *Knudsen* left Port Arthur, Texas, on the 1st of March
1942, under British Admiralty orders, bound for Halifax and then in
convoy to Liverpool. She motored southeast, rounded Key West and
Carysfort Reef off southern Florida, motored most of the way up the
Straits of Florida, then turned east through the Northwest and Northeast
Providence Channels. Her voyage was accomplished at slightly below

her stated speed of 12 knots, in part due to adverse weather. As a result she did not round Great Isaac Light until the 4th of March and passed Nassau that night. The following day O. A. *Knudsen* and her 40-man crew emerged from the Northeast Providence Channel, left Eleuthera to starboard and Hole in the Wall Light, Abaco to port, and entered the wide rolling Atlantic. By sunrise they were a good 75 miles east of the Bahama Islands.

They had been zig zagging (a defensive manoeuvre to throw off attacking submarines) since rounding Key West. Every two, four, or six minutes the ship turned at an odd angle to throw off any pursuers. Though they had no doubt learned of the sinking in recent weeks of the *Pan Massachusetts*, *Republic*, and *Cities Services Empire*, the crew could be forgiven for considering themselves safe in the Bahamas – after all, no ships had been struck there. They may well have been routed through the island specifically to avoid the threat of attack off Cape Canaveral, where her sisters had been struck so recently.

The 5th of March 1942 was a very busy day both for the civilian sailors on the O. A. *Knudsen* and for the navy men on U-128. U-128 took the high road and the O. A. *Knudsen* took the low road, and their paths were to intersect east of Hole in the Wall Abaco. The day before at 11:00 am (all times local, or Eastern Standard time) Ulrich Heyse recorded that the wind was negligible at only five knots or so, the seas slight, the barometer 1021 millibars and temperature 66 degrees Fahrenheit, and there was a slight swell from the east. At 2:30 pm, the submarine altered course from the north to the south-southwest, as Heyse had decided to proceed "again to the Northeast Providence Channel and through this, advance to the Florida Strait from the south" – in effect circumnavigating the northern Bahamas.

By 6:30 pm, the sub's course was 170 degrees just west of south when they picked up the beacon of Elbow Cay Light at Hope Town, Abaco. The light was built in 1864 and could be seen from 17 nautical miles away. Heyse could not resist commenting that it was "burning – as in peacetime." It was bearing 247 degrees from the surfaced sub. Having confirmed his position, Heyse took U-128 on a series of dives to enable the sound-gear operator to use his devices to probe the depths for the tell-tale sounds of a merchant ship nearby. The sub dove between 6:45 and 7:07 pm, heard nothing, and came back up for air. At 7:15 pm, it switched to just one diesel motor to save fuel. At 9 pm, Heyse commented on the bright moonlight – not a good harbinger for submarines designed to attack undetected at night. Between 9:30 and 9:42 pm, the submarine dove again.

At 11 pm, the course was changed to due south, as U-128 skirted the coast of Abaco about 30 miles off, passing Cherokee Sound to starboard. Between 11:41 pm and midnight, the sub dove again, this time to 150 feet, to listen for the sounds of ship propellers, with no results. The O. A. Knudsen was just behind the loom of Great Abaco Island, and had not yet emerged from behind the island, therefore her propeller sounds would have been blocked and invisible to the enemy craft. That would soon change, as the O. A. Knudsen motored at about 12 knots around Hole in the Wall Light just after 11 pm and carried out her zig zagging course to the northeast.

At 15 minutes after midnight on the 5th of March, U-128 was only about 34 miles east-northeast of Hole in the Wall Light, and motoring close to the surface, heading 215 degrees, or south-southwest. Heyse decided they had gone close enough. At 1 am, he ordered a course change to 65 degrees, or east-northeast, the exact course (within a few degrees) that the O. A. Knudsen was just setting. The weather conditions were the same, but the temperature had gone up to 68 degrees Fahrenheit. Again, between 1:30 and 1:45 am, the stalking submarine dove to listen for ships – this time to 200 feet. At 1:50 am, both engines were started and the submarine moved quickly on the surface to the northeast. During the course of 24 hours, the submarine had run 140 miles, for a slow average speed of six knots, as it was hunting.

By 6 am, Heyse was heading 45 degrees and the wind had risen to about seven knots with seas one to two feet. The temperature in the morning sun rose to 73 degrees. Suddenly, at 6:45 am, came the affirmation: "tanker in sight!" The O. A. Knudsen had been seen bearing 210 degrees, or off the submarine's starboard quarter. The sighting triggered a series of cold analyses for which Heyse and his fellow officers had been trained for months. Heyse jotted his observations into the sub's war diary:

"Positioned between him and the sun. Attempt to get ahead and therefore in a more favorable position with regard to illumination, tanker has general course about 60°, comes from the NE Providence

Channel, zig zags each time about 90° to either side. I get on course 60° ahead of him in shooting position. Must start the attack four times because of his zig zagging."

Heyse would have been frustrated, but then again he had time, and plenty of sea room with no interference to expect. At 7:36 am U-128 dived. She had not been sighted on the surface by the *O. A. Knudsen* men because the sub was coming out of the sun, an ideal position from which to attack. In the next 57 minutes, the submarine had to make a series of jarring course changes – from 50 degrees east to 164 degrees south, then 350 degrees north to 290 degrees west, then 100 degrees southeast, trying to line up a shot on the moving target, which altered course every few minutes precisely to throw them off.

Finally, at 8:33 am, Heyse had his submarine in position to fire. He utilized both motors to maintain a course of 90 degrees due east and with visibility a near perfect 12 miles, he released three torpedoes at the *O. A. Knudsen* from ten feet below the surface. The *O. A. Knudsen* was 90 degrees off the submarine's port bow, roughly 5,000 feet distant, and making nearly 12 knots. Torpedoes raced out of tubes I, II, and IV. It would take them about two minutes to reach their target at that speed and distance. Heyse recorded the results:

"Detonation, then another and a little bit later a third detonation. Steamer stops and apparently does not follow its rudder any more, sinks deeper on an even keel, after 10 minutes a list to starboard. Masts stand tilted a bit inwards, radio antenna yard hangs down." The report from the ship gives the tanker listing to port and records only one hit on the vessel. It is possible that Heyse was hearing the end-run-detonations of the other two torpedoes as they ran out of propulsion, missed the target and hit the sea floor and self-destructed.

In fact, out of an initial salvo of three torpedoes, only one had struck – in the port bow of the ship. This may have been because the ship was going slower than Heyse anticipated. The fact that the crew of the *O. A. Knudsen* did not see the other torpedoes can be explained by the allocation of the ship's surviving lookouts: two on the bridge aft and one at the gun – which was also aft. The first two torpedoes would have passed ahead of the ship, as it was anticipated by the submarine's officers to have reached that point already. The two torpedoes went unnoticed, because there was no one at the front of the ship to see them. The nearest person was a crewman named George Schmidt (or Smith) who was described as both French and English. He was working on a derrick of the number six tank at the time and was killed instantly, blown off the derrick by the explosion beneath him.

Realizing that the ship would not sink immediately, Heyse lined up to deliver a *coup-de-grace*, a tactic which was well practiced in the submarine service. But here he was foiled by his adversary, the determined Captain Bringedal. At the very moment that Heyse fired a fourth torpedo at his "dead" ship, at 8:42 am, a mere nine minutes after the initial attack, the O. A. *Knudsen* rumbled to life and began steaming at full speed for land. In Heyse's words: "At the instant of the shot the tanker goes ahead at speed and changes course from about 10 degrees true to a NW-course. Missed." He had calculated the speed of the O. A. *Knudsen* at one knot, but Bringedal had converted this in a short time to an impressive nine knots.

At 9:30 am Heyse notes, perhaps with reluctant admiration noted the remedial action taken by the ship's crew: "Tanker loses a lot of cargo from the hit or by deliberate pumping of the tanks. Oil layer on the water, as a result the tanker has [four to seven feet] of freeboard, the list becomes less." Twelve minutes later, he ordered the fifth torpedo of the morning into the ship. At 9:42 am, Heyse noted in the log that his second *coup de grace* has been sent, this one at 40 knots, with a target speed calculated at four knots, 100 degrees off the submarine's port bow. He noted:

"After 30 seconds running time a hit with a dull detonation, probably below the bridge. Afterwards submerged back and forth in the vicinity of the tanker, to observe the behaviour of the enemy or the sinking. Layer of oil on surface of the water, submerged view very much obscured. Tanker has the starboard stern davit swung out, ...cannot see the boat (also because of bad visibility)." It would appear that because U-128 was remaining below the surface, and her only means of observing the scene above was through a periscope, its view was obstructed because the ocean was covered in a layer of oil.

At 12:26 pm, U-128 rose to the surface for the first time since it dove to attack five hours before. Heyse reported that immediately the horizon "all around" was scanned for enemy aircraft or vessels. But the sub only remained on the surface for literally a minute before diving. At

1:00 pm, Heyse and his team were able to identify the ship both visually and by using an identification book called *Groner*, after its author. By this time, they had taken the opportunity to get close enough to their quarry to read the name on the stern. He noted that "From *Groner* the tanker is identified as "O. A. KNUDSEN" from Haugesund. Has retained shipping company mark (red rings) around the stack in spite of other camouflage painting."

At 2:15 pm, Heyse's radio operator picked up the *O. A. Knudsen's* first successful Mayday / SSS (for submarine sighted), which was somewhat garbled. As Heyse took it down, he heard both the ship call for help and the shore-based station WAX in Hialeah Florida calling multiple times on the 600 bandwidth, asking for clarification. Then, there seemed to be a warning sent out by the 7th Naval District about an enemy submarine or at least an attack at 23.10N by 74.34W.

As a cautionary measure, U-128 then descended to 215 feet depth to "wait on the behaviour of the tanker and the approach of twilight."At 6:30 pm, U-128 surfaced again. He proceeded on both engines, course 215 degrees south-southwest. Heyse noted: "At twilight closed the tanker and on the way readied the artillery. Condition of the tanker: it floats as if blown out on an even keel with little or no way. No fire. See several portholes amidships and the stern indicator light, no people." There were, in fact, people on the ship. Then Heyse wrote "Stopped to the starboard side of the tanker distance [2,000 to 4,000 feet]."

At 7:45 pm, U-128 moved in for the kill. Heyse wrote "With a total of 19 shots, observed 7 hits with the 10.5 cm, of which the 3rd shot caused fire and demolition of the bridge. 6th and 7th hits in the stern starting fires. After the 3rd hit immediately bright fire over the entire deck. Cargo of heavy oil runs out and also catches fire on the water. Tanker burns from bow to stern with explosions, the sea around him burns. No lifeboats seen. Tanker breaks with explosions behind the bridge, bright tongues of flame, while running off very heavy smoke observed from the direction of the oil fire on the water."

Leaving the carcass of the *O. A. Knudsen* to burn and sink, U-128 and its crew headed east at 9 pm. By then, Heyse recorded that the sea conditions picked up a bit, with wind at eight to 10 knots, seas two to three feet, and 1014 millibars on the barometer. The temperature was

64 degrees Fahrenheit. He noted that, but for his long encounter with the tanker, he would have entered the Northeast and Northwest Providence channels. However, his plan was "superseded by meeting O. A. KNUDSEN and had to give way." One can imagine his elation at having sunk the largest Norwegian tanker at the time. During the attack, his crew overheard Heyse swear under his breath "no wonder it took so long to sink - the ship was German-built!"

Aboard O. A. *Knudsen*, the torpedo had struck the #6 tank which fortunately held the kerosene, and not the more flammable gasoline. As Gunner Waldmar Lund put it, the torpedo "caught us unawares – we had neither seen nor heard anything. ...One man [a lookout] was up at the top of the mast [aft] when the torpedo struck and he got a good shaking up but he managed to survive." George Smith was not so fortunate. He was working exactly where the explosion impacted the most, and Lund said that he "disappeared, and we never saw him again."

Throughout the entire day, Bringedal and Heyse orchestrated a duel of wills. Captain Bringedal initially ordered the First Engineer, Harald Stavdal, age 29, to stop the engines. He told the Radio Operator, Nils Olsen, 39, to send continuous SSS signals, indicating attack by submarine. However, since the aerials had been knocked down, the messages did not get through to anyone, including the U-boat listening nearby. The Captain then had the starboard lifeboat amidships – on the side opposite from the attack – lowered. Into this boat climbed 31 men. Eight officers and men remained on board. Since Olaus Johansen was the oldest crew member and had been badly injured in the initial explosion, it can be assumed he was non-essential and in the sailing lifeboat.

The men selected to remain on board were all Norwegians, perhaps to avoid any miscommunication using different languages. They included the Captain, Chief Officer Jacob Tvedt, age 34, Third Officer Georg Berntsen, 39, Second Engineer Karl Hansen, 32, and Bosun Kaare Lund, 26. There were also three Able-Bodied Seamen, among them, Andreas Friestad, 21, and Ole Mikkelsen, 22, who, like Lund, doubled as a Gunner and Able-Bodied Seaman. After assessing the damage and concluding that aside from a slight list to port and the damaged radio aerials, the ship's engines worked and the vast majority of her other tanks – 26 out of 27 in fact – remained sound, Captain Bringedal made the decision to put the engine back in gear and head for the nearest land, Abaco, some 86 miles distant to the west-southwest.

After the fourth torpedo fired by Heyse shot harmlessly astern of the tanker as it turned to port, from ten degrees north-northeast to west-southwest, the O. A. *Knudsen* resumed its Admiralty-proscribed zig zag pattern towards shore. The ship managed nine knots, three knots slower than the 12 of which it was capable.

U-128 was not idle. At 9:10 am, the sub headed south-southeast at 120 degrees, then 20 minutes later turned west to 250 degrees, then at 9:30 am, came to northwest 290 degrees, trying to line up a fifth shot on its quarry. Operating under both electric motors, it finally lined up a shot and fired at 9:42 am, from such close range (about 1,600 feet) that the projectile struck the ship the same minute. The second hit on the ship struck the number nine tank further aft, which contained volatile gasoline cargo. The resulting explosion "blasted open" most of the port side of the ship, according to Captain Bringedal. The remaining men abandoned ship in the port lifeboat. Thus began a waiting game, with both the submarine – still submerged – and the two lifeboats lingering near the ship to see if she would sink. At noon, the master ordered the starboard lifeboat containing 24 men to head for the nearest land, while the motorboat (the port lifeboat) stayed near the ship. At 12:26 pm, the submarine surfaced briefly to ascertain the name of the ship, but re-submerged within a minute. U-128 was never seen by the survivors in the boats.

At about 1 pm, Captain Bringedal boarded the ship for the first time since he had abandoned her. He chose Chief Engineer Stavdal to accompany him, along with the Bosun, Kaare Lund, the Radio Operator Nils Olsen, Greaser Otto Sirkel, and an Able-Bodied Seaman, Arne Eide. Olsen tried to send off an SOS on 600 megahertz at 1:30 pm, however, it was not successfully transmitted. At about 1:35 pm, the six men joined the nine men in the motor lifeboat. They pushed off from the ship.

Soon thereafter at about 1:50 pm, the same crew managed to board the ship again – the second time Bringedal re-boarded his charge. They "proceeded to repair the broken aerial; the Radio Operator made a new tuning, which was successful." At 2 pm, they transmitted "SOS

TORPEDOED, POSITION 2617 NORTH 7515 WEST, PLEASE
SEND ESCORT." The signal was picked up by WAX, a radio station in
Hialeah Florida as well as Key West, which relayed the information to
the US 7th Naval District headquarters in Miami.

The US Navy records of WAX (Tropical Radio) in Hialeah show
that the "first and only" message was intercepted at 2:38 pm. It seems
clear from the record that the US Navy was efficient at getting the news
out, but inefficient about doing anything about it, in the way of sending
assistance. Twenty minutes after it was received, at 2:58 pm, the message
was relayed to the District Intelligence Officer. Twenty-six minutes later,
at 3:24 pm, the evaluated message was sent to the Commandant,
Seventh Naval District. Along with the actual message which the O.
A. *Knudsen* sent, was the following analysis:

"THIS WAS FROM IJIYJ [a callsign or ID] WHICH IS O.A.
KNUDSEN, NOR. M/V TANKER OF 11,007 GROSS TONS
ENROUTE PORT ARTHUR TO HALIFAX AND POSITION IS IN
THE MAIN SHIPPING LANE FOR ENGLISH PORTS. SHE IS
ABOUT 12 HOURS BEHIND SCHEDULE FROM PORT ARTHUR
AT HER RATED SPEED OF 12 [knots]. HOWEVER WEATHER
CONDITIONS JUSTIFY THIS POSITION." This message was not
logged in the Eastern Sea Frontier Enemy Action Diary until the
following day, 6th March 1942 after 10:00 am. However, clearly it had
made it to the decision makers in a timely fashion.

There was a complaint made later, by the US Navy, that
intelligence sources in Nassau had informed them that the O. A.
Knudsen had already sunk, and therefore, there would be no need to send
naval ships or airplanes, except to effectuate a rescue of the ship's crew.
However, the accuracy of this report is undermined by the fact that
Nassau never acknowledged receiving any radio message. They could
not relay intelligence which they did not receive.

The rest of the world – the naval establishment at least – now
knew about the distressed tanker. It would have been reasonable to
assume that help would be on the way, as they were roughly 200 miles
or about two hours by air from the Florida coast. On the U-128 war log,
the confirmation that the ship's SOS was received in Florida was grimly
noted. Meanwhile Bringedal, according to the First Mate Tvedt, threw

overboard the confidential codes and papers in a weighted bag before they abandoned ship for the second time.

Then, after 2 pm the ship's officers and crew left the ship. Like Heyse in U-128 nearby, they were waiting to see if she would sink. In the words of the survivors, "the ship was left until dark in order to insure the safety of the crew." If it did not sink, then the survivors planned to re-board her and motor once again for Abaco. At the same time, Heyse on U-128 was determined to sink her. Since neither party seems to have communicated with each other, they had no idea of the other's intentions or movements. This lack of communication nearly spelt the end of all the men who later re-boarded her.

At 7:30 pm, well after sunset, Bringedal, Stavdal the Chief Engineer, Olsen the Radio Operator, Lunde the Bosun, two ABs and Gunner Lund, and the Oiler Sirkel bravely returned to the ship under cover of darkness. U-128 was unaware that they had done so. The ABs struggled to transfer 25 gallons of gasoline, presumably in small drums, from the ship to the motor life boat. Lowering these to a lifeboat was no easy task. However, the low freeboard of the laden and damaged tanker must have meant there was not much vertical distance – about five feet - between the deck of the ship and the lifeboat. Some of the men went below to see if the motor was still functioning. Since the engines would have all been well beneath water by this time, this can only be considered highly daring of them. Chief Engineer Stavdal reported that "only small parts were broken – the engine was still useable." He told Captain Bringedal that "it could be possible to bring the ship into port at a very slow speed."

At 7:45 pm, the men were just getting ready to bring the ship's engines back into play and motor for land, when what appeared to be two submarines began shelling them. "Upon coming out on deck they were confronted by a shelling by two submarines, one from astern and one from forward." The submarine's shells were fired every half-minute – though there was only one, though shells seemed to be raining down from every direction. Out of 40 shells estimated to have been fired, half, or 20, hit the ship. The third and crucial shell struck the old Japanese 4.7-inch gun aft, and sent metal shards flying everywhere. Waldemar Lund was struck in the left eye by a shard. This part of the narrative is

best told by Lund himself, in a radio interview in New York several
weeks later:

"Our cannon...exploded with an ear-splitting roar. All the men
except one [Radio Operator Olsen] were injured, I got a terrific blow on
the nose and a shell splinter in my left eye. It bled considerably and I
could not see. I stood holding onto the ladder. Then the others called
out that they were going into the lifeboat again. ...I was the last man
on the ladder. The others shouted to me to jump overboard, which I
did, blindly. Once in the water, I could see again, since the salt water
cleaned the one eye, and I swam over to the life-boat. We rowed away
with all our might and just in the nick of time, since the ship was now
aflame. Half a minute more and we would not have managed to get
away. As it was, every one of us was burned."

Captain Bringedal then ordered the boat, which had eight men
in it, to come up to the ship on the port side. Lesser men might have
fled, but the men in the motor boat, under the command of First Officer
Tvedt followed orders and approached the ship. The men refused to
leave the ship until fires had broken out. As Tvedt later reported to the
Admiralty, "before the motor boat could get alongside to remove the
party, the Captain got splinters in his face and left foot, the Chief
Engineer [Stavdal] in both arms, the Boatswain [Bosun] in one shoulder
and the arm, and A.B. seaman Lund in the eye and A.B. seaman Eide
in the head, and the oiler, Sirkel in the nose." As the men clambered
aboard the lifeboat at 8 pm, the volatile gasoline cargo was ignited from
the explosion of the shells and the O. A. *Knudsen* erupted in a massive
fireball. Fortunately for the Norwegians, flaming gasoline on the sea
surface did not engulf the boat. Ulrich Heyse, looking on from a
distance, observed burning gasoline on the sea surface. He noted that it
emitted a dense smoke, visible even at night. Heyse also observed an
explosion. In his opinion the ship cracked just forward of the
accommodation, and was clearly doomed.

The O. A. *Knudsen* would burn throughout the night,
presumably sinking sometime in the morning of the 6th of March. Finally
convinced that his prey was doomed, U-128 headed east towards Europe.
It had taken five valuable torpedoes to sink the ship, but now the sub
could fly another victory pennant for having destroyed the largest

Norwegian tanker then afloat. Neither skipper witnessed the stubborn ship's actual sinking.

Heyse was not the only one elated at his successful patrol. At 4:31 pm on the 6th of March, as the men from the O. A. *Knudsen* were struggling to rendezvous on the wide sea in two different boats, U-128 received the following signal from U-Boat headquarters: "To Heyse. Kptlt (Ing.) Noack on 1 March is promoted in rank. Heartiest congratulations. Flotilla Commander." The Commander of the Second Flotilla (Front) *Kapitän zur See* Viktor Schütze in Lorient would send more promotions and laurels over the airwaves soon. During this patrol Heyse would also be awarded the Iron Cross First Class, as well as the U-boat war Badge 1939, both precursors to the Knights Cross with the Iron Cross, which he received in 1942.

A post-mortem on the sinking, in which the officers of the O.A. *Knudsen* vented their feelings about not having been rescued, was conducted by half a dozen ensigns and reserve naval officers in Miami weeks later. Those interviews reflect how the men felt as they gave their burning tanker up for lost. "In a calm but bitter voice," wrote Ensign W. G. Warnock, Jr., and Boatswain J. G. Fickling, US Naval Reserve, "Mr. Stavdal [the Engineer] placed the blame for the loss of the vessel (which he asserted was one of the finest tankers on the sea) upon naval authorities charged with safeguarding Caribbean shipping. At no time during the day was the vessel in danger of sinking, and her engines could have been capable of carrying her in safety to nearly any port if airplanes or patrol boats had been sent out to drive off the attacking submarines."

Stavdal, First Officer Tvedt, and Second Officer Hansen stated that "eventual loss of the vessel was due to fire, set by shelling, and not to torpedoes. ...All three of the officers informed that failure of any aid to arrive during the approximately 11.5 hour period during which they attempted to save the vessel (from 08:25 to 20:00, EWT, March 5, 1942) was indicative of greater United Nations weakness in Western Hemisphere waters than they had ever encountered elsewhere in the world, including off the coast of Nazi-held Europe." In a tone which could only be adopted by foreigners and which Americans would probably have been reluctant to adopt towards their own navy, Tvedt went on to say that "Axis submarines would not have the nerve to loaf around all day in order to sink a vessel in European waters, as they did in the sinking of the O. A. KNUDSEN." Stavdal opined that "it was a cat-and-mouse game as far as the submarine was concerned."

Another ship nearby – the Norwegian *Nueva Andalusia* – reported a ship ablaze at the *Knudsen's* position, yet no allied aircraft was ever deployed in the tanker's defense. The US Navy's Eastern Sea Frontier Enemy Action Diary for 11:00 am March 6th makes the following entry: "Info Center advised the master of NUEVA ANDALUSIA reports burning object, probably ship (0030 G.M.T. March 6) at 26-33 N., 75-41 W. (N/E of Eleuthera Island, Bahamas). Probably was SS O. A. KNUDSEN torpedoed."

This timing corresponds with the time that the O. A. *Knudsen* was abandoned in a burning state. The relative positions of the ships were also easily within line of sight of each other, particularly as one was a burning pyre in darkness. As to why Captain Olav Solhøy of the *Nueva Andalusia*, did not divert to rescue survivors of the O. A. *Knudsen*, no doubt the skipper was concerned for the safety of his own vessel and crew. The general rule of thumb for rescue at sea is that it must be undertaken unless doing so would, in the opinion of the rescuing master, place his own vessel and crew at risk of loss.

In fact, it was quite brave of the *Nueva Andalusia* to transmit a notice to shore via radio at all, as doing so may have exposed it to the menace of U-128 which was just heading out of the region, and whose duty it was to monitor the radio for targets. It is noteworthy that Heyse didn't hone in on the nearby ship after he heard the message. Probably this was due to the fact that the sub had used all 15 torpedoes and expended its entire remaining cache on the O. A. *Knudsen* attack. The crew were no doubt exhausted, and the prospect of taking on a large, armed ship with just a deck cannon would have been daunting. The more likely scenario is that Heyse was submerged and simply didn't intercept the message, as he makes no mention of it in his war log.

The motor boat headed for Abaco as soon as it pulled free from the *Knudsen*. Though ship was reported to be 86 miles from land when struck, they had motored west at nine knots for roughly three quarters of an hour, meaning the life boats were roughly 80 miles from the Hole in the Wall Light. At 3 am on March 6th, the boats were hit by a squall. Tvedt related that "the wind got stronger in the night with a heavy rain shower."

Leif Norman Bentsen, Ordinary Seaman on the O. A. Knudsen.
*Aged 23 at the time, he was in
the lifeboat which left the* Knudsen *soon after the attack.
He lived until 1994.
Source: Bentsen family members, Larvik, Norway, c/o Sten Kittelsen,
Oslo and Larvik*

The 15 men in the motor lifeboat travelled until 5:30 pm that day, for a voyage of 20 hours and 30 minutes, before they were able to catch up to the lifeboat which had been proceeding under sail with 24 men. Considering the large swathe of ocean, it is impressive that the boats met at all, especially since the men were so low to the water that their line of sight was very limited. It took the starboard lifeboat nine hours more than the motorboat to cover the same distance. The motorboat then took the sailing boat under tow, and together they set off for Hole in the Wall Light, which would have been about 20 miles distant. It is likely that as soon as the sun set around 6:30 pm, they would have seen the lighthouse beam, since it projected to 23 miles. Indeed, the survivors said they could see the reassuring beam by 7:00 pm. At 11:30 pm, the boats approached the shore after covering the distance in six hours.

Hole in the Wall Lighthouse and buildings,
southern tip of Great Abaco Island, Bahamas.
Source: marinas.com/view/lighthouse/355_Hole_in_the_Wall_Lighthouse_AB_Bahamas

Due to the heavy breakers encountered, they gave up trying to find a suitable landing place. Tvedt wrote that "…the boats were steered along the coast in an attempt to find a landing place, but were forced to abandon the plan because of the breakers." This is simply good seamanship, giving an unknown shore a wide berth at night. It took the motorboat 27.5 hours to reach land, and the sailing boat 35.5 hours. The night of 6th and 7th of March was fairly calm, in the lee of land, with a southeasterly wind. There was a persistent swell which crashed against the base of the cliffs at the Hole in the Wall Light at the very southern tip of Great Abaco Island. The light illuminates the deep water northern edge of the 40-mile wide Northeast Providence Channel. Begun in 1836 and completed in 1838, it was the first lighthouse built in the Bahamas by the Imperial Lighthouse Service. The light stands at 168 feet height and its single white flash illuminates the sea for 23 miles.

Unbeknownst to the men of the *O. A. Knudsen*, the three-masted schooner *E. P. Theriault* out of Bridgetown, Barbados was loading lumber at a jetty serving the lumber mill at Cornwall, southern Abaco, while U-128 was attacking the Norwegian ship. Built in Belliveau Cove, Nova Scotia in 1919, the schooner was 326 tons and owned by A. A.

Reid of Bridgetown. Then on the evening of Friday the 6th of March 1942 the wind picked up from the southwest, exposing Cross Harbour Abaco and the jetty to a "heavy southwester with high seas." Captain Foster, of West End, Cayman, was Master of the *E. P. Theriault* and decided it was safer to take his schooner around Hole in the Wall Light and to the lee, or eastern side of Abaco "….and return after the weather abated or the wind shifted so as to continue loading lumber."

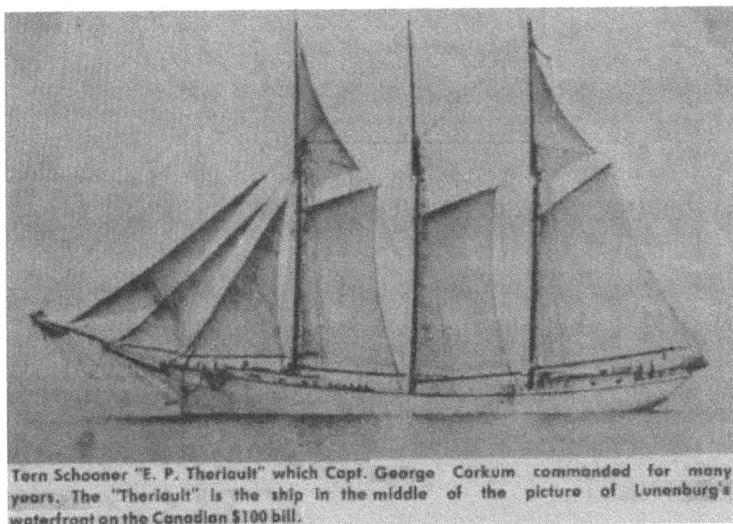

Torn Schooner "E. P. Theriault" which Capt. George Corkum commanded for many years. The "Theriault" is the ship in the middle of the picture of Lunenburg's waterfront on the Canadian $100 bill.

The Bajan schooner E. P. Theriault, *which rescued survivors of the O. A.* Knudsen *and took them to Cornwall,* Abaco, arriving on the 7th of March, 1942. Photo source: uboat.net/allies/merchants/ships/1692.html

The following day, Saturday the 7th of March, early in the morning, *E. P. Theriault* was navigating towards the re-assuring beacon after the midnight change of watch. Suddenly, at 2:00 am, the eerie arc of white light from the lighthouse illuminated something incongruous and startling – what could it be? There were two small lifeboats bobbing in the water outside the breakers. The men were calling in heavily Germanic accents – and signaling with small lights. Could they be Germans attacking the Bahamas? Who were they? Captain Foster eased off the *E. P. Theriault's* sails and bore down on the boats to hear their story. The other captain called over that they were shipwrecked Allied seamen from Norway. They were on their way to Miami, Captain Bringedal told him, and amazingly were prepared to keep motoring and sailing there. Apparently the Norwegian didn't give up easily

Faced with an unexpected humanitarian mission, in a remote British colony which had barely been touched by the war, Captain Foster and his crew responded in the finest traditions of the sea. They invited the injured and crowded men on board from the two lifeboats and accommodated them as best they could. It took some effort, but Captain Foster "insisted on them going to Cornwall and getting medical assistance from Nassau." Since the blustery winds from the southwest had now abated sufficiently for them to return to Cornwall, Captain Foster rounded Hole in the Wall Light and made his way north. By sunrise, about 5:30 am, they were passing the abandoned settlement of Alexandria. By 6:30 am, they had rounded Cross Harbour Point, seven miles up the coast. The nearest settlement was a lumber camp named Cornwall. In it were a team of laborers, at least three families, a small church, and even a telephone.

The motley group approached the community by the export pier, which was the terminus of a small temporary railroad. The *E. P. Theriault*'s anchored off the jetty to continue loading and discharged the survivors back into their boats. Word was passed quickly to the managers and workers at the mill — there were over three dozen shipwreck survivors that needed to be looked after. Work would have to be put on hold for the day. Soon the owner of the Abaco Lumber Company mill, local Member of Parliament for Abaco, John Wilson (J. W.) Roberts, was alerted.

From that point, whatever was needed was put at the disposal of the survivors, including the telephone to contact Nassau. Thanks to a call from the wireless telephone operator and Customs Collector C. V. Albury to the Colonial Secretary in Nassau, the motor boat, *Content S.* was dispatched, along with Dr. Lyon. Lyon was sent by the Chief Medical Officer for the colony, Dr. John Merrill Cruikshank, as well as a nurse. A rail car moved the men from the rail head to the community – a distance of about three miles. The lumber mill was essentially cut off without reliable road access to Marsh Harbour, the main community on the island. There were several itinerant lumber camps named Cornwall in Abaco, the first, according to philatelic resources, was in 1935 near Cornwall Point, on the west coast of Great Abaco Island. From there the camps were moved to four other sites, including possibly Sawmill Sink (a well known blue hole), until the final, or sixth camp was set up near Cross Harbour, southern Abaco, between Sandy Point and Hole in the Wall, around 1940. It was to be the final Cornwall camp in Abaco, having been disbanded in 1943 and relocated to Grand Bahama under a different name and new ownership.

The Norwegians wryly noted that "a sailing craft supplied information on a landing place," suggesting that the motor lifeboat and sailboat simply followed the schooner, however C. V. Albury is clear on the point that Captain Foster "....sighted the two lifeboats and changed his course and picked them up." It is possible that the *O. A. Knudsen* officers and *E. P. Theriault* crew decided to cut free the second, sailing lifeboat. Later Captain Granville Bethel of nearby Cherokee Sound, found an abandoned World War II lifeboat near Crossing Rocks, on the southeast coast of Abaco, north of Hole in the Wall. He towed it to Cherokee Sound, renamed it *Beluga*, and was engaged by the government to use it to supply mail and freight to the community of Crossing Rocks, then without access by road, for the next few decades. The crew from the lifeboats no doubt savoured being on a larger vessel, seeing fresh faces, and eating fresh food.

The most likely landing place can be deduced by considering two factors: they were landed at a railhead ("Cornwall, Abaco Island, where a landing was affected at the end of a railroad track at 08:00 EWT"), and it took them six hours to reach the rail head. First, there was but one rail road terminus in the area at the time, and that was on the eastern end of Cross Harbour. Some accounts give the arrival at Cornwall between 7:00 and 7:30 am. These facts mitigate in favour of the little convoy achieving about two and a half, perhaps three knots. The distance from a point just a bit off the Hole in the Wall Light to the southwestern tip of Abaco is four miles, from there to next headland is six miles, and from the headland to the rail terminus is two miles. Total distance: 12 miles. Likely destination: the jetty at Cross Harbour.

The coastline at Cross Harbour showing abandoned
Cornwall settlement at lower left.
Source: author's collection, courtesy of
Orjan Lindroth for diverting his airplane.

Lund described the place as "... a Negro island with only three white families." Said Lund, "...We were quartered in a chapel and given first aid and bandages by a Negro nurse...." Johansen must have been gingerly carried ashore in an improvised stretcher. The Survivors Statement indicates that "the British Admiralty was notified of the crew's plight via radio to Nassau." The men must have been greatly relieved to be onshore, despite the sand flies of the coast and the pervasive mosquitoes of the interior. They would have slept soundly, though for the injured it must have been a challenge to manage their pain and adjust to being on solid land for the first time in months. The next day, the little community had to transport 38 out of their 39 new charges back to the rail road terminus to meet a rescue vessel.

Content S. arrived at Cross Harbour the next day, the 8th of March. She was a 120-foot luxury yacht built by J. M. Densmore of Quincy, Massachusetts in 1920. Originally named *Percianna II* and owned by Percy L. Hance, a stock broker and socialite from New York, it was the flagship of the new Sea Horse Yacht Club in Rye New York, before the club burned down and was absorbed into the Shenorock Shore Club. In 1934, Hance sold it to Howard E. Spaulding of Shelburne Vermont and Palm Beach Florida. It lay unused in Florida for a number of years before being re-flagged to the Bahamas and re-purposed to inter-island trade, for which it was not ideally suited.

In 1940 Nassau merchant Richard Wilson Sawyer purchased her with the name *Content* and added the "S" presumably for "Sawyer." Her captain was Stanley Weatherford of Great Guana Cay, Abaco, whose relatives confirm that he commanded her. According to "Pappa" Floyd Lowe, born 1920 and the patriarch of Green Turtle Cay Abaco, the yacht was the "wrong ship" and "not a boat for mail service" on the Abaco-Nassau run, being narrow and deep draft and fitted out as a yacht, without the large cargo holds which would make such a ship profitable. Sawyer seems to have recognized this, as *Content S.* was only dedicated to Abaco service for about a year. It was better suited for its other purpose – carrying passengers in comfort. He chartered her out to the Duke and Duchess of Windsor for a tour of the islands early in their tenure in the colony.

The 120-foot yacht Content S. *under her original name* Percianna II *in New England waters, 1920s. Purchased by R. W. Sawyer of Nassau, she rescued men from* O. A. Knudsen *and* Athelqueen *from Abaco in March 1942. Survivors mostly slept on deck.*
Source: *Rosenfeld Collection, Mystic Seaport Museum, Mystic Connecticut, USA*

Olaus Johansen was forced to remain behind with Dr. Lyon. According to the radio operator and Customs Collector C. V. Albury he was "…so badly burned and in a delirious condition that he could not be transported by boat." He was given doctor's care but unfortunately to no avail. Leaving Johansen must have been hard on the crew. Though he had only joined roughly four weeks before, Lund at least clearly respected him. Johansen was the oldest man on board. It is likely that, with only hours to live, he was unable to fully appreciate that he was being left behind by his crewmates. But for the crew which prided itself on having stuck it out together since the fall of Norway two years before, it must have been difficult indeed to leave one of their own in an unfamiliar place.

The story came out (censoring the name of the ship and other details, such as which island they landed on) the very day that the survivors landed in Abaco. The citizens of Nassau were abuzz with the news that weekend, as locals prepared to welcome the first victims of the U-boat war in their waters. "Survivors or Torpedoed Ship Land in Bahamas" read the front page of the Nassau *Daily Tribune*, Saturday March 7, 1942: "It was officially stated today that survivors from a torpedoed ship have landed at an island in the Bahamas and that the Government has taken prompt measures to bring them to Nassau. A doctor and supplies have been sent by the quickest possible means." Inter-island communications seemed to be working rather efficiently (the *Tribune* carried the story in the evening paper, the *Guardian* the morning). The voyage from Cross Harbour to Nassau is just over 52 miles. It would have taken about five hours at an average speed of ten knots. It can be assumed that the voyage began late Sunday morning and that the survivors arrived that afternoon sometime after 3 pm.

Waldemar Lund, half blinded, records that on Sunday the 8th "...we came to Nassau and were received at the pier by the Duke and Duchess of Windsor. I hardly caught a glimpse of them, since I was taken to the hospital immediately, but I heard they had been very kind. We were well treated in every way, the sick and the well alike. All of us were given complete outfits by the Red Cross, though we heard that they came as a gift from the Duke." Clothing and articles were supplied as a result of Lady Solomon taking the unusual step of contacting the owners of shops on Bay Street on a Sunday evening and having them open their stores to allow the *Knudsen* men to help themselves on the government's account.

According to an unpublished manuscript by Mrs. Maxine Sandberg, who interviewed participants in Nassau in the mid 1960s, "Lady Solomon with the First Aid Detachment and the Chief Medical Officer [Dr. Cruikshank] went down to meet the men. The officers were put in one hotel and the enlisted men in another. The shops happened to be closed on the day that this happened, but they opened so that the necessary supplies could be gotten as the men had absolutely nothing. Lady Solomon recalls that the Duchess was extremely concerned when news of the arrival of these men became known and called on the telephone to say: "What are you going to do about them?" Lady Solomon had already been in touch with the shops. Both the Duchess and the Duke came down to see the men and received a rousing cheer."

There being no Sunday papers at the time, here is how the Nassau *Guardian* of Monday 9th March described the O. A. *Knudsen* survivor's arrival in a front-page article entitled "Survivors from Torpedoed Ship Brought to Nassau": "Thirty-eight survivors from a torpedoed ship, who were landed at an Out Island in the Bahamas on Saturday morning, were brought to Nassau early yesterday afternoon in the *Content S.* They were met on the dock by His Royal Highness the Governor and the Duchess of Windsor, the Colonial Secretary, the Hon. W. L. Heape, C.M.G., and other officials."

"Mrs. [later Lady] Kenneth Solomon, Deputy President of the Bahamas Red Cross Branch and Mrs. H. V. Brown were also there to ascertain the requirements of the men. The Captain and the men who had sustained injuries were taken to the Bahamas General Hospital and the others who seem to be quite fit are at the Rozelda Hotel temporarily. The Duke and Duchess went to the Rozelda to see the men settled in and Mrs. Solomon and Mrs. Brown supervised the out-fitting of the men with clothing such as socks and pajamas, suits and boots and toilet articles."

That evening the Nassau *Daily Tribune* author continued, writing that "A large crowd gathered at the landing. The Captain and thirty-seven men have arrived in Nassau. Three were stretcher cases and these were taken to hospital. Several wounded men were able to walk. One man has remained at the island. He was too ill to be moved. Dr. Lyon and a nurse have remained with him [Johansen]. It is understood that one man [Smith] was killed in the explosion when the torpedo struck the ship.

The hospital to which all injured or ill survivors of Allied ships were taken was known as the Bahamas General Hospital. It was located off Shirley Street in downtown Nassau. The first record of a general hospital in the colony was to "poorhouse" opened in 1809. By 1905 this had grown to a hospital with "four sections - for the sick, indigent, lepers and insane. Treatment was free, but patients were referred to as 'inmates,' and those who could afford it arranged for medical care at home." As recently as 1925 an outbreak of typhoid was reported amongst American visitors to Nassau, but no systemic improvements to hospital care were provided until after the war, with the commencement of Princess Margaret Hospital, opened in 1955.

The Bahamas General Hospital as it would have appeared before the Princess Margaret Hospital was built in 1952, replacing it. This is where six of the O. A. Knudsen survivors as well as men from several other merchant ships torpedoed by Italian or German submarines were treated during WWII. Since 1921 the Chief Medical Officer for the colony was Dr. John M. Cruikshank.

Dr. John Merrill Cruikshank in front of the Chief Medical Officer's quarters, following the hurricane of 1929. He would go on to Fiji as CMO for all British possessions in the Pacific.
Source: Dr. Harold Munnings,

The Centre for Digestive Health, Nassau.

Nassau had recently enjoyed a resurgence of American tourism which abruptly tapered off after the US entry in the war months before. It was, to use a tired phrase, a backwater to the action, where changes in beach dress codes still made the news. A contemporary author observed in 1940 that "...pretty women in the becoming coif of the Red Cross knitted and rolled bandages, held raffles and lotteries for war charities, zealously collected tinfoil and metal scrap. A home Guard drilled and a flying club trained pilots. Some local boys had gone to the armed services. American commissions inspected naval-base sites. Now and again a business-like Dutch or British cruiser slipped in or out of port on raider patrol. But, even in Nassau, the war was remote. People danced gaily in the Royal Victoria Gardens, sipped drinks in the Porcupine Club [on Hog Cay, later Paradise Island], swam and lunched at Emerald Beach and otherwise carried on much as usual. Air-liners brought in tourists. The homes of the rich American and winter residents were all open and occupied. Night clubs and hotels were filled. Even a group of English school children, bombed out of their home grounds and evacuated to Nassau, reveled in the warm climate and strange scenes, the terror from the skies and torpedoing on the way out forgotten." The convoy with the school children from the Belmont School to Nassau was indeed torpedoed, but not the specific ship carrying the pupils.

The wheels were set in motion to repatriate the O. A. *Knudsen* men from Nassau to Miami and New York right away. On the morning of Monday the 9th of March Mr. Brown of Curry Shipping Company in Nassau and Miami paid a visit in person to John H. E. McAndrews, the American Vice Consul in Miami. He laid out the facts of the loss of the O. A. *Knudsen* and told the consul that six men were in the hospital in Nassau. In his report to the State Department McAndrews crossed out that Johansen "was left" in Abaco and replaced it with "At the present moment one sailor is in Abaco, too badly burned to move." He also added in hand writing over typed text that "None of the crew are nationals of Axis nations." He added that "Most men have all their papers, but some have only a part of their papers." He requested clearance for the men to leave Nassau as soon as Wednesday the 11th of

March as far as New York. According to McAndrews, "Norwegian
Shipping & Trading Mission wires Captain to have crew proceed at
earliest possible time." The pressure was on Captain Bringedal.
Meanwhile the men needed a few days to rest and recuperate from their
ordeal.

      The Rozelda Hotel was a modern concrete building on East
Street in downtown Nassau built during the early 1930's. The hotel was
built and owned by Roland Symonette (later Sir), who would go on to
become the leader of the UBP (United Bahamian Party) and first
Premier of the Colony in 1964. Historian Michael Craton observed that
"a native of the poor white settlement of the Current Eleuthera, who
had made a fortune successively, in rum-running, shipbuilding, retailing,
construction, and real estate, "Pop" Symonette was seen as the
quintessential 'Bay Street' type." More than any other hotel, the Rozelda
was consistently chosen by the colonial government to house and feed
257 survivors of half a dozen Allied ships whose survivors landed in the
capital. This may be because it was not just a hotel, but offered furnished
apartments for rent on a reduced weekly rate, rather than the nightly
tariff. The local papers cited the Rozelda, Lucerne, Windsor and Prince
George hotels at the primary repositories of survivors. The Red Cross
Commandant Therese Straton wrote that even the men housed at the
Royal Victoria Annex were fed twice daily at the Rozelda, so clearly the
property was an assembly point for the men as they recovered and
prepared to be repatriated.

      The Duke and Duchess of Windsor, when they visited a hotel to
greet the men, give them gifts, or buy them a symbolic beer, did so at
the Rozelda rather than the less modern Lucerne or the more upscale
Royal Victoria. According to Symonette's son Craig, the hotel derived
its name from a portmanteau of the two most important ladies in
Symonette's life at the time: his wife Rose and his daughter Zelda. It
would later become the Carlton House, host to the Iron Bar. Renovated
and modernized in the mid-1960s, the property was razed within a
decade or two and now serves as a parking lot between the abandoned
estate named Cascadilla and the office of realtor H. G. Christie, opposite
an historic police station and behind the courts and the legislative
buildings.

East Street, Nassau, Bahamas (Rozelda Hotel)

The Rozelda Hotel.
Source: The Rumelier Collection

The Lucerne Hotel was owned at the time by Roger Moore Lightbourn and family, who "insisted their visitors be well served." Located next to the Trinity Church and between Christ Church Cathedral and St. Andrew's Presbyterian Kirk, the hotel and its bar did not have such a holy history. During the prohibition, Irish barman Tom Lavelle dished out a concoction called "Coast-to-Coast Flip" in honour of rum-runners, and the hotel was run by a burly matron from New England known simply as "mother." According to legend, the only time the bar's patrons toned down its antics was during church services next door, on Sunday mornings. The annual bash held in the hotel was called the Bootlegger's Ball and the most strident competition came from another bar on George Street named Bucket of Blood.

The name "Hotel Lucerne" can be read on the signpost between palm fronds on the middle right. The proximity of the hotel to Trinity Church, in the background, is clearly evident. "The manageress was known as Dog Face Di, and despite the unflattering description, she was known to keep the gangsters housed at the Lucerne quiet when services at Trinity Church were being held. At one time the south wing of the Lucerne was use as the girl's school of Trinity Church." Sailors of shipwrecked vessels during WWII gratefully thanked the Trinity rectors for service.
Source: Ronald Lightbourn, "Nostalgic Nassau,
Picture Postcards 1900-1940"

By 1942, the hotel had already hosted two Allied shipwreck survivors – Robert Tapscott and Roy Widdicombe of the *Anglo-Saxon*, sunk by the German raider *Widder* in 1940. Described as a "three-story wooden structure of the traditional Bahamian style, with balconies on three sides of the building, offering a cool retreat from the tropical climate," the hotel would have been a welcome reprieve for men accustomed to being exposed to the scorching sun for days at a time. Since the Lucerne and the Rozelda were the only two local hotels who offered a discounted weekly rate to the government and others, the Lucerne was more often than not nominated to house survivors like those from the O. A. *Knudsen*.

The other hotel the men were hosted in was known as the Windsor Hotel and was not far away, on the corner of Bay Street and Frederick Street. Remarkable for the liberal use of arches in its design, the hotel is presently owned by George and Useph Baker as the Windsor Shop.

Windsor Hotel, Bay Street Nassau, on the southeast corner of Frederick Street. It is the building with numerous arches. The man on they bicycle is Mr. Lightbourn, whose family owned the Lucerne Hotel on Frederick Street nearby.
Source: Photo courtesy of Mr. Ronald Lightbourn, c/o Captain Paul Aranha

The proximity of the men to several churches apparently had an impact, as Captain Bringedal penned a thank-you letter to Reverend Herbert S. Clarke of Trinity Methodist Church whilst still in Nassau on the 16th of March. Bringedal specifically thanked Clarke for his "kind wishes and active sympathy on my behalf and the wounded members of my crew." Clarke served the parish in Nassau between 1937 and 1947 and was succeeded by Father W. H. Armstrong. The task of entertaining the 32 members of the O. A. *Knudsen's* crew that were not hospitalized was eagerly undertaken. They were entertained at the Masonic Hall by the Imperial Order of the Daughters of the Empire (IODE).

*The Duke of Windsor, a Mason, outside the Masonic Hall,
Nassau with civic leaders.
Source: Courtesy of the Masonic Lodge, Nassau, Bahamas.*

A few days later, under the heading "Tanker Survivors
Entertained," the Nassau *Guardian* on March 10, 1942 recorded that
"The five men who [were taken] to the Bahamas [General] Hospital
upon their [arrival in] Nassau are improving after [two days. The] rest
of the men are [being taken] care of and some have [been] entertained
during their [stay]. ...Some of the survivors are young lads, have been
away from home for as long as [three years]". Of course all was not
celebratory for the wounded, and probably not for the men who were
physically fit, either – it must have been quite a culture shock to have
been delivered from their harrowing recent experience to resting in an
idyllic setting where peacetime conditions prevailed and rationing was
not widespread.

On the 9th of March, the day after his companions left, Able
seaman Olaus Johansen died of wounds in the care of Dr. Lyon and was
buried in Cornwall. As C. V. Albury described it, "...he died during the
night and was buried at Cornwall." The Nassau *Guardian* duly reported
the glum news: "It was learned here [that the] seaman who was left [in
the care of] Dr. Lyon in a critical [condition on one] of the Out Islands
[by] his fellow shipmates [from a] torpedoed ship, ...died this morning."

His death certificate states that "This death occurred in consequence of war operations. Burns." Olaus was listed as a 55-year-old male seaman who died in the District of Cornwall.

Olaus Johansen as a fisherman in Norway
Source: Photo courtesy of Rebecca Mason, UK, great-granddaughter of
Olaus Johansen

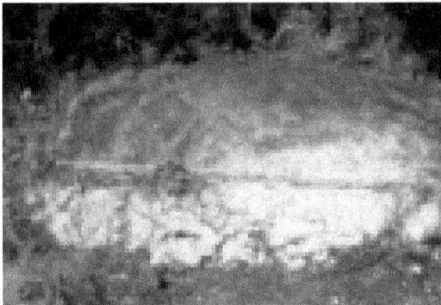

Photo of what is believed to be Olaus Johansen's grave near
Cross Harbour, Abaco
Source: Author's collection / Bethel, Marsh Harbor

The Norwegian grave of Olaus Johansen showing he was believed to have died in Cornwall, Vermont, USA, before the family learned of his passing in Abaco, Bahamas in 2011.
Source: Rebacca Mason, UK, great-granddaughter of Olaus Johansen

Among those known to have been hospitalized were Able Seaman and Gunner Ole Mikkelsen, Boatswain Kare Oddvar Lunde, Stuart Colin Cameron, a Canadian Oiler, and Able Seaman and Gunner Waldemar Lund. It is thought that Captain Bringedal was also hospitalized, for splinters in the face and foot, since on the 15th of March Consul John W. Dye states that the officer in charge of the party leaving Nassau for Miami was actually First Mate Jacob Tvedt.

The *Guardian* continued to report on the warm reception laid on for the men of the *O. A. Knudsen*, who were soon joined by 30 mostly Greek officers and crew from the *Cygnet* (arrived Nassau 12th March), 58 Brits from the *Daytonian* (arrived 15th) and *Athelqueen* (arrived 17th). "A large number of contributions of fruit, vegetables, and other foodstuffs have been received at the IODE Canteen in the Masonic building, for the survivors from torpedoed ships and the military forces in Nassau ... The seamen and soldiers have made themselves entirely at home in the friendly atmosphere of the Canteen and every night they entertain themselves with games of cards, darts, Chinese checkers, ping pong, backgammon and other games and a radio and two gramophones furnish music."

It is interesting to note that clearly the officers and crew of the *O. A. Knudsen*, the *Athelqueen*, the *Daytonian* and probably the *Cygnet* mingled in Nassau. "Ole MIKKELSON stated that it was rumored in

Nassau that survivors of an unknown English ship recognized the attacker of their ship as an Italian submarine." Since the O.A. *Knudsen* survivors never saw their attacker, they could be forgiven for thinking that she was Italian. The survivors of both British ships – the *Daytonian* and the *Athelqueen* – which were sunk so soon after the O. A. *Knudsen*, saw and interacted with their Italian attacker.

The *Daytonian* crew in particular saw the Italian flag being unrolled and interacted with Commander Fecia di Cossato. Of the two, it is more likely that the *Daytonian* crew spread this rumor, as the *Athelqueen* men did not arrive in Nassau until the 17th of March. The *Daytonian* men by contrast were landed on the 15th by the *Rotterdam* and would have had at least a day or two to mingle with the O. A. *Knudsen* sailors.

On Sunday the 15th of March, the State Department (Welles, Acting) authorized a waiver of visa and documents for the *Knudsen* officers and crew. It was a busy day for Captain Bringedal. During the morning he composed and mailed thank-you letters to the IODE, the Bahamas Red Cross ("we will long remember the treatment accorded us in the Bahamas"), and the Bahamas General Hospital ("for the treatment which sick members of my crew and myself have received at your hands"). He also wrote Mr. J. W. Roberts of Cornwall, Abaco ("for the courtesy and help you gave us after my ship was torpedoed. We will always have a grateful memory of the kindness of yourself and associates"). Finally he thanked HRH the Duke of Windsor "for the interest and assistance that you and the Duchess personally have shown and given us on our arrival in the Bahamas and during our stay. Would you please express our thanks and appreciation to the Officials of the Bahamas Government who have done so much for us."

Then, just after twilight on the 16th March 1942, Captain Bringedal and all crew except Lund (who had to have his eye removed) and one other man, Stewart Cameron, a Canadian Oiler, departed Nassau. Totaling 36 men, they utilized the services of the Albury & Company vessel *Ena K.* which had plied the route between Nassau and Miami literally a thousand times since 1927. According to historian Kendall Butler, the *Ena K.* was 87 feet long and was built of wood by Thomas Berlin Albury in Harbour Island, Eleuthera. The trip would have taken 18 hours. They arrived in Miami at 1:00 pm on the 17th of March.

Inter-island and Miami-Nassau trading vessel Ena K. *at the dock in Nassau, 1937. She carried the majority of Allied survivors from Nassau to Miami after periods of recuperation.*
Source: "The Harbour Island Story," Anne & Jim Lawlor, page 134

Albury and Company also conveniently served as ship's agents and handled procurement and administrative matters for captains, crews and ship owners in the Bahamas as well as Miami. However it was Curry Shipping which liaised with the consular officials to get the crew visas to visit the US, arranged for the British Tankers firm to wire funds to the Master, and taken care of all and sundry details. The local papers continued to update readers as to the status of the invalids and survivors, detailing their departure a week or so later for Miami, then New York and printing a letter of thanks from Captain Bringedal. Coverage of the men followed them to the United States, even though most of them only spent less than 10 hours in Miami. The Nassau *Tribune* published a piece entitled "Survivors Ready to Face Subs Again" on the front page:

"Thirty-four survivors of the Norwegian ship sunk near the Bahamas left two mates in serious condition in Miami Beach hospital and two in watery graves, but they were ready to fight again when they reached New York Thursday [after] watching helplessly while shells pounded their ship into a blazing hulk." During their stay in Miami, the survivors were subjected to many hours of questioning by a veritable battery of young Ensigns from the US Navy and US Naval Reserve.

Lund left Nassau for Miami along with Cameron on the 20th of March. After a few days in Miami, Lund transited and arrived in New

York, where he provided a radio interview. "Since all went well, I could leave a fortnight later," he writes. He must have been quite a personable and charming man, since he adds "In Miami the official who heads the port authorities is a Norwegian, and there I was taken on a sightseeing tour of the town for a whole afternoon." His generous host in Miami was actually a Norwegian ship's pilot named Captain Henry Warren. Born in 1882 and thus 60 at the time, he "first went to sea as a cabin boy at twelve years old, came to Miami in the early 1900s, and was one of the three founding members of the Miami Bar Pilots Association" in 1911. Lund continues: "Now I am waiting [in New York] to get a glass eye and then the Navy will have to decide what it wants to do with me" The author Lise Libaek, added "this young gunner went to the Norwegian Medical Office in New York city and said: 'Don't you dare put me out of active service; one eye is absolutely all you need for taking sight through a cannon.' "

Captain Knut O. Bringedal continued sailing as master. He took command of his next ship, the *Norvik*, in New York on the 20th of April 1942, just several weeks after returning there. This ship, too was sunk – by U-522 under *Kapitänleutnant* Herbert Schneider – in a convoy action south of the Azores on the 9th of January 1943. All but two of the crew of 45 was rescued by other ships in the Convoy, TM-1 from Trinidad to Gibraltar. This was a suicide mission at the end of December 1942 – of nine ships sent, only two arrived safely in port at the other end. Bringedal then served as Mate on the *Heranger* from 20 February 1943 in Glasgow to the 30th of May of the same year.

Captain Bringedal was considered one of the finest masters in the fleet of the Norwegian Shipping and Trade mission in New York. His opinion and advice were often sought out for the advancement of other officers. When Winston Churchill, as Prime Minister of Great Britain, composed and mailed a commendation to Bringedal and his men, Ole Bull for Oivind Lorentzen of the Mission wrote to Bringedal aboard the *Norvik* on January 4th 1943 that "We are exceedingly pleased to note that His Majesty the King of England has awarded you the Certificate of Commendation and ask you to kindly accept the heartiest congratulations of the Norwegian Shipping and Trade Mission." Thorald Pedersen at the Mission in London signed a similar congratulatory letter on 4 December 1942. Bringedal was specifically cited in the US government wartime manual *How to Abandon Ship* for having returned to his stricken vessel no fewer than three times to send radio messages, save his ship, and gather supplies.

It would appear that while serving aboard the *Heranger*, Bringedal was able to take a few week's shore leave. The newspaper in Roland Iowa reported on 13 April 1943 that he visited his aunt, Mrs. Malinda Areneson (nee Twedt). "Capt. Bringedal has had the misfortune to have two ships torpedoed from under him since the war started, but was fortunate in losing only three men. He is now stationed in Brooklyn, where he is awaiting the command of another ship. Capt. Bringedal stated that he has a wife and child in Haugesund, Norway, whom he has not seen since 1938, but he has word from them occasionally, sometimes through Sweden and at other times through the Red Cross." He went on to visit a sister in Morris, Illinois before returning to New York.

On 12 June 1943 in New York Bringedal assumed command of the *Marie Bakke* until 17 August. He served as relief captain of the Norwegian motor tanker *Vav* from 22 December 1943 and 27 April 1944, when he left the ship in Boston. His final command of the war was the *Kaptein Worsoe*, which he led from 14 June 1944 to 16 June 1945, discharging in New York. After the war his last command of the period, named *Geisha*, took him back to Bergen, Norway, where he arrived on the 8th of September 1945 and was finally reunited with his family. Married to Ingeborg for decades and the father of a son and daughter, he died in Norway on 12 April, 1968.

Waldemar Lund was cleared to continue his gunnery career despite the loss of his eye. He served aboard the *Frithof Nansen* of Oslo from January to June 1942, and the motor tanker *Vanja* from June 1943 to January 1944. Then he joined the *Titania Tonsberg* between January and November 1944, the *Edvard Grieg* between January and June 1944 and the tanker *Petter* of Arendal, on which he served from July 2nd 1945 until the 19th. Lund lived until 2000 and died at the age of 84. O. A. *Knudsen* Motorman Ludvik Slettene's career was far from over, though his life would end in the final weeks of the war. In April 1945 he served as motorman on the Norwegian ship *Karmt* which was sunk with less than a month of war left, a mere two miles from the white cliffs of Dover.

Five men, including four Norwegian motormen and a Belgian were killed instantly in the explosion. Ludvik Slettene was one of them.

Steward Arnulf Samuelsen was born in Drobak and was 29 years of age at the time. In New York, he joined a Norwegian general cargo ship which was, like the O. A. *Knudsen*, from Haugesund – the 1,383-ton *Manghild*. Exactly two months after the O. A. *Knudsen* was torpedoed, the *Manghild* hit Virgin Rock in Placentia Bay, Newfoundland in heavy fog. The crew were landed in Newfoundland, but the ship was declared a total loss on May 23rd.

Deck boy John Francis Boyle, listed as born in Glasgow on the 31st of October 1922, was 21 when he survived the O. A. *Knudsen* sinking but had already experienced a full life. According to his granddaughter Nikaela, "He worked on tankers and freighters. He was mostly on a German oil tanker. He was sunk several times on other ships, and received a medal for saving his ship from an incoming torpedo." Apparently "He was tried in New York eventually for something relating to mutiny. He was ordered back on a ship and he jumped ship on the way out of port and never went back. He stayed in the US from then on."

First Engineer Harald Stavdal, born in Solum, was sadly lost in the war – off South Africa on another ship. On March 9th, just over one year since the O. A. *Knudsen* was sunk, the ship the 4,768- ton *Tabor* was struck by a torpedo from U-506 off Cape Agulhas, South Africa. She was on a ballast voyage from Port Said Egypt to Cape Town via Aden. Stavdal managed to escape the inferno which the engine room had become, but he was badly burnt over his entire body and died on the first evening in the boats. Motorman / Mechanic Bjarne Børresen next appears on board the Norwegian ship *Glittre* of 6,409 tons, registered to Stavanger. On the 23rd of February 1943, the ship was struck in mid-Atlantic by a torpedo from U-628 and later finished off by U-603. The 34 survivors out of a crew of 37, including Borresen, were landed in Saint Johns Newfoundland by one of the escorting corvettes HMS *Dianthus*, which picked them up mid-ocean.

Able Seaman and Gunner George Napstad was more fortunate in that he survived the war. Later, he served aboard the *Grena*, which was the last Norwegian ship sunk by the Axis in the Indian Ocean during World War II. She was sunk by the Japanese submarine I-26 under Commander Kusaka on the 17th of March 1944 off the Arabian coast at Abadan roughly 30 miles away. George Napstad survived the ordeal. He was transferred to Suez on the 14th of April 1944 aboard the Dutch ship *Noesaniwi* where he stayed at the Merchant Navy Club to await joining another Norwegian ship.

Heyse had intended to utilize the Northeast and Northwest Providence channels to re-enter the Straits of Florida and essentially circumnavigate Abaco and Grand Bahama, however he decided instead to head back to home base in France. To do this the sub steamed northeast towards Bermuda on the 6th, and 7th, when it was attacked by aircraft. According to the US Office of Naval Intelligence Interrogation report, "Having used all his 15 torpedoes, the commander set course for Lorient, again passing close to Bermuda. In this area U-128 was attacked by an airplane which dropped either two bombs or two shallow set depth charges. No damage was sustained. It is probable that this was the attack delivered by two PBM planes of VP-74 at 1202 Q March 7 1942.

The first bomber released two depth charges set at 50 feet just as the stern of the U-boat disappeared, but unfortunately they were duds. The same plane made another run later releasing two depth charges, and the other bomber dropped two more. The assessment of the attack was 'No damage'." This is corroborated by Lawrence Paterson, who wrote "...near Bermuda Heyse received the brunt of a brief air-attack, two shallow-set depth-charges falling wide, shaking the boat as it crash-dived to safety." According to the KTB or war diary of U-128, her position on 7th March, was 28.57N, 70.54W instead of instead of 30.05N and 65N. However at noon the next day she was at 30.45N, 67.18W, which is closer, so it can be said that submarine and aircraft were in the same general area, and there were no other submarines in the same vicinity at that time. The fact that both Axis and Allies have a record of the same incident at the same rough time and location mitigates in favor of the report's veracity. At the relevant time the PBMs and other aircraft were stationed at the US lend-lease base in Bermuda.

On return to France, ONI notes that "Admiral U-boats, Dönitz, was present at their reception and congratulated Kapitänleutnant Heyse on his claim of 30,000 tons of United Nations shipping sunk."

U-128 returning to Lorient France from its patrol in the Bahamas, March 1942. Note the well-wishers lining the dock to the left.
Source:
seawolfproductions.com/shipwreck%20museum/Florida%20Wrecks/pan% 20mass/Aubrey%20Withee/AubreyWithee.htm

After this patrol U-128 went on four more patrols, the following three of them under Heyse, in which it sank a further nine ships. Patrol number three resulted in the destruction of 35,620 tons of Allied shipping, mostly just northeast of Trinidad, though the sub never re-entered the Caribbean Sea or the Bahamas area. U-128's final patrol began on the 6th of April and lasted only until the 17th of May, when the boat was sunk by Allied aircraft. On the 16th of May, U-128 was attacked by a US Mariner aircraft off Bahia Brazil, piloted by Lieutenant H. E. Gibbs who dropped six depth charges and observed a swirl in the sea. The following day a US depth-charge attack forced the U-boat to the surface. With the boat disabled and foundering on the surface, each aircraft initiated up to twenty strafing attacks. The submarine managed to move forward, however it could not dive. The crew assembled on the conning tower on the opposite side and some of them tried to signal surrender.

The pilots vectored two US Navy destroyers. On seeing the destroyers, Stienert decided to surrender and he ordered the crew to abandon ship. US aircraft dropped a life raft from the air into which at least 51 survivors climbed or clung. The US destroyers, *Moffett* and

Jouett, not daring to approach the submarine too closely, shelled her from a distance, sinking it. Four of the survivors who made it to the destroyers subsequently died. As reported by the ONI in their report, "*U.S.S. Moffett* was able to save 51 men.... 47 men, the commander, his executive officer, two midshipmen and 43 ratings and enlisted men, were landed at Recife on May 18, 1943." The report continues: "...No doubt the good treatment they had received played its part in the unlimbering some of the prisoners, most of whom were happy that for them the war was over. They were, in the words of some prisoners, 'very lucky'." Indeed, they were fortunate, and unlike two-thirds of their comrades and a number of the officers and crew of the *O. A. Knudsen*, they would survive the war.

Regarding the morale and loyalty of the *O. A. Knudsen* crew, the men were unified and "emphatic in their statements that there was nothing suspicious about the actions of any member of the crew prior to, or during, the attack." The interviewers went on to state that "...it should be noted that the officers and men are in accord in describing the crew as calm and diligent in carrying out all orders throughout the attack." This was not the case for all shipwrecked sailors to be interviewed by the US Navy and ONI.

Ten weeks later the *E. P. Theriault* had to be abandoned by Captain Foster and his crew when U-753 under Alfred Manhardt von Mannstein ordered them into boats and set charges to explode in the schooner's hull 55 miles west of the Dry Tortugas, Florida. Though it caught fire the ship did not sink, instead it washed ashore in the Bay of Cardenas, Cuba, its cargo was salvaged, and it continued to trade as the *Ofelia Gancedo* out of Havana, where the survivors managed to reach on the 27th of May. Captain Foster returned to his native Cayman Islands.

THE DUCHESS OF WINDSOR

Wallis Simpson, the Duchess of Windsor personally greeted every Allied survivor of submarine attack who landed in Nassau during World War II. She did so in the capacity of the second President of the Red Cross, which was founded in the Bahamas by Lady Dundas, wife of the previous governor. Simpson's husband, HRH the Duke of Windsor (the erstwhile King Edward VIII) was the Governor of the Bahamas between 17 August, 1940 and 16 March, 1945 – he was the only British royal in modern history to hold a civilian job, and it was to be his last. The Windsors were based in Government House in downtown Nassau through most of the war, though they enjoyed a peripatetic travel schedule to the US as well. Their presence not only uplifted the lives of over 257 Allied merchant sailors, for whom meeting the Duchess was something they all shared in common, but it also boosted tourism to the islands, endowing Bahamas with an aura of international glamour.

Dozens of books have been written about the influential Duchess, who succeeded in toppling a king where Hitler and the Axis had failed. Two unpublished manuscripts, one from the 1940s, the other from the 1950s, have been consulted for this book. Bessie Wallis Warfield was born on the 19th of June 1896 – interestingly, no certificate verified her gender. Her father died within a year. Her early life was characterized by poverty punctuated by largesse provided by moneyed relatives; though she attended the prestigious Oldfields School, her mother lived in a building akin to a tenement house.

On the 8th of November 1916 Wallis married her first of three husbands, Earl "Win" Spencer, a US Air Force officer and heavy drinker who occasionally beat her on the increasingly rare times they spent together. Having to witness two airplane crashes in the space of a week while at Spencer's air base in Florida made Wallis afraid of flying for the balance of her life. This was to have an obvious impact on her and the Governor's choice of travel between the Bahamas and Florida during the war. She followed Spencer to Hong Kong and had several affairs there, notably with an Italian diplomat who would become the son-in-law to Benito Mussolini (this is rumored to have led to a botched abortion which left her barren). The marriage ended on 10 December 1927.

On 21 July 1928 Wallis Spencer married Ernest Aldrich Simpson, an American of British descent who served in the prestigious Coldstream Guards and whose father co-founded the ship brokerage firm of Simpson Spence and Young, which is still extant today. The marriage lasted until Simpson's firm's fortunes changed and Wallis became the mistress of Edward, Prince of Wales, the heir to the British throne then occupied by King George V, a grandson of Queen Victoria.

Things moved quickly and momentously. King George died on January 30, 1936. Edward became King Edward VIII, though he was never formally crowned, the next day. A divorce from Simpson was granted to Wallis on the 27th of October 1936. The following month Prime Minister Baldwin gave the king three options: marry Simpson while remaining king and destroy the elected government while creating a constitutional crisis, drop the idea of marrying Wallis Simpson, or abdicate in order to marry her. On top of her unpopularity with British royals and the public at large, a key issue was that the Church of England, of which the King was head, forbade re-marriage by persons whose spouses were still alive (Wallis had not one but two living ex-spouses at the time).

On 10 December 1936 King Edward VIII abdicated – gave up – the throne of England and it passed to his younger brother the Duke of York (who immediately became King George VI). His statement that "I have found it impossible to carry the heavy burden of responsibility, and to discharge my duties as King as I would wish to do, without the help and support of the woman I love" has been famous since and is part of popular folk lore and music in the Bahamas. Leaving England for Austria, he reunited with Wallis after a legally required cooling off period on the 4th of May 1937 in Paris, France, where she had moved.

They married on June 3, 1937 at the Château de Candé, lent to them by Charles Bedaux, who was later arrested by the Allies for treason against the US and France (he killed himself in prison in Miami during the war rather than face a trial). After fleeing first to Southern France, then Spain and finally outside Lisbon Portugal where they became involved with intrigue with German diplomats, the couple were moved on orders of Prime Minister Winston Churchill first to Bermuda and then, on the *Lady Somers*, a commercial passenger ship, to Nassau. They arrived on the 17th of August, 1940 in sweltering heat. In a characteristic flaunt of protocol, the Duchess preceded the new Governor off the ship. On being installed the following day, the Duke of Windsor displaced the popular Governor since 1934, Sir Charles Cecil Farquharson Dundas. He and Lady Dundas were transferred to Kampala, Uganda.

By all accounts the Duchess of Windsor performed her job as head of the Red Cross well. It involved the welcome and care of over 257 survivors from ships sunk by German raiders or U-boats, starting with Tapscott and Widdicombe from the ship *Anglo Saxon*, sunk 3,000 miles away. Discovered in Eleuthera on the 31st of October 1940, the two emaciated and sole survivors of the British merchant ship were flown to Nassau the following day and visited in person by the Duke and Duchess.

This was a propaganda coup, since the men had survived ten weeks of privations on the high seas, and the seamen and royalty willingly acquiesced to be used in such a way (Widdicombe would be sunk on another ship within a year and Tapscott would run back to sea and ultimately kill himself). The next month a second batch of convicts from the French penal colony on Devil's Island, off French Guiana arrived in the Bahamas. In the exigencies of war the camp was no longer maintainable and so the convicts were simply cast adrift by their former wardens. Naturally these foreigners and former criminals were met with suspicion by the local populace and governmental confusion as to what to do with them, Ally or no. After weeks of wrangling it was decided to cast them loose again, with some food and water, on the high seas. This was done.

The Duke and Duchess of Windsor at Government House,
Nassau during WWII.
Source: guardian.co.uk/culture/2010/nov/13/william-boyd-any-human-
heart-murder

The Duchess had her work cut out for her and the staff of nurses, who drew their initial support from the Imperial Order of Daughters of the Empire. When she wrote to her beloved Aunt Bessie on the 16th of March 1942 that "We have been taking care of men landed here from three more ships – a job for the Red Cross…" she was referring to the Norwegian survivors from the O. A. *Knudsen*, the British survivors from the *Daytonian*, and the Greek survivors from the *Cygnet*. About the care of these vulnerable and often injured sailors Simpson would write in her memoir

"A few months after Pearl Harbor, Nassau got its first real taste of the war. The U-boats suddenly appeared in the Caribbean and off the Florida coast, to prey on the tankers and ore boats coming up from South America. In the space of ten days five shipwrecked crews landed in Nassau. With the other ladies of the Red Cross, I did what I could to make them comfortable while they awaited evacuation. As that terrible spring wore on we began to receive some truly heart-wrenching cases – men who had drifted for days without food or water under the searing tropical sun."

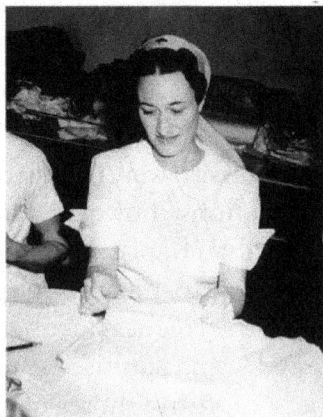

*The Duchess of Windsor in her Red Cross uniform
doing volunteer duty, Nassau.
Source: e-reading-lib.org/bookreader.php/1007828/Sebba_-
_That_Woman.html*

Her letter of 16 March 1942 continues: "...I am endeavouring to open a canteen for the boys to keep them out of the grapevine! ... We have just finished a Red Cross Fair in the garden [of Government House] and raised more than we expected – thank goodness as the outfitting of these seamen is a drain on our resources...." Her biographer Michael Bloch, who can only be described as an apologist for the Duke and Duchess, writes that "The sight of the shipwrecked moved her to great compassion."

Radio Operator Alan Heald, having just survived the sinking of the *Athelqueen* off Abaco, writes that on arrival in Nassau "...we were badly clothed and unshaven but we lined up to be received. It was a surprise to find that the Governor was the former King Edward VIIIth and his wife the former twice-married Mrs. Simpson. At that point someone came down the line and said to each one of us 'when you meet him you address him as Your Royal Highness, but when you meet her you address her as Your Highness because she's not royal.' We never found out who he was, but we presumed he was the adviser to the public on royal protocol." This was probably Captain George Wood, an aide-de-camp to the Duke in Nassau.

Certainly the presence of the Duchess of Windsor as principal care-giver to the survivors lent an element of glamor to the otherwise pitiful conditions in which the men were rescued. Most of them spoke glowingly of their interactions, however brief, with the Duke and Duchess. One survivor, Nathan Kaplan, cadet on the *Potlatch*, cherished a pair of silk pajamas given to him by the Duke, and others kept photographs of them with the Duchess taken on arrival. The British, in particular, were impressed – and surprised – to have their recent king welcoming them in person on the shores of an otherwise overlooked colony.

Wallis Simpson's fear of flying indirectly lead to their acquiring the 57-foot Elko-built power boat, named Gemini *for her star sign,*
which is still operating today.
It was given to them by an American after they moved to Nassau.
Source: yachtserenity.com/storyserenity.html

U-BOAT ACTIVITY 5 TO 10 MARCH 1942

The week between the loss of the O. A. *Knudsen* on 5th March and they *Cygnet* on the 11th belonged largely to three Italian submarines from the Betasom flotilla in Bordeaux. Carlo Fecia di Cossato continued an extraordinarily successful patrol by sinking the Dutch steamer *Astrea* as well as the Norwegian ship *Tonsbergsfjord*, both on the 6th of March. Two days later the submariners sank the Uruguayan ship *Montevideo*, which had ironically been the Italian ship *Adamello* before being requisitioned by the Uruguayan government.

The *Giuseppe Finzi* under *Capitano di Corvetta* Ugo Guidice sank the British ship *Melpomene* on the 6th of March. *Melpomene* was requisitioned from the French. The same day *Finzi* sank the neutral Swedish ship *Skane*. Four days later Guidice found and sank the Norwegian ship *Charles Racine* north of Puerto Rico. This attack led to the diversion and ultimate demise of the British tanker *Athelqueen* which was transiting to the north towards the Bahamas.

The period from 7 to 9 March belonged to *Kapitanleutnant* Ernst Bauer, aged 28. Bauer would go on to sink a record eight ships in the region, accruing 38,468 tons. He followed up the attack on the *Mariana* off Mayaguana by dispatching the American ships *Barbara* and *Cardonia* within sight of each other off the northwest coast of Haiti. The *Cardonia* men managed to struggle ashore in life boats on Isle Tortue, Haiti, where they were at first mistaken by locals for Germans invading the island.

Two days later, U-126 dispatched the Panamanian tanker *Hanseat* in the Old Bahama Channel, between Bahamian and Cuban waters. This incident was misconstrued by the otherwise well informed historian Capt. Samuel Eliot Morison, who wrote "In a few instances there is suspicion of collusive sinkings. ...The [*Hanseat*] crew abandoned ship at invitation of the U-126 commander before the attack; German officers boarded her and obtained confidential communications; and the crew later admitted that this was the third ship lost by them in that manner."

With the benefit of declassified documents not only on the *Hanseat* but other ships sunk in the area, it is clear what actually happened. By a strange coincidence three of the same company's tankers were all attacked in the same area on the same week: the *Esso Bolivar* on the 8th, the *Hanseat* on the 9th, and the *Penelope* on the 14th of March. It is possible that members of the crews of all three ships were reunited for their repatriation trip from Guantanamo to Miami and thence to New York. If that were the case, then there would have been veracity to the statement that the crews of three ships all sunk by the Axis were together, or something along those lines. Adding to a sense of suspicion of the crew, the *Hanseat* was built in Germany in 1929 and up until 1935 was owned and operated by the Baltisch-Amerikanische Petroleum Import GmbH of Germany. At the time of her loss the crew, under Captain Einar Brandt, were mostly Danish.

CARLO FECIA DI COSATTO & R.SMG. *ENRICO TAZZOLI*

The *Enrico Tazzoli* was one of three submarines of the *Calvi* class, so named after the first submarine in the series, the *Pietro Calvi*. The others were the *Giuseppe Finzi* and *Tazzoli*. All three patrolled to the greater Bahamas area during the war – the *Finzi* twice. The design of the submarine was of civilian origin, whereas submarines afterwards were designed by Naval draftsmen in the Regia Marina, or Royal Navy or Italy. They were designed for blue-water, or ocean-going operations in the open sea and the salient feature was double hull throughout. As Christiano D'Adamo writes:

"Typical of this class was an increased range and an improved habitability, thus making the vessels very suitable for long cruises. Unfortunately, these units, slow in maneuvering, were better suited for isolated attacks against slow merchant ships than group actions. Overall, they should be considered successful since the *Calvi* sunk 29,603 tons, the *Finzi* 26,222 and the *Tazzoli* 96,553."

The dimensions of these three submarines were 276.57 feet overall length, 25.3 feet wide, and 17.06 feet deep. The submarine's displacement tonnage was 1,550 tons on the surface and 2,060 tons submerged. She was propelled by 4,400 horse-power diesel engines which were backed up by a 1,800-h.p. secondary motor. These turned two propeller shafts and provided the vessel with 17.1 knots of speed on the surface and 8 knots submerged. As D'Adamo writes, "The standard propulsion system consisted of diesel engines for surface navigation and electric motors for submerged one. The *Ammiragli* and *Balilla* class had a third diesel engine attached to a Dynamo used to produce electricity for surface navigation, thus providing for low-speed long-range capabilities." He notes that Italian submarines never fully researched or installed the Dutch-designed schnorchel device, which enabled the submarines to recharge their batteries and motor under diesel power while submerged.

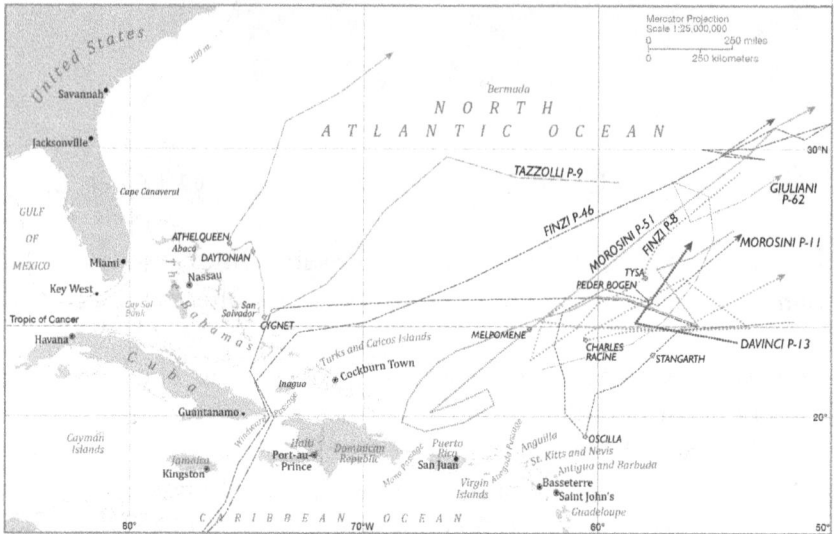

The range of a *Calvi* class submarine was 11,400 nautical miles at 8 knots on the surface, based on a carrying capacity of an impressive 75 tons of diesel. The primary armament consisted of eight torpedoes, each of 533 millimeter-diameter, fired from both fore and aft, as well as two 120 X 45-mm canons, located just forward and aft of the conning tower. There were an additional four anti-aircraft guns mounted on deck, each of 13.2 millimeters.

One of the unusual features of the submarine was that it was capable of carrying – indeed it required a full crew of – 72 men, versus the 48 to 55 required for a typical Type VII or Type IX submarine. The crew breakdown was typically seven officers and 65 crew members. Since one of the most outcome-determinative persons on the submarine was the commander, it will be worth devoting several paragraphs to Carlo Fecia di Cossato, one of the most successful submarine commanders both in the Bahamas region and worldwide during World War II.

Carlo Fecia di Cossato was born in Rome on the 25th of September 1908 to Carlo and Maria Luisa Gene. His was a noble Piedmont family and he was invested with the title of Earl, part of the Savoy dynasty. He attended the Royal College at Moncalieri, run by the Barnabiti brothers. Naval service ran in di Cossato's family: his father had lost an eye on the China station and his brother Luigi had received the silver medal for bravery for leadership during landings in Bargal,

Somalia in 1925. Because Luigi had died during other exercises in Calabria, Carlo was denied his request to serve as an aircraft observer.

Carlo Fecia di Cossato
Source: piombino-storia.blogspot.com/2010/09/capitano-carlo-fecia-di-cossato.html

In 1923 he completed the equivalent of high school and entered the Naval Academy in Leghorn, graduating in 1928 with the rank first of Midshipman and then of Acting Sub-Lieutenant at the age of 19. His early assignments were aboard the submarine *Bausan*, a cruiser named *Ancona*, and a destroyer named *Nicotera*. After further classes he was assigned to the cruiser *Libia* in China, where he led amphibious troops in Shanghai. In 1933 the *Libia* returned to Italy and di Cossato participated in the defense of Massawa, in the Italian colony of Abyssinia.

After a brief staff assignment under Admiral De Feo in East Africa, Di Cossato's next assignments were all in Libya – on the torpedo boat *San Martino*, Pollux and *Alcione*. During the Spanish Civil War he served on submarines, taking part in two special missions to the coast of Iberia. In 1939 he enrolled in submarine school. He became a Lieutenant aboard the submarine *Menotti* of the 34th Squadron in Messina. Then in the fall of 1940 he was transferred to Bordeaux to join the Betasom flotilla, the joint venture between the Regia Marina and the German Kriegsmarine.

Di Cossato served as second in command to Victor Raccanelli on the *Enrico Tazzoli*. Together they sank the Yugoslav steamer *Orao* off Scotland, and the British *Ardanhan* on 14 January. Then in early 1941 he was promoted from *Tenente di Vascello* (Lieutenant), then to *Capitano di Corvetta* (Lieutenant Commander). The next promotion, all going well, would be *Capitano di Fregata* (Commander). Then on 5 April 1941 Raccanelli was removed from command and di Cossato was promoted and given his own command. After vigorous testing the boat began its first patrol just two days later. A week later they found and sank the British ship *Aurillac*. The Norwegian ships *Fernlane* and *Alfred Olsen* followed. Di Cossato was establishing a level of success for himself in submarines.

On July 15ᵗʰ 1941 di Cossato and crew began another cruise from Bordeaux, this time to Freetown, Sierra Leone, West Africa. He attacked a convoy on 10ᵗʰ August without success. On the 12ᵗʰ of August di Cassato was given unconfirmed credit for damaging a ship called either the *Sangara* or *Zangara* of British registry. On the 19ᵗʰ of August he sank the Norwegian tanker *Sildra*. Later in the year, just before Christmas, the British cruisers HMS *Devonshire* and HMS *Dorsetshire* used Allied Enigma code-breaking to intercept and ship two of the most active German raiders of either world war: the *Atlantis* under Bernard Rogge, and the *Python*, in the southern Central Atlantic. This left over 414 men in need of rescue. As a result Admiral Dönitz activated all the larger Italian submarines they could spare, reducing their manning to a minimum to make room for the passengers. In an extraordinary rescue, Tazolli and other Italian and German submarines managed to load 254 men on their deck casings and in a slow convoy proceed back to Saint Nazaire France by Christmas.

On a macro level, D'Adamo writes that Dönitz, "attempted to integrate the Italian forces in the wolf-pack strategy, but the Italian boats were technically poor, slow to dive and possessed a large and easily detectable profile. As a result, most Italian submarines operated in the Central and Southern Atlantic in solitary missions." Indeed it is precisely these kind of missions which the *Finzi*, *Tazzoli*, *Morosini* and *Calvi* undertook to the Bahamas area – lone wolves supported above all else by each other in the transfer of fuel and torpedoes in the operational area.

Enrico Tazzoli began her patrol on the 2nd of February 1942, sailing from Bordeaux. Her assigned area was to the east of Florida and the Bahamas – because she was so busy sinking ships she would never have the need to approach Florida directly. *Tazzoli* was the first Italian sub sent to the region, but not the first to arrive, as the *Finzi* preceded her. On the way to the patrol area she encountered and fired three torpedoes at the British tanker *Rapana* in daylight on March 3rd. Due to interference from the sea conditions, all missed, and the boat continued westwards.

Three days later, on March 6th, the *Tazzoli* came upon the Dutch steamer *Astrea* and sank her. Later on that same day (a claim which is not supported by geography – the distances between the two reported sinkings being too far apart for even a fast boat to have covered in the same day), *Tazzoli* destroyed the Norwegian tanker *Tonsbergsfjord.*

War trophy: the Italian crew of the submarine Enrico Tazzoli *display a life ring from the Norwegian merchant ship* Tonsbergsfjord. *Note the large portals, which German U-boats did not have, and the head of an Italian sailor peering through one of them at upper right.*
Source: Antonio Maronari, "The Submarine Which Didn't Return"

Because the 32 surviving crew met survivors of the *Montevideo,* sunk by the same sub, and were rescued by the same ship (the *Telamon*) the story of how the *Tonsbergfjord* reached Haiti and then Curacao makes for colorful reading. The *Montevideo* was sunk on the 8th of March – she was a steam ship from Uruguay which had been built in Italy (ironically) as the *Adamello* in 1920. Claims that the neutral ship was sunk by Germans inflamed anti-German nationalism in Uruguay and led to protests and that country's eventual abandonment of its neutrality. Uruguay's neutrality had crucially allowed the German cruiser *Gräf Spee* to seek refuge there after the Battle of the River Plate earlier in the war.

CYGNET

The *Cygnet* was built as the steam ship *Mirach* in 1917 by the Rotterdam Dry Dock Company of the Netherlands. She was launched on the 3rd of March 1917 and completed in June. Her original owners were the N.V. Van Nievelt, Goudriaan & Company's Steamship Company, also known as Nigoco. Her flag was Dutch and home port Rotterdam. In 1939 *Mirach* was sold to the Goulandris Brothers of Piraeus and Andros, Greece and London, who renamed her *Cygnet*. Technically the ship was owned by the Halcyon Steam Ship Company Limited. The new owners flagged the ship to Panama and registered her to Panama City. Her gross tonnage was 3,530 tons and her overall length 373.2 feet. The ship's beam was 49'11" and draft 21'7". Her cargo carrying capacity was 6,367 tons. A 1,600 horse power engine propelled *Cygnet* at an average speed of ten knots.

Panamanian-flagged, Greek-owned, Dutch-built ship Cygnet, *ex-*Mirach *under her former name.*
Source: wrecksite.eu/wreck.aspx?194990

On her final voyage, the crew of 30 was led by Greek Master Captain John Mamais. Twenty seven of the men on board were Greek, with one citizen each from Canada, Romania and Spain. *Cygnet* was carrying a cargo of bauxite from Georgetown, British Guyana to Portland, Maine. It seems the ship topped up on rubber, in addition to carrying bauxite. According to locals on San Salvador, Bahamas, there were many bales of rubber which later floated free.

The charterers for her final voyage were Saguenay Terminals Company of Montreal, Quebec which was part of the Aluminium Company of Canada. The *Cygnet* completed a partial loading of cargo in Guyana and sailed on the 3rd of March 1942, exactly 25 years after she was launched. Probably it could not load a full cargo and still get over the bar of the mouth of the Demerara River, and so had to top up, or complete loading cargo, elsewhere. This it did in Saint Thomas, Virgin Islands, where *Cygnet* loaded more bauxite and sailed on the 8th of March.

Routing instructions were issued by the British authorities in British Guyana and by the Americans in Saint Thomas. They called for the ship to follow the coast as close as practical. It can be assumed that

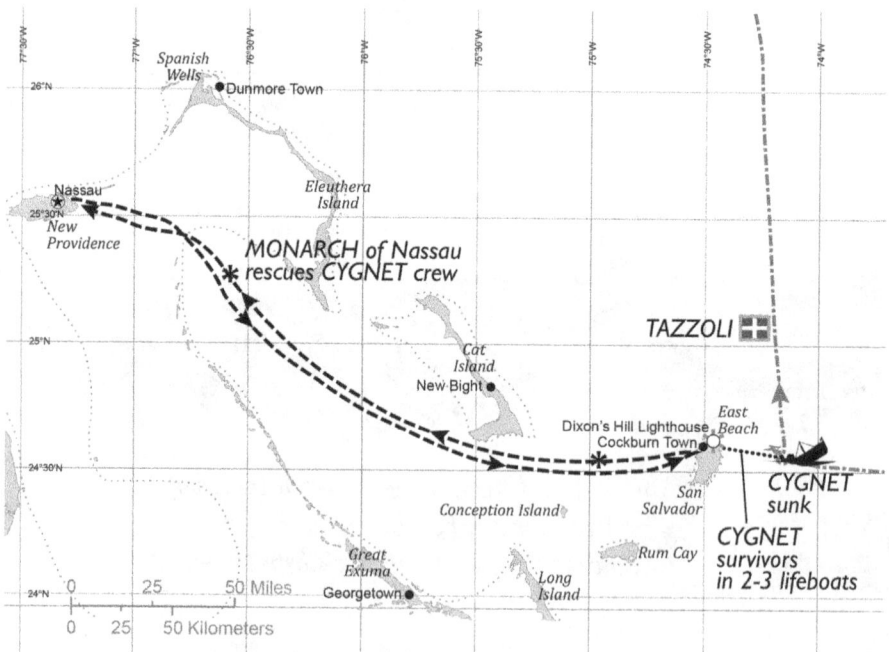

the *Cygnet* gained the open Atlantic through the Anegada or Mona Passage rather than the Windward Passage, as that would have been an easier route to take. Whether she passed north of the Turks and Caicos or used the Crooked Island Passage is not known.

The voyage proceeded uneventfully until the late afternoon of Wednesday, the 11th of March, 1942. Greek Radio Operator George Lemos, 29, was sitting in the radio shack. There was a lookout on the deck, and three lookouts on the bridge: Captain Mamais, age 37, Chief Officer Antonios Falangas, 31, and a helmsman. The weather was clear, the sea slight, and visibility good. The ship was not armed and was not zig zagging. Since it was a bright afternoon, they were not using any lights.

At 4:48 pm Chief Mate Falangas saw a torpedo emerge from beneath the ship on the port side, quite deep, heading towards land at a right angle to the bridge, which it appeared to have barely missed. At that point the ship was using the lighthouse at Dixon Hill, on San Salvador as a navigational reference. They were just over six miles away from the light, which was bearing 305 degrees. The *Cygnet* was steering almost due north - 350 degrees - and was making roughly nine knots.

The lighthouse at Dixon Hill, northeastern San Salvador Island, Bahamas. Source: homeaway.com/vacation-rental/p16121

Falangas called Captain Mamais over to see the torpedo's wake. Suddenly there was an explosion forward, by the number one hatch. The Chief Engineer, Constantinos Vlachakis, age 34, happened to be on deck at the time of the impact. He saw the torpedo approaching and when the torpedo hit, he witnessed the heavy cargo hatch being blown off and "a cloud of dust and debris rise several hundred feet with the explosion." He immediately ran aft to the engine room and stopped the engine. From the bridge, the Captain and First Officer watched in horror as the donkey engine (a steam contraption for enabling men to do heavy lifting such as raising and lowering the gangways) was shattered into little bits by the explosion.

Antonio Maronari, a member of the crew on the Italian submarine *Enrico Tazzoli* recorded events from the attacker's point of view:

"We are en route the Bahamas... Land ahoy! shouts Passon [a crew member] at 20:30 hours [German time]. Distant and blurred, there lies the island of San Salvador... Rather than proceeding immediately to the Crooked Pass (between that harmonious island and Long Island in the Bahamas group), as previously agreed, the Captain decides to stay here for a few days to make the most of this excellent area.

Botta [another crew member] has intercepted the transmission of a nearby ship, followed by another transmission, in which a coastal radio station signals to the American steamers an enemy submarine is in the Caribbean Sea. The *Tazzoli* perhaps? We are six miles offshore of San Salvador... It's 22:00 hrs. The gunner Corneli, whilst on the lookout at starboard, has spotted a ship. We accelerate at full speed and we perform a fast manoeuvre at 23:00 hours in order to attack underwater.

The Commander has taken position at the attack periscope... besides him, the Chief Torpedoman is ready to press the 5th and 6th switch of the launch device...

5 out! 6 out! It is 23:45 hours.

...It has barely been a minute.

"Hit! Surface...!" shouts the 'Pirate of the Atlantic' as a tremendous roar rumbles into the abyss."

The torpedo struck forward, about eight feet below the water line. So large was the hole that according to the Chief Engineer, water was up to the well decks before the lifeboats could even be lowered. Immediately, the ship took on an angle of sinking by the bow, or head. She also drifted to starboard but did not list heavily to that side. Fortunately none of the crew was badly injured, and all of them proceeded in an orderly fashion to launch the lifeboats. The exact number of boats launched is not known, but photos of the ship show large boats on either side, plus at least one jolly boat, or harbor launch, on the bridge deck on the port side. From this evidence, one may conclude that at least three and possibly four boats were launched.

Lemos was able to get an SSS signal off by radio, but he was unaware of the exact position of the ship, so he ran to the bridge to jot down the position. However, the officers were already abandoning ship. He saw the men in the boats beckoning him to join and he did so. Although Lemos was thus unable to give shore stations a position, as the Chief Engineer wryly noted, "Sent SOS but did not send position – no time. Position sent from San Salvador Island (they saw it)." Indeed he was right, as the attack was being witnessed with great excitement by residents on the nearby island, who also heard the explosions of shells.

Meanwhile the *Enrico Tazzoli* surfaced about one mile off the starboard quarter. They fired a warning shell to be sure that the boats stayed clear of the ship, which they fully intended to destroy. The boats pulled clear to a quarter to a half mile astern. The diarist Maronari wrote:

"We head towards the slightly heeled ship, the boats of the castaways already floating around it. In seconds, we are laying the guns. After a few minutes the boats are already far: we can open fire without fear of hitting them. A few castaways greet us waving their arms. We return the salute in disbelief. Then, without worrying about the proximity of the land, from which they can easily see and follow all the action, we open up [fire] on the ship that is down by bow. Seven 120 [calibre] rounds pierce the hull at the waterline. Amid the smoke, we distinguish the name of our fourth victim on the taffrail: *Cygnet - Panama.*"

"The deck is upside down and the high smokestack vents steam: one of the rounds has landed on the bridge, operating the siren which is now emitting a whining sound. From afar, the castaways are motionlessly watching on... ...it may even seem that they are commenting on the accuracy and the effects of our fire."

"At this time the Commander recalls an American radio program a few days back, in which the speaker said that: 'Never have the Italian submarines reached the shores of the United States.' The ship slowly sinks. We run at full speed towards the survivors on the boats and, as we approach, the Lieutenant and the crew spontaneously shout 'good luck.' Commander Cossato waves the "Tricolore" flag in the air and shouts in English:

Tell the Americans 'it isn't true. The Italian submarines have come here to sink their ships!' The castaways respond by frantically waving on and shouting cheerfully. These exchanges are extraordinarily friendly, especially since in a similar circumstance in which we would rather expect a series of accidents."

First the submariners sent shells hurling into the starboard side, then they rounded the bow and shelled the port side. The Greeks underestimated the number of shots fired according to the Italians. The Chief Engineer described their firing as "leisurely." Others said they fired a shell about every minute. Asked whether the Italians communicated with their Greek victims, the Engineer said that the "enemy merely waved." He said the sub looked old, and rusty.

Clearly convinced that the ship was doomed, di Cossato motored off in a northerly direction at about 5:45 pm. They had been on the surface for roughly 50 minutes. According to some of the crew, the submarine submerged as it headed north. But, since Maronari wrote about seeing the boilers explode and the glow of the burning ship in the dusk, it would seem that di Cosato was rather unconcerned about a counter-attack, and he remained on the surface for a while. In either event, the *Cygnet* was observed to sink by her crew at 6:20 pm on the 11th of March, about one hour and 30 minutes after the initial attack.

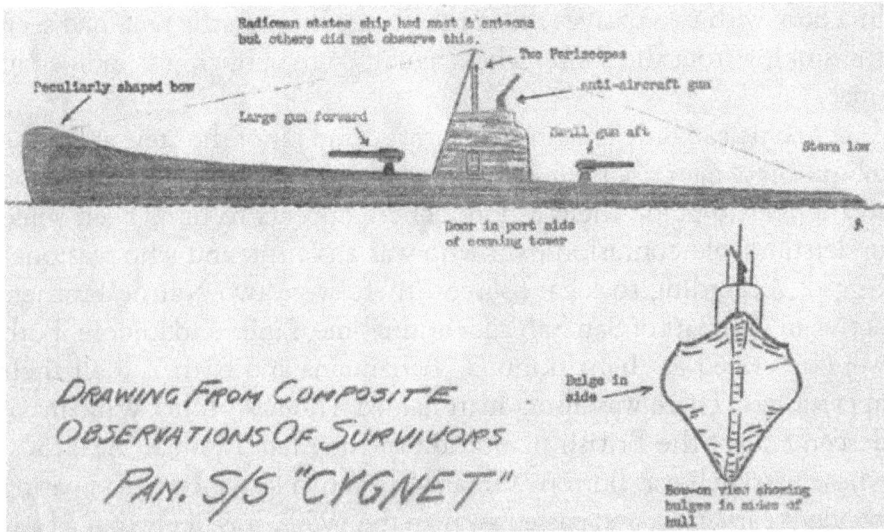

Drawing of the *Tazzoli* as described to US Navy personnel in
Miami Florida 22 March 1942.
*Source: Survivors Statements, National Archives and Record
Administration (NARA) Washington, DC, USA*

Maronari related the final moments of the *Cygnet*, as seen from
the deck of its attacker that night. "To the east, the shadows of the
sunset already stretch to the ocean. Flaming clouds to the west swallow
to last tendrils of gold. They move slowly driven by night breezes. In
this wonderful play of lights sparkle in the trees and the long lighthouse
tower, *Cygnet*, the condemned vessel, still shows, emerging on the lazy
waves. Suddenly the sky darkens. A red glow, followed by a piercing roar,
breaks the flow of our thoughts. *Cygnet* has jumped in the air, water has
invaded the boilers, causing the explosion and then the greedy ocean
swallows these other 4,784 tons."

Though the distance to San Salvador may seem negligible at six
miles, it took the men some ten hours to cover, by rowing, with little or
no breeze to propel their sail. This was an average of about half a mile
an hour. The locals were waiting, even though they did not arrive at the
dangerous reef line until four in the morning. According to Third
Officer Dods, "Mr. A. B. Nairne, a one-legged American who came out

in a dory with two natives to lead the boats through the reef, had seen the sinking from the shore. The account of the attack was radioed at once."

One can only imagine the surprise and joy of the crew at having a boat full of men risk their own safety to come out through an opening in the reef to guide them ashore. There appears to have been some understandable confusion over who was a Nairne and who was one-legged. According to local sources, there were two Nairne brothers active in that part of San Salvador at the time, Emile and Elmore. Both were described as "light-skinned" Bahamians and both had all their appendages. There was also a man named Thomas (Tom) Williams, a descendent of the British plantation-owning family since the 1780s, whose patriarch was Burton Williams. Tom had lost a foot in a boating accident earlier on, and passed away in the 1950s. It is likely that a boat sculled by Williams and carrying one or more of the Nairne brothers came out to rescue the *Cygnet* men, and in the excitement the survivor confused their names.

A local boy who was about 10 years old at the time "remembers hearing an explosion and waiting for word to reach about what had happened. He also remembers the sailors being transported to town - an uncle or cousin had one of the few vehicles on the island at the time. He thought they came ashore at East Beach in two row boats. They were then shipped over to Nassau on the regular mail boat. ...he thought the boat was a Dutch ship. He remembers that the ship was carrying rubber, and that for a little while after the incident that large bails of rubber would wash ashore. People would collect these and send them off to Nassau to sell."

Whether by the luck of good timing or because of the message was quickly sent from San Salvador to Nassau, the *Cygnet* crew were able to board the inter-island steamer *Monarch of Nassau*, under Captain Roland Roberts of Eleuthera, the very next day. They traveled in comfort, as the ship was fitted with 16 first class and 16 second class accommodation with a state-of-the-art ventilation system. In 1938 it was on the Miami-Nassau run and was disparagingly refered to by a Miami reporter as "a prissy old tub with a hifalutin name." Late in 1939 John Hawes (*aka* Father Jerome, the Hermit of Cat Island, a Catholic priest and architect) sailed on the *Monarch of Nassau* to Cat Island.

Under Carl Sawyer's ownership, it rammed and sank a ship named *Fire Island* in Miami. Later in the war she traded between Miami, Kingston and the Greater Antilles. She was sold and presumably broken up in the US Gulf after 1951.

The Monarch of Nassau *in the builder's yard, Cheshire, UK, as the* Sir Charles Orr, 1930. *She was delivered from the UK to Nassau in just 19 days by Captain E. R. Westmore and six crew.*
Source: John Bowen, Model Shipwright, Number 90, December 1994, p. 58

The entire *Cygnet* crew arrived in Nassau on Friday, the 13th of March – the same day that the *Daytonian* met a fiery end at the hands of the *Enrico Tazzoli* off the Northeast Providence Channel. The *Cygnet*'s crew was only the second batch of survivors of submarine attack to arrive in Nassau, after the *O. A. Knudsen* less than a week before. The news was announced guardedly in the local papers thus: "Thirty officers and men from a freighter which was torpedoed in Bahamas waters Wednesday night are all safe and were landed in Nassau today. They are being taken care of by the Greek Consul and the Red Cross."

In Nassau the officers and crew were well looked after by the local Greek community, which was led in part by Consul Christopher Esfakis, Acting Greek Vice-Consul, F. Scarlatos and the Greek Orthodox Church, led by Father Spirtos. On the 18th of March, Captain Mamais filed a Letter of Protest, on the instructions of the owner, in which he "hereby gives notice of his intention of protesting" the sinking of his ship by enemy combatants. The Notary Public was

Stafford Lofthouse Sands, Esq., who later became a prominent politician and the Minister of Finance for the colony.

The Halcyon Shipping Company appointed R. H. Curry and Company Limited of Nassau to be agents in the Bahamas. To handle the crew's needs and get them from Miami to New York, they used sub-agents Messrs. Albury and Company of Nassau and Miami. The general manager in Nassau suggested that the ship owners pay the Florida agents directly, "to avoid dollar exchange as there is considerable red tape in this connection." He also observed that the charity, which the survivors were receiving, was saving the owners money: "With regards to clothing for the men, the Red Cross and the Greek Community in the Bahamas have very generously assisted, and we do not think the men will need any more clothing."

During the nine days that the *Cygnet* crew laid over in Nassau they were joined by hundreds of other shipwrecked mariners – from the O. A. *Knudsen* sunk 5th March, the *Daytonian* whose survivors arrived the 15th of March, and the *Athelqueen*. The IODE and the Red Cross scrambled to drum up funds, clothes, cigarettes and basic amenities for the men. Local papers were filled with drives for supplies such as a refrigerator for the men, as well as listings of social events like movie screenings, dinners, dances, etc. to entertain them. Some of the men were taken into private homes, others were put up gratis at the Lucerne and Rozelda hotels, and some of them had to stay in the hospital. Given the crowding in local hotels from roughly 150 other survivors, most of the men would have stayed in private homes opened by member of the Greek community. Captain Mamais submitted that at least four of his men had minor injuries.

A Mrs. Alexiou, matriarch of the Greek community in Nassau Bahamas recalled, "…some were in bad shape, tired sun-burned, bruises and minor wounds, talked about trouble with sharks. They were taken to the hospital for a couple days, looked much better and rested after that. They were put up in an apartment which the Greek Orthodox Church owned on Frederick Street near their house - near what is now the Central Bank. She was newly-wed and went with her husband and Father Spirtos to see them in the hospital. Her husband used to bring them to their restaurant – Gleneagles - to eat. They were in town for a couple of weeks, then permission came for them to travel to USA. [She

has] never seen or heard of [them] since. ...other Greek families -
Damianos, Maillis, Esfakis, Psilinakis, Mosko - all helped."

An open letter of thanks from Captain Mamais was published in
the local paper the following day. It read: "The Captain, officers and
crew from the torpedoed Greek freighter who arrived in Nassau
yesterday have asked us to express their deep appreciation for the
kindness and hospitality extended to them by the Bahamas Red Cross,
the Acting Greek Consul, the Greek community and everyone else who
helped. In asking us to express their thanks, they said 'Please make it
very nice because everyone has been so kind and we cannot say how
much we appreciate their goodness.'"

As is usual when sailors or travelers lose their documents (they
had to abandon their home in a matter of minutes, and most of them
had only the shirt on their back), the sailors had to be issued new visas
and passports. The American Consul, John Dye, worked closely with
the agents and the owners to arrange these. Money was sent from New
York for the Captain to advance some funds to the crew. On the 17th
of March, Dye telegrammed the Department of State requesting transit
certificates for the "27 Greek 1 Spanish 1 Canadian 1 Rumanian
seamen." The Greek Consul paid for the cost of the telegrams. At 7:57
pm on the 19th, "Welles, acting" for the US government granted the
waivers. Perhaps surprisingly, given the speed with which they were
forced to abandon ship, about half of the men were able to produce some
form of identification.

After roughly one week, on the 21st of March, they secured
passage on the inter-island motor vessel *Ena K.*, which provided a
regular sea link from Nassau to Miami. On arrival in Miami, they were
taken to the United States Naval Reserve Armory at Northwest South
River Drive. George Morrison was interviewed by Ensign A. T. Carter
at 4:30 pm, Radio Operator Lemos and Third Officer Dods by Ensign E.
L. Valier, USNR the same day. Chief Engineer Vlachakis was debriefed
by Ensign Millard H. Shirley, and Chief Officer Falangas was
interviewed by Ensign George V. Salzer, Jr. on the 31st of March. The
men stayed at least ten days in Miami before they took a train to New
York, to meet with the owners and obtain their next assignment.

Meanwhile the *Tazzoli* continued it deadly patrol. The next day
Maronari observed "It is 1:00 am. The sun sets behind the island of San

Salvador by drawing an outline of fire with the profiles of the hills and coastline, sunk in the great light path, a long fiery black shape. ..the night has swallowed all the latest tendrils of gold. The air cools and suddenly a light breeze ruffles the surface of the sea, which has become gray. A pulsating light shines on the north coast of the island. The lighthouse of San Salvador works even in time of war? Is this an American's joke?"

"The night brings with it thoughts and reflections on the events. A quick review of that day allows us to rather lazily examine things and events, now routine for us. In the control room, in the quiet shadows of blue lights, the engineer, Firrao gossips with the lieutenant, who grumbles: 'Don't hit my head when you pass!'"

"If we have been seen from the shore, the better. That fills me with an intimate and profound joy.... The wet berths welcome us and the lazy waves of the Atlantic gently lull the Corsair crew of the boat to sleep. The night passes, with every four hours the tranquil echo of the heavy tread on the guard plates above us...."

UBOAT ACTIVITY MARCH 10 – 15 1942

In the five days between the loss of the *Cygnet* and the *Tazzoli's* next victims the *Daytonian* and *Athelqueen*, two Axis submarines entered the region and four ships were sunk. On the 11th of March Ernst Bauer in U-126 continued his sinking spree in the Old Bahama Channel by destroying the US ships *Olga* and *Texan* on the 11th and *Colabee* on the 13th of March.

Ernst Bauer during patrol with his new Ritterkreuz. *Bauer sank more ships in the Bahamas area aboard* U-126 *than any other submarine commander, German or Italian.*
Source: U-Boot-Krieg in der Karibik, VerlagsArchiv

Two days later, on the 15th of March, ace *Kapitanleutnant* Albrecht Achilles, age 28, entered the region briefly by transiting out of the Caribbean into to open Atlantic, homeward bound via the Anegada Passage. During his patrol, he had penetrated into the Gulf of Praia to attack two ships in Port of Spain, Trinidad on 19th February, followed by an audacious entry to Castries Harbour, Saint Lucia to attack the *Umtata* and the *Lady Nelson* at berth on the 10th of March. The attack required him to reverse out of the narrow channel under fire.

The Italian submarine *Morosini* under *Capitano di Corvetta* Athos Fraternale entered the region on the 15th of March. A few days before, he had dispatched the small British ship *Manaqui*, steaming alone for Kingston. Sadly all hands were lost - his attack was later confused with the loss of the *Stangarth*, a larger ship, which was sunk in a different location and different time by the German submarine U-504.

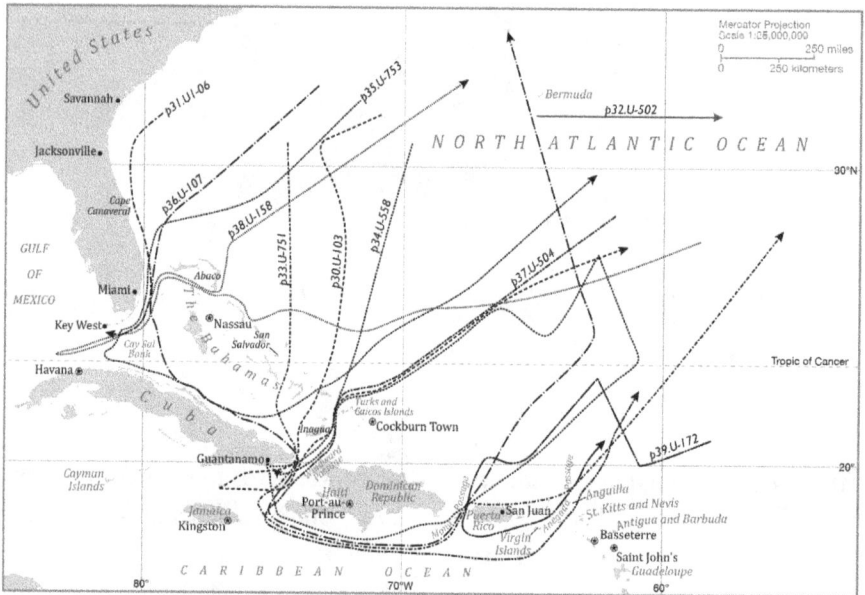

DAYTONIAN

The *Daytonian* was a British steam ship built in 1922 by D. and W. Henderson and Company Limited of Meadowside, England. Her original owners were the Leyland Line, which eventually sold the ship to the Thomas and James Harrison Company, also known as the Charente Steamship Company, of Liverpool. At the time of her last voyage, the *Daytonian* was chartered to, and under the control of, the British Ministry of War. Early in the war, the *Daytonian* found itself in a series of back-to-back convoys, starting on 18 November 1939 and then back and forth to Halifax for two years until August 1941.

The ship's dimensions were 413'6" in length, 52'6" in breadth and 29'2" in depth. Her quadruple-expansion steam engine propelled the *Daytonian* at a respectable 12 knots. Her gross tonnage was 6,422 tons and cargo capacity was 9,480 tons. She was armed with a four-inch gun aft, two Hotchkiss machine guns of .303 caliber, two Marlin machine guns and two Lewis guns.

British steam ship Daytonian *in port*
Source: Linda Ryan, daughter of Henry Mapplebeck, Third Officer of
Daytonian 1941-1942

On the 8th of March 1942, the *Daytonian* left Mobile, Alabama for a voyage to Halifax. In his personal diary, Third Officer Mapplebeck recorded that it was "cold rough weather." The general cargo of 7,500 tons consisted of steel, lumber, and cotton. Her ultimate destination was Liverpool. The voyage took her around Key West, up the Straits of Florida and around Great Isaac Light through the Northwest Providence Channel and past Nassau. Since leaving Mobile the weather was reported to have been fine. From the Northeast Providence Channel, she was proceeding towards a point 200 miles south of Bermuda, from which she was to turn north for Halifax as per routing instructions.

Daytonian's Master was Captain John James Egerton and the Chief Officer John Marsden. Most of the crew of 58 was English, but there were two Welshmen, Able Bodied Seaman Howard Jones and Deckhand John York, a Scotsman, Deckhand William Thompson, and a Canadian, Fireman Ernest Sampson. The Third Officer was Henry Mapplebeck of Hull, aged 27. Married less than two years before, his wife Barbara was pregnant with their first child at the time, and he loaded his cabin with a crib, nappies, and baby clothes in the US, as all were on short supply in war-torn England.

At noon local time on the 13th of March 1942, the *Daytonian* was some 75 miles east-northeast of Hole in the Wall Light. The ship was heading east-northeast at 72 degrees true and making nine knots and not zig zagging. The weather was mild, with a light southeasterly breeze, a smooth sea and good visibility. Suddenly, the mast-head lookout saw a torpedo streaking deep down the starboard side, just aft of the bridge. It was too late to take evasive action. A torpedo fired by *Enrico Tazzoli* under Carlo Fecia di Cossato, fresh from sinking the *Cygnet* off San Salvador, found its mark in the *Daytonian* and dealt a crippling blow. The diarist Antonio Maronari on board the Italian sub relates that:

"The Commander is motionless in his place. However, since the last few minutes, it seems like the binoculars are glued to his eyes. Then he suddenly leaps from the chair and climbs into the periscope. "Alarm"

"Yes Sir!" A funnel has appeared down the horizon, at times emitting moderate puffs of smoke. "Come starboard! Full speed ahead!" The heat begins. With change course to 200 at maximum speed, we come closer. It's a big ship and it's moving quite slowly. At 17:15 hours we descend by 30 meters and perform the set–up, reaching periscope depth. The whole operation has taken place with astounding precision. The ship heads towards us. We will launch [the torpedoes by] the stern. A strange light revives the Commander's lifeless eyes. The eyes of the men gaze in the direction of the invisible target.

"Launch stern tube.... Ready 6... Ready 7... 6 out! 7 out!"

Two nearly instantaneous detonations struck the ship in the center, under the bridge. Suddenly, a third explosion violently shakes us. Some of the lights go off and few muffled yells can be heard in the twilight. An airplane must have identified us whilst we were attacking at periscope depth. We're stuffed! I thought I had seen something in the sky above the ship during the attack, but at the time I thought I might have been wrong. The commander thoughtfully mumbles as we hastily descend to safe depth."

On board the *Daytonian*, the torpedo penetrated the engine space, disabled the boilers and decommissioned the engines. Fortunately none of the engine room crew were killed. The ship came to a gliding stop. Captain Egerton ordered the two port lifeboats, on the side opposite from the explosion, to be lowered, and they promptly made away from the ship with about half of the crew. On inspection, it was learned that both boilers were under water but had not exploded. The engine room team had managed to secure the watertight bulkhead connecting the boiler room and the engine room. However, this was not enough to prevent water from entering the engine room. In the engine compartment, water was four feet high and rising quickly. Because there was no submarine visible and thus no target to fire at, the guns were not brought to bear.

The Radio Operator, William Anthony "Herb" Cox managed to send off continuous SSS and SOS messages. Though Nassau Radio (VPN) received this message, it did not reply. Operating since at least 1922, VPN had a range of 400 nautical miles and sent messages between 7 am and 3 pm. Key West (MAR) and Lake Worth Florida (WOE) confirmed that the Mayday messages were received. Lake Worth asked the ship directly for a clarification of the position and Key West called Lake Worth to confirm it had received the SSS.

Captain Egerton threw the confidential codes over the side of the ship in an iron box with holes perforated in it. Confidential mail from the British legation in Caracas, Venezuela for the Secretary of State for Foreign Affairs in London were later torn into small pieces and thrown into the sea from the lifeboat. At 12:30 pm, 10 minutes after the attack, Captain Egerton ordered the abandonment of the ship. By 12:50 pm, both starboard lifeboats rendezvoused with the two port boats. All 58 men got safely away. The attack proved too much for the frail heart of Thomas Jones, age 65, an English Able Seaman. Apparently he suffered a fall to the deck during the attack, and had to be carried into the lifeboat by his shipmates. Shortly afterwards, Jones suffered a fatal heart attack and died that afternoon (he was buried at sea).

Meanwhile, on the submarine the crew was convinced (incorrectly) that they had been attacked by an Allied airplane and proceeded cautiously: "Confirmation comes from the various chambers that the explosion hasn't caused any damage to the hull or to the control room. We carry out the silent set–up at a depth of 45 meters. The hydrophones can't pick up any sound. We come to surface at 06:45 hrs. Everything's clear at the horizon.

"Man stations!" We haven't fully emerged from the sea depths that the cannon and machine guns are already armed and aimed. The

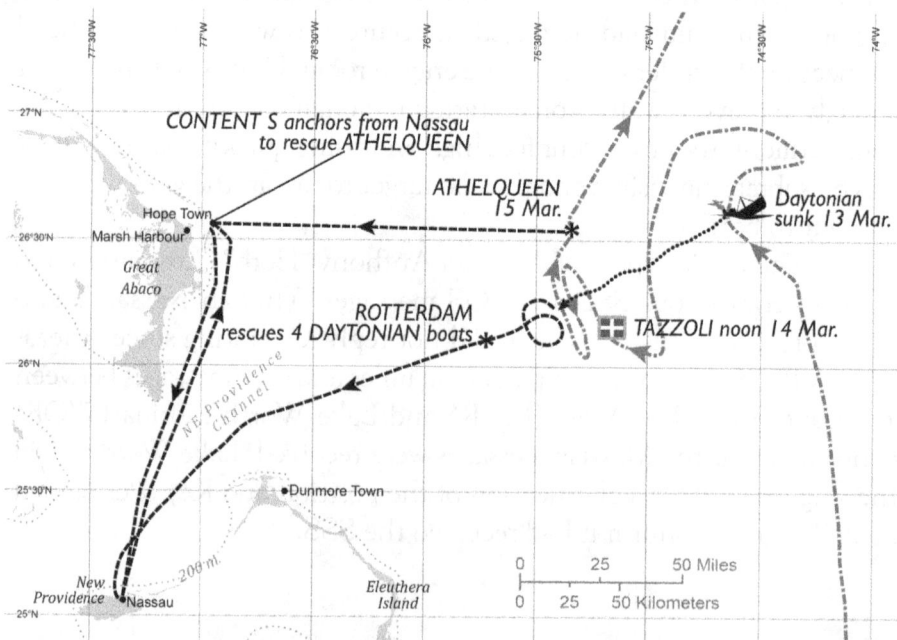

CONTENT S anchors from Nassau to rescue ATHELQUEEN

ATHELQUEEN 15 Mar.

Daytonian sunk 13 Mar.

Hope Town
Marsh Harbour

Great Abaco

ROTTERDAM rescues 4 DAYTONIAN boats

TAZZOLI noon 14 Mar.

NE Providence Channel

•Dunmore Town

New Providence Nassau

Eleuthera Island

0   25   50 Miles
0   25   50 Kilometers

ship is on the right. The aft gun is swung in our direction. Obviously, when we launched [the torpedoes], the enemy gunners found the periscope cropping out of the water. Here then is the explanation of the third explosion! The flagpole is flying the British flag. The ship is overloaded, and many large crates are stacked even higher between the two funnels."

At 1 pm, the *Enrico Tazzoli* came cautiously to the surface, wary that there could still be gunners on board the stricken merchant ship. At first, the submarine only partially surfaced. Then she fully surfaced half a mile off the starboard beam, and circled the *Daytonian*. By now the ship was roughly seven feet above water forward and had only three feet of freeboard aft, and generally appeared to be on an even keel. The last of the life boats was only 200 yards or so astern of the ship and quickly moved out of the way.

The submarine then began shelling the ship, aiming for the port quarter. In the words of Maronari, "We approach and begin hammering the ship with cannon. We too almost suffer as a massive fire rages through the enormous bridge-house. The water laps lazily around a name that stands at the stern of the ship in large white letters: *Daytonian - Liverpool*."

The *Tazzoli's* firing was more accurate than with the *Cygnet*, with 12 out of the 13 or 14 rounds scoring hits. Forty-five minutes later, a tremendous explosion ripped through the amidships portion. At 1:45 pm the ship sank on an even keel – an hour and 25 minutes after the initial attack. The men in the four lifeboats had ample opportunity to observe the submarine. They noted that she had "a large red spot on the starboard stern, indicating possible damage and repainting."

Di Cossato brought his sub amongst the life boats. He was dressed smartly in an Italian Naval uniform and as many as 20 of his men were on the deck and conning tower. According to the survivor reports, "…..the Italian sub commander questioned the master in perfect English, offered aid, and unfurled an Italian flag." The "enemy officer inquired if all hands were all right and if they wanted anything. The captain replied that the men were all right and that they wanted nothing." The *Tazzoli* left five minutes after the sinking, heading off to the east at 1:50 pm, "the sub's crew waving a friendly good-bye."

The Italian account of the *Daytonian's* final minutes is more vivid: "The *Daytonian* begins to sink, more and more and soon, soon.... Gurgles, roars, hisses escape ....[she] slips into the depths of the ocean.... scrap, trash cans, tables, boxes, floating in a mess ... Around the vortex a large patch of oil grows rapidly, as though blood gushing from the wound of a human being shot dead. This painful simulation leaves a deep impression. We run to the east, with more than 6,434 tons to our account."

The men in the boats were left to their own devices, and could only hope that since their radio messages were heard, help would be on the way. Staying within three to four miles of each other, they set off westwards for Abaco. Because of the light breeze, they did not make much progress, and meandered around for dozens of hours. As Mapplebeck laconically put it in his diary, "Torpedoed 11:20am, abandon ship, steer for Bahamas, c/s [course] 280 W." The next day, Mapplebeck reported "Fine weather, sighted nothing. Hope all well." He records that in the first 24 hours the boats covered "about 58 miles, setting on a/c [actual course] 250 W, speed about 2 knots judge [distance] from Abaco about 95 to 90 [miles]."

Two days after the sinking, at 2:10 am on the 15th of March, the number two lifeboat under Chief Officer Marsden found itself in the immediate vicinity of a submarine. This could only have been the *Tazzoli*. The sub headed west-southwest charging its batteries audibly, and passed only 400 yards from the lifeboat. At 2:25 am, it turned to starboard, crossed the wake of the lifeboat, and headed to the east-northeast.

Just 35 minutes later, at 3:00 am, the Dutch tanker *Rotterdam* came upon and rescued the first lifeboat. Her Master, Captain de Rata, reported that "...after picking up two lifeboats, a black spot, apparently another lifeboat was sighted on the starboard. The black object then paralleled the *Rotterdam* at the same speed, much in excess of possible speed of a lifeboat. After five minutes the object disappeared. The Master and First Mate were reasonably certain it was a conning tower of a sub. No lights were displayed on it, whereas each of the lifeboats signaled with flashlights. The Master suspected that the sub, if any, mistook the *Rotterdam* for a warship and fled."

Presumably the *Tazzoli* had been stalking the *Rotterdam* and because of its sheer size, turned away to the northeast to find other prey (it found the *Athelqueen* in the same area the following day). Over the next three hours, at great peril to itself, *Rotterdam* manoeuvred around the area picking up all four boats from the *Daytonian*. By 6:00 am she had collected all of them, and proceeded to the nearest large port, Nassau and landed the men there at 3:00 pm on the 15th or March. As Mapplebeck put it, "Convoy [to] port 3:30 am picked up by Dutch tanker *Rotterdam* landed Nassau, met Duke of Windsor, all well." To his wife he adds "missing you dear, off colour."

The next day both the Nassau *Guardian* and Nassau *Tribune* carried the same censored summary: "The crew from a third torpedoed ship were picked up and brought to Nassau yesterday afternoon after having been in their lifeboats for two days. Fifty-seven were saved, one died of shock immediately after the torpedoing." Mapplebeck reports a "quiet walk" and "no news, time dragging, entertained at night."

English Sailor Leslie Edmondson was hospitalized, however not for injuries sustained in the attack – rather for venereal disease. The Canadian Fireman, Ernest Sampson was able to obtain repatriation back to Canada and left the island for Kingston Ontario on the 25th of March, before his crew-mates. The rest of the men stayed in Nassau for nearly three weeks. On his third day, Mapplebeck went shopping, to the pictures at night, and was able to send a cable telegram to the UK. On Tuesday March 17th, the papers glowed about the warm and hospitable reception which had been laid on for the men from the *Daytonian* as well as survivors from the *O. A. Knudsen* and *Cygnet*, in an article entitled "Survivors Here Outfitted and Entertained."

On Thursday March 19th, Mapplebeck visited the yacht club, and "met duke duchess, nice day, bought baby stuff." The following day he went shelling on the coast. At night he was "up the canteen" at the Masonic Hall on Bay Street, and managed to send a letter. On Saturday the 21st, he commented on the "Usual routine, canteen, etc. beautiful weather, but dying to be home." On Sunday, he took a drive to the beach and went out to dinner at the Westinghouses. The following day it rained and he reported a quiet day in the canteen "morning + night." The following day, the English officers went together to the broadcasting house to enjoy a quiz program there. It was a wet day, and Mapplebeck commented on the blackout in the town. He was able to receive a cable from home. This was a particular relief to him as a doctor had told his wife that she could not bear children without placing her life and that of the child in peril.

On Wednesday the 25th of March, Mapplebeck was entertained to both lunch and dinner. His ear ached badly, for which he may have sought treatment by the Red Cross. The following day, he did a little shopping and received "orders to go," for which he was "glad to be on the way." The next day he was at the Bahamas General Hospital, probably for the ear infection. The weather was fine and there was a football match to follow. Their departure wasn't as clear and simple as the crew may have thought. United States Consul John Dye had to work with the "local government" in Nassau as well as the State Department in Washington DC to waive the usual "documentary and visa requirements" for Captain Egerton and a total crew of 56.

*A photo showing Daytonian Fourth Engineer John McCullam Holmes
(foreground) and Third Officer Henry Mapplebeck (third person) "shelling"
at the beach. It was very rare for survivors to have cameras after their
ordeal, and even rarer for the few photos to have survived intervening years.
Source: Linda Ryan, daughter of Henry Mapplebeck, Third Officer of
Daytonian 1941-1942*

Originally, they were to have arrived in Miami on the 31st of
March, however a reply to a telegram request of the 27th March was
not provided until 8:03 pm on April 1st, when "Welles, Acting," replied
via telex that the waiver was authorized. For practical purposes this
meant that plans to catch the next steamer to Florida could not be made
until the following day, the 2nd of April. On the 28th, the "nice weather"
continued, and Mapplebeck went out to dinner again. On Sunday, the
entire crew went to church, then "out for cocktails." He reported that
he was "bored stiff." On the 30th, he reported the sailing has been
delayed and that his is in the hospital for a quiet day of fine weather.
On the first of April, Mapplebeck was at the canteen, and the following
day he went alone to the pictures, possibly at the Savoy Theater. After
noting that he went to the canteen at night he adds "all set," presumably
meaning that the crew is packed and ready to leave.

*Officers and men of the Daytonian in Nassau, March, 1942. On the left
is John Holmes, Fourth Engineer. Henry Mapplebeck, Third Officer, is
seated in the middle, hands clasped, with moustache.
Some men in the photo may be Nassuvians.*

Source: Linda Ryan, daughter of Henry Mapplebeck, Third Officer of
Daytonian 1941-1942

On Good Friday, the 3rd of April 1942, the 55 remaining men
boarded the British steamer *Ena K.* and sailed for Miami (Thomas Jones
was dead, Ernest Sampson was in Canada, and Leslie Edmondson
remained behind in hospital). As Mapplebeck put it, "Out picnic am.
Many farewells, sailed 3:20 pm for Miami." The ship averaged about ten
knots, arriving in Miami at 10:00 am after a passage of roughly 19 hours.
In Florida they were interviewed by US Navy officials, but very quickly
processed. Mapplebeck described it as a "Rush day, board train 10.00 pm
for New York. New experience. Stops." All of the shifting from house
to boat to train would have been particularly challenging for
Mapplebeck as he was laden with goods for his wife and their soon-to-
be-born daughter, Linda. The men spent all of Easter Sunday, the 5th
of April, in the train northbound. They arrived in New York, presumably
at Pennsylvania Station, at 6:30 am and had breakfast there.

As in Miami, the *Daytonian* men's layover in New York was but
brief. Two and a half hours later, at 9 am, they left for Montreal, where
they arrived at 10pm the same day. They were put up at the Ford Hotel
in that city. By Tuesday the 7th, he wrote "Day cold, fed up, no heat,
mooched around. Wish I was home."

Three of the survivors (Mapplebeck, John McCullam-Holmes,
and Leslie Taylor) had their letter of appreciation to the local Nassau
community published in the papers. In it, they compared their reception
in Canada: "…[I]t's been snowing for the last twelve hours. Would you
believe me, they won't give us money to buy raincoats, in fact, for all
they care we would be going around in our birthday suits. It's just as well
the people in Nassau were so generous, otherwise we should be in a bad
way. We are still smoking the cigarettes you gave us when we left, and
shall have to stop smoking when they run out as we can't get any money.
One thing that really touched the heart strings was your marvelous
gesture in giving us those lovely shell brooches for our wives."

*A "nautilus" shell willed to Henry Mapplebeck by a Nassau resident, also
an enthusiast for the hobby of shelling, and mailed by his widow after the
war. This shell is quite rare in the Bahamas.
Source: Linda Ryan, Mapplebeck's daughter, taken by his great-
granddaughter Alexandra*

Fortunately in the following week, while Mapplebeck was
looking for work on other ships, he was able to connect and stay with
his uncle John, receive news from home and meet with extended family,
which cheered him up considerably. On the 13th of April 1942,
Mapplebeck and presumably the rest of the crew were discharged.
Mapplebeck's conduct was described as "very good," and Captain
Egerton added on the 20th that he "...proved himself to be a capable
efficient and trustworthy officer, at all times attentive to his duties and
strictly sober." He had served aboard *Daytonian* for 13 months.

The following day Mapplebeck was issued a transit certificate by
the US consul and took a train by himself to Boston to join SS *Daghestan*
as 2nd Officer. On Wednesday the 22nd he "joined ship homeward."
After shopping in Boston the following day (he had been paid out in
Montreal), they sailed on Friday the 24th of April at 1 am. Mapplebeck
noted "...fine weather, nice captain, all quiet." They arrived in Glasgow
at 10 pm two weeks later, on Friday the 8th of May, "sent wire, received
reply."

On the 9th of May 1942, Henry Mapplebeck was given a
discharge from the *Daghestan*. After a train ride from Glasgow he was
finally able to return home to his expectant wife Barbara in Liverpool.
Four months later, on the 20th of September 1942, the first of their three
daughters, Linda, was born. She had a crib and nappies from the

Americas. Mapplebeck went on to serve in the Home Guard, then as a stevedore superintendent in Liverpool before retiring due to ill health. He died in 1988 at age 62.

As an after note, the *Rotterdam* was built at Friedrich Krupp Germaniawerft AG in Kiel in 1925. At the time it rescued the *Daytonian* survivors, the ship was in ballast. The *Rotterdam* was lost only months later. On the 27th of August, U-511 under Friedrich Steinhoff fired several torpedoes into convoy TAW 15 (from Trinidad to Aruba and Key West via Guantanamo) as it prepared to enter the Windward Passage from the Caribbean. *Rotterdam* and *San Fabian* were sunk and the *Esso Aruba* damaged. Ten men were killed. The survivors were picked up by a submarine chaser and landed in Guantanamo.

ATHELQUEEN

The British tanker *Athelqueen* was completed by the Furness Shipbuilding Company of Middlesbrough, England in 1928. She was fitted with two modern motor oil engines and had two propellers. Her owners were the Athel Line, also known as British Molasses, or the United Molasses Company Limited, of Aldwych, London. She was registered to Liverpool. *Athelqueen's* dimensions were 471 feet three inches long by 62 feet five inches wide and her tonnage was 8,780 gross tons.

British tanker Athelqueen *under way.*
Source: freepages.family.rootsweb.ancestry.com/~treevecwll/athelqueen.htm

Athelqueen's engines generated 3,800 horse power and propelled the ship at 10.5 knots. The ship was armed with a 4.7-inch gun, another gun capable of firing 12-pound shells, two Lewis machine guns, two Marlin machine guns, two other strip Lewis guns, and four P.A.C. rockets with kites. The P.A.C. stood for "parachute and cable," and was an anti-aircraft weapon. The theory was that the ship would fire a parachute on a cable high into the air and it would snag and ideally bring down enemy aircraft which were strafing or bombing the ship. These weapons were manned by one Royal Marine in charge of three Naval and two Army Gunners, as well as volunteers from among the crew, which totaled 50 men.

During her early life the *Athelqueen* traded in the Far East. On the 1st of September 1933 the ship was the site of a deadly explosion off Yokohama, Japan. So bad was the destruction that Chief Engineer Knott, the First Officer Putt, and Apprentices A. M. Rae, Carpenter, M. Johansen, and Deckhand W. Read were all killed. During World War Two, the ship completed eight trans-Atlantic convoys from Halifax to Liverpool. She appears to have carried her specialty dedicated cargo of molasses in all instances.

On her final voyage, *Athelqueen* was in ballast. Her Master was Captain Charles R. J. Roberts, age 33, born in Bootle and residing in Liverpool. On board *Athelqueen* for her final voyage were three Apprentices; Mark John Foster, Roy Sampley, age 20, and Phillip Roland Freshwater, 22. Harold Jones, age 21 served as an Able Bodied Seaman, William Proctor, 30, as a Senior Third Engineer, and David W. Firth, age 52 was a Greaser on board. The First Mate or Chief Officer was George Keedwell, age 57, the Second Mate was Edwin Harvey Simmonds, 23, and the Third Mate James Read Hearse, 25.

Athelqueen's First Radio Officer was George Leslie Anderson, age 23. V. L. Coleman, a Deckhand, 41, was to prove himself in the role of gunner on the voyage ahead. The Third Radio Officer, was Alan B. Heald, 19 from Leyland.

Alan B. Heald of Preston, England:
Third Radio Officer of the Athelqueen.
Source: courtesy of Alan B. Heald

Captain Roberts was clearly a man of forceful personality and opinions and vied for the best, fastest and safest convoy for his ship and his men. The Captain didn't want to dither in a slow-moving convoy to bring her back westwards across the Atlantic. She would be in ballast, or empty of cargo. Roberts advocated that his ship join a relatively fast convoy of 10 knots, given that his ship was capable of 10-and-a-half knots, and was equipped with double engines.

Even though there was a 10-knot convoy leaving at about the same time, the Naval Control Shipping Officer performed some research and determined that the captain before Roberts had registered the *Athelqueen* as a nine-and-a-half-knot ship. Exasperated, Roberts was resigned to joining what he described as "a slow Freetown convoy" sailing from the UK to Sierra Leone. The independently routed ships would peel out of the convoy in the vicinity of the Azores.

The convoy which *Athelqueen* joined was Convoy OS 20. It left Liverpool on the 22nd of February and arrived in Freetown on the 12th of March 1942. There were at least 34 ships in the convoy, including 15 ships that split off en route and seven ships which for various reasons never sailed. The two which were ultimately sunk from this convoy were lost in the greater Bahamas region. They were the *Charles Racine* and the *Manaqui*. Both were sunk by Italian submarines. The *Charles Racine*, a Norwegian tanker, was attacked on the 9th of March and sunk on the 10th some 500 miles northeast of Puerto Rico by the Italian submarine *Giuseppe Finzi*. The *Manaqui* was sunk on 16 March 1942 outside the immediate area, and southeast of Barbuda, succumbing to torpedoes from the *Morosini* under *Capitano di Corvetta* Athos Fraternale.

At 5:30 pm on the 28th of February 1942, the *Athelqueen* was ordered to disperse from Convoy OS 20 and proceed to Port Everglades, Florida independently. She was roughly 1,000 miles southwest of Liverpool, 350 miles northeast of the Azores, and a full 3,000 miles from the entrance to the Northeast Providence Channel in the Bahamas. Roberts opted not to zig zag across the Atlantic but preferred instead to take a direct course. The next two weeks continued "without incident." On March 10th the *Athelqueen* would have been 350 or so miles southwest of Bermuda at the time (at an average of 10 knots) and thus 600-plus miles northwest of the *Charles Racine* sinking, and only 400 miles or so from the entrance to the Northeast Providence Channel.

At 9 am on the 11th of March, "an American plane, probably based in San Juan, Puerto Rico, circled the ship several times and then flew off southward without making any signal." The *Athelqueen* continued on her course, until about 5 pm "...either this or another American aircraft returned, circling around and signaling with his Morse lamp, but as we had to look right into the sun to see him at all, we had great difficulty in reading his signal. However we managed to read S.O.S. several times and he signaled "S.O.S. Follow me..." I altered course and followed the direction he indicated by flying backwards and forwards towards a south easterly direction. I knew that a ship had been torpedoed in this direction and thought perhaps we were being directed to pick up survivors."

The *Athelqueen* turned on all its lights so that survivors in boats could see the ship and signal it for help. However, they became a much easier target for the Axis submarines in the area. This was the beginning of a crucial 27-hour diversion for the ship which Roberts blames for the loss of the *Athelqueen*. Roberts had reason to be nervous. The *Charles Racine* sent off at least three SSS and SOS messages which were transmitted and heard by the *Finzi*. There were at least two submarines in the region at the time, as testified to by the fact that the *Finzi* was refueling the sister submarine the *Morosini*. What is unusual about the request for the *Athelqueen* to divert to the *Charles Racine* is the fact that *Athelqueen* was some 600 miles northwest of the reported position of the *Racine*.

On the 9th of March, the *Finzi* had proceeded to a rendezvous with the *Morosini* northeast of Anegada. According to the *Finzi's* war diary, the transfer began on the 9th of March but was interrupted by the sighting of an enemy tanker, the *Charles Racine*. The *Finzi* broke off its fueling operations to sink her with at least four torpedoes launched between just before midnight on the 9th of March and just after dawn at 6 am on the 10th. The *Finzi* completed the transfer of 21 tons of fuel on the 13th and departed back to France, arriving back at Le Vedron on the 31st of March.

There were 41 men on the *Racine*, all of whom got away in four different boats. As it turned out, three of the boats with Captain Arthur Svendsen and a total of 34 men were rescued by the US Navy Destroyer, *USS Moffett*, under Lieutenant-Commander Gilbert Haven Richards Junior on the morning of the 12th of March. They were taken to San Juan and from there to New York on the 22nd. The fourth and final boat, with seven men in it under First Mate Nils Nilsen, were rescued by an Argentinean ship and taken to Trinidad. All were saved. (USS *Moffett* helped sink U-128 off Pernambuco, Brazil on the 17th of May 1943).-

The men of the *Athelqueen* meanwhile spent an exhausting night looking for survivors of a ship about which she did not know much, and in a location that was not provided. In the words of Captain Roberts, "I was very annoyed at having had to steam for 12 hours away from my course and risk the dangers of a night torpedo attack by keeping my lights burning and then not finding any survivors or receiving further directions. If the plane had signaled the position of survivors I could have found them." At sunrise, not finding any other airplanes to take directions from and not knowing what he was searching for or where, Captain Roberts ordered the helm put about to the northwest, doing a u-turn, back towards their last position and the Bahamas. At around 4:30 that afternoon, on the 11th of March, the *Athelqueen* reached its original track and resumed its course southwest for the Northeast

Providence Channel. As Captain Roberts summarized the diversion, with noticeable bitterness, he and his men had "lost a full 24 hours and accomplished nothing."

The 12th of March seems to have been uneventful on board the *Athelqueen* as they undoubtedly lay on steam for the Bahamas and their original itinerary. Then on Friday the 13th the men on the *Athelqueen* learned that colleagues on the British freighter *Daytonian* had been torpedoed by an enemy submarine on the same track. In fact, the *Daytonian* had been emerging from the Northeast Providence Channel, for which the *Athelqueen* was then headed.

Roberts wrote that following his learning via "a signal" about the demise of the "DETONIAN" (he was misspelling the name), he received a message from the British Admiralty regarding the *Athelqueen's* route. "My course was through the north-west Channel," he writes, "but I received a message from the Admiralty altering my route round the north-west coast of the Bahamas and taking me through the position in which the DETONIAN had so recently been torpedoed. However I altered course on the 14th and proceeded as ordered by the Admiralty."

This is confusing, as it appears that the Admiralty's instructions are consistent with the *Athelqueen's* original itinerary. If that were the case, though, why would Captain Roberts refer to so pointedly to "Admiralty altering my route" and "I altered my course"? One explanation may be that the Admiralty was in fact trying to route the *Athelqueen away* from the attack on the *Daytonian*, north of Abaco and Grand Bahama, rounding the northwest corner of the colony and steaming down the Gulf Stream. There may have been a misunderstanding. From what Captain Roberts writes, he was intending to use the Northwest Providence Channel and the Admiralty ordered him to do so.

Ships transiting through the northern Bahamas from the open Atlantic utilize first the Northeast Providence Channel then the Northwest Providence Channel, the two being named by their position relative to Nassau. The entire route is roughly 100 nautical miles, from Great Isaac Light off Bimini to Hole in the Wall light. On the 14th and 15th of March, while Roberts on the *Athelqueen* steamed towards his ship's doom, Carlo Fecia di Cossato had finished with the *Daytonian* and was waiting for more prey. Between a span of 10 and a half hours he had the *Enrico Tazzoli* patrol the Northeast Providence Channel. Daringly, considering they had just sunk an Allied ship there, the submarine remained on the surface all day. They were hoping that a large Allied prize would be routed to that shipping chokepoint. Though the *Tazzoli* had missed seeing and attacking the Dutch steamer *Rotterdam* just the day before, the *Athelqueen* was about the drop into its lap.

At 10 am on the 15th Roberts noted that the *Athelqueen* passed over the position of the sinking of the *Daytonian*, about 135 miles east of Elbow Cay Light and Hope Town, Abaco. *Athelqueen* proceeded on an almost westerly course (285 degrees true), for the next five hours, averaging just over ten knots and covering 55 miles distance. At 3:00 pm ship's, or local time, on the 15th, *Athelqueen* was 80 nautical miles due east of Hope Town.

At 12:26 pm local time, di Cossato in the *Tazzoli* sighted *Athelqueen* on the horizon roughly 11 miles distant. The diarist Maronari noted (wrongly) that she was "obviously coming from an African port," and that "the sea was incredibly calm." At 1:45 pm, after lining up the best angle to approach and fire torpedoes, the *Tazzoli* dove for the attack, apparently unnoticed by the *Athelqueen* lookouts, probably since the sub was positioned in the same direction of as the blinding sun. According to the *Tazzoli* log, di Cossato sent two torpedoes at the *Athelqueen* at 2:35 and 2:38 respectively and they took 78 seconds to reach their target. Only one of them appears to have hit.

On board the *Athelqueen* there were five men on watch: three gunners on the poop deck aft by the 4.7-inch gun, one on the bridge and the highest standing on top of the bridge. The torpedo was seen by lookout atop the bridge roughly a quarter mile distant, three quarters forward of the port beam. The lookout shouted his sighting to the Second Mate, Edwin Simmonds, who was officer of the watch and standing one deck below. Before sounding the alarm, Simmonds turned the *Athelqueen* on an emergency course to starboard, in order to minimize the target for the torpedo. This maneuver seemed to work, as the lookout on the bridge observed the torpedo running roughly 100 yards off the port side and parallel with the ship for a short time.

Then the torpedo "suddenly turned in towards the ship and struck us in the engine room on the port side, about 20 feet from the stern of the ship" recounted Captain Roberts. Since it is not believed

that Italian or German torpedoes at the time and in this theater were
magnetic or capable of turning so sharply and quickly towards their
target, it can also be assumed that the torpedo which struck the ship was
the second torpedo fired. However some eye-witness accounts
counteract this assumption.

Roberts noted that the impact was muted: "None of the crew
saw a flash from the explosion, nor did they see any column of water
thrown up." Immediately after impact, the engine room and bunker
(fuel) tanks began to fill with sea water, though all the men in the
engine spaces managed to make to the deck safely. The weather was fine
and visibility good. There was negligible and variable wind and the seas
were only slight. Roberts was below in his cabin. He reported that his
cabin door was blown open by the explosion and that the ship
experienced "….a small explosion and a small amount of concussion."
Soon thereafter, as he rushed into the alleyway, he experienced a "much
larger explosion" which may have been the boilers exploding as they
were hit with colder Atlantic water. The second explosion occurred only
ten seconds after the first. When Roberts made it to the deck, he
observed that "The ship did not list, but rapidly settled by the stern."

Ship's model of the Athelqueen, *showing deck,*
forecastle and accommodation layout.
Source: SuperSkyline89, flickr.com/photos/28583390@N07/4691821775/

Roberts and his officers and men immediately began preparations
to abandon ship. On the deck, there was not much visible damage,
however internally the ship was badly wounded. "…All the internal

fittings in the accommodation and wireless room collapsed." Roberts continued that "...in spite of this the Wireless Operator [George Anderson], managed to fix up enough of his equipment to get out an S.O.S., to which a reply was received from the American authorities. Indeed the *Enemy Action Diary* of the Eastern Sea Frontier noted that at 3:12 pm "SS ATHEL QUEEN (8780 ton British Tanker) torpedoed and shelled east of Great Abaco, Bahamas." The men on the stricken tanker could take some consolation from the belief that help would be on its way, in the form of Allied aircraft or rescue vessels. Roberts ensured that the confidential codes were dropped overboard in a weighted bag.

Attention was focused on abandoning ship. For over a quarter of an hour, the men were allowed to go about their tasks unmolested by the submarine lurking beneath the waves nearby. Second Mate Simmonds ran aft to begin launching the boats. Recognizing that if the bow could be flooded, the trim of the ship might be stabilized (though the ship's engines were still immobilized), Roberts and First Officer George Keedwell ran forward and opened the valves which would normally enable the forward tanks to flood. However, because the *Athelqueen* was tilted so far aft, where the torpedo or torpedoes had allowed the tanks and engine spaces to flood, the water would not flow forward to the bow fast enough for an effective counterbalancing. The weight that the two most senior officers were placing at the high end was not enough to bring the other, the lower end out of the water. It was a good idea undermined by the reality of the gravitational pull on the part of a ship that was already submerged.

Roberts and Keedwell then returned aft to assist with the launching of the lifeboats. The only life boat which had been swung out in readiness for deployment (it was literally hanging over the side, held to the ship by davits) was the only boat damaged by the upward push of the explosion when the torpedo hit on the port quarter. As a result, it sank as soon as it was launched. The other boats were not damaged. Three of them were launched in a short space of time. The port aft boat, directly above the explosion, was undamaged, because it was housed between decks.

Meanwhile the *Tazzoli* was not idle, and neither were the *Athelqueen*'s gunners. At 2:58 pm, or 20 minutes after the initial torpedo attack, the submarine surfaced on the starboard quarter roughly 2,000 yards away. The gunners were ready, and Marine Gun-layer V. L. Coleman, promptly opened fire with the 4.7-inch gun, which he had evidently loaded in preparation for just such an opportunity. Roberts was later to commend Coleman for not waiting for orders, noting that "The ship was down by the stern, making it very difficult to get a foothold on the sloping deck and fire accurately. However these shots made the submarine crash dive." As an indirect result of his action, Coleman put one of the deadliest submarines in the region out of commission for a patrol which had claimed over half a dozen ships in just 10 days.

Realizing that it was being fired on (though all three shots missed), the *Tazzoli* crash-dived to avoid being hit. Di Cossato wrote in the log that the sub surfaced at 2:58 pm local time, "but noticing that the tanker's stern gun is ready to fire, we dive and surface again 36 minutes later. Crucially, di Cossato by his own admission did not judge its distance from the ship or the submarine's forward momentum correctly. The *Tazzoli* collided with the middle of the starboard side of the sinking ship, badly damaging its bows and putting the forward torpedo tubes out of commission. Maronari observed that di "Cossato miscalculated the distance and when he tried to take another peek with the periscope, he still had not crossed to the other side and sighted the enemy ship so close that he could distinguish the bolts on the hull. The submarine tried to go deeper but seconds later, there was a shock and the submarine had obviously collided with the enemy ship."

Moronari reported that a powerful jolt forced the crew to tumble, and a cry went out of "What happened over there?" After a pause came the reply "all normal," to which di Cossato mumbled "thank goodness," accompanied by a great sigh. Di Cossato took the submarine to 132 feet to test the vessel's seaworthiness. No water leak was reported in the submarine and everything appeared under control. "*Tazzoli* surfaced and it was observed that the bow was smashed on a length of three meters and the torpedo tube doors were apparently deformed and no longer usable." As Maronari wryly observed, the sentiment on board was that "We'll see later." They had a sinking ship to contend with and put out of its misery.

Enrico Tazzoli's damaged bow following a collision with the
Athelqueen *off Abaco.*
Source: *freepages.family.rootsweb.ancestry.com/~treevecwll/athelqueen2.htm*

It was a devastating end to one of the most aggressive patrols of the war. The *Tazzoli* was to see a number of otherwise easy prey fall by the wayside unharmed as a result of Coleman's bravery. There is no record that the men on the ship felt the ship lurch due to the collision, as they were occupied with saving themselves. While the submariners licked their wounds and checked frantically for any signs of the ingress of water, which would signal that the key pressure hull had been ruptured, the men on the *Athelqueen* had bought some time – though not much - to abandon ship in an orderly fashion.

Soon the *Tazzoli* re-surfaced and the men from the Italian crew frantically ran forward to assess the damage to the bow and report back to their anxious skipper. From Roberts' perspective, the submarine "… .surfaced ahead and lay there, knowing that we had no guns forward with which to attack. I realized that she was waiting for us to abandon ship and therefore gave orders to lower the boats." Maronari noted that "The tubes III and IV were ready but it was observed that the enemy crew was lowering a boat and moving very calmly to evacuate. In these conditions, firing another torpedo could have caused butchery. It appears that di Cossato wanted to move his submarine ahead [to be outside the field of fire of the enemy gun crew which was located aft] of the enemy ship to attack from the opposite side." Italian submarine historian Platon Alexiades noted that "probably he hoped to surprise the enemy gun crew or perhaps fire his torpedo on a side where there was no lifeboat being lowered."

Simmonds again proved his mettle by "rushing around collecting sextants and chronometers." As a result, Simmonds was not able to retrieve his personal belongings. According to Roberts, all 50 men abandoned ship in the three operative lifeboats at 3:15 pm. The gunners snuck a working Lewis machine gun on board their boat as well. As the men rowed away from their mother ship, Roberts noticed from the Plimsoll line on the side of the ship that the *Athelqueen* seemed to be leveling off – in other words that the water flowing to the bow seemed to be having the desired effect of righting the ship's trim. He wrote that "…I thought that within an hour we should be able to re-board her if the submarine did not interfere."

As the men pulled clear of the ship, di Cossato began circling the *Athelqueen* and firing into it with their deck guns. According to di Cossato's log, seven minutes elapsed between re-surfacing at 3:34 pm and when they opened fire at 3:41 p m. The British crew counted that between 40 to 60 shells were fired into the *Athelqueen*, mostly at the super-structure which was still above water (in reality there were 128 shells fired - the confusion may stem from the fact that more than one gun was fired). Roberts noted that "…the submarine did not seem to be concerned about how many rounds they fired. I counted 60 rounds from her guns until finally I saw my ship sink at 1530."

According to her master, the *Athelqueen* had taken half an hour to die, but had spared taking any lives. According to di Cossato, the attack took over an hour. In fact some reports state that the attack took four hours between 4 pm and ending when the *Athelqueen* sank at 8 pm. The difference between 30 minutes and four hours suggests that both renditions are erroneous. Since the torpedoing, boat launching, ship firing on the submarine, colliding, sub laying off the bow and firing 128 shells (which usually took 30 seconds to load), all would take considerable time, it is likely that the incident lasted closer to two to three hours rather than half an hour.

Maronari was on deck at the conning tower of the *Tazzoli* and recounted the final minutes of the *Athelqueen* thus: "Both deck guns were manned and they opened fire delivering quickly some 128 rounds and the merchant ship was engulfed with fire. Apparently the reserve ammunition on her stern was hit and started a firework display forcing the submarine to move away by a few hundred meters but this explosion was apparently the *coup de grace* and the ship took a heavy starboard list and settled… The water around her was covered with fuel, oil and debris."

Maronari was poetic in describing the last moments of the *Athelqueen*. He wrote how the air whistled with tracers and exploding ammunition. Di Cossato fired the final torpedo from the sub's stern tubes and *Athelqueen*'s stern swerved to the right side. According to Maronari, the ship's bow, "salt encrusted and covered with algae, thrust upwards with halyards pointing skyward. …There was a horrendous roar of torn sheet metal," he wrote. "Pieces of scrap jumped into the air, then the boilers exploded and the ship disappeared into a massive gorge in the water. The water swirled for a long time, spewing forth oil, naphtha, and other wreckage. Then the water slowly calmed and silently closed forever over the tanker." The *Athelqueen* lies to this day in 14,692 feet of water. The submarine crew hoisted the sixth and final victory pennant for the mission.

Carlo Fecia di Cossato, commander of the Enrico Tazzoli, *after a patrol. Source: piombino-storia.blogspot.com/2010/09/capitano-carlo-fecia-di-cossato.html*

After the *Athelqueen* sank, di Cossato took his submarine amongst the survivors' boats to ask questions. Roberts described his nemesis as "….mousy-colored, very sun-burnt and wearing a blue shirt with blue shorts. He spoke with a distinct German accent. I talked with the captain of the DETONIAN later, he said that the Captain of the submarine which sank him was an Italian and showed a large Italian flag. The submarines seemed much the same on comparison but we certainly saw nothing of a flag, neither German nor Italian. The submarine looked clean and her nose appeared to be bent as if she had been diving in shallow water. The Captain told us that we were 80 miles from land and then leisurely steamed off on the surface, apparently without a care in the world."

All was not well aboard the *Tazzoli* and the comparatively dampened reception they gave the *Athelqueen* survivors was because their own craft had been badly damaged. The Italian crew knew that they were effectively out of the war for the next few months, except as observers, and ideally survivors. As a result, there was no jocular showing of the Italian flag after this casualty. In his log, di Cossato did identify his victim as the "ATHELPRINCE," an English tanker of 8,782 tons. Since this was a sister-ship to the *Athelqueen*, he was near enough to the mark. He rather laconically noted that "during the submerged attack we collided with the bow of the tanker. The resulting distortion to the bow damaged the forward tubes. When submerged we noticed a leak in the port diesel room and decided to return to base and not to use the two remaining torpedoes" – the ones in the forward tubes, which had been damaged.

Di Cossato did not record the exact time at which the submarine left the scene, but having sunk the ship, and the men in the lifeboats having been interrogated, and bearing in mind that an SOS had been sent and the Allies had confirmed receipt of the messages, the *Tazzoli* turned away from her week of conquests in the Bahamas. She arrived in Le Verdun, France, and then Bordeaux at 6:20 pm on the 1st of April after having had a highly successful patrol lasting nearly two months.

The *Athelqueen* crew began a two-day open-boat voyage in the three surviving lifeboats. They set off at roughly 4 pm on Sunday, the 15th of March. Roberts recounted how he "…ordered all the boats to keep together and to steer for Abaco Island, which was sighted about midnight on the night of 16/17 March." The voyage of 85 miles lasted 32 hours. Roberts and the officers in charge of the individual boats were able to maintain good discipline and morale, at least up until land was sighted.

According to Roberts, "As the sea was a bit choppy I decided not to land on the lee shore [on the lee, or windless side of the boat] but to row round to the lee side of the island [on the windless side of the island] and look for a more sheltered spot. I was ahead of the other two boats and closed the land intending to pull round the northern end of the island, when suddenly the boat began pitching and rolling and then grounded on a reef. I shouted to the other boats to pull away out to sea and wait until daylight when I would try and rejoin them. We pulled hard to get the boat free but the tide kept sweeping us in more and more on the reefs. The crew were becoming very tired so I decided to turn and pull as hard as we could towards the shore and risk the boat being capsized. The boat suddenly freed herself and we landed without damaging the boat to any great extent."

Roberts continued: "meanwhile the Third Officer's boat had also reached the edge of the reef, and the first thing they knew was that the boat pitched and hit the reef, violently throwing the Third Officer right out of the boat. The crew, thinking that the boat had been holed and that the Third Officer had jumped for it, got panicky and five of the men jumped overboard and started swimming for the shore. The Third Officer managed to climb back into the boat, which was undamaged, but owing to the darkness was unable to see these five men. After searching around, decided they must have swum for the shore, he therefore pulled out to sea and remained until dawn in company with the Chief Officer's boat. Two of the men who had jumped overboard managed to reach the island but the other three were drowned or eaten by sharks. As soon as it was daylight the other two boats rowed in and landed safely on the beach."

He continued; "....It seemed hours before daylight came and when it did we could see no sign of the men who had left the boat, but coming towards us was a small boat in which were two men – one steering and one in the bow indicating directions. We were secured to this motor-driven boat and towed to the beach, where we were met by the islanders and taken to houses where we were given food and found a place to rest. I think the main burden fell on the local Methodist minister and his wife whose home was swamped by the addition of some 20-odd crew members."

Alan Heald related that "Abaconians fed us and found places for us to sleep. A Roman Catholic priest asked if we would like him to contact our families and we all said yes, but no messages were ever received by our people, perhaps because of war-time restrictions on radio traffic. One islander took me round his 'plantation' consisting of coconut palms and sugar canes and another - a young woman - made me a straw hat."

After several days on the island Heald noted, "our thoughts [were] about getting off Abaco and back to the wartime world, …but as there was no landing strip for aircraft and no quay at which boats could tie up, we were at a loss to think of alternatives. However, it was announced one morning that our rescue transport had arrived and was standing off the beach where we had landed… ….When the time for us to embark came we were accompanied to the shore by many local people, and as we got into our lifeboats again and became attached to the small vessel which had towed us in, the islanders began to sing something that was very familiar to me, it was the hymn the first line of which runs 'God be with you till we meet again.' Young Hope Towner Vernon Malone, born December 11th, 1937 and thus just over four years old at the time, remembers that the *Athelqueen* men were "very friendly" to him, and that he "cried when they left."

Heald was under the impression that the ship which rescued them was the royal yacht *Victoria and Albert*. Though this is incorrect, and the 120' *Content S.* was in fact a good deal smaller than the *Victoria and Albert*, he could be forgiven for having been impressed with the *Content S.* which had been the luxury yacht *Percianna II* only a few years before. "On arriving at the yacht we walked up the gangplank and left our boats to be used by the islanders. I was glad about this, for we had no financial means of compensating those who had looked after us and to see them acquire some material gain was, in a sense, satisfying, although it cost us nothing personally."

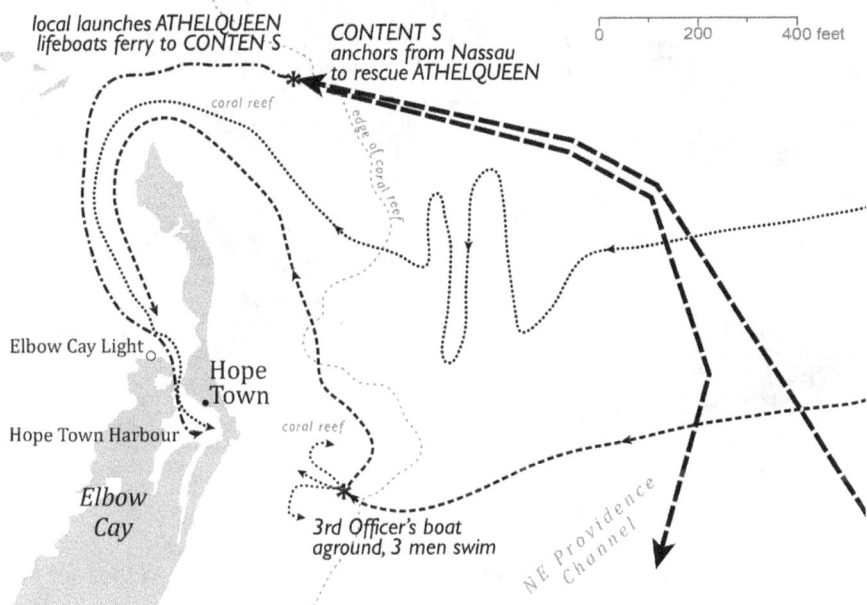

local launches ATHELQUEEN
lifeboats ferry to CONTEN S

CONTENT S
anchors from Nassau
to rescue ATHELQUEEN

0   200   400 feet

coral reef

edge of coral reef

Elbow Cay Light

Hope
.Town

Hope Town Harbour

coral reef

Elbow
Cay

3rd Officer's boat
aground, 3 men swim

NE Providence
Channel

Mail Day, a painting by Bill Gillies, showing the Athelqueen *lifeboat being utilized as a launch shuttling to and from Hope Town Abaco and anchored mailboats such as* Content S, Stede Bonnett, *and* Priscilla *which were used into the early 1950s. Named* Athelqueen, *or simply "the queen." Originally equipped with a mast and sail, Vernon Malone says the wooden lifeboat was burned at the end of its useful life in the mid-1950s. Source:* Under A Different Sky, *by Dave Gale, author interview with Vernon Malone*

"There was no room on the ship," Heald wrote, "to allow us to sleep in normal accommodation, but we were quite happy to sleep in deck chairs on the open deck because it was so warm. The ....yacht was not in the usual wartime camouflage; it was in its everyday livery. Because it was so conspicuous it came in the middle of the night and went back to Nassau only after darkness had fallen again."

The original motor launch for the Content S., *being restored in Portsmouth, Rhode Island, 2013.*

Source: *Earl McMillen III, McMillen Yachts,*

www.woodenyachts.com

The *New York Times* reported the sinking of the *Athelqueen.* "The British also lost another ship off the Bahamas, a dispatch from Nassau stated. In their invasion of the waters of the Western Hemisphere, the enemy submarine packs seem to have followed a pattern of striking hard in one locality, then shifting to another. Bahama waters are undergoing – or have undergone – their share in the cycle, for this was the fourth ship sunk in that area in nine days."

The same article continued: "A dispatch to the *New York Times* last night said that forty-six survivors from a torpedoed ship had arrived in Nassau Wednesday night. It was the second British ship recently hit in Bahama waters. In addition, a large Norwegian vessel and a Greek ship have been sunk. The sinking of the British ship occurred last Monday. The survivors reported that a tragedy occurred when one of the three lifeboats, within sight of land, struck a reef. Three of the men who had survived the torpedoing were drowned attempting to swim ashore, only a mile away." The Associated Press, in a round-up of the losses in Bahamas waters said that 171 had survived and six had died in four sinkings." Given censorship and other obfuscations and the different governments, the degree of accuracy is quite impressive.

The Nassau *Guardian* of Thursday 19th March reported that "Forty-six more survivors of the fourth lot from torpedoed ships to arrive in Nassau within ten days – were brought here last night after being landed at an Out Island in the Bahamas, from lifeboats. ...The Captain and officers are staying at the Rozelda Hotel and the rest of the ship's company are at the Lucerne. Members of the Red Cross met the men and outfitted them with necessary clothing last night and this morning. His Royal Highness the Governor and the Duchess of Windsor visited the survivors this afternoon." Heald related that "on arrival in Nassau we were housed in various hotels but we were ordered to go to the

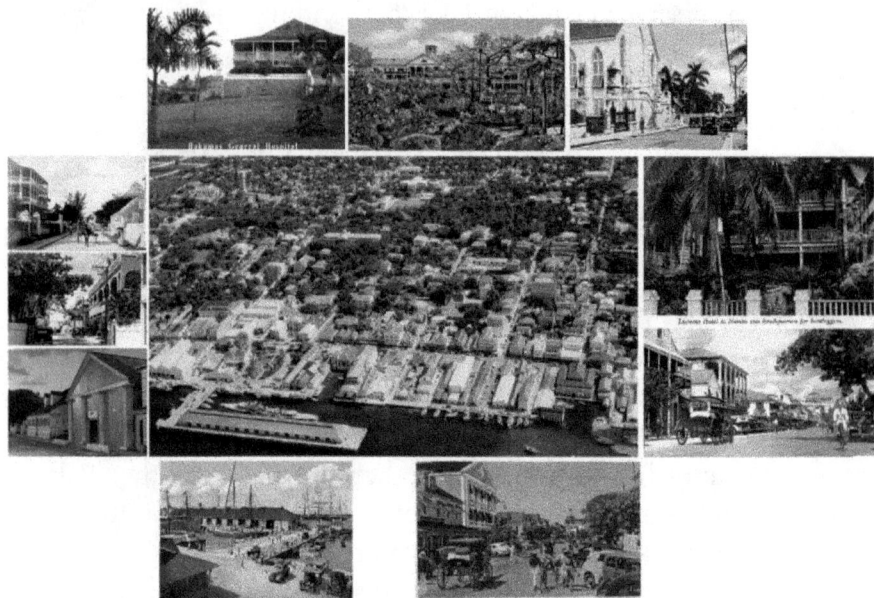

Downtown Nassau, surrounded by insets of significant landmarks - clockwise from top:-
Royal Victoria Hotel; Trinity Church; Lucerne Hotel; Windsor Hotel; Masonic Temple;
Landing Place at Prince George Wharf; Nassau Theatre (red building); Rozelda Hotel; Royal Victoria Annex.

Rozelda the following morning because the Governor wanted to meet us. We were badly clothed and unshaven but we lined up to be received.

*Collage of the various hotels, churches, docks, hospital
and cinemas various crew visited 1942.
Source: Courtesy of Captain Paul Aranha, from various sources.*

Looking after these disheveled men was a grass-roots affair. An article from the local papers read: "A large number of contributions of fruit, vegetables, and other food-stuffs have been received at the I.O.D.E. Canteen in the Masonic building, for the survivors from torpedoed ships and the military forces in Nassau. There is a great need there, however, for a Frigidaire, as the only appliance for preserving the food is a small ice box. The Canteen Committee would be very grateful if someone having an extra Frigidaire would lend it to the Canteen for this deserving cause. The seamen and soldiers have made themselves entirely at home in the friendly atmosphere of the Canteen and every night they entertain themselves with games of cards, darts, Chinese checkers, ping pong, backgammon and other games and a radio and two gramophones furnish music. Many of the men are fond of the old English game of cribbage and would be very appreciative if a cribbage set could be donated to the Canteen."

A local benefactor in Nassau who chose not to give his name to the press provided funding for the survivors of the *Athelqueen* to cable home to Great Britain news to their families that they were alright and had been rescued in the Bahamas. No doubt this was an invaluable service and an immense relief to the survivors'families in the UK. It seems that at least five cables were paid for, which is about 10 percent of the crew, so it is possible that messages from multiple crew members got through on each cable. The same week, the Red Cross thanked the public for generous donations of money, games and foodstuffs for their canteen, which was located on Bay Street, the main commercial thoroughfare on the island.

Heald recounts that "Whilst in Nassau, the ice-importing family - the Farringtons - took an interest in me and looked after me very well. I got friendly with one of their sons who was student at a military academy in Jacksonville, Florida. He and his friend Peter took me around and I went with them to the [Trinity] Methodist church where I met the minister who was known locally as Father Armstrong. He kindly provided Sunday lunch for me. I also went to a local dance hall where I met young people who had been evacuated from England. I still have a four shilling note from my time there. ...The [Farrington] family was warm and generous and I remember going to the local Methodist church with them and having lunch with the minister."

On March 21st, US Consul Dye telegrammed the Secretary of State in Washington DC (paid for by the local government), requesting they waive documentary and visa requirements for "Master C.R.J. Roberts and 44 others of crew to enter United States on twentythird at

Port Everglades Florida." Receiving no reply, on the 23rd he sent another telex marked Urgent and saying "45 seamen still here…. Please confirm granting waiver." Finally, at 9:52 pm on March 25th, Welles authorized the waiver. It was received by Dye the following day, the 26th March.

Based on the authorization the *Athelqueen* men were put aboard a passenger ship that very day and arrived at Port Everglades on the 27th of March. They reported for further duty to agents of the Athel Line of the UK who were located in Port Everglades. One man, Arthur William Kemp, a Junior Second Engineer, remained behind as he required hospitalization – it is not known for what. Kemp was finally repatriated to the US on the 24th of July – four months later – via the *Ena K*, arriving Miami on the 25th. Francis J. H. Dever, Inspector in Charge of Immigration in Miami assisted Dye in getting Kemp back to the States and ultimately back to sea.

Roberts published an open letter of thanks to the people of Nassau and Abaco in the Nassau *Guardian*, on the 26th of March, under the heading "Acknowledgement." Partially garbled, it reads: "Captain Roberts, the [leader of]… the men of shipwrecked [ship wishes to] thank His Royal Highness the Governor and the Duchess [as well as] members of the Red Cross for the [kind] administration shown them in [their hour] of need, and for their [welcome] into the colony. The good work …carried out by this [group]… has been especially appreciated on account of the friendliness accompanied the [carrying out the]…routine of their duties. Captain Roberts wishes to thank also the many expatriates in the colony who have helped them [offering] willing co-operation and eagerness [to assist] along many paths. To the many other [kindnesses] made during their stay, all of the ship's hands wish to express their enormous gratitude and …it is with much regret that they leave a Garden of Eden."

Memorial to Athelqueen *and her survivors made from local limestone,*
Hope Town, Elbow Cay
Source: Wyannie Malone Historical Museum, Hope Town

According to Heald, "Repatriation was a short boat trip to Florida, then a three day train journey to Montreal where we stayed for a month before going to Saint John, New Brunswick, where we were accommodated on a ship bound for England." He suffered the misfortune of being sunk on two ships immediately following the *Athelqueen.* These sinkings would have occurred between April and May of 1942. It would appear that the ship carrying him (and others) from Saint John, New Brunswick, to the UK, was attacked not once but twice, or that the ship which rescued them was also subsequently sunk. In any event, though Heald survived all three attacks, he was listed as unfit for further sea service and moved to shore, where he tested radio sets for use at sea. The experiences were so gruesome that Heald refuses to discuss the sinkings with anyone, including his own children.

Roberts remained incensed at the fool's errand that his men had been sent on, and his inability to obtain a straight answer or admission from authorities. He wrote in his report to the British that "I reported the incident of the aircraft which had been the means of taking us off course to the American authorities at Florida before I went up to Morehead City [US] for 14 days. When I returned to Florida the authorities informed me that they were unable to discover anything about this plane and asked for further information."

Enrico Tazzoli was forced to break off the patrol and make back for Bordeaux. She arrived on the 31st of March, culminating one of the most successful single missions to the region and of the war as a whole, with a ship attacked on the average every day for a period of six days. *Tazzoli* spent April and May undergoing maintenance and repairs, and the crew rested. Her next patrol would be to the Caribbean, but the submarine would access that area by a more southern route and bypass the Bahamas. She left port on the 18th of June and by the 2nd of August intercepted and sank the Greek *Kastor* near the equator. On the 6th of August, *Tazzoli* sank the Norwegian ship *Havsten*. Two men were taken prisoner. Following this success, the boat returned to France on the 5th of September. Again, two months of repairs in the naval yard were required, having motored 10,348 miles over 71 days.

Di Cossato began his last patrol on the *Tazzoli* on the 14th of November, 1942, bound for the coast of Brazil. On the 12th of December, they intercepted and sank the British ship *Empire Hawk* and apparently, on the same day, though it is not confirmed, the Dutch ship *Ombilin* (named by others as the *Sumatra*). On the 21st of December, the boat is credited with attacking and sinking the British *Queen City*. On Christmas Day 1942, the crew found and sank the American *Dona Aurora*. Two of the crew were taken prisoner, and though seven died, 62 survived. It was to be the last ship sunk by *Tazzoli* under di Cossato's command. The submarine returned to Bordeaux on the 2nd of February 1943.

After roughly four years in submarines, di Cossato was transferred back to torpedo boats. He assumed command of the *Aliseo* in the Mediterranean. The *Tazzoli*, meanwhile, was stripped of its armament to enable it to serve as a supply boat to Japan. It left Bordeaux on the 16th of May 1943 loaded with 165 tons of material. The following day communication with the submarine was lost. According to Cristiano D'Adamo, it is likely that the USS *Mackenzie* sank the submarine by a depth-charge attack on either the 16th or the 22nd of May. As a result, all the officers and crew of the *Enrico Tazzoli* remain on "eternal patrol."

The loss of his former crew mates so soon after he left them made di Cossato distraught. He suffered severely from what might today be called "survivor's guilt." Nevertheless, he again proved himself a dashing and capable commander when aboard the *Aliseo*, in an extremely fluid situation; in September 1943 he sank a number of German ships escaping the port of Bastia on the island of Corsica. However, he was overtaken by events larger than himself. The Italian navy surrendered, and as a consequence, officers were no longer required to swear allegiance to the king, but rather to the new government. Di Cossato could not accept those terms, and refused to serve. For this he was imprisoned and ignored.

Then the royal court would not receive him in Naples. To a man whose family for generations had fought for noble causes, and whose busy life had been devoted to the same goals, it was too much for him. Unable to reunite with his family in the north due to the fighting there, and unwilling to take up arms with the Allies, he became deeply depressed.

The authorities were unsure exactly what to do with di Cossato. From Naples, in the last letter to his mother, dated August 21st 1944, he wrote: "For months I have been thinking about my sailors of the *Tazzoli* who are honorably on the bottom of the sea, and I think that my place is with them." Carlo Fecia di Cossato took his own life the day he wrote his final letter, which he ended with the instructions: "Hug Father and sisters, and to you, Mother, all of my deep, untouched love. In this moment, I feel very close to you and you all and I am sure that you will not condemn me."

PART II:

U-BOAT ACTIVITY 16 MARCH TO 6 APRIL 1942

Between the loss of the *Athelqueen* on the 15th of March and the *Kollskegg* on the 6th of April six submarines entered the region and four vessels were attacked and sunk. U-124 under Johann Mohr merely dipped tentatively into the area east of Savannah on the 20th of March. The balance of end March and early April belonged largely to the Italians. The sinking of the *Stangarth* credited for many years to the Italian sub *Morosini* under Fraternale, was actually sunk 16 March by U-504 under "Fritz" Poske, who observed crates being shipped to the Middle East floating in the debris. The *Stangarth* was heading to the Middle East to help the Allied war against Rommel in North Africa. In fact Morosini sank the *Manaqui* further to the south and east. *Stangarth* had not even left New York by the time Fraternale claimed to have sunk her. Since no Allies survived either sinking, accounts of both attacks exist only in the attack reports by the respective commanders.

Morosini also managed to catch and sink the Dutch ship *Oscilla* on the 15th of March. The following week Fraternale sank the former Antarctic whaling fleet tanker *Peder Bogen*, registered to the UK, also well east of the Bahama Islands on the 23rd of March. On the 25th of March the Italian submarine *Pietro Calvi* under Emilio Olivieri passed well east of the Bahamas, en route to a patrol area off South America. It sank the *Tredinnick* of Great Britain 1,100 nautical miles northeast of Anegada.

Closer to the Bahamas, U-124 was followed on the 3rd of April by U-154 under Walther Kölle, who initially at least just skirted the area to enter the Mona Passage. Even during this short passage through the area, Kölle managed to sink the 5,034-ton US-flagged molasses tanker *Comol Rico* on the 4th. The very next day Kölle sank another US-flagged molasses tanker, *Catahoula*, just north of the Mona Passage. Survivors of both ships were rescued by the US Navy destroyer USS *Sturtevant*, DD 240, which was later lost to friendly mines off Key West. On the 5th of April, Reinhard Hardegen aboard U-123 made his second voyage to the region, coming south from Cape Hatteras for a week during which he ravaged shipping of the coasts of Florida and Georgia.

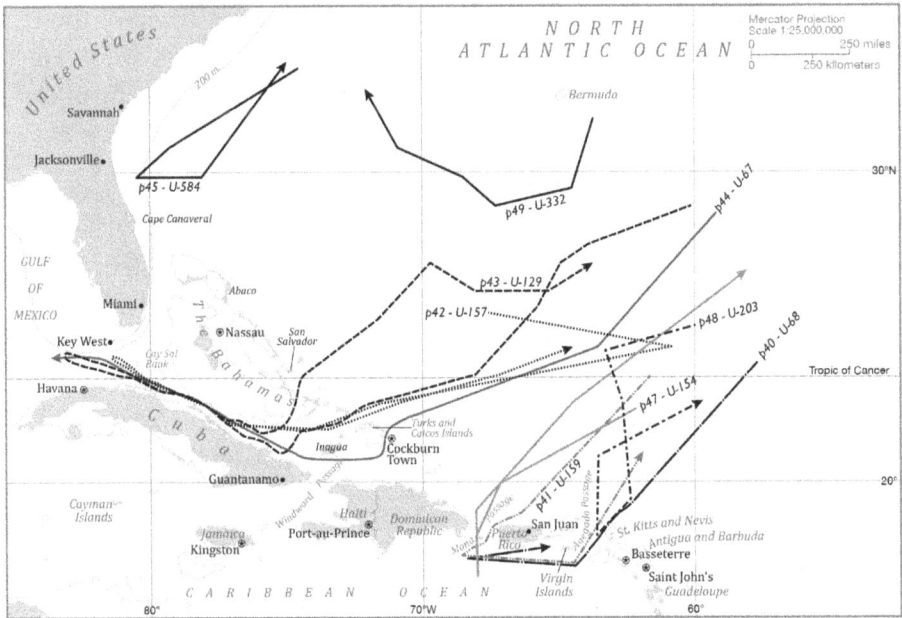

KOLLSKEGG AND BUSHRANGER

The sinking of the Norwegian tanker *Kollskegg* between Cape Hatteras and Bermuda is another instance of unflappable determination to survive. The fate of the survivors also demonstrates how difficult it can be in a three-dimensional, international plane, to track survivors. They were sunk from beneath the sea, some of them met each other on the high seas, and they were rescued by whatever ship happened to be nearby and taken wherever the ship was heading at the time.

Kollskegg was built by the Eriksbergs Machine Works in Gothenburg, Sweden and delivered in January, 1940. Her gross tonnage was 9,858 tons and she was 528 feet in length, 65 feet wide and 36 feet deep. Her two oil-burning engines generated 861 net horsepower and propelled the ship at 13 knots. The tanker's owner was the Odd Berg Company of Oslo and during the war she was controlled by the Norwegian Shipping and Trade Mission (Notraship). During her final voyage the *Kollskegg* was on charter to the Anglo-American Oil Company.

Norwegian motor tanker Kollskegg with wartime Norwegian identification painted on sides.

Source: Dame Siri Holm Lawson,
warsailors.com/singleships/kollskegg, from Bjørn Pedersen's collection

On the 29th of March 1942 the *Kollskegg* sailed from Curacao loaded with a full cargo of 8,000 tons of Colon Residue (a type of crude oil) and 6,300 tons of fuel oil. Her master was Captain Leif Søyland, who oversaw a total crew of 42 souls. The crew included 33 Norwegians, seven British, a Swede and a Chilean. Under her previous master, Captain Ole Sørensen, the *Kollskegg* had survived an attack by a dozen German aircraft, was struck by five bombs, and beached in a burning condition. She was repaired in the UK between July 1940 and June 1941.

The *Kollskegg* was destined for Halifax and then the UK. The initial portion of her final voyage was uneventful – she cleared the Windward Passage and southern Bahamas and was heading a shade east of north. Though the ship was not zig zagging, her two guns aft, one 4.7-inch, the other .37 millimeters, were manned, for a total of five lookouts. There was a gentle wind from the west south-west, visibility was good and the sea was calm.

Just before 2 pm local time on the 6th of April, a torpedo from U-754 under 28-year-old *Kapitänleutnant* Hans Oestermann slammed into the starboard side of the ship in tank number 15, just below the wheelhouse. Before hearing from Captain Søyland, who was below at the time, Second Officer Kåre Larsen stopped the engines, sounded the alarm and told the deck crew to prepare to abandon ship. In the ensuing panic, 10 men got away in one of the lifeboats. Soon the master was able to gain the bridge and restore order and instill calm and purpose in the bridge team. During the interim, two young British mess-boys, Norman Hunter, age 17, and George Morrison were drowned in the rush to launch and board the boat, leaving eight survivors in charge of the boat, which had drifted away from the tanker.

Though the ship initially listed up to 25 degrees to starboard, the machinery was still working and the list did not prevent the ship from moving. Søyland decided to head towards the nearest land, which was Hampton Roads, Virginia. Course was changed to 283 degrees west and speed increased to 12 knots. Though one a lifeboat was lost overboard, empty, another which had been lowered was retrieved. However in order to escape from the enemy submarine, which remained unseen, the boat with eight men in it was abandoned.

The Naval Operating Base in Bermuda picked up a radio message sent by British radio Operator William F. Morris, and dispatched an aircraft to the ship's last position that evening, without result. A no-doubt befuddled Oestermann caught up with the tanker and just after 6 pm hit the ship with another torpedo, this time in the engine room. This *coup-de-grace* sank the tanker in four minutes, killing Second Engineer Arthur Gundersen, 27, and Chief Steward Henry Pedersen, age 47. Thirty men managed to get away in two lifeboats to begin their ordeal adrift.

Twenty one hours later the master's lifeboat was found by the Panamanian ship, *Bushranger*. The *Bushranger* was built as the *Stakesby* in 1922 by the Sunderland Shipbuilding Company. After being requisitioned by the US government from the Finnish firm of Gustaf B. Thordén in December 1941, the ship was given to the Alcoa Steamship Company, which renamed her *Bushranger* and flagged it to Panama. On the 4th of April 1942, the *Bushranger* began a voyage which would take her several months. She was bound for Havana, Cuba and then Paramaribo, Dutch Guyana (Suriname) and other South American ports to discharge general cargo, followed by a return voyage with bauxite to Saint Thomas, Virgin Islands, then Key West and New York. Her master was Captain Martin Strandley, age 32, who oversaw 42 other men.

To the great good fortune of the *Kollskegg* survivors in Captain Søyland's group, the *Bushranger* rescued the 30 men in the lifeboat to the west of the *Kollskegg*'s final resting place. It was just before dusk on the 7th of April. The survivors had been adrift for 21 hours. Considering that the *Bushranger* was to be sunk on her voyage in the Caribbean, it was also fortunate that the ship diverted to the Bahamas to deposit the survivors. Four days later, on the evening of the 11th of April, the *Bushranger* anchored off Nassau harbor and deposited the survivors ashore. There was no mention of their arrival in the local press, though three of the men were hospitalized.

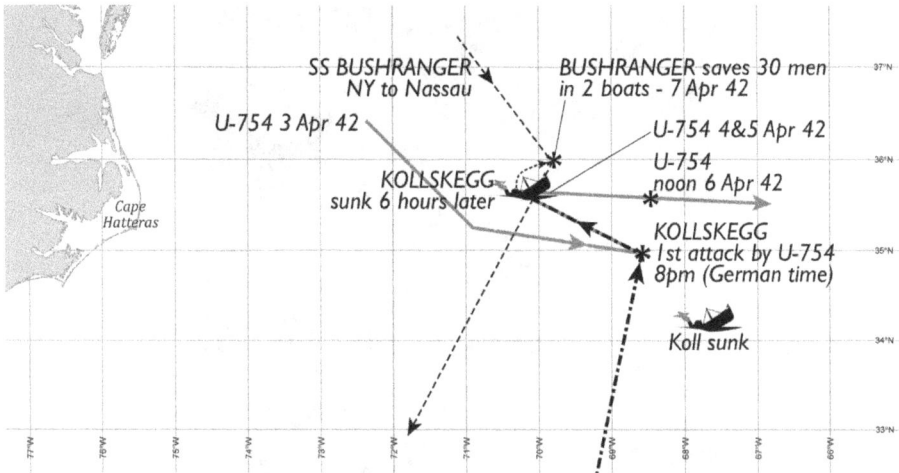

In Nassau Captain Søyland was interviewed extensively by Allied naval authorities, and he subsequently gave reports in Miami and New York. Three of the crew was hospitalized. British Able Seaman Thomas Browne was treated for injuries received in the torpedo explosion. Norwegian Motorman Einar Grønning and his colleague, Able-Bodied Seaman Harald Haugvik were admitted for another malaise, described in survivor reports as "social disease." A request to repatriate 30 of the survivors through the US was registered by Consul Dye as soon as the 14th of April. The waiver was granted on the evening of the 18th.

Meanwhile, there was still no word as to the fate of the eight *Kollskegg* men who had initially cast off in the lifeboat. These men had an impromptu rendezvous mid-ocean with the lifeboats of the ship *Koll*, ironically from the same Norwegian tanker company. On the 14th of April, the Canadian warship HMCS *Niagara* rescued the eight *Kollskegg* survivors after eight days adrift and landed them at Halifax. News of their survival eventually reached their mates.

The Duke and Duchess of Windsor greet Kollskegg
survivors at the Rozelda Hotel, Nassau,
Source: *"Survivors Meet Royalty – Survivors of Sunken Ships Keep*
Duchess Busy," and is dated 23 April 1942,
by the San Antonio Express-News, *Texas*

After nearly two weeks in Nassau, the 27 fit members of the *Kollskegg's* officers and crew travelled to Miami aboard the passenger freighter *Ena K*, arriving on the 23rd. There they were interviewed by members of the District Intelligence Office for the Seventh Naval District. Within a week they were transported to New York, mostly likely by train. The Second Officer, an Able-Seaman, the Third Engineer and Electrician provided statements in maritime hearings on the 30th of April. Then most of the men went right back to sea from the hiring halls of Manhattan and Halifax.

Three men remained behind in Nassau. Nineteen-year-old British Ordinary Seaman Thomas Frederick Browne for injuries and Einar Grønning, a 29-year-old motorman from Stavanger for illness. They left Nassau aboard the *Ena K.* on July 1st for Miami. Able-Bodied Seaman Harald Haugvik, aged 21 remained behind in Nassau for over three months, recuperating from his "social disease." He finally left Nassau on the passenger freighter *Betty K.* on the 17th of July and arrived in Miami the following day, where he was received and processed by Francis J. H. Dever, Esq., Inspector in Charge of Immigration in Miami. The *Betty K.* was also built in Harbour Island, Eleuthera by Thomas Berlin Albury. She took over the Miami-Nassau service from the *Isle of June* in September, 1938. *Betty K.* had 12 passenger cabins upgraded in Nassau for service between New York and Miami.

The *Bushranger* continued on to Havana and its destiny. The ship was sunk on the 1st of June 1942 by *Kapitänleutnant* Harald Gelhaus, age 26, southwest of the Cayman Islands whilst on her return voyage to the US. Seventeen out of her complement of 43, including Captain Strandley, were killed.

U-BOAT ACTIVITY 7 TO 20 APRIL 1942

The U-boat Ace Reinhard Hardegen, who kicked off Operation Drumbeat off New York and Cape Hatteras in January 1942, came south and spent between 6 and 14 April patrolling off the coasts of Georgia and Florida off Jacksonville and Cape Canaveral. During his incursion Hardegen and crew mates on U-123 damaged the US-flagged tankers *Esso Baton Rouge* and *Oklahoma* on 8 April off Brunswick, Georgia. The following day Hardegen dispatched the US-flagged merchant ship *Esparta*, also off Brunswick.

Then on the 11th he sank the *GulfAmerica* off Mayport, Florida. The sub was so close to shore that locals watched spellbound from the nearby beach resort – one of them even attempting to reach the scene in a small boat. Out of consideration for the onlookers Hardegen took his sub between the shore and his victim in order to try to shell the aerial antennas out of commission, lest he miss and hit the onlookers. The *Korlsholm* of Sweden was dispatched further south on the 13th of April, followed the same day by the US-flagged ship *Leslie*.

Next into the area was U-130 under Ernst Kals, who entered the region from the Mona Passage on the 4th of April, headed north then northeast and exited west of Bermuda on the 18th. In that time, he managed to attack and sink the *Grenanger* of Norway on the 11th. On the following day he sank the US tanker *Esso Boston*, also southwest of Bermuda and well northeast of Abaco in the Bahamas.

The rescue of the men in the motor lifeboat from the *Grenanger* is worth retelling. On their second day the British ship *Almenara* found them and offered to take them aboard. However the Norwegian master of the *Grenanger*, Captain Finn Rusti, decided that the rescuing ship did not have sufficient lifeboats for the safety of the extra passengers in the event it was sunk, so the Norwegians opted to put back to sea, which they did after receiving food and water. A week later the motorboat had somehow found the other lifeboat from *Grenanger*, a sailing lifeboat, and both were spotted by an aircraft off Sombrero Island and ultimately towed to Saint Thomas by the USS *Courier*, AMC 72. The original pencil-scratched note which was dropped to them by the American pilot is preserved to this day. The *Almenara* was ultimately sunk, by a mine off Italy, on September 20th, 1943.

Hand-written note from pilot of a Marine Scout Plane to
Grenanger *crew in lifeboats, 18 April 1942.*
Source: Chris Voorhees, Riverton Utah, USA, BuyandSellWWII.com

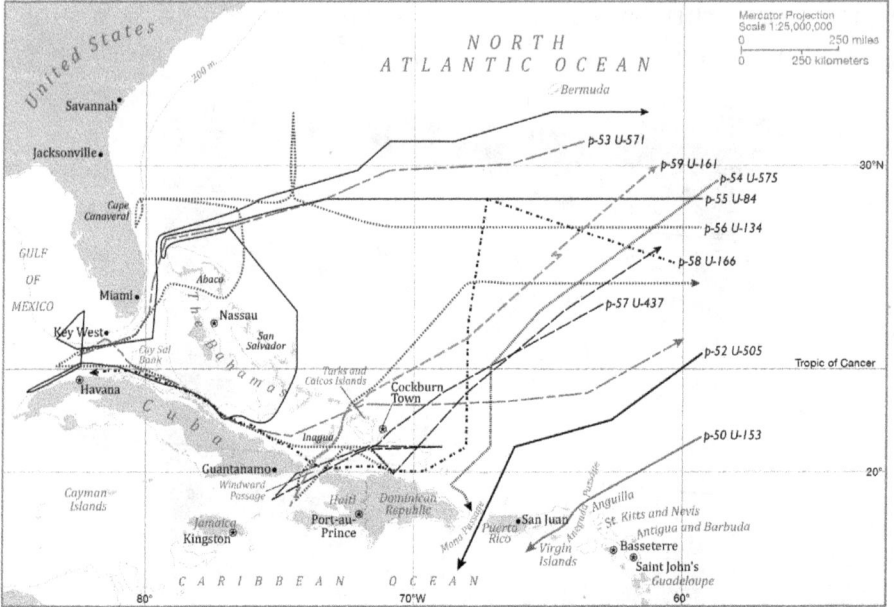

VINELAND

The next patrol to the region was led by Walther Kölle. His submarine, the U-154 was to return to the area four times in the course of the war – a record only tied by U-129. Kölle's submarine headed from north of Anegada into the Mona Passage. Along the way he sank two Allied ships, the Puerto Rican tanker *Comol Rico* and the US-flagged *Catahoula* on the 4th and 5th respectively.

U-154 entered the Mona Passage on the 6th of April, and left the region for nine days. The sub returned through the same narrow passage between Hispaniola and Puerto Rico. Then it turned west for a cruise north of the Turks and Caicos and east of Acklins and Crooked islands. Kölle then proceeded to a point roughly 300 miles north of the Mona Passage, doubled back to a point north of the Dominican Republic, and then steamed along westwards to the north of the Turks and Caicos, where he encountered the only Canadian ship sunk in the region.

The officers and crew of the Canadian ship *Vineland* have the distinction, along with those of *Fauna* and *Vivian P. Smith*, of having been rescued and repatriated by the islanders of the Turks and Caicos. The *Vineland* was launched in 1919 by the American International Shipbuilding Company of Hog Island, Pennsylvania. Originally she was built as the steam ship *Sapinero*, named after a rural enclave in Colorado which was subsequently inundated by the Blue Mesa Reservoir in 1963. She was commissioned for the United States Shipping Board. Under their ownership she performed at least one "immigrant" voyage and earned a place in the archives of Ellis Island.

In 1925 the *Sapinero* was sold to the Gulf West Mediterranean Line (the Tampa Interocean Steamship Company), headquartered in New Orleans. Eight years later she was formally transferred to Lykes Brothers Steamship Company. *Sapinero*'s next and final owners were Canadian.

SS Vineland *under Panamanian colors.*
Source: The Mersey Story, Thomas Raddall, Liverpool, NS,
Bowater Mersey Company 1979

In 1928, Izaak Walton Killam purchased 150 square miles of timber on the Mersey River in Nova Scotia and founded the Mersey Paper Company. He was an understudy of Lord Beaverbrook, also known as Canadian press baron Max Aitken, who went on to own Gun Point, an estate facing Spanish Wells in North Eleuthera. In Liverpool, Nova Scotia, Killam built a large mill and loading port for the export of rolls of newspaper print. In 1930, the firm started the Mersey Shipping Company Limited to move the product to market. This was renamed the Markland Shipping Company Limited in 1937. The company's ship, the *Markland,* served the *Washington Post* as well as the *New York Times* and papers as far afield as New Zealand and Australia.

After the outbreak of World War II, Mersey Paper Company officials realized that the *Markland,* which was British flagged, could be requisitioned for the war effort at any time, leaving them without a ship. Indeed in June of 1940 she was. As a contingency the firm purchased the *Sapinero* in March of 1940 and renamed her *Vineland.* A master from Nova Scotia, Captain Ralph Albert Williams, was placed in charge of a total complement of 37 men, including three Royal Canadian Naval Reserve gunners to man a two-inch gun on an aft platform. His brother Charlie commanded another of the company's ships.

Captain Ralph Williams of Vineland, *the V for which he was fond of saying stood for "Victory"*
Photo source: his daughter, Mrs. Edna Greenwood.

The *Vineland* was envisioned to carry finished newsprint to Australia and New Zealand, with interim voyages carrying pulpwood and coal from Cape Breton to Liverpool. In order to avoid having the *Vineland* requisitioned like the *Markland*, they registered the new ship under shell companies like the Scotia Shipping Company, and flagged it to Panama, though her home port was still listed as Liverpool, under the Markland Shipping Company.

Flagging the ship to Panama was only partially successful, as the Canadian Shipping Board's Department of Transport called the ship to service, carrying bauxite from the Virgin Islands to Portland, Maine. By early 1942, efforts were well underway to re-flag her to Canada. Officers from the Markland Shipping Company were corresponding with Furness, Withy and Company Limited to have the ship registered to Ottawa at the time of her loss.

The *Vineland* was a steam-propelled cargo ship which could carry 7,800 tons of cargo. Her gross registered tonnage was originally 5,106 tons, but by 1942 this had reached 5,587. The ship's length overall was 401 feet, her beam was 54.2 feet wide, and the draft was 24.5 feet deep. Her registered speed was 12 knots. However, by 1942, she was 23 years old and her quadruple-expansion, single-screw engine was not likely to achieve that. On the 10th of April 1942 *Vineland* left Portland, with no cargo and in ballast, bound for Saint Thomas. Her instructions were to load bauxite there. This was to be her second voyage carrying bauxite.

The ship hugged the American coast on the voyage down, not setting off for the open ocean until after it had passed Cape Hatteras. On the way through the torpedo junction, Ralph Kelly, one of her crew, observed "around Diamond Shoals off the Carolinas, you could see where the submarines had chased ships right up onto the shoals, and they were sinking. They were afire, there were a lot of bodies around. We [sic] seen bodies pretty near every day."

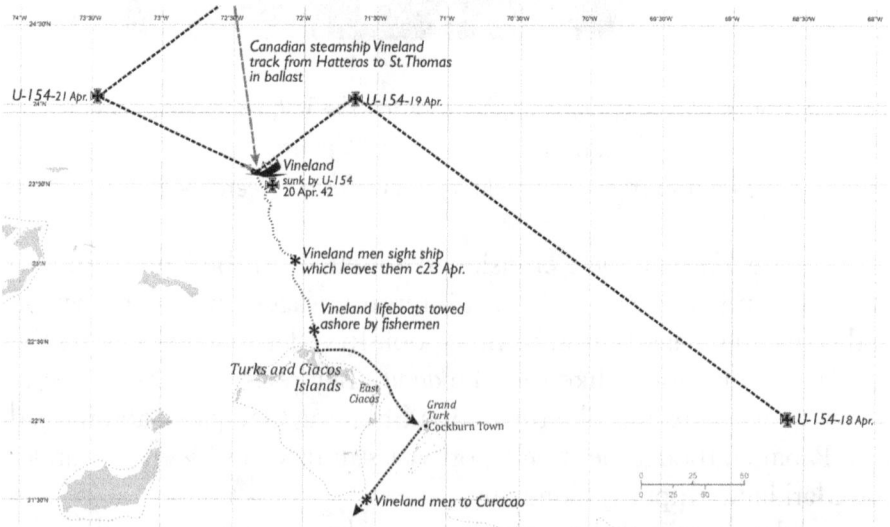

Canadian steamship Vineland track from Hatteras to St. Thomas in ballast

U-154 -21 Apr.

U-154 -19 Apr.

Vineland sunk by U-154 20 Apr. 42

Vineland men sight ship which leaves them c23 Apr.

Vineland lifeboats towed ashore by fishermen

Turks and Caicos Islands East Caicos

Grand Turk
•Cockburn Town

U-154 -18 Apr.

Vineland men to Curacao

At 2:03 pm local time on the 20th of April 1942, while in a position roughly 90 miles north of Mayaguana and North Caicos U-154 under Walther Kölle fired two G7a-type torpedoes at the ship. None of the lookouts spotted the sub, periscope or torpedoes being fired, since the U-boat attacked from the direction of the strong mid-day sun. The weather was described as fine, with only a gentle swell. The first one struck aft and a second missile porpoised to the surface and missed astern. Ralph Kelly was serving as a mess boy and was leaning over the rail at the time, and saw the torpedo hit. "It hit between the gun crew and myself, right back by number four hatch. I was about fifty feet from where it hit. ... While we were gettin' ready to put the lifeboats over the side, we seen the second torpedo go by us."

Vineland *crew Erlin Conrad at age 19 in Nova Scotia*
Source: *Erlin Conrad c/o Karen Ohrt, daughter, 2013*

The damage from the first torpedo was significant enough that the aerials were brought down. There was no time for the radio operator to rig an emergency aerial and call for help. Nor could the gun be brought to bear. Kelly was in a lifeboat with the Chief Cook. Because the oil from the galley stove spilled into the lifeboat, soaking everyone in it, a number of the crew leapt into the water. One of them was Oiler J. Lawrence Hanson. "This other young fella jumped out. What happened to him, they think either the gang plank or the funnel from the ship hit him." Kelly and the cook then went around collecting men in the lifeboat. Three boats got away from the ship with everyone except the young Hanson, who was drowned (one report says that his body was retrieved and carried back to Halifax but this is implausible). Two boats went down one side and the third on another.

After all of the crew had scrambled off the ship, Kölle fired a *coup-de-grace* which hit amidships and broke the stern section completely off at 2:20 pm. But the Hog Island-built ship stubbornly refused to sink, even after U-154's crew sent five rounds of deck artillery into her waterline at the bow. Then the ship's crew reported a dozen shots fired. Afterwards, the *Vineland* sank quickly, roughly 20 minutes after the initial attack.

Wryly noting that the sinking occurred on Hitler's birthday, Kelly described his aggressors as "reasonably good, didn't bother us. He [Kölle] just went in and out of the lifeboats like that, takin' pictures of us." Captain Williams was so wary of being taken captive by the Germans, that he threw his braided Captain's cap away, lest he be recognized as the master. Kelly continued: "the Germans gave us cigarettes, asked the captain where he was goin' to and what he was going to carry, if we needed medical aid, and told us the nearest course to land. One course was ninety miles and the other was a thousand, so you could take your pick..." U-154 left the men heading east on the surface. After the U-154 left they assembled and split the men evenly between the boats.

Left on the open ocean with no ship and no sub, the men started to row and sail southwards, toward the Turks and Caicos. Though the Bahamian islands of Mayaguana and Acklins were roughly equidistant, they were further downwind. On the evening of the third day, the survivors sighted what they assumed was an Allied passenger ship on its way to rescue them. However, whether the ship sighted the survivors or not, it turned away and steamed over the horizon. As a result, the *Vineland* survivors were convinced that it was a German supply ship and that they had been spared captivity, though there is no evidence to support this theory. For the remaining three days of their five-day voyage, the winds were light and the men made little progress, though the islands were tantalizingly close. Kelly described those days as "just driftin' around" and said it might have been a week.

For at least one of the crew, the lifeboat voyage was traumatic. According to the family which tended to him on Grand Turk, the "man was badly injured having gone overboard to repair an awning. Something came up from the depths and bit his foot so badly that he stayed at the hospital on Grand Turk while the others returned to duty." Several locals reported that there was a teenager about the *Vineland*, which they confused for being a British ship (of course they never saw the ship). "One young crew member, who seemed to be just a boy, really, was a nervous wreck, having been torpedoed three times."

On April 23rd, the three lifeboats which had managed to stay together, were discovered by the British sloop *Emily Conway*, which was built in 1940 and owned by James M. Clarke of Blue Hills, Caicos Island. According to the Turks and Caicos Islands *Annual Colonial Report*, "the S.S. *Vineland* was torpedoed, but her crew of 35 was picked up by a Caicos sloop." The fishermen towed the lifeboats to Chalk Sound, Providenciales. The men had suffered from sunburn, as well as dehydration, but were otherwise fit. None of them required hospitalization. Apparently two of the boats landed on one side of the town of Providenciales, and the third on another. According to one survivor: "On the first little island, the life boats were on different sides, so I don't know what happened with the other two. Where we were there was one old man and one boy and no supplies. But the old man did give us some banti roosters to kill and eat."

Kelly writes that "Fishermen picked us up, native people in the Turks Island. That night we got ashore, they scrubbed us and scrubbed us, trying to get the oil out. ...For some reason or other they wouldn't let us stay there." This is likely because a small fishing village would have been hard-pressed to adequately provide for 36 hungry men. Captain Williams states that the *Emily Conway* (he named her the *Emily F. Convey*), took them to Grand Turk on the 24th of April. Kelly continues "...this fishin' boat took us from there to Grand Turk and that's where we stayed for a couple of weeks. They gave us clothes that they didn't think they'd need at that time. They sold us all their cigarettes they could possibly spare because they were on rations too, you might as well say, 'cause a ship only come around about every six or eight weeks'. "

The Herriott family, having originally emigrated from Bermuda in the 1830s, had built the largest edifice on Grand Turk, wedged between the salt pans and the ocean. Named the White House, it still stands today. Family lore has been well kept by Georgina Dunn Belk, who provided a number of anecdotes relevant to the arrival of Captain Ralph Williams and the crew of the *Vineland*. Her aunt writes that "as children, we saw evidence of the torpedoing of ships by the German submarines when some of the survivors of a torpedoed merchant ship were brought to East Harbour by fishermen who discovered them drifting in lifeboats. Our family, along with other families who could, took them in until they could be transported back to the United States." One of the *Vineland* survivors says that "on Grand Turk the women made clothes for some of us."

The White House, Grand Turk, where some Vineland *officers and men were accommodated.*
Source: Dr. Edward Harris, Bermuda Maritime Museum, and Georgia Dunnk Belk, descendant of the Harriotts,
royalgazette.com/apps/pbcs.dll/article?AID=/20130323/ISLAND09/7032 39983 &template=printart

Life on shore was bleak, but not as bad as for others surviving wartime winter in Canada: "Ships from the Maritimes had even poorer food to feed the crew and for them a meal ashore at the White House, where [the hostess] would have a chicken killed for them as honored guests, was memorable." The islanders had become, by necessity, adept at scavenging the bounty of wartime submarine attacks. "Essentially, anything that floated ened up on a beach and Turks Islanders would come to the door of the White House selling items they had found including life boats, life rafts, oil drums, ropes and tarps, timber and furniture. But the most treasured finds were the crates of dried tin food, so when large tins of white powder washed up the beach [we] brought it from the salvager. It has the appearance and consistency of porridge. Cooked and eaten for breakfast, it had the consistency of glue but was more or less edible."

One of the Herriotts continues: "We had five seamen in our home from the sunken British merchant ship with supplies that left New York for South America to pick up raw rubber.... [the *Vineland* was en route to the Caribbean and South America]. The rescued men were picked up one afternoon by our fishermen. (Daddy told us later that the men were covered in oil and some were burned quite badly). Five of them were settled into our home after Cleo and I had gone to bed. We didn't know about our guests until we came down the next morning for breakfast and there they were at the dining room table with my father and mother having their morning tea." She continued: "our torpedoed British seamen stayed with us and the other families four or five days until a ship came for them. We borrowed additional cots from family, and they took over our bedroom upstairs, and we moved into our parent's room and slept on the floor."

Presumably the officers stayed at the White House. Eight of the men were accommodated at the Louise Ariza boarding house in Grand Turk. Osvaldo Ariza remembers that his mother "put up survivors there" and that "most were Canadian." He remembers hearing that a young boy from the ship said he had been torpedoed three times, and that Captain Williams was fond of telling local school children that the "V" in *Vineland* stood for Victory. Another of Mrs. Ariza's sons remembers one of the cooks aboard the *Vineland*, a man named Hutter. The Arizas and Mr. Hutter remained in contact for years after the war.

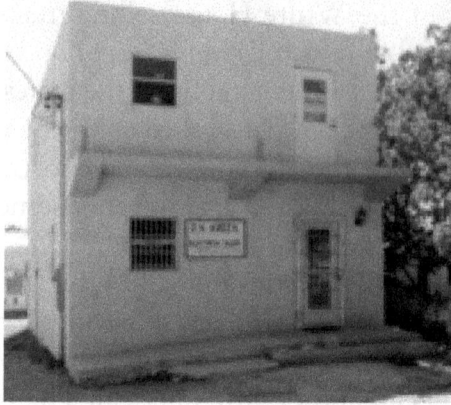

The Louise Ariza boarding house on Grand Turk where some of the
Vineland *men stayed.*
Source: Sherlin Williams

During their stay in Grand Turk, Captain Williams managed to get word through to the Naval Officer in Charge in Trinidad. Through that channel, the British Admiralty in Jamaica learned that *Vineland* had been lost and all her complement barring the one man killed were in the Turks and Caicos. The British Admiralty in Jamaica promptly informed Ottawa and Washington, as well as the Canadian Shipping Board's Commander Heenan. By April 29th, efforts to re-register the ship were promptly scrapped.

After 13 days on Grand Turk, or about May 10th a Dutch inter-island passenger ship took them to Curacao. Their farewell was poignant and a community event. One of the Herriots recounts how "When arrangements were made for them to return on a ship that came to pick them up, Daddy, Cleo and I went down to the waterfront where all the survivors had congregated, as did most of the men of the island. They were loaded into small boats and taken out to the ship. ...and they were returned to the United States where they were to be assigned to another ship carrying supplies to England."

Despite nearly being torpedoed a second time en route to Curacao, they made it to that major oil refining center and were given "shaving equipment, suits, socks, underwear, you name it. And they even gave us money to spend," wrote Kelly. The harrowing repatriation of

Vineland's men was not over. After less than a week in Curacao, they boarded a German-built, Dutch-run ship laden with ammunition, bound back to Halifax. Fortunately for all involved, it was an uneventful voyage of 14 days during which "everybody was scared stiff" wrote Kelly. They didn't arrive back until early June, over six weeks after their torpedoing. That autumn, Ralph Kelly joined the Royal Canadian Navy. By his tally he avenged Kölle's attack on the *Vineland* by attacking three submarines during the war.

Survivors of the Vineland *on arrival back in Halifax.*
The sign reads "Reserved: Survivors Only"
Source: local paper, c/o Erling Conrad's papers, c/o his daughter Rev.
Karen Ohrt

On April 21st, Kölle turned northeast and made a bee-line back to France. He passed just south of Bermuda and exited the area on 24th of April. On this patrol (which began on March 11th and ended on May 9th), U-154 sank five ships, including the *Delvalle* and *Empire Amethyst* in the Caribbean, for 28,715 tons. It was an impressive bag, and in some ways close to his last. Kölle had earlier served on the *Gräf Spee* before she was scuttled off Uruguay. He rose to senior naval officer of the Flushing base before joining U-boats in November 1940. His patrols to the region lasted 60 and 80 days respectively. His next patrol was to

Mexico and the Caribbean. He surrendered command of U-154 to Heinrich Shuch after his third patrol and moved ashore to staff positions.

Age 34 at that time, Kölle's career total of ships sunk included only two other steamers, *Tillie Lykes* and *Lalita*, bringing his total to seven ships for 31,352 tons. It is safe to say he made his career in a single patrol through the Bahamas. In September of 1943 he took part in commando raids to occupy the Italian port of Genoa. He was later chosen as Second Officer of a new commerce raider, named *Hansa*, however the ship never sailed. He achieved *Fregattenkapitän* in March 1945, right before Germany's fall, but was not decorated. His three patrols for 164 days were all on U-154. Walther Kölle lived until the age of 84, dying in 1992.

Vineland survivor Erlin Conrad, summer 2013,
c/o daughter Rev. Karen Ohrt

U-BOAT ATTACKS 21 TO 30 APRIL 1942

Between the attacks on the *Vineland* and the *Federal* on the 20th and 30th of April respectively, 10 submarines entered the region. They managed to sink three ships. U-201 under Adalbert Schnee ducked into the region west of Bermuda on the 21st to 23rd of May 1942 only long enough to sink the British ship *Derryheen* on the 22nd. He followed that success with an attack on the US passenger liner *San Jacinto*, an Awilines ship headed from New York to Puerto Rico. Fourteen perished, but 169 managed to survive. Captain Robert W. Hart was not among the survivors landed in Norfolk by the USS *Rowan* – passengers saw him return to the bridge of the sinking ship and heard the report of a pistol shot shortly thereafter. In an ancient tradition of the sea, Captain Hart went down with his vessel.

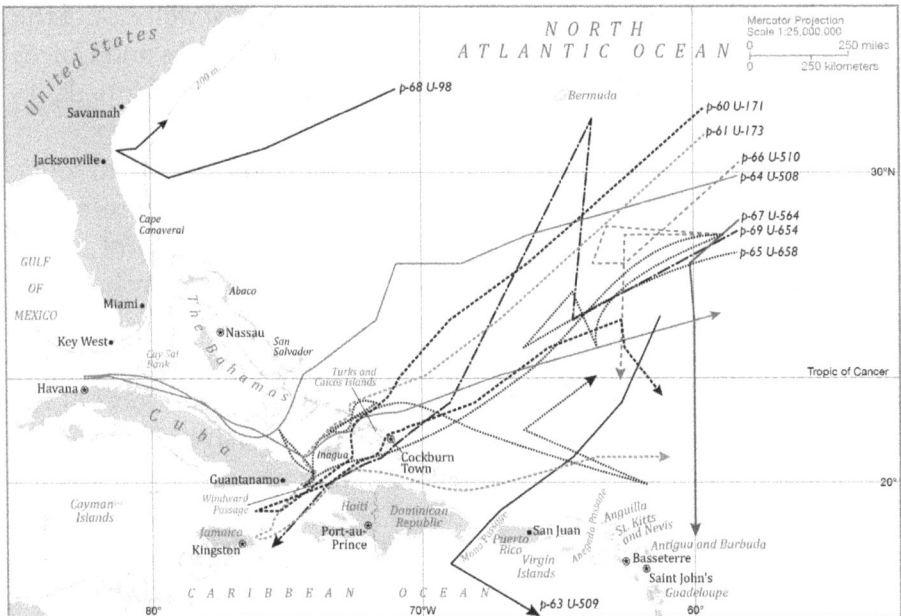

Next into the area came U-654 under Ludwig Forster who cruised northeast of Abaco between the 24th and 29th of April. He was followed by Sigfried von Forstner in U-402 who dipped into the region westbound from Bermuda towards Hatteras between the 25th and 28th of April without sinking any ships. This short incursion was followed by Harro Schacht in command of U-507. Starting on the 24th of April Schacht utilized the Caicos Passage and Old Bahama Channel to exit the area into the Gulf of Mexico via Key West. He returned on the 18th of May, used the Straits of Florida to transit the Northwest and Northeast Providence channels, and exited the region west of Bermuda on the 22nd of May, homeward bound, without having sunk any ships in the Bahamas area.

On the 26th of April U-125 under Ulrich Folkers transited inbound, north of the Dominican Republic into the Caribbean via the Windward Passage. He returned on May 21st also via the Windward Passage, using the Caicos Passage to exit the region east of the Bahamas on the 27th. U-109 under Heinrich Bleichrodt came south from Hatteras on the 27th of April, skirted the north of Grand Bahama, and patrolled off Cape Canaveral Florida before exiting the region west of Bermuda on the 13th of May. Klaus Scholtz on U-108 was next to the region, motoring south from Bermuda towards Anegada starting on the 27th of April. On the 29th he dispatched the US tanker *Mobiloil* well east of the Bahamas, Then Scholtz patrolled extensively off the Turks and Caicos between May 3rd and 14th before exiting the area south of Bermuda on the 18th.

U-506 under Erich Würdemann entered and exited from south of Bermuda 28 April and 30 of May. During the interim he transited the Providence channels to access the Straits of Florida and patrol in the Gulf of Mexico. On the return voyage between 24 and 30 May he opted to pass north of Grand Bahama, heading east. U-333 under Peter Erich "Ali" Cremer entered the area south of Bermuda on the 28th of April and exited west of Bermuda on the 10th of May after using most of his torpedoes in a series of effective attacks off Cape Canaveral which saw the demise of the *Halsey*, *Amazone*, and *Java Arrow*.

U-98 Herbert Schultze patrolled north of Grand Bahama and off northeastern Florida between 28 April and the 18th of May. U-582 under Werner Schutze dipped into the area south of Bermuda between

28 and 29 April without sinking anything. A day later Ace Reinhard "Teddy" Suhren in command of U-564 guided his submarine down the Straits of Florida as far as the Cay Sal Bank off Cuba, then proceeded north to a point off what is now Freeport, Grand Bahama, but was then just barren coastline. While in the Straits he dispatched the *Ocean Venus, Eclipse, Ohioan, Delisle, Lubrafol* and the Mexican tanker *Potrero del Llano*. Leaving a swathe of destruction he exited the region west of Bermuda on the 22nd of May.

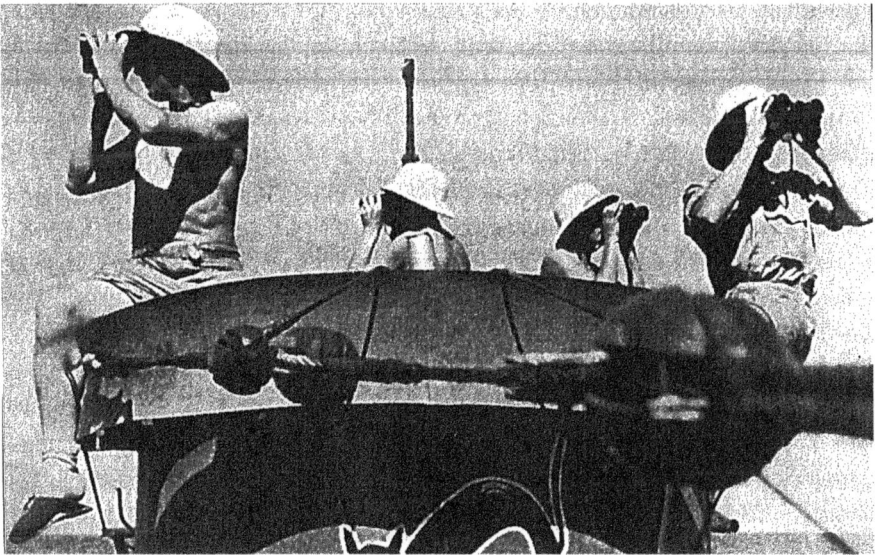

The conning-tower watch ever vigilant aboard U-564 in the Caribbean area under Teddy Suhren.
Source: U-Boot im der Karibik, VerlagsArchiv, U-Boat Museum / U-Boot Archiv, Cuxhaven

FEDERAL & IVAL

The sinking of the *Federal* is worth noting as the first Allied U-boat casualty in the Old Bahama Channel, and because Bahamians helped rescue the survivors. *Korvettenkapitän* Harro Schacht spent 14 days transiting the Bahamas. He was the first to utilize the Old Bahama Channel along the north coast of Cuba. On the 30th of April Schacht sank the *Federal*, an American ship of 2,881 tons off Gibara, Cuba. The *Federal* was en route in ballast from Tampa to Banes, Cuba to load molasses. Her 33 men were under the command of Captain Walter Furst. It was not a clean sinking. The U-boat was detected by lookouts when three miles away and submerged. The tanker, meanwhile made full steam for the safety of nearby Gibara.

Rather than expend valuable torpedoes on his quarry, Schacht opted for a running duel with shells. The sub surfaced alongside the ship and poured 30 shells into it, killing a cook and a mate. Thirty-one men got away aboard two rafts and a lifeboat. U-507 then approached the stricken ship and at short range pumped another 100 shells into it, sinking it an hour later and killing three more men. Because of the brazen nature of the attack, which occurred in broad daylight a mere five miles from a busy port, the casualty attracted a lot of attention. Two US navy airplanes circled overhead, looking for signs of the submarine. The US Army transport ship *Yarmouth* diverted to investigate. However her master, fearing for his ship's safety, left the scene without rescuing *Federal* survivors.

Fortunately for the survivors on the *Federal* there was a Bahamian schooner named *Ival* in Gibara port at the time. After witnessing the attack on the ship several miles away, *Ival's* willing crew were requisitioned by Cuban authorities and immediately set out to help. Local Cuban officials boarded her to take part in the rescue. The subsequent tale of Bahamian heroism was recounted on the front page of the Nassau *Tribune* on Thursday 14 May 1942:

"Mr. Wilfred Toote recounted how the Bahamian schooner 'IVAL' (Captain Rupert Bowleg Jr.) rescued 25 seamen immediately after the torpedoing of an American freighter off the Cuban coast recently. Apparently, the 'IVAL' was in Gibara Harbor when the attack occurred only five miles outside the port. The ship was torpedoed and then shelled, and the explosions could be clearly heard along the shore. The 'IVAL' with Cuban naval officers on board, put out in a mild breeze

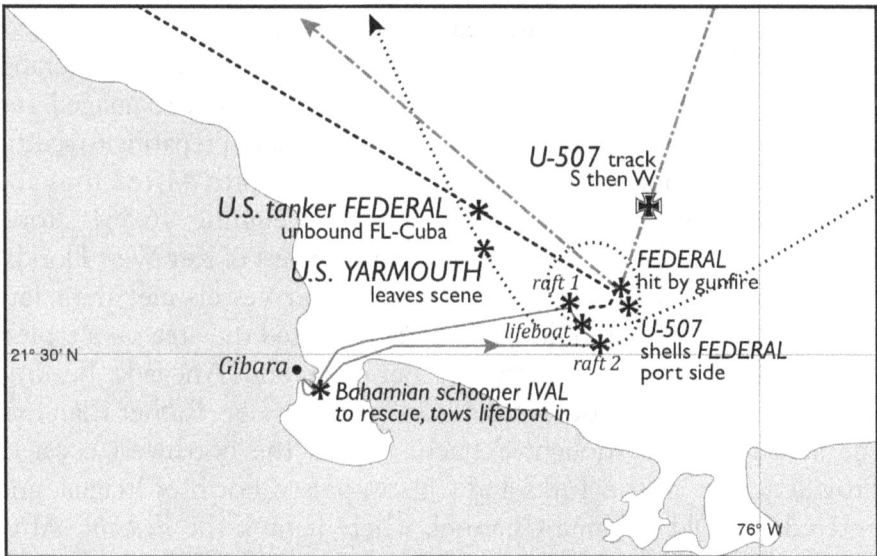

and guided by the smoke, picked up twenty-five men in the choppy sea."

The article continues; "'When the men saw the Union Jack,' Mr. Toote said, 'they stood on the raft and cheered.' Five of the 35 crew members were killed in the explosions, and the remaining five were rescued by another vessel which put out at the same time as the 'IVAL'. " It would appear that there is a factual error, inasmuch as only 28 men escaped from the *Federal*, and her total crew was 33 not 35 men. If five of the survivors were rescued by another boat, then the *Ival* must only have rescued 23 men (not the 25 reported). It is possible that in the confusion, Mr. Toote counted some Cubans among those rescued. Mr.

Toote states that he rescued men from rafts. The men on the lifeboat were said to have followed their rescuers ashore. So it appears that the *Ival* emptied all of one raft of survivors and split the survivors of the second raft with another vessel.

It was not the end of *Ival*'s voyage. The article concludes that "The '*IVAL*' on which Mr. Toote was Super-cargo, returned to Nassau [13 May] from a trip to Haiti and Cuba. She was chartered for the voyages by Mr. Reginald Christie, who was also on board."

Aside from sinking the *Federal*, Schacht's patrol on U-507 stands out for the impressive array of Allied ships – mostly American – which he destroyed in the US Gulf region off New Orleans: the *Norlindo*, *Munger T. Ball*, *Joseph T. Cudahy*, *Alcoa Puritan*, *Ontario* (Honduran), *Torny* (Norwegian), *Virginia*, *Gulfprince* and *Amapala* (damaged and salvaged after an Allied plane surprised the Germans preparing to scuttle the ship) for a total number of nine ships sunk worth 44,782 tons and one ship damaged (the *Gulfprince*) weighing 6,561 tons.

The *Norlindo* was actually sunk northwest of Key West Florida, outside the Bahamas area, whereas the other vessels met their fate deeper inside the Gulf of Mexico. U-507 entered the area on a typical trajectory from midway between Bermuda and Anegada heading southwest in the direction of the Windward Passage. Rather than exit the area that way, though, Schacht skirted the northwest coast of Providenciales in the Turks and Caicos, passed north of Inagua, and entered the Old Bahama Channel, where it sank the *Federal*. After exiting the Old Bahama Channel via the San Nicholas Channel south of the Cay Sal Bank (controlled then, as now, by the Bahamas), U-507 left the region on the 4th of May, only to return via Key West two weeks later, on the 18th.

At that point Schacht initiated another first. His was the first German U-boat to transit the entire Straits of Florida from off Key West to Grand Bahama, which he did on the 18th, 19th, and 20th of May. Thereafter the boat headed back to Lorient, exiting the area on the 22nd of May not far from the west coast of Bermuda. He had begun the patrol on the 4th of April in Lorient and ended it there on the 4th of June 1942.

U-BOAT ACTIVITY MAY 1-17, 1942

Between the attacks on the *Federal* on 30 April and the *Fauna* on 17th of May 1942 five submarines entered the larger Bahamas area. These and their compatriots managed to sink 18 Allied ships in as many days. On the 3rd of May Ulrich Gräf in U-69 entered the area south of Bermuda bound for the Mona Passage, via which he entered the Caribbean proper on the 8th without having sunk any ships. Dietrich Hoffmann brought U-594 into the region for a 27-day incursion on the 5th of May, west of Bermuda. The sub patrolled off San Salvador from 8 to 10 May before heading to Cuba, then around Inagua and back north to patrol north of the Greater Antilles until the 21st. Then Hoffmann doubled back and entered the Caribbean via the Windward Passage. The men attacked no ships but lost a man overboard during a crash dive on 25 May. Between June 2nd and 8th the sub transited from the Windward Passage to exit the region south of Bermuda.

Gräf was followed on the 8th of May by U-103 under Werner Winter. At first he motored south from off Hatteras between 7 and 13 May, using the Crooked Island Passage to enter the Caribbean via the Windward Passage. Then between 31 May and 5 June he used the Caicos Passage to exit the area south of Bermuda. Next came U-106 under Hermann Rasch. Between 13 and 20 May Rasch motored down the Straits of Florida to enter the Gulf of Mexico via the Florida Keys. He returned to transit the region from 2 June, up the Straits of Florida, around Grand Bahama, and exited the area south of Bermuda on the 9th of June.

Between 13 and 14 May Juergen von Rosenstiel took U-502 briefly into the region via the Anegada Passage. He was followed by U-751 under Gerhard Bigalk 14 May, who spent five days heading straight south from off Hatteras to the Caicos Passage and the Caribbean via the Windward Passage. En route he sank the US freighter *Nicarao* east of

Eleuthera. The crew of the *Nicarao* saw so many local schooners and
inter-island trading vessels that they were convinced the schooners were
complicit in the destruction of their ship. There were also lights seen
on the sinking ship after it was abandoned, which might have been from
a few of the crew left behind on the doomed ship. The date was 16 May
and the survivors were picked up by the US tanker *Esso Augusta* the
following day and landed in Norfolk on the 20th of May.

Survivors of the Nicarao, Purser Frank C. Bunn, Jr. with satchel,
board a bus in Norfolk.
Source: NARA, College Park, Maryland

U-753 under Alfred Manhardt von Mannstein cruised south
from west of Bermuda down the Straits of Florida between 14 and 19
May, at which point it entered the Gulf of Mexico. The sub returned
from the Gulf on the 1st of June, proceeded down the Old Bahama
Channel and utilized the Caicos Passage on the 5th before exiting the
area for La Pallice on the 8th of June. On May 15th Günther Krech took
U-558 directly south from east of Savannah to the Caicos Passage and
the Caribbean via the Windward Passage. On the way to leaving the
area on the 20th he sank the *Fauna* on the 17th, west of the Turks and
Caicos.

Allied losses in the month of May began with an effective attack
on the British ship *La Paz* on the first by U-109 under Bleichrodt. Two
days later the same commander sank the Dutch freighter *Laertes*, also of
the east coast of Florida. The same day U-506 under Würdemann
ignored larger prey nearby in order to sink the converted schooner *Sama*

not far from Orange Cay, south of the Bimini Islands, Bahamas. On the 5th Scholtz in U-108 sank the 5,010-ton American ship *Afoundria* off Il Tortue, an island off the northwest coast of Haiti.

Women and children survivors of the Afoundria
being landed in Guantanamo Bay Cuba
Source: National Records and Archives (NARA) College Park, Maryland.

Meanwhile "Teddy" Suhren in U-564 was very busy in the waters off Cape Canaveral. He dispatched the British *Ocean Venus* on 3 May, her compatriot the *Eclipse* the following day, and the US-flagged *Delisle* a day after that. The American ship *Ohioan* fell to Suhren's expert aim on the 8th and the Panamanian *Lubrafol* the following day. On the 14th the experienced skipper made a mistake. Saying that he confused the brightly lit Mexican flag on the side of the tanker for that of Italy (why would he have sunk the ship of what was then one of Germany's Allies?), he sank the Mexican tanker *Potrero del Llano* off southeastern Florida.

Rasch's sinking of another Mexican tanker, the *Faja de Oro* on the 21st of May, with a combined loss of life of 23 Mexican officers and crew led to protests in Mexico and indirectly to that country's declaration of war against Germany less than 10 days later, on the 1st of June, 1942. Suhren was the third-most-successful U-boat skipper in the region, with six ships sunk there for 37,635 tons. Close behind Suhren, ranked 10th regionally with four ships of 21,293 sunk, was Peter-Erich "Ali" Cremer, in U-333. All four of those vessels were sunk in less than a week, three of them off the coast of Florida. The Dutch ship *Amazone* and the American ship *Halsey*, as well as the US ship *Java Arrow* were all dispatched on the 6th of May. Cremer effectuated his attack on the *Clan Skene* of Britain to the northeast of the Bahamas on the 10th of May. Nine of her Indian crew were killed in the attack, the survivors were rescued by the USS *McKean* and landed in Puerto Rico after drifting for 36 hours with a broken radio.

On the 11th of May U-502 von Rosenstiel found and sank the British 4,963-ton ship *Cape of Good Hope* well northeast of the Virgin Islands. One boatload of survivors managed to reach the Dominican Republic 18 days later. The captain and his group were able to sail to the British Virgin Islands, where they were towed into Road Town, Tortola after 11 days by the sloop *Sparrow*, out of Virgin Gorda and under the command of Captain Robinson O'Neal.

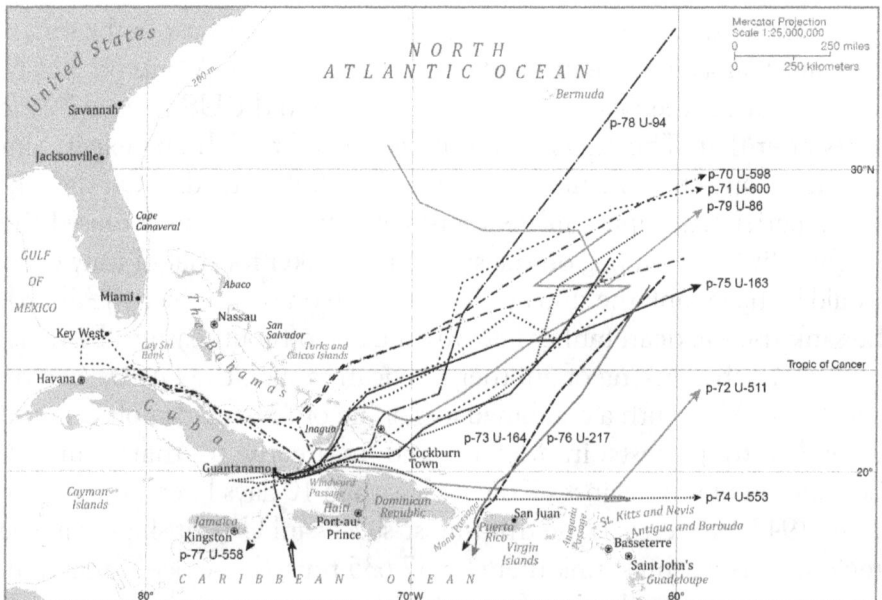

FAUNA

One remarkable aspect of the sinking of the ship *Fauna*, off the Turks and Caicos is that she was actually trading with these islands rather than just passing through them. Her survivors spent several weeks circumnavigating the Turks and Caicos in a lifeboat and local sailboat. The *Fauna* was a Dutch 1,272-ton steam merchant ship constructed in 1912 by Rijkee and Company of Rotterdam. Her dimensions were 262 feet long, 36 wide and 16 feet deep. An 800 horsepower triple-expansion engine drove a four-bladed propeller which boosted the ship at 9.5 knots. Her owners were the Royal Dutch Steamship Company (KNSM) of Amsterdam. In 1942, long after the Netherlands was overrun by the Germans, the company was being operated out of 25 Broadway in New York City.

Steamer Fauna *in her Dutch livery.*
Source: wrecksite.eu/imgBrowser.aspx?3883

Compared with many of the other non-sailing merchant ships struck in the Bahamas area during the war, *Fauna* was a small ship. The O. A. *Knudsen* by example, was nearly ten times as large in terms of gross tonnage. The *Fauna's* cargo reflected her small size. She carried five barrels of gasoline and 15 barrels of kerosene, presumably for the generators on the small island of Grand Turk where there were salt works, and a general cargo including matches, cement, machinery, and flour. The gasoline and kerosene were stowed on deck. The master was also entrusted with 22 bags of regular mail plus one bag of registered mail.

A crew of 29 men was under the command of Captain Jacob den Heyer, a Dutchman. Four of the crew were British, including a "servant" named John White, age 42, sailor Othniel Dickenson, age 46, sailor Ben Eve, age 49, and a fireman Sam Sanny, age 25. Of the 25 Dutch men on board, two of them, Wilhelm Johann Kervezee, age 29, and Tonnis Bierling, age 42, were gunners manning a 3-inch gun aft. *Fauna* left New York on the 6th of May 1942 destined for Grand Turk, to be followed by a stop in Port au Prince, Haiti, where she was to deliver some Lend-Lease cargo. The ship was under orders of the British Naval Control. *Fauna* took some 11 days to cover roughly 1,300 miles. It is possible that she joined the coastal convoys as far as Georgia before striking out for the eastern Bahamas. The fact that the convoys only sailed during the daytime and put into port at night would account for the slow progress. She was less than a day from her destination on the 17th of May when she was intercepted in the Caicos Passage by U-558 under Günther Krech.

The position of the subsequent attack was east of Mayaguana Island, west of Caicos Island, and just 10 miles or so north of Northwest Point, Providenciales, in the Turks and Caicos. The passage is some 30 miles wide at this point. The Captain described it as "very narrow… and… not generally used as a shipping lane or route." This is a puzzling statement given that the Caicos Passage is a deep, wide shipping channel commonly used to gain access between the Windward Passage and the open Atlantic. Captain den Heyer may simply have been referring to the ship's proximity to land.

At seven minutes before midnight the men on watch were no doubt anticipating their imminent relief from duty. The ship's course was east-northeast at the speed of 10 knots. It was a clear night with a slight swell and no wind to speak of. Without the moon, visibility was one to one-and-a-half miles. There were three lookouts on station, one on the forecastle up forward, one manning the gun aft, and a third on the bridge.

Meanwhile, Günther Krech was tracking the *Fauna* from seaward, or the ship's port side to the north. His crew began their first patrol into the Bahamas area aboard the U-558 on the 15th of May. Having left Brest on the 12th of April, U-558 refueled from U-459 on the 29th northeast of Bermuda. He opted for a straight line from Hatteras to the Windward Passage. When the *Fauna* was struck, the survivors supposed that the sub must have been waiting there for resupply.

Kapitänleutnant Günther Krech of U-558, *which sank the*
Fauna *off the Turks and Caicos*
Source: uboat.net/men/krech.htm

Suddenly a single torpedo pierced the number two cargo hold, roughly two feet below the water line. The explosion ignited the cargo of matches stowed there. The large hole blown in the *Fauna*'s side immediately flooded the number two - and soon after the number one - cargo holds, then the engine and boiler rooms. Hatch covers from both holds were blown into the air, the radio shack and the ladder to the bridge were destroyed, and the port-side motorboats were knocked clear off the ship. There was no opportunity to send a radio distress message or to man and train the guns.

Given the circumstances, the men behaved with restraint commended by Captain den Heyer. This is particularly true of Third Mate Jan Noordveld, Third Engineer Jan Rab, sailors Nicholaas Plugge and Maarten de Jong, and Kervezee, the gunner, who "stayed on board to see everything clear" and in doing so perished. Soon the *Fauna* was listing to starboard at an alarming 26, then 30 degrees. The men on watch grabbed personal papers and cash and made their escape. Within 10 minutes, 27 men had leapt into the water or clambered into the only remaining lifeboat – the one from starboard. Just before midnight, and only five minutes after the attack, the men saw U-558 approaching from the starboard beam. Krech brought the submarine to within three quarters of a mile, kept it darkened, and circled the bow of the stricken ship. When U-558 made it to the port quarter, aft of the beam, it switched on its searchlight to help the men in the water to make it to the lifeboat.

Then the sub circled the lifeboat and asked for the name, tonnage, and destination. One officer came down to the deck of the submarine to do the questioning in English. Den Heyer responded in German, but still there was a misunderstanding about the spelling of the *Fauna*, and the Germans ended up writing *Towa* instead of the correct name. After this brief interrogation, the sub motored through the wreckage and then set off in a northeasterly direction 12 minutes after the attack.

As the lifeboat set about gathering survivors from the water the *Fauna* performed a death-roll. A heavy explosion rocked the ship, on which six men remained – this was possibly a boiler exploding when the sea water hit it. At first the ship stayed on course, but then it veered to starboard. Finally, after roughly 50 minutes, at 43 minutes past midnight on the 18th of May, the *Fauna* rolled over to port, the side with a gaping hole in it, and sank quickly. The Germans did not attempt to board the blazing wreck.

Of the six men who remained on board, four of them – Noordvelt, Rab, Plugge, and de Jong – managed to escape and swim to the lifeboat. G. C. van Baardwyk, age 40, a Trimmer from the engine room drowned along with Keverzee. Both men were seen on the deck by their crewmates just before the sinking. Captain den Heyer observed that "it is believed they went back below, and were trapped."

Once they had collected all 27 survivors, the men set out for the nearest land. Strictly speaking this would have been Northwest Point, Providenciales, however winds and currents pushed the lifeboat west and south. As a result, they managed to make landfall on the unpopulated island of West Caicos at 11 am the same day. Though there appears to have been a settlement named Yankee Town near Lake Catherine, den Heyer and his men "found no people there."

The same day, the lifeboat set off to the north, and after 14 miles they rounded Northwest Point and headed southeast, looking for signs of habitation. While they were under way, the boats were discovered by two local fishing boats. Captain Ralph A. Ewing, owner and skipper of the schooner *Sister E.* (also known as *The Sisters*), was the first one back to shore at 1 am on Tuesday the 19th of May. The local craft, weighing 10 tons and built in Blue Hills in 1922, was loaded with roughly half of the *Fauna* crew. It is not known what happened to the large lifeboat – perhaps it was towed to port, rather than discarded.

According to historian Kendall Butler "the Ewing family was prominent in High Rock, Blue Hills, Providenciales. Hilly Arthur Ewing [was a] boat builder." Doris Ewing was nine years old at the time and remembers her father Captain William Ewing returning to Blue Hills aboard his boat *The Flirt*, with the balance of *Fauna*'s survivors. She says that "the boats used to go down by Inagua and the Caicos Passage to look for food and clothes floating in the sea that came from torpedoed ships." In this instance the islanders discovered more than they expected in the jetsam of war.

The men were found in poor condition – cut up and bruised – and several of them were naked and covered in oil. The children were kept at a discrete distance from them. Captain Ralph enlisted the help of his wife to clean them up, and they would have enlisted the help of the island mid-wife, who was the senior care-giver in the community. Doris Ewing relates that her "mother and aunts and other men and

women, from North-side, bandaged them up and fed them." Local
historian Sherlin Williams relates that "The Midwife was the only
healthcare giver to be found in each of the three settlements. ...No
young women in the entire island during those days would have been
allowed to be exposed to naked men. Only mature persons in age bracket
of the wives of boat owners, whose children were already grown, would
have been in direct contact in their condition."

   During their overnight stay in Blue Hills the Dutch sailors were
put up in the local schoolhouse.

The old school house in Blue Hills, Providenciales
where Fauna *survivors stayed.*
Photo: Sherlin Williams, Turks and Caicos historian.

   In Blue Hills the *Fauna* survivors were offered a local sailing boat
for onward passage. At the time, the government in the colonial capital
of Cockburn Town Grand Turk reimbursed local sailors for providing
assistance to stranded sailors. They also reimbursed islanders for
returning items salvaged from torpedoed shipwrecks on the coast,
though in some instances, items like tinned food and clothing was
simply taken and used by the islanders. The islanders faced great
difficulty finding a market for the salt they harvested, due to the danger
to shipping in exporting it. "Although demand was up, delivery of salt

became difficult. With an enemy presence in the Caribbean and North American waters, steamers stopped their business and export of salt to the eastern seaboard dramatically declined." As a result, skippers in Blue Hills were eager to take the survivors east to the capital, with or without direct payment from the *Fauna* captain.

The men set out later that day for a longer voyage – to South Caicos Island. After two days, in daylight on the 21st of May, they reached Cockburn Harbor, South Caicos, which is also known as East Harbour. Historian R. E. Sadler, in his study *Turks Islands Landfall* confirms that "The K.N.M.S. Steamer *Fauna*, bound for Grand Turk with supplies, was a victim of submarine attack, but her crew of 27 landed safely at South Caicos." The men remained on South Caicos for a week. During that time, three of them – Rab, who had an injured leg, Noordveld, who was burned, and Oiler Johannes Stroomberg, 46, who had a cut foot, were treated for their wounds. After a period of recuperation, the men all set off again on about the 27th of May for Cockburn Town, Grand Turk, which was their original destination. Again the three injured men were treated, and again they opted to remain and recover for a week.

In the capital town some of the *Fauna* sailors were put up in a guest house named the Dora Do Do on Middle Street on Grand Turk. Built in the 19th century, its matron was Dora Williams – because she was believed to practice Obeah, or Voodoo, her nickname was "Dora Do Do." Another establishment where they stayed was the Coverley boarding house, owned and operated by Felicia Grand and her husband Vincent Coverley. Probably den Heyer and his officers stayed at the Coverley house, as Sherlin Williams adds that it was "where VIPs visiting the island lived." The waterfront building, between the Anglican Church and the sea, has since been demolished.

The Dora Do Do guest house in Cockburn Town, Grand Turk, Turks and Caicos, where Fauna *men stayed.*
Source: Sherlin Williams, at the request of the author

Despite no doubt taking pride in assisting the stricken seamen, and also in harvesting the goods of value that washed up on their shores as a result of submarine depredations, the fact remains that the impoverished islanders still very much needed ships like *Fauna* to arrive with their cargos intact. It was essential for their survival. During the war "staples such as rice, beans, hominy and lard became scarce. Rice and grits that arrived had to be washed and flour sifted to remove the weevils. [People] gardened, although water was scarce due to the drought, and the family fished, trolling along the Edge of the Deep. ....
Sails were patched until the patches had patches...."

In a letter addressed to "The Commissioner of Turks Island, Grand Turk, B.W.I." from the Dutch Central Transport Workers Union in exile in New York, dated 24 July 1942 and signed by P. J. van der Berge, Secretary, the union thanked the islanders "for the help rendered them by your good office and the good people of West Caicos and East Harbour." The union was asked by the *Fauna* men to "express their sincere and heartfelt thanks." The letter went on to tell the Commissioner that "their assistance to shipwrecked Dutch seamen will always be remembered by the Dutch people and the Dutch labour movement. ....Our warmest thanks goes to the people of Turks Island and your good self, who left nothing undone to mitigate the hardships of our men and help them recover from the ordeal to which they were subjected after the sinking of their ship by enemy submarines."

On or about the 3rd of June the 25 survivors set off for Cape Haitian, a port city on the northwest coast of Haiti separated from Grand Turk by 115 miles of open ocean. The two British sailors, Dickenson and Eve, opted to remain behind. Perhaps they didn't feel up to another open boat voyage. It is not clear whether the rest of the survivors used the same local sailing craft or obtained transit on another vessel, probably the latter, which would have been safer. Taking another ship to Haiti would also help explain the delay of a week, since they would have been reliant on another skipper's schedule.

Once they landed in Cape Haitian and reported their predicament, the men were transported by automobile to the capital, Port-au-Prince. Captain den Heyer was debriefed by the US Naval Attache in Port au Prince. From there, they were given another ride to the city of Saint Marc. This meant a car journey over the mountains of at least 75 miles and many hours. Again, two men opted to remain behind: a Dutch Fireman named Francisca, age 40, and the English "Servant" John White, age 42.

On the 11th of June 1942, the 23 remaining men, led by Captain den Heyer, boarded the ship *Gatun* bound for New Orleans, where they arrived on the 20th of June. The refrigerated steamship *Gatun* was built in 1926. She was owned and operated by the Standard Fruit and Steamship Company and her master at the time was Captain MacLean. Aside from carrying bananas from Haiti and other islands to its home base in New Orleans, she was utilized by the US Army during the war. Presumably, the *Gatun* was part of convoy that travelled via Guantanamo and Key West.

On arrival in New Orleans, Captain den Heyer was interviewed by W. S. Hogg of the US Navy. He then precoded post-haste to New York, in order to report on the loss of his ship to the owners. Presumably, the remaining 21 Dutch crew were re-assigned to other Dutch vessels by the Dutch consulate. Sam Sanny, the English Fireman, made it home to his wife Cornelia in Brooklyn.

Meanwhile, U-558 had limited success in its eight-day transit of the Bahamas area. However, it inflicted heavy losses in the Caribbean and sank an additional ship on the return voyage. The submarine attacked and sank the HMS *Bedfordshire* on 12 May, off Cape Hatteras, then the Canadian *Troisdoc*, damaged the *William Boyce Thompson*, and sank both *Beatrice* and *Jack* in the Caribbean as well as the *Triton* on the way home – northeast of the Caribbean. The total tonnage sunk by the patrol was 19,301.

Krech was amongst the first U-boat skippers to utilize the Mona Passage between Hispaniola and Puerto Rico on the 29th of May. Over the next four days, he steamed northeast leaving the region on the 1st of June 1942 bound for Brest, where the boat was based with the First Flotilla, arriving on 21 June. On the return trip, U-558 refuelled from U-459, in mid-June west of the Azores. Günther Krech, 27 at the time, became one of the better known U-boat skippers of the war. In April 1941 he had achieved the rank of *Kapitänleutnant*. He became famous in part due to his success in sinking over 20 ships of over 100,000 tons. He is also remarkable for his youth and early recognition: he earned the Knights Cross shortly after this patrol. In over 10 patrols of 437 days, Krech sank 17 ships of 93,186 tons and damaged two others for 15,070 tons as well as effectively destroying a further ship of 6,672 tons. On 20 July 1943, U-558 was sunk by Allied aircraft in the Bay of Biscay, with Krech and four others surviving. They were kept in captivity by the Allies for the remainder of the war and for some time thereafter. Krech lived until age 85, passing away in June 2000.

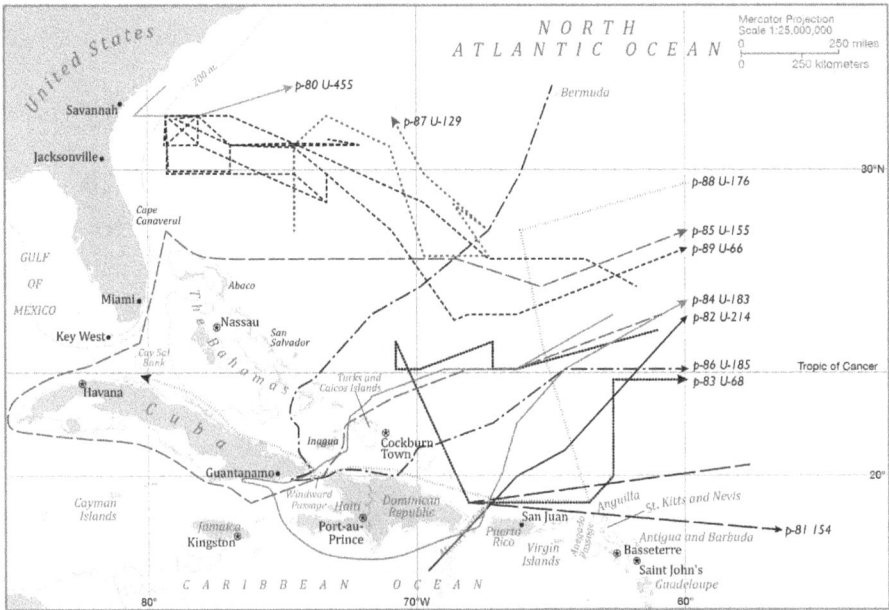

PART III: JUNE TO AUGUST 1942

U-BOAT ATTACKS 18 MAY TO 27 JUNE 1942

Between the loss of the *Fauna* on the 17th of May and the *Potlatch* on the 27th of June, a dozen German submarines attacked the waters around the Bahamas and 23 Allied ships were sunk, for an average of more than two ships a day, or one every eleven hours. Harald Gelhaus leading U-107 expended a considerable effort in 11 days of patrolling the region starting on 22 May just east of Savannah and heading southbound to transit the entire length of the Straits of Florida as well as the Old Bahama Channel. He entered the Caribbean via the Windward Passage on the 29th of May only to re-emerge through the Mona Passage on the 19th of June.

On that day, while transiting back north of the Antilles, Gelhaus bagged his only "ship" in the region, the small, 35-ton coastal sailing schooner *Cheerio*, which had been coasting in the pre-dawn light between Puerto Rico and the Dominican Republic. Though the nine men were rescued by the US Coast Guard Cutter CG 459, her owners, officers and crew later petitioned the US government for reimbursement for their loss. The submarine headed north, leaving the region west of Bermuda on the 23rd of June.

U-504 under Fritz Poske returned to the region for more predations on the 22nd of May. Poske headed south of the Turks and Caicos and straight for the Windward Passage, which he entered on the 27th. The sub didn't return until the 20th of June, in order to simply transit the Anegada Passage for two days. U-158 under the aggressive and talkative skipper Erwin Rostin entered the region south of Bermuda westbound on the 24th of May, having sunk the British ship *Darina* well east of the Bahamas on the 20th.

Grateful survivors of the Darina *being fed aboard their rescue ship – note the ill-fitting belt.*
Source: NARA, College Park, Maryland

After encountering and dispatching the Canadian laker ship *Frank B. Baird* on the 22nd, Rostin transited the Northeast and Northwest Providence Channels between the 27th and 28th. He exited the area at the base of the Straits of Florida for the Gulf of Mexico on the 31st. In the Gulf he sank a number of ships outside of the area before returning to the Straits of Florida on the 26th of June, northbound. Rounding Grand Bahama on the 27th he then sank the Latvian ship *Everalda*, taking two prisoners. This final kill was to seal his fate – that and his loquaciousness. When Rostin radioed his success to headquarters in France, the Americans were able to bead in on the submarine, which was subsequently discovered northwest of Bermuda on the 30th of June and sunk from the air.

U-172 Carl Emmermann transited the area from north of Anegada into the Mona Passage inbound between the 2nd and 6th of June 1942. U-172's torpedoes sank the American ship *City of Alma* on the 3rd of June and north of the Dominican Republic the sub sank the small US freighter *Delfina*. Roughly three weeks later he exited via the Anegada Passage on the 2nd and 3rd of July.

U-68 under Karl-Friedrich Merten, an established Ace, just clipped the corner of the zone by transiting the Anegada Passage inbound to the Caribbean on the 3rd to 4th of June. Merten exited the area via the same route on the 26th and 27th of July. Merten sailed himself into the history books as the most decorated commander to serve in this region during the war. Though the patrol began in Lorient on the 14th of May 1942, the submarine put into El Ferrol Spain, where U-68 was given fuel from the German supply ship *Max Albrecht* and also undertook repairs. This would make this the first German submarine patrol to the region which ended in Spain.

Helmut Witte brought his sub U-159 into the region on the 3rd of June, entering the Caribbean via the Mona Passage on the 5th of June. Witte sank the *Illinois* on the 2nd of June well east of the Bahamas. He returned to exit via the Anegada Passage on the 24th and 25th of the same month. U-157 under Wolf Henne began its final patrol in the region on 6 June, heading for the Caicos Passage, which it transited on the 10th. From there Henne marched his sub up the Old Bahama Channel, stopping to dispatch the American ship *Hagan* off Cuba on the 11th. This alerted American forces to the sub's presence, and they were waiting for him as he approached the chokepoint between Havana and Key West. On the 13th of June the sub was detected, hunted and sunk with the loss of all hands between Cay Sal Bank in the Bahamas and the Florida Keys.

Hans-Ludwig Witt brought U-129 into the area on the 9th of June 1942. For 10 days the men transited the Caicos Passage and Old Bahama Channel, exiting the area off Havana on the 19th of June. The day after his arrival Witt dispatched the Norwegian freighter *L. A.*

Christensen, and on the 12th of June he sank the British ship *Hardwicke Grange*. Twenty-three men in one of the *Hardwicke Grange*'s lifeboats navigated to the southern Bahamas or Turks and Caicos and heard surf breaking on the reef when they were fortuitously rescued by the British tanker *Athelprince*, sister ship to the *Athelqueen*, and landed in Cuba. *Hardwicke Grange*'s Second Officer, E. L. Warren stated to the British Consul in Nuevitas that "We were picked up on the 24th June by the tanker SS *Athelprince*, actually the night before we had passed within 1 ½ miles of some rocks which we had not been able to see." It would thus appear that the survivors were mere meters or minutes from landing in the Bahamas or Turks and Caicos before being rescued.

Meanwhile U-129 continued its onslaught, sinking the US vessel *Millinocket* off the north-central coast of Cuba on the 17th of June before passing west of Havana. Witt returned to Lorient between the 22nd and 31st of July along the same route, except that he opted for the Mayaguana Passage, slightly more to the west, on the way back. U-67 under Günther Müller-Stöckheim returned to the region on the 9th of June, plodding steadily through the Caicos Passage and up the Old Bahama Channel to enter the Gulf of Mexico near Key West on the 16th. On that day, U-67 was responsible for sinking the Nicaraguan freighter *Managua* off Key West. Müller-Stöckheim retraced the same route, passing Key West eastbound on the 17th, Caicos Passage on the 19th and exited the region on the 23rd of July, bound back to Lorient.

On the 15th of June Joachim Deecke in U-584 arrived north of the Bahamas on a special mission: to land saboteurs on the beach via inflatable boat at Punta Vedra Beach, Florida, which is south of Jacksonville. His mission accomplished, along with having deposited a number of boxes of explosives, on the 18th, the boat cruised briefly north of Grand Bahama before heading for Hatteras and departing the area on the 20th of June. The *Guisepi Finzi* under *Tenente Vascola* Amondola patrolled the area north and east of the Bahamas between roughly 27 June and 22 July 1942, receiving extra fuel and provisions from compatriot submarines in the area also operating in the Betasom joint-venture with the U-boat arm. Hartenstein in U-156 sank the British ship *Willimantic* on the 24th of June 1942.

As he approached the Anegada Passage Wilfried Riechmann, on his second war patrol with U-153 and an untested crew encountered and sank the British freighter *Anglo-Canadian* on the 25th of June. Reichmann followed this with the loss of the *Potlatch* and *Ruth* in two-day intervals: the 27th and 29th of June. The sub then motored into the Caribbean to meet its fate at the hands of USS *Landsdowne* off Panama. On the same day that the *Anglo-Canadian* was sunk, Rolf Mützelburg brought U-203 into the region. The following day his team sank the Brazilian freighter *Pedrinhas*, and the British ship *Putney Hill*. Mützelburg, who had just celebrated his 29th birthday on the 11th of June, lost his life in a diving accident southwest of the Azores on the 11th of September 1942. The sub lurched, causing him to hit either the saddle tank or the deck with his shoulder and head. Even a medic from the nearby supply sub U-462 could not save him.

Walther Kölle began his second patrol to the area aboard U-154 on the 25th of June. It took him just three days to enter the Caribbean via the Mona Passage, which he did on the 27th. On July 31st he returned towards Lorient by the same route, exiting the region on the 4th of August. There were seven ships sunk and one merely attacked in the region between 23rd May and 27th June 1942. U-125 under the command of Folkers destroyed the US ship *Lammot du Pont* on May 23rd. Würdemann in U-506 sank two British ships within days of each other: the *Yorkmoor* north of Abaco on the 28th of May and the *Fred W. Green* on the 31st of May further east.

In the Windward Passage Harald Gelhaus was busy in an area whose proximity to the American base in Guantanamo would make it a dangerous hunting ground as the war wore on. Gelhaus in U-107 sank the British ship *Western Head* on 29 May. The *Western Head* was owned by the Maritime Navigation Company Limited, of Nassau. Krech in U-558 sank the Dutch vessel *Triton* on the 2nd of June well east of the Bahamas.

On that same day occurred one of the strange near-misses of the theater: U-753 under Alfred Manhardt von Manstein was heading south down the Old Bahama Channel at night when it very nearly collided with the motionless and blacked-out American sugar-carrier *Domino*. Startled men on both vessels just managed to fire off a few confused rounds at each other before the currents and their own momentum separated them. Perhaps wisely, von Manstein decided against following up on the attack – no doubt his watch-standers received an earful.

Another odd occurrence, though on the southeastern extreme of the area, was the sinking of the abandoned tug *Letitia Porter* by Ulrich Gräf in U-69 on the 5th of June. There was no record of a tug having been abandoned by its crew in the region at the time. Thus the riddle became a mystery until Rainer Kolbicz put the pieces together. It turns out that when the Dutch freighter *Koenjit* was sunk by Werner Hartenstein in U-156 on 15 May, part of its cargo was the small 15-ton tug *Leticia Porter*. The tug popped free from the mother vessel when it plunged to the depths, and ended up drifting for 23 days a distance of 175 miles north-northwest until it came into the sites of Gräf's U-69 and was finally sunk.

WILFREID REICHMANN AND U-153

A rare photo depicting Wilfried Reichmann atop the conning tower of U-153, most likely in Lorient, France June 1-6, 1942. Reichmann, aged 36, is likely the man seated to the left in the white commander's cap. The younger man standing with megaphone is likely First Watch Officer Oberleutant zur See Wolfgang Felsch, aged 25. Note broad axe on starboard side, and the Viking ship emblem on the front of the conning tower.

The German submarine U-153 was in commission for just under one year before being sunk on its first long patrol. Its only commander, *Korvettenkapitän* Wilfried Reichmann, moved to U-boats after having passed a 4 ½ year officer s training and served a various shore establishments (Naval Schools, Naval and Army Staffs) as well as many commands at sea (torpedo boat, minesweeper, and frigates). Over 17 years starting in 1924, these included stints on the training ship *Niobe* in South America, the cruiser *Schleisien*, torpedo boat *Falke*, minesweeper *M-132*, training yacht *Asta*, and frigate *F-8*. Over its short career U-153 accounted for more than twice as many German dead (97, two submarines) than Allied killed (44 dead on three merchant ships). Out of a crew of 55 officers and men on her final patrol, only three of the men had ever served aboard other submarines, and so far as is known only one of them, the Second Watch Officer, had ever been in action. Overall U-153's men appear to have done their best to live up to their U-boat, U-Axe's motto: *be bright, cheerful, and strike at them hard.*

Wilfried Reichmann was born on the 10th of October, 1905. He enrolled in the German Navy in the spring of 1924, meaning he belonged to the Crew of 1924 which initially comprised some 80 volunteers. Reichmann jumped the queue to become commander of a submarine without serving as either a watch officer or observer during a war patrol. As explained by Peter Monte of the *Deutsches Uboot Museum* in Cuxhaven, "...he was a rather experienced Naval Officer joining the U-boat force in 1940, already 35 years of age. Also unusual, he did not go through the usual training for potential Commanding Officers, i.e. after basic training a few tours as Second Watch Officer and First Watch Officer plus one tour as Commanding Officer under training overseen by an experienced C.O. [One] reason for this might be his rank, since he made *Korvettenkapitän* (Commander junior grade) on 1st of July 1939."

The original order for the Type IXC German submarine U-153 was signed on the 25th of September, 1939. This was mere weeks after the declaration of war between the UK and Germany and the subsequent sinking of the *Athenia* by U-30 under Fritz Lemp. It would be a year before the ship yard, Deschimag AG Weser in Bremen, would commence construction on its 995th vessel. The keel was laid on the 12th of September 1940. Known as *Schiff-und Maschinenbau*

Aktiengesellschaft, or ship and engineering corporation, AG Weser was the result of a merger in 1926 of eight shipyards. Krupp purchased the majority stake in 1941. Overall AG Weser in Bremen would construct a total of 24 Type IXCs, almost half of the total 54 ever built. The total cost of construction was 6.5 million German Reich Marks, or roughly $2.5 million at the 1940 exchange rates (in today's currency that would be roughly $41.25 million US dollars).

Launched after nearly seven months of construction, the submarine was 740 tons, 253.3 feet long, 22.3 feet wide, and her draft while surfaced was 15.5 feet with a total height of 30 feet 10 inches. She displaced 1,232 tons of water when submerged. The submarine was powered by twin nine-cylinder 4,000 horsepower M.A.N. diesel engines which could propel her at 18.3 knots, or 22 miles per hour while surfaced. Her range at 10 knots was 24,880 nautical miles when surfaced, easily enough to reach Panama from France (c.5,000 miles), and then patrol and return. In addition to the diesels, the U-Boat had two 1,000-horsepower electric motors and 62 battery cells for operating whilst submerged. Underwater her top speed was 7.3 knots. She could submerge as deep as 330 feet, to a maximum depth of 750 feet before being crushed like a can by the pressure. Her range under water was 117 nautical miles before she had to surface and ventilate to recharge the batteries.

The main difference between a Type IX and a type IXC boat was an increase of fuel capacity by 43 tons to 208 tons. This resulted in an extension of 2,300 nautical miles over its predecessor design. Also an extra periscope was added in the conning tower. The sub's total horsepower output was 4,400 surfaced and 1,000 submerged. U-153 could be equipped to carry and lay 44 TMA or 66 TMB mines. U-153's armament consisted of 22 torpedoes fired from four tubes in the bow and two in the stern. On deck she carried a 10.5-centimeter gun with 110 to 180 rounds of ammunition as well as a 3.7-centimeter cannon with 2,625 projectiles and a 2-centimeter gun with 4,250 rounds. The submarine was manned by between 48 and 56 officers and men, the minimum required being four senior officers and 44 crew.

The U-boat was commissioned three and a half months after its launch. Reichmann was its only commander. The boat's first assignment was to the 4th Flotilla for training. They were based in Stettin, Germany, just over the border in Poland and now renamed Szczecin. Training was conducted over 11 months between July 1941 and 31 May, 1942. During this time the young crew would create a name and logo for their new charge. According to Georg Högel, in his book *Embleme, Wappe, Malings,* "U-153 carried an emblem on the front of its conning tower which consisted of a golden Viking ship prow plus an axe and shield with flower. Even today, the emblem is associated with the name "U-axt" (U-Axe)."

Not only did they embellish the conning tower with a color emblem, but the crew added an axe on the starboard side – this would be verified by survivors of ships sunk by the submarine later in the war. The impression is of an untested crew who are determined to be good sports, and envision that their boat will make an historic contribution to the war effort. Amongst the only officers who had served on different U-boats were Chief Engineer Döbereiner aboard U-25, and that was only during January of 1940. Junior Boatswain Albert Deska, age 24, had served on U-68 under *Kapitänleutnant* Karl-Friedrich Merten, however not on war patrols. Second Watch Officer Eduard Thon had not yet left U-158 to join U-153.

U-153 *and its crew during commissioning ceremony,*
19 July, 1941, presumably in Stettin.

Work-up and training was extended because of a tragic accident. U-153's early operational career was marred by the death of 45 of her comrades in a collision. On 15 November 1941, after less than four months of training, Reichmann and his crew rammed into the new submarine U-583. Both boats became locked in a fatal grip and spiraled together towards the sea floor. At the last minute U-153 broke free and managed to make the surface again. U-583 did not, and all of its mostly young crew perished.

After an exhaustive search, the only signs of U-583 were two life jackets. They were empty. Kapitänleutnant Heinrich Ratsch and his entire crew were drowned under 300 feet of water in the cold Baltic Sea. Ratsch, from Berlin, was 27 years of age at the time of his death. Writers for various online forums have speculated that given watertight doors, it is possible that the forward and aft torpedo rooms were made airtight, and that men could have survived. Three hundred feet is after all less than half the crush depth of an undamaged submarine. According to the *Spokesman Review* of August 16, 1979, a letter on wax paper signed by "Lt. Heinz Ratsch" was discovered in a metal canister 36 years later. It read in part "…our submarine is resting on the sea bottom, engine and torpedo rooms flooded. Five men besides me are alive." Since Ratsch claims in the note to have been attacked by a four-engine British bomber on 11 November, the note can be dismissed as a hoax. But the possibilities of U-583's men dying a slow death of asphyxiation, waiting for a rescue which would never come, must have haunted the survivors aboard U-153, who all survived the collision, though thoroughly shaken up.

Repairs added time to the work up before the eager crew could begin their first war patrol. Reichmann was hospitalized and out of commission for nearly two months, from the 7th of January (seven weeks after the collision), until the 13th of February, 1942. Whether his hospitalization had anything to do with the stress of having inadvertently killed 45 men is not known, however it must have had quite an impact on the commander. It must have been terrifying for the survivors, to endure a massive impact then begin a death spiral into the depths, held in the clutches of another vessel, only to be released at the last minute. No doubt they could hear their colleague's submarine sink, the sounds audible through the hull as well as sub-sea listening devices.

U-153 began its second and final patrol from Lorient on the 6th of June 1942. On the 27th of June Reichmann sank the US freighter *Potlatch* well east of the Anegada Passage and east-northeast of the Virgin Islands. It was a long attack and was to have ramifications for survivors who landed in the Bahamas one month later. The following day, heading west, Riechman in his Type IXC U-boat entered the Caribbean via the Anegada Passage. Unbeknownst to its crew the sub was motoring towards its fate off Panama.

POTLATCH

The 6,065-ton American steam ship *Potlatch* was built as the *Narcissus* for the United States Maritime Commission, part of the War Shipping Administration, in 1920. Her builders were the Moore Shipbuilding and Dry Dock Company of Oakland, California. The ship was sold to the Weyerhaeuser Steam Ship Company of Tacoma, Washington State in 1940. *Potlatch* was a big ship of 12,000 tons carrying capacity, and by 1942 she was rusty and battered. Constructed of steel, her dimensions were 403 feet long, 53 feet wide, and 32 feet deep. She had two steam turbine engines turning two propellers which pushed the ship at 11 knots. *Potlatch* was armed with a single 4-inch gun, two .30-caliber and four 20-millimeter machine guns.

Potlatch *in New York harbor early June 1942, days before her final voyage to the Middle East with military supplies.*
Source: Steamship Historical Society of America archives, sshsa.org.

The master of the *Potlatch* was John Joseph "Jack" Lapoint who oversaw a total of 55 men, including 16 Naval Armed Guards. Amongst the 39 merchant marine crew were two Cadet-Midshipmen. On her final voyage the *Potlatch* loaded "military cargo, trucks, tanks and tinplate" in New York under charter to American Export Line (this is misleading, as she carried tank trucks on deck, not actual attack tanks). The ultimate charterer was the War Shipping Administration (WSA). Crew member Henry Jensen, 17 years old at the time, later dictated a detailed report of the incident. He relates that "we were fully loaded [below decks] but we didn't sail. First we stayed tied up for days. Then we began to make strange short trips to docks and darkened warehouses of an additional deck cargo." Another source relates that the *Potlatch* was "delayed proceeding" from at least the 4th to the 10th of June, 1942. During this lay over the US Coast Guard photographed the ship lying at anchor with a number of trucks and rolling stock stowed on deck.

Henry Jensen, narrator of a detailed account published serially in Liberty *magazine.*

The *Potlatch* left New York on the 10th of June 1942, bound for Suez via a stop in Trinidad and Cape Town. Because of engine trouble *Potlatch* limped along the coast, utilizing the Chesapeake and Delaware Canal to pull into Lynnehaven Bay, Virginia for repairs. The men didn't set off for Trinidad until 21 June, 11 days after leaving New York.

Enlisted members of the Potlatch's *16-man Naval Gunner group. 16-year-old Jake Jatho is second from the right, standing. Estil Dempsey Ruggles is sitting, lower right.*
Source: Jake Jatho

For reasons known best to him, Captain Lapoint deviated from his routing instructions, heading east of the proscribed course. Cadet Carbotti told his family that Lapoint confided that he planned to outsmart the U-boats by placing the ship where it would not be expected. German and Italian submarines were thick in the area, though, and during daylight on the 27th of June the ship was sighted by lookouts on U-153 under Reichmann. The *Potlatch* had stopped several times earlier in the day. The ship was some 1,700 miles from New York, 550 miles east of the nearest land in Antigua, and over 1,100 miles from Great Inagua in the Bahamas. Though the weather was clear, a breeze of 15 to 18 knots was coming out of the southeast, the direction the ship was headed. There were six lookouts on duty – one was in the crow's next, one was on the bridge, another on the flying bridge and three aft by the 4-inch gun

Potlatch route south from New York toward Trinidad – as conceived by US Navy routing officers and the ship's actual course, and point at which it was sunk. From the US National Archives, naval history files. Dated on or after August 1942, after the survivors had been interviewed and the position of her sinking determined.

At 3:52 pm local time a torpedo from U-153 slammed into the port stern of the *Potlatch*,between 10 and 12 feet below the waterline. It penetrated the number four cargo hold. "There was a whoosh and the whole ship seemed to move a hundred feet or more," wrote Jensen: "There was a vibrating roar, and the *Potlatch* shivered the way a dog used to do in the rain." Basilios Palaelogas, the Third Assistant Engineer, was badly injured. The damage was fatal to the ship, resulting in an "extremely violent" explosion which led some of the men to think they had been torpedoed twice. Some of the deck cargo of crates and trucks was blown into the air and then the sea. The ship was immediately flooded, the deck plates buckled, steam heating coils burst, and the steering gear was thrown out of commission.

According to the Gunner Estil Dempsey Ruggles, the ship seemed to go down in two minutes flat. John Burke and Hugh Kilpatrick were presumably trapped in the mess room by the violent explosion - they were never seen alive again. Up on the bridge Captain Lapoint asked the radio operator, a young man named Dalby, to send an SOS, but he didn't follow up on the order. Instead of grabbing the sextant and charts, Captain Lapoint went below to get the ship's papers and a promissory note for $20,000. Though the gunner tried to fire from the ship's machine gun, there was nothing to fire at, and the stern of the *Potlatch* was going under.

Many of the members of the crew had harrowing experiences in escaping from the fast sinking ship. Telling himself "You gotta keep cool," Jensen ran aft towards his station at the port lifeboat, just forward of where the torpedo struck. There was debris flying around – a piece cut him above both knees, and another lodged in his forearm. Chief Mate Larsen was hit by shrapnel and badly cut over his eye nearby on the boat deck. Suddenly a second explosion from the number four hold – possibly the boilers or cargo exploding – sent the heavy cargo hatch flying by "seventy feet in the air, a geyser of oil and water supporting it." Then "there was a grinding noise below, and steam, oil, and debris of all kinds were churning upward through the engine-room skylight. The ship was lurching and setting rapidly."

As the ship sank by the stern, the cargo lashed all over the deck began breaking free and sliding with deadly effect down the decks of the ship towards the water. Stanley, an ordinary seaman, ran out of the alleyway as a truck charged down the deck. It slammed him flat against the galley bulkhead. One of the hands that he had thrown up to protect himself was sheared off by the impact. Lapoint later reported seeing his body, the head crushed to "a pulp." Jensen released the gripes on the port lifeboat, then he and gunner Jake Jatho (also 17) leapt into the boat to release the oars and push it off. The injured Third Engineer Palaelogas was put in with them. As they were lowering the boat from above, the forward line jammed with a kink in it. As a result, the stern end of the boat kept going down and soon the boat was hanging vertically from the front. In Jensen's words, "The boat hit the water. A wave immediately swamped it and it was sucked into the torpedo hole under our feet. Jonah [Jatho] hauled himself up, but I was lower down and in the water up to my knees, hanging on by my left hand. I saw a small bare foot floating by me; I grabbed it, but the suction tore it out of my grasp and it disappeared into the ship. Later I found out that it was Palaelogas, our injured assistant engineer, who had been put into the boat. It seemed as if the whole ocean was pouring into the *Potlatch*. My shoes and socks were sucked right off my feet."

Jensen managed to pull himself to the lower main deck, which was below the boat deck he had left. He ran forward and crossed the alleyways on top of the crates. On the starboard side the lifeboat had already pushed off. As he relates: "Then I saw the colored chief steward in his clean white jacket, standing by the mast. I yelled 'Come on, McKenzie!' But he didn't answer me. His eyes were rolled up on his head, his knees sagged, and his mouth was hanging open. His hands were dangling helplessly. He was out with shock and had no life preserver on. But there was nothing I could do for him. The main deck was six inches under water and going down under me, while great explosions of air burst from the sides of the ship."

As Jensen swam away from the suction of the ship he heard a crash and when he looked back "...there was the *Potlatch* with her bow shooting up into the air, trucks and boxes tumbling off her like toys. The whistle gave a last pathetic toot and she slid under. It was exactly three minutes from the time we were hit, according to the deck cadet's wrist watch."

Captain Lapoint's ordeal was just beginning. Describing what happened to himself in a formal report he wrote: "Master jumped from starboard side, from top of gangway, caught in suction from starboard across to port, fouling in smoke stack stays, considerable lumber from cases, catwalk, hatch covers, etc. Also in suction at smokestack. Master managed to get free from stay [a wire] but unable to get clear of suction and debris and again fouled jumbo stay and wireless aerial foretop mast going down again, finally getting free, life jacket bringing master to surface."

Captain John Joseph "Jack" Lapoint, Master of the Potlatch.
Photo source: San Francisco Examiner, *July 1943*

His injuries included a pounding sensation against his right ribs, what he thought was a punctured lung. He was bleeding from the mouth, and had extensive dark blue and yellow contusions on his instep, calf, thigh, hip, knee and ribs. His right leg was feeling numb, he felt he had broken a rib and noted that "…entire right side, right chest and right side of back has severe pain." He also experienced pain breathing and moving forward. As a precaution he nominated Larsen to be his replacement in case he was incapacitated. Lapoint was determined to make for the US Virgin Islands. The confidential codes were thrown over by the Master and officers, however they did not sink right away. A prescient crew member found them floating in a box and submerged the codes until they saturated and sank, thus preventing U-153 prowling nearby from getting them.

Despite his injuries, Captain Lapoint took command of the starboard life boat. Fortunately three of the rafts were cut - or broke - free. The starboard life boat would not launch at first, as "the line had gotten kinked and was preventing it from being lowered." As Ruggles says, the line "was about as big around as my forearm. I grabbed an axed and cut it with one blow, then we scrambled on board and pushed away before the suction could get us." Altogether 49 men managed to get away from the doomed ship in just a few minutes. However "...the shock had dulled the senses of most of the crew. They forgot to cut sea painter, holding the lifeboat to the ship. ...in another few minutes the crowded lifeboat could have spilled its precious cargo into the sea." Chief Cook Beckles was still on board the ship and realized what was happening. He frantically looked around for an axe and found one. Beckels managed to cut the painter, or line, and free the boat. He was later awarded the Mariner's Medal for his actions.

Meanwhile, Reichmann brought his submarine in among the wreckage. Seeing two of the huge crates still floating, the U-boat crew fired into them with deck guns ("rifle fire") and sank them. Ruggles and Jensen said that as many as 30 German sailors lined the decks and conning tower, though this would have been nearly two-thirds of the complement.

Drawing illustrating the interaction between Reichmann and officers aboard U-153 and the men of the Potlatch. *If this were a photograph it would be the last image of the men of U-153*

The men were pre-occupied with saving themselves, and most of the crew believed that Lapoint had indeed drowned with the ship. When an officer from U-153, almost certainly 25-year old First Watch

Officer Wolfgang Felsch, asked for the master. When he was told by
Jensen and others that the captain had gone down with the ship, he
pursed his lips in impatience. Felsch asked in fairly good English for the
cargo and destination as well as the name of the ship. Since some of the
life rings still said *Narcissus*, the crew gave this erroneous information
as the ship's name (even though some of the crates were marked
Potlatch), and the German accepted it. Next the submariners asked if
there was anything that the survivors needed. When told that they
needed water and cigarettes, the Germans shared two packets of
German cigarettes. The submariners told the men that they were 400
miles due east of Saint Thomas. Whether intentionally erroneous or
not, this information turned out to be an underestimate of about 250
miles.

The submarine crew was described as well tanned. Jensen
described their questioner as "not more than twenty-three." When told
the name of the ship was *Narcissus* the questioner confirmed with the
man holding the notebook said "*Ja*," "...checked the name off in his
book and flipped up his mustaches. I could have bashed his face in"
wrote the 18-year-old Jensen. Felsch then asked the Second Officer of
the *Potlatch*, Frederick Sorensen, about the ship's armament, but the
merchant and navy crew did not want to volunteer this valuable and
potentially damaging information to their enemies. On their refusal to
answer "the sub commander became angry, threatened those on the raft
– and the information was given." Jensen said that "the sub commander
gave a signal, and the two submachine guns were turned and pointed at
my chest. Someone behind me shouted 'Four 20-millimeters and one
four-inch gun!' That broke the tension. The machine guns were pointed
skyward.

'For what company are you sailing?' The commander asked
quietly. The United States Government.' 'Government, government?
What company I asked you?' ... 'The Shipping Board, as in the last war.'
....In a different tone he asked 'Is there anything I can do for you? Is
anyone hurt?' to which Jensen's reply was 'Not that I know of.' 'Good
luck, gentlemen,' the commander said as he saluted us. We returned the
salute. As they moved away they began using their deck guns to sink
trucks – and Lord how they missed!"

*Photo of actual interrogation of survivors from a British merchant
ship by U-Boat crew, similar to that experienced by the Potlatch men,
except that they were on a raft, not a lifeboat.
Source: U-Boot-Krieg in der Karibik, VerlagsArchiv*

According to Lapoint, "...the raft was shoved clear of the sub,
which cruised among the wreckage, picking up several of the tires
attached to the wheels which were floating around, taking some on
board." The sub remained in the vicinity of the *Potlatch* sinking until
nightfall, lurking amongst the wreckage and picking up more tires and
materiel. The 49 men in the single lifeboat and four rafts were faced
with a challenge: how to subsist and navigate at least 600 miles in a
boat without a motor that had to tow three crowded bits of deadweight,
with limited supplies. Their mother vessel was 25.5 feet long and could
accommodate about 25 men comfortably, but they had nearly double
that number. There was no navigational equipment except a compass
which was off by several degrees, so they would have to rely on the stars
and sun.

The boat had a main sail, a smaller jib sail, and a piece of canvas
eight feet by four feet. It also had a barrel of water containing 18 gallons,
and stores of crackers, chocolate, and tins of pemmican, described as
"dried meat pounded into a paste with melted fat." On the first day the
men were given their largest meal of the voyage: half of a bar of

chocolate, a single cracker, and a two-ounce ration of water. Thereafter, the rations were reduced a little, based on a 30 day survival plan.

The disposition of the men at the outset was: seven men each on two of the rafts, and eight each on the others for a total of 30 on the rafts. The balance of 19, were in the lifeboat. At about 8 pm on the first day, having searched for their six missing crew-mates for four hours, the lifeboat hoisted its red sails, secured the four rafts in a convoy behind it, and headed to the southwest. To help the rafts see the lifeboat, Lapoint rigged a lantern on the tip of an oar.

The evening of the second day of their ordeal, the survivors were forced to abandon the first raft, the one closest to the lifeboat, because it was damaged as the stuffing was waterlogged. This called for a redistribution of men among the remaining three rafts and the life boat. The number of men on Jensen's raft rose to 10. With them came the bad news from the lifeboat: that the captain had neither sextant nor chart.

The following day was Monday the 29th of June – the third day in the raft for the *Potlatch* men and the day that the freighters *Ruth*, *Tysa*, and *Thomas McKean* were all sunk in the area. Hunger was becoming evident on the men. The captain observed that the injured were showing signs of "slight improvement." Meals were served at 8:00 am and 5:00 pm. Lapoint decided to cut free a second raft, but the wind from the east-southeast at over 10 knots meant that they would have to wait till the following day.

The four life rafts being towed by the one life boat of the Potlatch, *late June 1942, early in the voyage of survival.*

On the fourth day the seas became rough with large swells. The number three raft's tanks were leaking and it was floating deep, so Lapoint decided to abandon it. The transfer took place at 11 am. There were now 30 men in the lifeboat, ten men in the raft attached to it, and nine men in the second raft. One person made a determined effort to catch fish and managed to spear a five-inch African Pompano. On the following day, their fifth day after the sinking, another survivor made a net from some frayed line and used it to catch two fish. The men had to bail continuously the water out of their lifeboats. Fortunately there were some rain squalls, which provided the opportunity for the men to collect precious fresh water

During the men's seventh day in the rafts and boats, Captain Lapoint noted that the swelling of Delatorre's leg had gone own and that Harriston's eye was healing. Even the master's injuries seemed to be getting better. However, he suffered from a new affliction of sunburn. During the morning of their ninth day, the towline connecting all three rafts to the boat parted. Lapoint ordered the sails dropped and the oars shipped so the boat could go back and retrieve the men in the rafts. The length of rope between the boat and rafts was shortened from about 35 feet to 10, which put more strain on all of the craft. The strain also began to show on the men who had to sleep sitting up.

On the 5th of July – the boat's 10th day - a significant incident occurred. A crewman, Jensen saw a speck on the horizon. The men sent flares to attract the attention of a lifeboat from the Dutch ship *Tysa*, sunk by the Italian submarine *Morosini* in the same general area. They were successful, and the Dutch lifeboat swooped down towards them but kept a cautious distance from the Americans. Keeping at a hailing distance away the boats made brief contact. The *Potlatch* men were told that they were about 100 miles from Antigua, and that the *Tysa* lifeboat would inform the authorities about the *Potlatch* survivors.

Based on their behavior during the encounter, it is clear that the Dutchmen were concerned that their own large, well-equipped boat might be swamped by numerous other survivors from *Potlatch*, and their own progress slowed by a transfer of survivors from the rafts to their boat. They were doing comparatively very well and were in no mood to linger. At no time did they offer to take anyone from the clearly over loaded rafts. The Dutch after all had a boat of roughly twice the capacity yet only half as many men.

Lapoint was not able to follow the *Tysa* lifeboat on the course they directed, as he still towed the rafts. It would have been difficult and perhaps impossible for the cluster of slow rafts and a boat to make precise navigational targets, and perform the kind of navigational feats that a free-sailing lifeboat with a minimum of crew could achieve. For the *Potlatch* survivors, the constraints were considerable: they were overloaded by double, under-nourished, and slow. They were, in effect, drifting with the wind and current.

The *Tysa*'s First Mate Roggeveen communicated his sighting of the *Potlatch* survivors to the Allies in Dutch Saint Martin. The US Navy stationed in Saint Thomas sent aircraft over to Saint Martin to verify reports of American survivors adrift in a boat and rafts. They initiated an air search but to no avail. Though airplanes were sighted often by the men in rafts and boat, they were too high to be seen. To compound the confusion, on the 29th of July the US military erroneously reported *Potlatch* survivors landed in Saint Kitts. The Navy must have been mixing the *Potlatch* survivors up with those from the steamers *Anglo-Canadian* and *Thomas McKean*, whose survivors landed in Saint Kitts starting on the 9th of July, and were transported from Antigua aboard the local schooners *Manita* and *Betsy R.*.

Tuesday the 7th of July was the 11th day for the survivors at sea. Fortunately some rain squalls enabled the men to collect some water off the sails. Lapoint observed that the supplies of crackers and chocolate were running low. The following morning, heavy seas necessitated more laborious pumping, which depressed the crew's morale. Fortunately, the wind and seas abated at dawn on their 12th day. Conditions became more difficult for the survivors. One person, John Miller (affectionately nicknamed "Stinky" by his crewmates) started eating bandages, drank iodine and plenty of sea water out of desperation. Salt water can cause fatal damage to the kidneys and liver, debilitating those who drink too much of it, dehydrating them and inducing insanity.

As they cleaned and divided some fish caught by the dip net, a four-foot shark, attracted by the blood, came close enough that Sorensen grabbed it by the fin and dragged it into the boat. Miller was holding it by its head, but it bit him on the arm and the wounded shark was lost overboard, to be devoured by bigger sharks swimming near the boat. Not only was a considerable supply of fresh food lost, but Miller was seriously wounded.

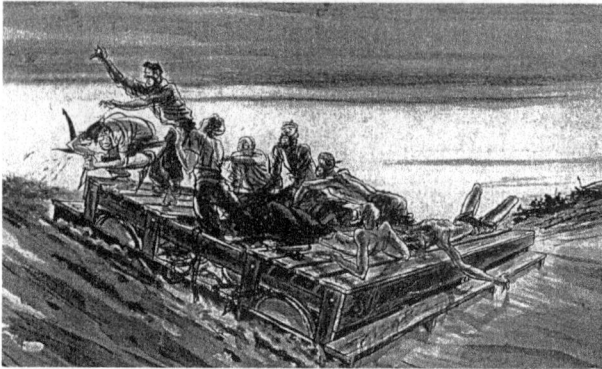

Shark leaping aboard one of the rafts and biting John "Stinky" Miller's arm.

On the 14th, some men suggested to Lapoint that they leave 10 volunteers on a raft so that the lifeboat could go ahead and get help, sending rescuers back to the raft. Lapoint overruled the idea, fearing that the volunteers might starve to death before help was able to arrive. Instead, he decided to abandon one more raft in order to enhance the speed of the lifeboat. On their 15th day, the 11th of July navy Lieutenant Dorsey Lybrand, in charge of the gun crew, and nine other men moved from the raft to the lifeboat. This left 40 men in the lifeboat and nine on the raft. The men consumed the final portions of pemmican.

Miller's arm was healing well, but he insisted on drinking salt water, essentially killing himself. At this point, the men were down to a half tablet of chocolate and two ounces of water issued twice daily. Some of the men supplemented their half ounce of malted milk tablets ration with raw fish that they caught - a total of 40 fish were caught during the voyage. A number of the men were suffering from severe sunburn. On the 14th of July – their 18th day – Dalby the radio operator tried to kill himself by leaping over the side. The men in the raft managed to retrieve him. Rain squalls enabled the men to capture an impressive 11 gallons of water. On the 19th day the captain said he believed that they were close to some land, possibly the Virgin Islands.

The decision was made to move all the men off the last raft. However Dalby the radio operator was despondent. He wanted to be left adrift, as he felt guilty that he had not managed to get a SOS message out, and blamed their predicament on himself. The captain had to order some men to bring him aboard by force, disarming him of an axe in the process. Lapoint had begun eating the berries from large clumps of seaweed which drifted past them, and some of the men followed his example to stave off hunger. Miller kept insisting on drinking sea water. He became "raving with fever" and men were assigned to prevent him with force from drinking more salt water. Fortunately, as their drinking water was running out, a heavy rain storm enabled the survivors to collect five gallons of precious fresh water.

By the 18th of July, the 22nd day after the sinking of the *Potlatch*, Miller was in a coma and his pulse rate was very low. They heard the sounds of airplane engines overhead. At 5 am on the 22nd day, Stinky Miller died. At 6:30 am Lapoint held a "simple prayer service and had Miller committed to the sea." Jensen wrote, "…a few planes flew overhead. The pilots of the planes probably thought these were fishing boats, and did not see the red distress sails or the flares that the survivors released," which was obviously very frustrating for them.

Burial of John Miller at sea from the lifeboat, after seven no doubt distressing days during which the 48 other men had to listen to his descent into madness and death.

The aircraft sent out from Saint Thomas to find the *Potlatch* survivors never did find the lifeboat. This is not surprising, given that they would have estimated the speed or the course of *Potlatch's* lifeboat to be faster than in fact it was. It would appear that the planes were flying in a west-northwest direction, towards Nassau or Miami. To boost morale Lapoint had the sail on the lifeboat lowered to enable the men to bathe in an effort to hydrate themselves by soaking moisture through their pores. This was particularly important as there was no rainfall, and the survivors were running out of drinking water. The survivors bathed repeatedly. The Captain estimated that each 15-minute swim was equivalent to two ounces of water.

The 24th and 25th days of their ordeal were very difficult. The sea became calm and the sun beat down mercilessly. They were just drifting and not moving forward. Most of the men sat with their heads bent down or stared out hopelessly for hours at the dancing horizon. Some of them began to lose control of their mental faculties. In fact, it was months after their rescue before some of them could remember much of what happened.

Morale was clearly sagging. The Cadets Kaplan and Corbatti say that they were encouraged to engage the men in sing-alongs and conversation to keep up morale from flagging further. There were 48 men of many backgrounds – from Europe, the Americas, the West Indies, brown and white, from ages 17 to at least 65. These men were all stuck together on a metal boat less than 26 feet long. They were locked in a struggle for survival which was both social, as in endured by the whole group, and concurrently individual and thus very personal. The stress was terrible. That night a number of arguments broke out amongst the men. Lapoint wrote laconically "Necessary to take more drastic measures. Quite a few are showing signs of weakening."

On the 26th day since the sinking of their ship, when they had had no water for several days, thousands of birds were spotted, which indicated that they may be near to some island. The routine continued though, with a 9:00 am swim. Perhaps because the water was shallower they were now followed by several sharks, and the noon swim had to be postponed. At 3:00 pm the sharks were following the boat more aggressively. At 4 pm there was enough of a breeze for the boat to start moving forward.

Jensen observed that "low clouds hung over one part of the horizon, ahead and a little to port and they looked as though they had been stopped they by some land. "Just before the light began to fail that evening," wrote Jensen, "I begged the skipper to take his glasses and search the horizon. To humor me, he finally did." Ruggles wrote that then Lapoint "...said, in a quiet voice, 'Now men, I don't want you to get excited, but there is something out there.' We gathered around him, staring ahead. Then his voice rang out, 'Land!' We went crazy, crowding forward, laughing, jabbering, pointing."

Jensen added that "Red, the Oiler, keeled over and fell to the bottom of the lifeboat in a dead faint. He was revived with some spirits of ammonia. The third mate, Allen Holmes Jackson of New York, was "completely unnerved" by the thought of the proximity to land. He was in great intestinal pain and was offered the last ounces of water, but could not ingest them and spit them out. "A moan passed over the whole lifeboat at this waste. The mate cried openly, and I don't mind saying that many of the rest of us were crying as we stood gripping the gunwale of the lifeboat to stare ahead at land."

It was dark by the time the lifeboat grounded on a sandy beach. Lapoint logged that land was sighted at 5:40 pm and that at 8:40 pm they "...Landed on shore, touched on scattered rocks and reef, few dents in way of bilges, boat not leaking. Made landing on Eastern side of island." They had covered a distance of 1,130 miles in 25 days, four hours and 40 minutes, for an average speed of 1.8 knots – quite respectable considering the number of men, their level of fatigue, and crucially the drag of the several rafts behind them, at least initially. When asked 60 years later about his first impressions of landing in the Bahamas, Ruggles said that he only remembers falling flat on his face in the sand. Lapoint observed that "Men on getting ashore unable to stand or walk. All had dizzy spells which passed in about half hour but none able to walk without staggering." Young Jatho rolled out of the boat and was trying to flop towards shore without the use of his stiffened legs when his commanding officer, Lybrand, ordered him to take a life jacket ashore, to which the young gunner retorted "get it yourself!"

Immediately those who could started looking for fresh water to drink – what Jensen described as a "mad search." But over six hours later, at 3 am all had returned to a fire that had been lit using an emergency flare, since all the matches had been used, lost or gotten wet. Lapoint and Hansen climbed a nearby ridge in bright moonlight and looked for lights or any sign of habitation or a port. They found nothing. Jensen described the results of the men's first forays as discouraging.

At sunrise the following day Jensen and others saw the wild donkeys which inhabit Inagua Island moving in the brush. Excitement rippled through the bedraggled encampment – if there are jackasses, there must be water. Some of the men dreamed of catching one of the beasts and having "jackass steak" but were unable to in their weakened condition. Instead some of the men decided to follow the animals to their watering hole. They collected empty bottles in the driftwood on the shore and set off inland. At 7 am Lapoint saw that with the neap tide caused by the full moon most of the rocks on the reef for a mile and a half out to the north and south were "well out of the water," and he worried about navigating the boat off the island, especially with such weak men.

Others remained at the camp and began collecting whelks and conchs to make a stew out of – but found their hunger overwhelmed their better intentions, and not much of the catch actually made it into the pot. Two attempts were made to obtain water near their encampment. Although the men dug, in one case an impressive 12 feet down, they came turned up only salty water. Although the survivors sighted goats and a dog, they found no sign of people

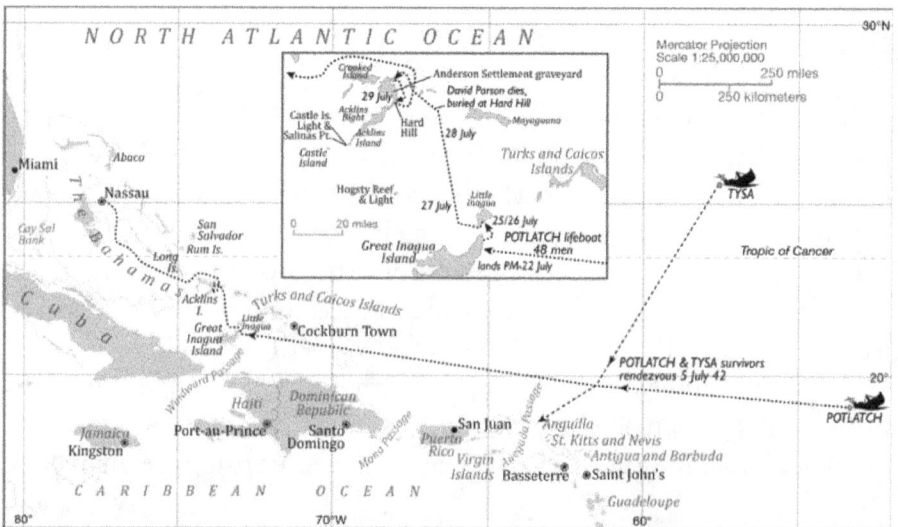

At 4:30 am the next day, the 24th of July – the 28th day of their ordeal – the men were back at it, digging for water again. At sunrise the fittest men were detailed to fan out and search for water. Recognizing that there wasn't enough food for his men on the island, Lapoint decided that they must push off within 36 hours. He and Hansen reconnoitered north along the coast. The men landed on the northeastern corner of Great Inagua, near Christophe Point, where the 80-foot ridge afforded them a view of Little Inagua, across a channel only six miles wide at its narrowest. Based on his observations, Lapoint clearly did not think he was on Great Inagua in the Bahamas – he couldn't reconcile the proximity of Little Inagua, which they could see, to his own conception that they had landed in the Virgin Islands. He and the mate set up ranges and markers on the shore to enable them to navigate their way back to sea through a narrow gap in the reef.

It took some six hours for the donkeys to divulge the location of their drinking hole, which was situated in some lava-like limestone rock. Jensen wrote that the men "smelled sulfur, and looking around saw a small wet hole in the rock about 200 yards away, which turned out to be a putrid green sulfur spring. Even so, it was water. We fell on it like maniacs, and then lay there most of the afternoon, crawling up to the hole from time to time for another drink. The water went right in and out of us." One of the men indulged so much that he drank 32 quarts of the precious liquid. The men were hungry too and Jensen ate some acrid-tasting leaves, which didn't either allay his hunger or make him very sick.

Lapoint organized all fit men to head for the spring, which was one and a half miles west of camp, post-haste. They slung the smallest keg, of ten gallons, on an oar between their shoulders. This they were told to bring back to camp for those too sick to move. Four hours later, at 8 pm, roughly half of the fit men came back to camp with the keg of water - the others remained at the spring to satiate their thirst.

Lapoint doled out two cups of water to each of the injured and sick. They then made a large fire for the night. Already the cooks were becoming adept at roasting conch on the fire and soon they would be adding water to make a stew. Lapoint resolved that if no signs of humans were found by noon the following day he and the men would push off to the next island, which they had seen from the ridge. Saturday the

25th of July was the 29th day of their ordeal and would be their last on Great Inagua. Although there was a lighthouse on the southwest coast of Great Inagua, the survivors were on the northeast coast of the island and could not see the light, as they were nearly 40 miles away.

Lapoint sent men with two empty kegs of water back to the spring with orders for all of the men there to assemble. At 6 am the weak and sick – including engineer's assistant Alfonso Delatorre and second cook David Parson – were placed in the lifeboat. The rest of the men from camp walked the boat along the shore northward in knee-deep water. For the next 10 hours the bedraggled group negotiated their way northwards up the coast, some of them pushing the boat in the shallows, the others carting water from the spring inland.

By 4 pm all the 48 men assembled with the extra rations of water. Ten of the men were given life preservers and told to hold onto a line strung from the back of the boat. Lapoint calculated that ten men would weigh three quarters of a ton, or 1,500 pounds – in fact due to their privations they all weighed considerably less. By 5:30 pm Lapoint was confident enough of clearing the reefs that he had the remaining ten men climb aboard. "But we had no sooner worked our way over that reef than we found others just beyond it," wrote Jensen. It was the beginning of a long night for all of the men aboard. As Lapoint noted, "wind changed to E, forced to continue rowing, unable to hoist sail, will drift back on reef. Making little headway. Men tire easily and only about half able to row…. Forced to row all night. …Several times during night drifted on edge of rocks. Just outside of reef, and hit hard twice. Boat not leaking yet but has taken severe punishment, having a steel keel is what saved us." By daybreak the lifeboat was in blue water and sailing again.

At sunrise they were able to see Little Inagua in the distance to the northwest and they raised sail and headed for it. They landed at 10:30 am without the drama and close calls of their night-time landing on Great Inagua. However they did strike a few submerged rocks as they approached a bay on the south side. Their voyage of 17 hours may have only been 10 to 15 miles and they might have made five knots per hour once underway – impressive considering the constraints of an overloaded boat and a wind that blew them towards land.

It was Sunday, the 26th of July and the 30th day of the crew's ordeal. Little Inagua is a small, square-shaped island nine miles wide and nine miles long at its thickest. Initially they did not find any water there. Jensen and his mates stumbled upon an itinerant fishing shanty. "In the afternoon," he wrote, "some of us found the pole frameworks of two thatched houses. A rotten and weather-beaten dugout canoe was pulled up on the beach nearby. We whooped in triumph. This time, we thought, there was sure to be a spring or some water at hand." Again they were disillusioned.

Though they beat around the brush on foot looking for a watering hole, the survivors soon realized that they had to get off the island before their strength was all gone. Having not eaten any substantial meal in weeks the men were slowly starving while they expended ever-increasing reserves of energy on rowing, foraging, walking, and sailing. Back on the boat Parson was literally dying in his companions' arms.

Lapoint and the men in the boat had found "plenty of fresh water bubbling up close to sea and running into the sea." They also became accomplished at finding and catching the slow-moving mollusk known simply as conch, with its tough but tasty muscular white meat. They must have gathered well over 100 conch, because Lapoint says their afternoon repast consisted of conch "which was gathered and boiled up; each man having half a cup of broth and several conchs and whelks."

Finding that they could not penetrate the thick brush, Lapoint decided to sail round to the lee, or western side of the island the following morning at slack high water. He had already estimated the local tides, based on observation. The following day was Monday, 27th of July 1942. It was their 31st day after the sinking of the *Potlatch*. First thing in the morning they filled all the water kegs with fresh water. Then the cooks served a shellfish broth – four ounces per person or roughly a gallon and a half of broth. At 11:00 am the 48 men piled back into the boat and bumped their way back to the open sea over reefs and rocks. Two hours later, at 1:15 pm they rounded the southern tip of Little Inagua, then sailed roughly west for five miles until setting a course to the north-northwest.

They could not sail due north, since the lifeboat simply could not point that high into the wind. Had they been able to go wherever they pleased they could have made for Little Caicos Island, only 25 miles to the north, or Mayaguana, 50 miles to the north-northwest. Instead they opted to go where the wind most easily pushed them – to the northwest, where Acklins Island lay some 75 miles away. The wind was roughly 15 knots and there were large swells coming into the Mayaguana Passage from the open Atlantic. Because of the waves, water seeped underneath the weather cloth as well as over the gunwale on the starboard. All night the men had to bail continuously. Parson's condition deteriorated badly. Also the third mate suffered from recurrent and acute intestinal trouble. Hansen's feet and lower legs were swollen, and some of the gunners were experiencing the same condition, perhaps a result of the sudden influx of fluids into bodies grown unaccustomed to it.

The wind picked up that night, rising to over 20 knots with rough seas. At 2:30 am on the morning of Tuesday the 28th of July, the 32nd day of the saga, they had to bear off, easing sail to make the trip more comfortable and running more along with the wind than against it. As a result, instead of pointing north-northwest they headed west-northwest. Just after sunrise, at 6:00 am they heard another airplane overhead. Then half an hour later they sighted the first ship since their own vessel was sunk. The ship must have been transiting the Crooked Island Passage to the south, probably using Castle Island Light at the bottom of Acklins as a bearing.

As Jensen said, "…we had no more flares to send up. Besides, we had had enough of phantom ships, and planes. Most of us had reached our absolute limit of endurance. We lay like so many stacked up corpses." At 10 am they saw what looked like a plane from the US Navy, flying from the southeast to the northwest (towards Nassau), however they could not tell if the boat had been seen. Even if it had, it might have been mistaken for the many local trading schooners in the region.

At 7 pm on Tuesday the 28th of July, the men sighted two small islands – the Plana Cays – but ignored them. It would have been suicidal for them to have attempted to land on the small cays —at night without charts or local knowledge. Wisely they resisted the temptation and sailed on. They were roughly halfway across the Mayaguana Passage and finally on their way to Acklins. At 30 minutes after midnight on Wednesday the 29th of July, the 33rd day of their voyage, David Parson died in the lifeboat of what was described as exposure and exhaustion – more likely the latter. He was 65 years of age. Certainly the men were exposed to the elements – scorching hot in the daytime and cold at night. Ruggles' body weight speaks to their privations: he weighed 160 pounds when he boarded the boat on the 27th of July and only 90 pounds when he reached a scale for the first time some 35 days later.

David Parsons, *Potlatch*.

David Parson, Second Cook on the Potlatch, buried in Acklins Island Bahamas, August 1942.

Just an hour and a half later, at 3 am the welcoming beacon of Hell Gate Light, on the northeastern tip of Acklins hove into sight. The 32-foot tall structure was erected in 1920. Lapoint wisely decided to heave-to a safe distance from the reefs until he could be certain he and the men would be taken care of ashore. At 6 am, in sunlight, the boat approached the light tower, but found bad shoals encircling it. Looking for somewhere sheltered to bury Parson, they spotted a small community – actually "dwelling houses" five miles ahead. It was the small coastal community of Pinefield on the northeast coast of Acklins. They sailed south, towards it.

The last leg of the survivor's voyage had taken some 40 hours to cover roughly 80 miles. It was 33 days since the *Potlatch* was sunk by the German U-boat, and roughly 23 days, since they had seen the mysterious Dutchmen sailing off towards rescue off Saint Martin. They were roughly three weeks overdue in Trinidad, but there is no evidence that there was any great alarm having been caused by her overdue status. Lapoint didn't know much about Acklins. In fact, he had to be told by locals the name of the lighthouse. In the words of Jensen, "By the light of early morning we came into a bay, sighted a few houses in a coconut grove, and headed in for them. We were too weak and numb to show any excitement. The first signs of life we saw ashore were two pigs and a goat. Then six Negro women and some children came running down to the beach. They backed up, muttering and gasping, when they caught sight of us. They must have thought we were ghosts risen from a watery grave. Our captain stepped out of the lifeboat and spoke to them softly and they replied in good English. When they realized what had happened to us they twittered like birds and ran off in all directions for food and water."

According to Newton Williamson, he and several other children were playing in front of their homes in Pinefield, overlooking the bay. Their de-facto leader was the oldest, his future sister-in-law Remilda Cox. Newton was only about six at the time. When they saw the lifeboat come through the reef and beach itself, they ran down to see for themselves. The adults – men as well as women - were out in the fields cutting cascarilla bark, a key ingredient for aperitifs like Compari and a local cash crop. Once Newton and the others realized that the mostly white men were in need of help, they dispatched several children to run and notify adults. This led to women arriving with some food, and Reverend Captain Collie in nearby Hard Hill ordering his sailing schooner *Go On* to be moved from Hard Hill up the coast to Pine Field. The 25-ton *Go On* had been built on Ragged Island in 1927 for the Maycock family and sold to the Collie brothers who used it for trade and transport between Acklins and Nassau.

Newton Williamson points to the gap in the reef which the Potlatch
lifeboat navigated in 1942.
Source: Mari Anderson and Fritz Damler

In Lapoint's more restrained prose he relates that at 09:15 am
they "landed and arranged with one colored family to cook up oat-meal
and meal mush for entire crew. This being only food suitable, available
in quantities, to care for 47 men. Paid $15.00 to Lady. Sent for Official
at [censored] to arrange for burial of 2nd Cook." Only 45 minutes later
the Constable, a man named Forbes, and town officials arrived in a
sailboat in order to lead the survivors to another settlement. According
to the American Consul General in Nassau, John W. Dye, "Local people
were very kind to them, fed and accommodated them for 2 days." Jensen
meanwhile was overcome and "burning up with fever" and collapsed in
the lifeboat. He wrote that the constable "....wore a white tropic helmet
with the badge of his authority pinned on it and he had a little curly
wisp of a moustache that addes the last touh to his official bearing." His
assistants lifted Jensen out of the boat.

Hard Hill is in the middle to east of the northern end of Acklins
and does not have a port of its own. There is a cemetery at Anderson
Settlement on the coast, a short distance from Hard Hill. Once they
arrived, the survivors had to walk perhaps two miles to the village.
Lapoint noted that "Several men had to be carried from beach to school
house account of badly swollen feet, ankles, and legs. Also Deck
Engineer [Delatorre] with broken leg. These men carried by natives."
They had to abandon the battered but loyal lifeboat where the landed

on the beach as it was badly dented and leaking from landing over so
many reefs and rocks in recent days.

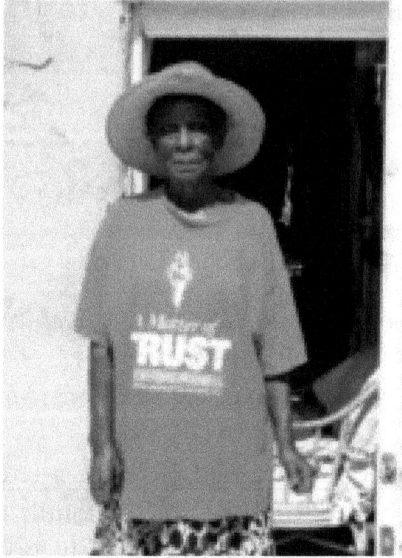

*The Reverend Clarisse Cox, ministers of the Methodist Church in Hard
Hill, Acklins and a daughter of Reverend Captain Collie.
Source: Mari Anderson and Fritz Damler*

Lapoint, ever industrious on behalf of his men, arranged for the
locals to prepare a meal of chicken and rice soup with vegetables. There
was no fresh fruit available. Jensen says that the local women washed
the bedraggled men and spoon fed them, since most were not strong
enough to hold a utensil. When he tried smoking a cigarette "it fell right
out. Finally, by leaning way back, I managed a few draws. I'd never tasted
anything so good in my life!"

After dinner Lapoint walked to a nearby settlement where he
managed to send a message to the District Commissioner on Fortune
Island and it seems from there to Nassau. Lapoint wrote that he
"Managed to buy 62 packages of American cigarettes. At the one and
only small store in settlement, purchased entire stock of canned goods,
consisting of 19 cans of peaches, 4 cans tomatoes, 1 lb. can of butter, 24
cans canned corned beef. Some condensed and evaporated milk."
Meanwhile Jensen and fellow crewmen were looking forward to their
first sound sleep in weeks, but could not quite manage it. Their minds

were plagued with obsessions about food and water. Fortunately for them, "the women had been up most of the night preparing our breakfast: tea, canned tomatoes, corn meal and corn bread. It was heavenly."

With normal people to compare to, Jensen was struck with just how emaciated the survivors looked. "We looked like leather-covered skeletons. Sparks [Radio Operator Dalby, who had tried to kill himself] weighed only 74 pounds. His stomach was so collapsed that even when he stood up we could see the outline of his backbone. I had fallen from 176 to 87 pounds." He goes on to recount how the men spent the day lounging in the cool shade of the school house, "drinking coconut water, eating a little corn meal, smoking and resting and chartering like a cage of monkeys. All we had been holding back for 32 days came out now." The process of re-acclimatizing their digestive systems to regular meals must have been painful and probably lasted several weeks.

Reverend Captain Collie sailed the *Go On* to Fortune Island (Long Cay) and brought over the native District Commissioner, H. V. Wiley, who Jensen described as "...a cheerful, fat little man who was dressed in a blue uniform, trimmed with brass buttons. His roly-poly face was topped with a Pullman porter's cap and two tufts of white curls stuck out from under each side of it. The Commission we full of pep and encouragement...." He "did his best to raise our spirits.... Clucked sympathetically when he heard of our hardship."

The school house in Hard Hill Acklins where the
Potlatch *men were accommodated.*
Source: Mari Anderson and Fritz Damler

There was one crucial errand that Lapoint had to accomplish before he could sign off. His diary of events concludes: "Parson buried. Casket and funeral services furnished." David Parson was buried at the Hard Hill Cemetery located in Anderson Settlement by local islanders. Jensen and his crew-mates were too exhausted to attend, but they "….saw lanterns moving about in the dark coconut grove, and we heard the wailing and chanting. David was pkut in the ground with reverence and by his own black people. He could not have had more sympathy or a nicer funeral back home."

The Methodist Mission Society church in Hard Hill where are memorial service with a young choir was conducted for David Parson by the Reverend Captain Collie of Acklins, August 1942.
Source: Mari Anderson & Fritz Damler

The final resting place of David Parson,
the Methodist Cemetery in Hard Hill, Acklins.
Source: Mari Anderson and Fritz Damler

The men left Hard Hill on the native schooner *Go On* in the morning of Friday the 31st of July bound for Fortune Island across the north of Acklins and Crooked Islands. Jensen wrote that "As we moved out of the bay, we saw the *'Potlatch* Jr.' as we called our lifeboat, lying half awash on the beach." They must have taken the northern route across the top of Acklins and Crooked Islands, as before they reached Fortune Island they were met by a rescue vessel sent from Nassau off Bird Island Light at Pittsdown Landing, also known as Landrail Point. The sailboat was proceeding north in the dark when a bright light burst upon them and a signal flashed reading "you are rescued!" The yacht "loomed up out of the dark and our negro Captain brought the cumbersome old "*Go-on*" so close and so delicately along side of her that you could have held a water glass between the two vessels without it being cracked."

Following this fortuitous rendezvous, the men and their rescuers aboard the fast motor yacht *Vergemere IV* skippered by Marion Carstairs left Bird Island Rock on the night of Friday 31st of July. Ruggles said that some men took shelter below decks on the floor of the cabin. Jensen wrote that "We slept that night on deck wrapped in the blankets" provided by Carstairs. Ruggles said that the boat was powered by diesel engines and that the weather was "calm enough, with no waves." This would have enabled the boat to plane and achieve very high speeds. They are confirmed (in consular and news reports) to have arrived Nassau 5:30 pm Saturday the 1st of August. The total distance travelled would have been 225 miles. Consul General Dye notes that "Miss Marion Carstairs gave the use of her vessel *Vergemere* and all fuel and other supplies gratis."

MARION CARSTAIRS AND *VERGEMERE IV*

Forty-one years old at the time of this rescue, Marion Carstairs had already rescued a number of people, local and expatriate, from Bahamian islands. In December of 1937, for example, she helped save the crew of the student yacht *Polaris* under Captain William Pond, stranded with nine persons on board the Joulter Cays, between Andros and the Berry Islands. The local newspapers hold several accounts of Miss Carstairs rushing Bahamians to the hospital in Nassau or saving foreigners from the rocks. She is one of the more colorful characters in the island's history.

Betty "Joe" (born Marion Barbara) Carstairs was a wealthy British power boat racer known for her speed and her eccentric lifestyle. She was born in 1900 in Mayfair, London, England. Her mother was the American heiress Frances (Fannie) Evelyn Bostwick, whose family had done extremely well with Standard Oil – her father was an original trustee of the company. Her father was Captain Albert Carstairs, a Scotsman who served with the Royal Irish Rifles.

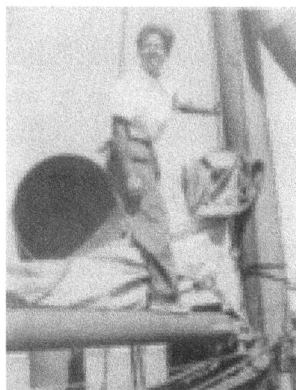

Marion Carstairs on the boom of a sailing boat.

Carstairs' mother married Captain Francis Francis. From her second marriage came two offspring whose descendants still inhabit the Bahamas. She married a third time. Their first daughter Marion moved to Paris at the age of 17 and learned to "live like a man" including having her first lesbian encounter. Carstair's sense of duty towards the British and American sides in both wars was as strong as her sense of adventure. During the First World War, like Hemingway she drove ambulances for the International Red Cross in France. While working with the Women's Legion Mechanical Transport Section in Dublin Ireland she seduced Oscar Wilde's niece Dolly Wilde. When most people were trying to put the war behind them, Carstairs went back for one of the more traumatic aspects of the war: burying the dead for Royal Army Service Corps in France.

In 1918 Carstairs entered into a sham marriage with French Count Jacques de Pret in order to take control of her inheritance from her erratic mother, who insisted she marry and settle down. As soon as her mother passed the marriage was annulled on the grounds of non-consummation. Carstairs also exhibited organizational and entrepreneurial flair that would come out in the Bahamas as well. Two years after the war she organized women drivers to found the X Garage, in which women drivers chauffeured clients around London and the surrounding area.

On a personal level, Carstairs was openly a lesbian and often dressed herself and her doll Lord Todd Wadley as a man. She tattooed her arms, and was like male race drivers addicted to speed and machines – particularly speed boats. By winning the 1926 Duke of York's trophy she became the world's fastest woman on water, later winning the Lucina Cup and the Royal Motor Yacht Club international race. Through proxies – by supporting their campaigns with lavish funds and in one case giving the engines out of her own boat - Carstairs attained the highest levels of boat racing. Record-setter Sir Malcolm Campbell and his boat *Bluebird* as well as John Cobb on *Railton Special* were beneficiaries of Carstairs in the period 1925 to 1930.

Marion Carstairs at the wheel of a racing motor boat in the 1920's or 30's.

Alas as Sir Harry Oakes had demonstrated, no amount of patriotism and loyalty can obviate an onerous tax burden. Carstairs found that she could not keep her inheritance safe from tax authorities in the UK, and resolved to exile herself. She chose the Bahamas and in 1934 she purchased Whale Cay in the Berry Islands (between Bimini and Nassau), for $40,000. She later expanded these properties by also buying the additional islands of Bird Cay, Devil's Cay, half of Hoffman's Cay, Cat Cay in the Berry Islands, and a tract of land on Andros Island to the south. Carstairs took pleasure in hosting a number of socialites and snow birds including Marlene Dietrich, Tallulah Bankhead and of course the Duke and Duchess of Windsor. She kept photographs of some120 of her sexual conquests in a sculpted library on Whale Cay.

Carstairs not only constructed a Great House for herself and her guests, but also a school, lighthouse, cannery and church for the benefit of the Bahamians who moved to the island to work for her. Driving around on a motorbike with her beloved stuffed doll Lord Todd Wadley, she ruled the island in the vein of a benevolent despot, arguing for reforms in the treatment of natives to the Duke of Windsor and the Bay Street Boys – to little effect. "I was a leader," confided Carstairs – "I could do anything."

Carstairs tried to contribute to the war effort. The Nassau *Tribune* of January 21, 1943 reports that "Miss Marion Carstairs arrived in Nassau today and is a guest in the Prince George Hotel. She has just returned from the U.S. where she had her yacht *Sonia* converted for war work." When the British Navy issued a request for boats to use as minesweepers, she immediately offered her finest schooner. "This ship," Carstairs wrote in a press release, "one of the most beautiful private schooners in the world, has been placed by Miss Carstairs unreservedly at the service of His Majesty's Navy." His Majesty's Navy turned it down as unsuitable. Carstairs offered her schooner to the US Navy, and again it was refused. When she asked a well-connected British Admiral how she could personally contribute to the war effort, as an officer in the Navy or skipper of a torpedo boat (a position for which she was uniquely qualified), the answer she received was "wrong sex, wrong war."

Carstairs relocated to Miami, Florida in the 1950s. After selling the island in 1975, she lived in Florida until her death in Naples in 1993. Her doll was cremated with her.

Portrait of Marion Carstairs in the United States Library of Congress.

Although a Captain Collins is reported to have commanded *Vergemere II* (ex-*Sonia*), by all accounts, including contemporary photographs, Carstairs herself skippered the *Vergemere IV* – the original motorboat which had been built on Whale Cay – to save the *Potlatch* survivors. Carstairs received word of the *Potlatch* crew's distress by "a little cutter" from Nassau and set out directly from Whale Cay to Crooked Island. Apparently the tom-boy Carstairs was initially mistaken as a crew. Jensen relates how one of his crew-mates yelled "Hey mess-boy" at the "sun-tanned, tattooed kid in shorts, 'Bring us some water!' The mess-boy came over with a big smile and we found it was Betty Carstairs, the speed-boat enthusiast." She gave Jensen a pair of her own khakis, which fit him well.

The launch of Vergemere IV, *Marion Carstair's private power yacht on Whale Cay. It was named after the Bostwick family estate, presently the Beach Point Club in Mamaroneck, New York.*
Source: Capt. Paul and Mrs. Kim Aranha, niece of Marion Carstairs

Delatorre wrote that "Whiskey heiress Betty Carstairs, on a nearby island, rushed down and transported us to Nassau in her yacht." There was an understandable and common misconception that Betty Carstair's fortune came from a very popular and much-advertised brand of whiskey named Carstairs. In fact her wealth originated with the Standard Oil fortune in Long Island, New York. Ruggles says that the men slept on the deck of the *Vergemere IV*, under the stars.

POTLATCH CONTINUED

The Nassau *Tribune*, the evening paper, got the scoop on the *Potlatch* survivors' arrival that same day. A front page article reads: "Forty-seven survivors from a torpedoed ship landed in Nassau at 5:30 this afternoon, having been brought from Acklins Island in a local boat after landing there on Thursday morning. The Duchess of Windsor, President of the Red Cross, and other members of the Red Cross were on the dock to meet the survivors who were taken to the Rozelda and Lucerne Hotels, where they are being taken care of and outfitted by the Red Cross. Eight of the men are in the hospital."

Survivors of the Potlatch photographed in front of the Rozelda Hotel. Michael Carbotti, far right, insisted on a quick shave before being photographed. Nathan Kaplan is on the left. The tall nurse on the left is

Mrs. Sawyer, the Greek nurse, Marion Carstairs, a Red Cross official, Duchess of Windsor, Allen Holmes Jackson, and ship's officer John Moe. Source: Hugo Vickers, Behind Closed Doors, from the Associated Press

Most of the survivors were in bad shape. Ruggles said that 90% of the men suffered from severe exhaustion, and even sturdy young Jensen had passed out in Acklins on arrival. "When Matte, who had lost 85 pounds during the 32 days at sea, and his companions tottered into the Nassau dock, they were met by the Duchess of Windsor, head of the Nassau Red Cross. 'A very nice woman,' said Matte solemnly, "she came to the hospital and to the hotel to see us the next day, too'." In Nassau "Lieut. Lybrand and Capt. Lapoint were invited to ride in the private car of the Duchess of Windsor. Hospital facilities were limited and the ten men who were in the most serious physical condition were given treatment there. The others were treated at the hotel." Another article dated 12 August says that Lybrand and Lapoint "were made comfortable by the Duke and Duchess of Windsor. On one of the days while the survivors were at Nassau the Duke and Duchess of invited Capt. Lapoint and Lieut. Lybrand to visit them. They spent an hour in conference discussing the sinking of the ship, etc."

Lieutenant Dorsey Lybrand, in charge of all US Navy gunners on the Potlatch. When Jake Jatho, a teenager under Lybrand, was told that Lybrand had become a lawyer and state senator decades later, he retorted "it figures."

Jake Jatho, shortly after enlisting in the US Navy at age 16.
Source: Jake Jatho

"'As anxious as we were to get back to the States,' said Carbotti, 'we had to admit she [Windsor] was showing us a swell time'." The Duchess of Windsor "found places for them in hospitals and hotels, fed them six-course dinners and had herself photographed with them. To blushing Cadet-Midshipman Kaplan she presented a beautiful pair of gaily-colored pajamas which he still wears despite the kidding he gets."

The Commandant of the Red Cross was Therese Straton. Mrs. Therese Limido Straton appears to have emigrated to the Bahamas with her husband, Dr. Norman David Swayne Straton, a dentist. Mrs. Straton balanced family and a career – whilst her husband built up a dental practice and her children Peter David, Coralie and Joan attended Queen's College preparatory school in Nassau, Therese rose to the top role of Commandant of the Red Cross and head of the St. John's Ambulance in Nassau. The responsibility and demand on her leadership skills must have been intense, since the Red Cross only opened a chapter in Nassau in 1939. By 1940 Therese was photographed demonstrating bandages to the Duke and Duchess of Windsor.

The war was more than a remote notion to Mrs. Straton. Not only did she undoubtedly have many friends and family back in the UK involved directly in the war, but her son Peter joined the Royal Air Force Volunteer Reserve as a Sargeant. In the fall of 1940 she and her fellow nurses assisted the severely malnourished Widdicombe and Tapscott back on their feet after some seven weeks in an open boat following the loss of the *Anglo Saxon* to the German raider *Widder*.

Original caption: "The Duke (1894 - 1972) and Duchess (1896 - 1986) of Windsor host the annual inspection of the Bahamas branch of the Red Cross (of which the Duchess is President) at Government House in Nassau, 1942. Here Mrs. T. M. Straton, Commandant of the Red Cross First Aid Detachment, shows them some medical supplies destined for England."

Then, starting in March 1942 and lasting until the *Potlatch* men were repatriated in early August of that year, the Red Cross was charged with caring for and repatriating 257 men. The Red Cross, sharing their burden with the IODE, St. Johns Ambulance, volunteers, churches, and the Masonic Lodge which turned their facility into a canteen, was responsible for caring from men from at least six ships. In short, Therese Straton had a busy war.

Ironically, in the newspaper that same day, reports on the recent visit of Labor Advisor F. A. Norman and the American investors from Maine, the W. Ericksons, having just returned from a flight to Inagua. They must not have seen the survivors while they were on the island or making their way through the Mayaguana Passage.-

The men of the *Potlatch* appear to have largely flown under the radar of the local newspapers, probably because they were so weak. Another reason may be that they behaved well. According to the American Consul Dye, the captain led by quiet but firm example. He wrote that "Throughout this experience the Master of the *Potlatch*, Captain John J. Lapoint has conducted himself in a really remarkable and efficient manner. His control of the thirst and hunger-mad men was kind but firm and was the means of saving many lives. Of all rescued crews of torpedoed vessels these men conducted themselves the best in Nassau due to the Captain's quiet appeal and good example."

Ruggles mentions that the men made it to the movies, and no doubt some of them patronized the IODE canteen, which was open for Allied servicemen working on the air base, and for US and British service men. The *Potlatch* men were the only shipwreck survivors on the island at the time, and the last of the war – *Kollskegg* survivors had left the island by end April, over three months before. It would appear that the apartments made available to the *Potlatch* officers and men in Nassau were shared by American or British expatriates or Bahamians.

According to Lieutenant Lybrand, who as senior naval officer on board, ought to have known, "Arriving in Nassau they were met by the Army and Navy officials, as well as officials of the British government." Delatorre wrote that on arrival in Nassau, "the Duchess of Windsor and a group of newspapermen greeted us, and our rescue was officially announced." The reception was all possible because of the days between when word of their rescue was first telephoned from Acklins, the time it took Carstairs to voyage to the remote southern Bahamas, and then pick them up and return. This would have given the press a window – unique in all of the Bahamas and Turks and Caicos rescues of World War II – of several days to fly to Nassau and cover the story, pro-actively rather than reflexively. Also their arrival in the capital happened over the weekend, when more people had the idle time to spectate.

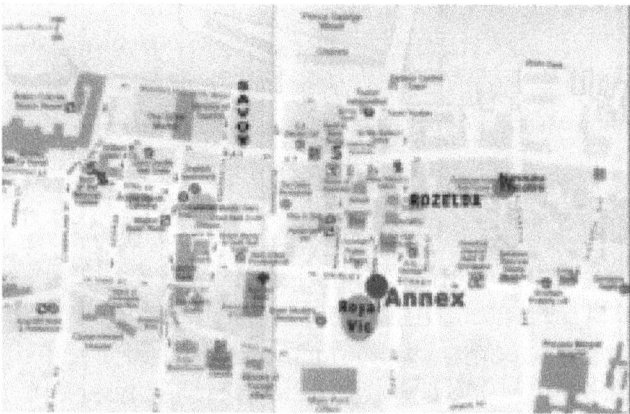

Map of modern-day Nassau with historical hotels, theaters superimposed.

The crew were separated in the city. Jatho wrote that ""When we got back to Nassau they took all the Navy guys to one hotel and mariners to another one." Ruggles wrote that "none of the gunners were in the hospital. Only the merchant mariners. The movie house was right next door to the hotel." How they could afford the movies is not clear if Ruggles is correct in saying that they never received wages. Clearly Lapoint and Dye ensured the men had enough for spending money and the basic essentials of dignity. A reporter who interviewed him a week or two later during his furlough wrote: "Jake didn't say as much, but it is reported that the boys in his crowd were given $100.00 each for grub and fun money ashore."

Ruggles wrote that "we didn't see any nurses until we got to Florida." This suggests that the Red Cross focused on the merchant mariners, not the US Navy sailors, who were free to pad over to the movie theater and immerse themselves. However Ruggles' is cited twice on Red Cross Commandant Straton's list of survivors, and the fact that Lapoint suggested he suffered from appendicitis suggests that he would have received at least some medical attention, though he wasn't one of the eight hospitalized. Another gunner, Solomon Goodman "…was able to get to a telephone and call his wife, who was in Hopewell [Virginia]. His wife… and his family did not even know that his ship had been sunk."

Straton says that a number of the men were housed in the European Annex of the Royal Victoria Hotel. The first of the truly grand hotels in the Bahamas, the Royal Vic was built starting in 1860, on the heels of Samuel Cunard securing a subsidy from the Bahamas government to establish a regular passenger and cargo service between Nassau, New York, and Havana. Business boomed for the first half of the decade as British, French and other merchants purchased cotton from the south in exchange for manufacturing equipment and manufactured goods which the southern states generally lacked the capability to make.

By 1898 the Royal Victoria, situated down town on a ridge behind the legislature, the courts and public goal, a few blocks from the harbor, was purchased by the famed hotelier Henry Flagler, known as the Czar of Miami. The purchase price was a reasonable 10,000 British Pounds Sterling and Flagler also purchased the Army barracks at Fort

Nassau. His priority at the time however was construction of the mammoth Hotel Colonial, right on the harbor, completed in 1922.

The Royal Victoria experienced a second boom, this one driven by profits from the smuggling of liquor into the United States during the prohibition. The halcyon days were to last over a decade, into the mid-1930s, and considerably replenish not only the pockets of local merchants and hoteliers, but also the coffers of the local government, leading the way for substantial improvements in public infrastructure.

Since 1922, when the Colonial Hotel burned down and the government contracted the Munson Steamship Line to rebuild it, the Royal Victoria was owned by Frank C. Munson, President of Munson Steamship Lines which operated from New York to Latin America and the Bahamas between 1899 and 1937. He left a widow, Cora Mallory Munson who came from a shipping family– the Mallorys of Mystic, Connecticut, who had been in maritime business for 130 years. To illustrate her interest in things maritime, on December 5th 1940 Cora put the jolly boat in which two men, Tapscott and Widdicombe had drifted for seven weeks, out on the verandah of the Royal Victoria.

According to Straton, the "European Staff Quarters was converted into a 1st Aid station and Emergency Quarters by the Duchess of Windsor." Straton continued: "The men stayed at the Annex, but meals were provided for them by The Carlton House Restaurant [known as the Rozelda Hotel and Iron Bar at the time], where we took them twice a day." Straton notes that "The Red Cross supplied clothing to the men where needed. As they were not seriously injured, but only suffering from minor complaints, the 1st Aid Station was able to cope with these. Vitamins were given to help the poor condition they were in due to exposure and lack of food." Ruggles, in an interview, said that they didn't all stay in the same hotel. He said that though they didn't have clothes to go out and about in, they were too weak to do so anyway. "It was better than a boat," he said.

The Royal Victoria Hotel Annex, for European staff. According to Therese Straton, Commandant of the Red Cross, Wallis Simpson commandeered these quarters for Allied survivors. It was located in central downtown Nassau, between the hospital, the goal, and the Royal Victoria, a short walk from the Rozelda Hotel on East Street, where their shipmates were staying.

On August 11th Dye continued, saying that the men "were at once well cared for in hotels, apartments, and the Bahamas General Hospital. The local Red Cross, headed by the Duchess of Windsor, provided them all with cigarettes and needed clothing and shoes. No compensation has been suggested for these articles by the Red Cross and it is believed none will be." On the 2nd of August he noted that "Master saved log, other papers, and letter of credit. All survivors well cared for here. ....The Captain having a letter of credit for $20,000 at hand paid all other expenses of the crew such as subsistence and wages." This certainly shows the value of Lapoint rescuing the ship's letter of credit.

Unlike survivors of ships like the *Cygnet*, where the agents had to be appointed and funds requested from different continents, in the *Potlatch's* case they coordinated directly with the US Consul General and a recently set up US Navy liaison office to have their needs efficiently met. The fact that Lieutenant Dorsey Lybrand and his crew of 16 Naval Armed Guard were among the survivors would have helped galvanize the US military to their aid. The *Potlatch* is also the only recorded United States-flagged ship to have had survivors landed in

Nassau. There is not a record of the customary "thank you letter" to those who helped the survivors to the people of Nassau from Captain Lapoint. They flew out of Nassau aboard two US Army airplanes on the 5th of August. Straton and colleagues were there to see them board busses from downtown to the airfield.

Compared with the other survivors, however, it must be noted that none of the men from the other ships had near so trying an ordeal except perhaps those of the *Kollskegg*, who were in the life boats for only 21 hours and on the rescue ship for another five days, from 7 to 11 April 1942. The *O. A. Knudsen* men landed and were fed within 24 hours, as was the case with the *Cygnet*, *Athelqueen*, and the *Daytonian* men were only waterborne for three days or so. The more challenging survival voyages on boats occurred in the Turks and Caicos – the *Vivian P. Smith*, *Fauna*, and *Vineland* crew had open boat voyages lasting up to a week, but none of these voyages compare in sheer length and degree of starvation with those of the *Potlatch*. Considering how many men were in shock before they even entered the lifeboat, it is not surprising that they were not remembered in Nassau like the "three Musketeers" from the *Daytonian*, who painted the town red, gaily celebrating their survival.

Dye further notes that "The U.S. Naval Liaison Office in Nassau questioned the master and crew of the vessel and reported fully to the Navy Department." The first detailed reports received directly from the master to the navy are dated the 9th of August, several days after their arrival in Miami on the 5th. They were subsequently interviewed by Ensign E. D. Henderson, US Naval Reserve, in Miami on the 14th of August, most likely after they had more fully recovered. Some of the officers and men told Henderson that there were tanks in the cargo.

Jensen's jocular nature followed him to Miami. He and the other merchant mariners were housed in the Marine Hospital there. Despite the luxurious surroundings he complained that "Those doctors couldn't seem to understand that we were hungry." When the men were allowed out of the hospital to take a walk they carried their freedom a bit further. According to Jensen they went on a culinary orgy, devouring 20 meals in 24 hours and gaining 15 pounds in the interim. He was surprised at some of the adulation the men received, as they were being touted as war heroes in light of their long survival. Jensen appeared in newsreels and on radio. In Washington DC Admiral Land provided the Mariner's Medal to Jensen and fellow crew. Lapoint was awarded the US Merchant Marine Distinguished Service Medal for especially meritorious service under unusual stress and hazards.

Ruggles told a news reporter that "In the newspapers, a Ripley's *Believe It Or Not* feature told how the survivors of a torpedoed US merchant marine ship "survived 32 days in a lifeboat before landing on an uninhabited Caribbean island and being led to water by wild jackasses." Ruggles received new set of dog tags to replace the ones that went down with the ship and was given a 30-day leave, after which he was assigned to another ship out of New York. He would serve on a number of ships, in both the Atlantic and the Pacific, before being discharged two days before Christmas 1945. He was awarded the World War II Victory Medal, Navy Occupation Service Medal, African-Middle Eastern Campaign Medal, Asiatic Pacific Campaign Medal and the American Campaign Medal. He says he never saw any of the other *Potlatch* survivors again, though he tried to keep in contact. When he finally arrived home "things were not very good" and he "just moved on" becoming a trucker. He ultimately settled in Garrison, Kentucky.

Estil Dempsey Ruggles (left) and Jake Jatho at a Potlatch *reunion, St. Louis, Missouri, 2012*
Source: Becky Jatho, daughter-in-law of Jake Jatho, 2013

Cadet-Midshipman Nathan J. Kaplan changed his name to Stark and moved to Kansas City, Missouri, where he rose to Vice

President of Hallmark Greeting Cards. Nathan Stark died on
November 12, 2002 in Washington DC at 82. Kaplan's colleague
Cadet-Midshipman Michael James Carbotti returned to sea following
the *Potlatch* experience. First he completed his studies at the U.S.
Merchant Marine Academy in Long Island New York. He then joined
the US Navy, became an Ensign and in 1946 was sailing aboard the
destroyer USS *Eberle*.   Ruggles said that after being processed
in Miami the officers, crew and gunnery men of the *Potlatch* "split off
in all directions." It is highly likely that as the US was only nine
months into the war, they all continued to serve in various capacities
in the US merchant marine (like Lapoint) or the navy (like Ruggles
and Carbotti). Ruggles said he was "extremely grateful" to Lapoint for
navigating them to land, and is convinced to this day that Lapoint
did, indeed have a sextant the whole time.

Engineers from the Potlatch; *Delatorre, Varnuk, Avery, Vierra, Kennedy,
Celian, reporting to* The National Maritime Union *in New York, August,
1932. They spoke highly of the officers.*
Source: National Maritime Union *Pilot*

The voyage of the *Tysa* survivors continued after the 4th of July
when the First Mate noted that he "Shouted to [*Potlatch* men] the
distance from land, that I should make a landfall on the following day
and that I would report them as soon as possible, continued our voyage."

They would not take one day but three for them to reach land. On July 7th at 4:30 pm after strenuous rowing and anxious sailing the men threaded their way onto the beach in Bad Bay, on Dog Island north of Anguilla. Soon the light keeper, described as "Indian" living in a shed with his "squaw," joined them and told them about a fresh water spring inland. Soon the crew returned with pails of water and all of them drank refreshingly. Roggeveen tried to send fire signals to Anguilla. The next day, 8th July 10 am they attracted the attention of a local fisherman who sailed into the bay. They convinced him to take them to Saint Martin, administered by both the Dutch and the French, which lay roughly 12 miles to the south. The 24 men arrived in Marigot, on the French side, the same afternoon at 3 pm and were well looked after by first French and then Dutch administrators. The Dutch governor invited them to Philipsburg, the capital, but some men had to remain on the French side until 15 British survivors of the *Willimantic* could be tended there first. The *Tysa* crew arrived on the Dutch side on Thursday the 9th of July and stayed in the government hotel and private homes. True to his word, Roggeveen told the US pilots about the 49 survivors from the *Potlatch* which they had encountered. All 43 officers and crew of the *Tysa* survived their sinking.Two days after the attack on *Potlatch*, Riechmann and his men sank the US freighter *Ruth* on the same track towards the Anegada Passage. In an act of compassion Reichmann collected three members of the *Ruth*'s crew (Harold Dayse, Andrews, Dowdin and Whitecotton) and put them in a lifeboat. The survivors spent three days drifting in the area before being rescued. For many years, based on erroneous information provided by the survivors, the *Ruth* sinking was reported to have taken place right off Acklins Island in the southern Bahamas. Either the crew were trying to protect their skipper by suggesting he used the Windward Passage rather than his own route, or as junior crew members they simply didn't know. In either event, all the men were discovered hundreds of miles upwind of the Bahamas, nowhere near Acklins, and rafts and boats drift with the prevailing winds, which are from the east, rather than against it. The fact that U-153 was sunk compounded the confusion, however, there would not have been time enough for U-153 to have motored from the *Potlatch* attack to Acklins between the 27th and 29th of June.

Aside from four *Ruth* survivors, the last people to see the U-153 officers and crew alive were *Potlatch* survivors. Usually the submariners are the last ones to see the faces of doomed seamen before they drown or die of exposure. In this case, the tables were turned and most of the Allies on the *Potlatch* survived, whereas all of the Germans in the U-boat were killed off Panama within weeks.

U-BOAT ATTACKS FROM 28 JUNE TO 10 AUGUST 1942

Between the 28th of June and the 10th of August, 17 Axis submarines entered the Bahamas theatre, sinking 19 ships there. The Italian sub *Morosini* under *Tenente Vascola* Francisco D'Alessandro entered the region northeast of Puerto Rico on the 28th of June and remained in the region, refueling from its compatriot *Finzi*, for a month, until the 29th of July. Mostly, it patrolled north and northeast of Puerto Rico. U-505 under Axel-Olaf Loewe arrived in the area the following day, heading southwest for the Mona Passage, which it entered on the 3rd of July, thus leaving the region for the Caribbean. During its brief transit, U-505 dispatched the American *Sea Thrush* on 28 June and the US-flagged *Thomas McKean* the following day. (U-505 was captured by an American hunter-killer group in the Sargasso Sea later in the war, and now serves as an exhibit at the Museum of Science in Chicago).

In the last week of June and the first week of July, five Allied ships were sunk in the greater Bahamas area. Johannes Liebe brought U-332 into the area for a brief incursion between Bermuda and Savannah from the 27th of June to the 2nd of July. The day after entering he sank the American freighter *Raphael Semmes*, also known as the *Ralph Semmes*, northeast of Puerto. Rolf Mützelburg of U-203, in the last few weeks of his life sank the American freighter *Sam Houston* in the same general area and on the same day. The following day U-158 under Irwin Rostin sank the Latvian *Everalda*, taking her Spanish skipper and a crewman who had jumped overboard as prisoners. Before the bloody month of June was out, the *Morosini* under Fraternale sank the Dutch ship *Tysa* Dutch on the 30th of June. On the 4th of July the American ship *Norlandia* was sunk northeast of the Dominican Republic by Günther Heydemann in U-575.

U-571 under Helmut Möhlmann entered the region just south of Bermuda on the 30th of June, and rounded the northern coast of Grand Bahama on the 5th of July. On the 7th of July Möhlmann and his crew sank the British freighter *Umtata* between the Cay Sal Bank and Florida Keys. The *Umtata* had been damaged by a torpedo from U-161 under Albrecht Achilles in a daring attack on Port Castries, Saint Lucia on the 10th of March 1942, and was being towed to the US for permanent repairs. Möhlmann followed this sinking with a successful attack on the American ship *James A. Moffett Jr.* on the 8th of July. The attack was noteworthy for an Ahab-esque scene: while descending from the ship to the lifeboat Captain Patrick Sarsfield Mahony caught his arm in the falls, or ropes leading from the boat and nearly lost his arm. He bled to death while awaiting rescue, which was effectuated by two amateur US Coast Guard Auxiliary craft, the *Mary Jean* and *Southbound*, as well as the destroyer USS *Nike*, all of which landed survivors at Craig, Florida.

By the 9th, U-571 had exited the region via Key West and sank the small Norwegian-built American fruit carrier *Nicholas Cuneo* in the Gulf of Mexico. Möhlmann returned to the region on the 16th of July, when it transited down the Old Bahama Channel, cleared the Caicos Passage on the 20th, and exited the region between Bermuda and Anegada on the 23rd of July.

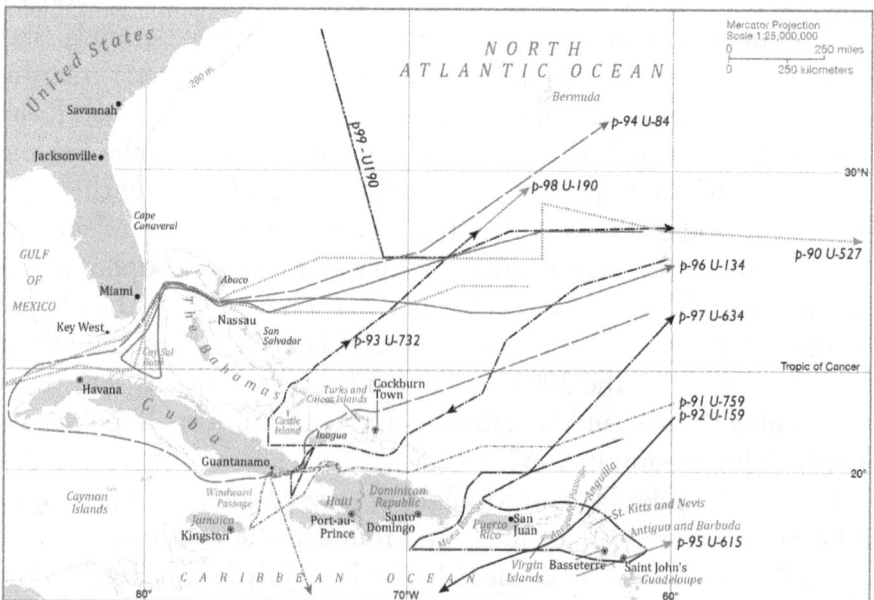

Günther Heydemann brought U-575 into the area south of Bermuda on 30 June 1942. The sub headed straight for the Mona Passage, which it transited into the Caribbean on the 5ᵗʰ of July, having sunk no ships in transit. U-84 under Horst Uphoff arrived in the area on the 1ˢᵗ of July. It would be a lengthy patrol during which Uphoff essentially circumnavigated the Bahamas. From the 5ᵗʰ to 8ᵗʰ of July the sub patrolled off the northwest point of Grand Bahama and the east coast of Florida. On the 10ᵗʰ Uphoff used Bird Island Light, Crooked Island as a reference (three weeks later the *Potlatch* men were rescued there).

He then entered the Old Bahama Channel and proceeded up the coast of Cuba before patrolling near the Cay Sal Bank from 13 to 19 July. On the 21st July U-84 sank the American freighter *William Cullen Bryant*, followed two days later by the *Andrew Jackson*. Both ships were dispatched between Key West and Havana. Uphoff then passed the north end of Grand Bahama on the 25ᵗʰ of July, leaving the area just south of Bermuda on the 29ᵗʰ and returning to Lorient.

Rudolf Schendel in U-134 also entered the area on the 1ˢᵗ of July, from south of Bermuda. Like Uphoff, Schendel opted to spend several days, from the 5ᵗʰ to the 9ᵗʰ of July, north of Grand Bahama. Then from the 10ᵗʰ to the 17ᵗʰ to U-boat repositioned to an area between Grand Bahama and Cape Canaveral, then further south in the Straits of Florida. On the 19ᵗʰ U-134 exited the region to enter the Gulf of Mexico, returning on the 26ᵗʰ to transit the Old Bahama Channel as far as the north coast of Haiti, where it arrived on the 2ⁿᵈ of August. Schendel then entered the Windward Passage between the 3ʳᵈ and 4ᵗʰ of August before transiting the Caicos Passage on the 5ᵗʰ and exiting the area back to La Pallice France on the 10ᵗʰ. It was a harbinger of patrols to come inasmuch as despite a month's worth of effort U-134 did not find or destroy any victims during its sojourn around the Bahamas.

Hans-Günther Kuhlmann in U-166 was more fortunate than his predecessor in his attacks at least until the sub was sunk. U-166 entered the area south of Bermuda on the 7ᵗʰ of July and headed south for the northeast corner of the Dominican Republic, near the Mona Passage. There, on the 11ᵗʰ, Kuhlmann dispatched the Dominican schooner *Carmen*, of just 84 tons. Heading west up the Old Bahama Channel Kuhlmann next sank the Ford Motor Company freighter *Oneida* off the

northeast coast of Cuba, near the Windward Passage, on the 13th.
Unbeknownst to him, Kuhlmann was leaving a trail for the observant
Allies to pick up and follow as he marched northwest sinking ships large
and small.

The loss of a small American fishing vessel laden with 40,000
pounds of onions and 19 swordfish, sunk between Cuba and Florida on
the 16th, makes for interesting reading. The 15-ton boat shared a name
with that of Kuhlmann's wife: Gertrude, on the 16th. The two-man crew
of the *Gertrude*, under Captain Walter Broward Crossland, was given a
chance to board a crude motorboat powered by a small outboard. They
attempted to reach Cuba, 30 miles away, but ran out of fuel and drifted
to the north, where a Civil Air Patrol plane spotted them and they were
rescued after 78 hours near Alligator Reef in the Florida Keys.
Kuhlmann's luck ran out four days later – U-166 was sunk by the US
Navy patrol craft PC 566 off New Orleans on the 20th of April. The
wreck of the sub was discovered in 2001 near the wreck of the passenger
ship *Robert E. Lee*, which it sank.

U-437 also entered the region on the 1st of July, a day when there
were a record 12 Axis submarines in the area. U-437 was commanded
by Werner-Karl Schulz, who took the sub directly southwest to the
Windward Passage, which he used to gain the Caribbean on the 5th of
July. On the 16th the U-boat returned via the same route, and spent from
the 17th to the 21st patrolling around the Turks and Caicos, and between
there and the north coast of the Dominican Republic. On the 21st U-437 bent a course for Saint Nazaire, leaving the region south of Bermuda
on the 25th of July without having sunk any vessels there. The highly
successful U-161 under Albrecht Achilles returned to the area on the
11th of July. On the 12th U-161 transited the Caicos Passage en route
from the Caribbean to Lorient, using the Windward Passage. Before
exiting the area south of Bermuda on the 18th, Achilles dispatched the
US freighter *Fairport* on the 16th of July.

Günther Pfeffer in command of U-171 initiated its cruise to the
Bahamas in Kiel, Germany. U-171 entered the Bahamas area from south
of Bermuda on the 13th of July. On the 17th it transited the Caicos
Passage, passing Great Inagua to starboard, and entered the Caribbean
via the Windward Passage the following day. Pfeffer returned via the
same route on the 14th of August 1942, this time opting to skirt south of

the Turks and Caicos and patrol north of Puerto Rico. The sub left the region north of Anegada on the 19th of August without having sunk any vessels in the area.

Heinz-Ehler Beucke in U-173 spent roughly 10 days in the region, starting on the 13th of July, when he entered south of Bermuda heading for the Caicos Passage. After rounding Providenciales on the 17th he entered the Caribbean via the Windward Passage on the 19th, and did not return until the 4th of August. At that time Beucke re-entered the Bahamas area, opted to skirt the northern coasts of Hispaniola and Puerto Rico, and exited the area north of Anegada on the 6th of August without having sunk any ships whilst there.

The Italian submarine *Reginaldo Giuliani* under Giovanni Bruno spent 10 days north and east of Puerto Rico, starting on the 16th of July 1942. The following day Bruno reported that he not only attacked a nameless ship, but that the submarine withstood an Allied counter-attack from the air. On the 23rd the sub rendezvoused with its compatriot, the *Finzi*, north or Puerto Rico to exchange fuel and intelligence. *Giuliani* exited the area north of Anegada on the 26th of July. Ultimately it ran into engineering difficulty due to an Allied air attack and was forced aground in Spain, where it ended up spending the balance of the war after the allotted time for neutral transit had lapsed.

U-509 under Karl-Heinz Wolff began an in-bound transit of the southeast corner of the region on the 21st of July. It exited the area into the Caribbean via the Mona Passage four days later, on the 25th, without having caused any damage to Allied shipping. Wolff was followed on the 26th of July by Georg Staats, in command of U-508, which arrived on the 26th of July, direct from Kiel Germany on a repositioning patrol which ended in France. Between the 31st of July and 1st of August Staats transited the Crooked Island Passage, leaving Long Island Bahamas to starboard and apparently just missing *Vergemere IV* as it headed from Crooked Island to Nassau on the same day. U-508 then forsook the Windward Passage in favor of marching up the Old Bahama Channel. Arriving off Key West on the 3rd of August, he exited the area for the Gulf of Mexico. U-508 spent the next two weeks or so patrolling the area around the entrance to the Straits of Florida, mostly west of the demarcation between Havana and Key West.

On the 12th Staats managed to attack the Special Convoy 12 and sink the Cuban ships *Manzanillo* and *Santiago de Cuba*. U-508 then re-entered the Saint Nicholas Channel to return to the Old Bahama Channel on about the 19th of August, passing north of the Windward Passage on the 23rd. The following day, at a point near the frontier between Haiti and the Dominican Republic the submarine turned north, passed between the Turks and Caicos and the Silver Banks, and exited the area south of Bermuda on the 27th of August, 1942, bound for Lorient. On 23 July 1942 Hans-Ludwig Witt in U-129 sank the *Onondaga* in the Old Bahama Channel. At least one passenger, Captain Mellin Edwin Respess, was killed. His Liberty Ship, the *Thomas McKean*, had been sunk by Alex-Olaf Loewe in U-505 exactly a month before. It is said that Captain Respess was traveling with his "negro ship's boy," who was also tragically lost.

Hans Senkel brought U-658 into the region on 27 July for a lengthy and somewhat complicated patrol. To start with the submarine patrolled in zig zags on the eastern fringe, west of the line between Bermuda and Anegada, for about nine days. Then on the 7th of August U-658 headed for the Windward Passage, passing east of the Turks and Caicos. Entering the Windward Passage on the 10th, Senkel quickly dispatched three ships in the Caribbean Sea (*Laguna, Samir,* and *Fort La Riene*), before heading north to an area between Great Inagua, Bahamas and Cuba, where he sank the smallish freighter *Medea* on the 13th of August. Staying in the area north of the Windward Passage for some four days, Senkel then crisscrossed the entrance to the Crooked Island Passage between the 18th and 23rd before heading east towards a point just north of Anegada. Arriving on the 26th he then back-tracked west for a day to a point north of the Mona Passage and finally headed northeast for Saint Nazaire on the 28th of August 1942. His was the third patrol in the area to originate in the German port of Kiel.

Karl Neitzel in U-510 seems to have been reading the same voyage orders as Senkel before him. For one week between the 30th of July and the 6th of August the submarine tracked back and forth south of Bermuda and west of the line connecting that island to Anegada. U-510's quest bore more fruit than U-658's, however, as Neitzel was able to sink the neutral Uruguayan ship *Maldonado* on the 2nd of August. The salvation of the *Maldonado*'s crew involved Bermuda, Canada, the US,

Germany, Switzerland, and Uruguay. It is also only the second incident in the region where prisoners were captured by the Germans, *Everalda* by U-158 being the first.

The *Maldonado* survivors abandoned ship in four lifeboats. After dispatching their vessel, Neitzel nudged the submarine amongst the boats and demanded that both the master and chief engineer board his submarine. By the time that Captain Giambruno was aboard, he apparently no longer required the engineer. The captain was taken aboard as prisoner, most likely to help verify the status of the ship. U-510 then submerged and headed off in a northwesterly direction, leaving 48 men hundreds of miles from land. Thirteen men in one boat were spotted by the USS *Owl*, rescued, and landed in Hamilton, Bermuda on the 6th of August. Another boat with 13 was retrieved by USCG 491. They were landed in Cape May, New Jersey on the 16th of August. The last batch of survivors of the *Maldonado* was sighted by a US Navy Catalina patrol plane on the 5th of August. The plane vectored the British troop transport *Capetown Castle* under Captain E. H. Thorton to the two boats with 22 men in them. They were landed in Halifax on the 8th of August.

Embarrassed at having seized the skipper of a non-belligerent neutral ship, the Germans released Captain Giambruno, who travelled through Switzerland and managed to return to Uruguay by November 1942. There were riots in the streets of Montevideo over the treatment of the Uruguayan ship and the men who manned it. Were it not for a remarkable series of rescues as a result of which none of the crew died or were seriously injured, the outcry would have been worse.

U-564 under Reinhard "Teddy" Suhren returned to simply skirt the eastern fringe of the area, starting on the 3rd of August south of Bermuda and proceeding to a point east of Anegada on the 8th. He was followed on the 6th of August by Ludwig Forster in U-654, who was coming back to the region for the second time. U-654 motored towards the Windward Passage, ducking east and south of the Turks and Caicos on the 10th of August and entering the Caribbean on the 12th. Ten days later it was attacked by an American Dibgy bomber north of Colon Panama and sunk. All 44 men on board perished. Between the 5th and 11th of August U-98 under Wilhelm Schulze entered the region west of Bermuda and motored to a patrol area off the coast of Jacksonville.

Without having sunk any prey, Schulze returned north along the Georgia coast for the region off Cape Hatteras.

U-600 under Bernard Zurmühlen circumnavigated Cuba between 12 and 29 August 1942. Zurmühlen's KTB, or *Krieg's Tag Buch* (war day book, or diary) includes detailed charts and sketches of his patrol. Entering south of Bermuda on the 8th of August, he passed east and south of the Turks and Caicos and exited south of Bermuda for La Pallice on September 3rd.

U-598 under Gottfried Holtorf entered the area from Kiel on the 7th of August, two days after losing Willi Bredereck, who drowned while refueling from U-463. The sub reached the Mayaguana Passage by the 10th. It then passed west of Inagua and motored up the Old Bahama Channel. In the crescent of deep water which forms the back end of the remote Ragged Island chain in the southern Bahamas Holtorf deftly pinned a disorganized convoy, TAW 12-J (Trinidad, Aruba, Key West northbound), which had been ravaged and partially scattered in an action against convoy WAT 13 (Key West, Aruba, Trinidad – southbound) the day before by U-658 under Senkel, U-508 under Staats, and U-600 under Zurmühlen in the Windward Passage.

In fact Zurmühlen vectored Holtorf to the vulnerable group. In an audacious dawn attack, Holtorf managed to pick off three British vessels in the space of an hour or so: *Michael Jebsen*, and *Empire Corporal* both sunk, the latter with the convoy commodore on board. Though also badly damaged, another ship, the *Standella*, managed to limp into Havana, where her crew had the dangerous and difficult task of locating and extracting the bodies of their six dead shipmates from the forepeak area before they putrefied in the tropical heat.

U-598 reached a point south of Cay Sal Bank Bahamas on the 16th. At that point Holtorf turned the sub around and headed back towards the Inagua area. For several days, Holtorf lingered north of the Windward Passage, looking for prey. Perhaps Holtorf was a victim of his success, as with convoys having been organized and defenses beginning to be beefed up, victims were hard to find. It is remarkable that he was not hunted down and sunk in the narrow Old Bahama Channel, as were U-176 and U-157. On the 22nd, the sub returned northeast for Saint Nazaire via the Mayaguana Passage again, and exited the area on the 28th of August.

VIVIAN P. SMITH

Kapitänleutnant Bernhard Zurmühlen in the Type VIIC boat, U-600, led the next attack in the region. He was a member of the Class of 1933 and worked with radios on a battleship and in signals on shore before joining U-boats in March 1941. He was serving under von Tiesenhausen on U-331 when that boat sank the British battleship HMS *Barham* in the Mediterranean in November 1941. He commissioned U-600 as its first (and only) commander in December 1941. The patrol to the Bahamas was its first patrol. En route to the Caribbean U-600 was refueled by U-463 west of the Azores in early August. He entered the area on the 8th midway between Bermuda and Anegada, then headed for the Windward Passage via the Turks and Caicos. On the 10th of August the Germans chanced upon a Barbadian schooner, *Vivian P. Smith*, the first Allied vessel which they had encountered together.

Vivian P. Smith was constructed of wood and launched on October 23rd 1915 in Lunenburg, Nova Scotia. Her builders were Smith and Rhuland and the principal shareholder (out of more than 40 listed on the registration) was William G. Smith. Presumably the yard built her on spec, or at their own cost, and that they were confident of a buyer. In April 1916, the journal *Canadian Fisherman* announced that "the new schooner, *Vivian P. Smith*, has been added to the fleet for Captain Roland Knickle."

*Francis W. Smith, sister ship to Vivian P. Smith, both
Canadian built and Barbadian registered.
Source: Photo courtesy of Will Johnson, Bridgetown Barbados*

The schooner was to have many owners. At her launch alone
her ownership was broken into 64 shares with almost as many
stakeholders, indicating that it was truly a community venture and also
a capitalistic venture for small stakeholders. By 28th of November 1927.
When she was sold out of Canadian and into Dutch registry, there were
23 transactions for the ship – either William G., Lewis H., or James H.
Smith owned her 10 times.

She was 102 feet long, 26 feet wide, and had a draft of 11 feet
empty - 14 feet when loaded with cargo. A sailing schooner with two
masts, *Vivian P. Smith* had an attractive elliptic stern, was built in the
carvel style, and her head was constructed in the billet style. She had
no internal bulkheads or ballast tanks. *Vivian P. Smith* had a net
registered tonnage of 97.42 and gross tonnage of 130.28. Her cargo
capacity was roughly 1,000 cubic feet of storage space. The ship was not
equipped with a radio and the record is silent as to whether an auxiliary
engine was added later in her career.

According to the ship's registry on file with the Canadian
National Archives, she was sold out of Canadian registry in 1927. From
there, she was owned by the indefatigable sailing clan the Hassels of
Bridgetown Barbados and Saba whose nautical lineage goes back
centuries. She was used for fishing off the snapper banks of British
Guyana. Captain Frank Hassell, the father of Eric, purchased her sister
ship, the *Francis W. Smith*. She shows up in newspapers in Trinidad and

Barbados bringing cargoes of ice or fresh fish from foreign ports and fishing grounds. Her arrival was advertised in the local papers.

At the time of her loss the *Vivian P. Smith* was owned by the Kenneth Johnson family of Bridgetown and was registered to Demerara, British Guyana, now known as Georgetown Guyana. Kenneth and his father Captain "Daddy" Johnson owned three other two-masted schooners operating out of Demerara. She was two days into a voyage from Grand Turk, Turks and Caicos, to Bridgetown, Barbados under the command of Captain Allen Frederick Jones. The total crew consisted of 11 persons, all of them British subjects, of whom nine were West Indian. She was laden with 206 tons of salt, with an additional deck cargo of live donkeys, as the Turks and Caicos were trying to rid themselves of the beasts by selling them to other islands. Unbeknownst to her crew, the *Vivian P. Smith* was being stalked by the U-600. As Sadler notes, "unfortunately the ship ...was torpedoed by a U-boat shortly after leaving, and the animals perished."

Conditions were smooth, with the wind at only three knots from the east-northeast, meaning the schooner must have had hardly any headway under sail. Since the captain gave her speed at the time as 5 knots, the schooner must have had an auxiliary motor since her heading was east-northeast and into what little wind there was. Visibility was good, it still being daylight at 3 pm local time. The schooner didn't have any confidential papers or armaments on board. Four of her crew were on the deck.

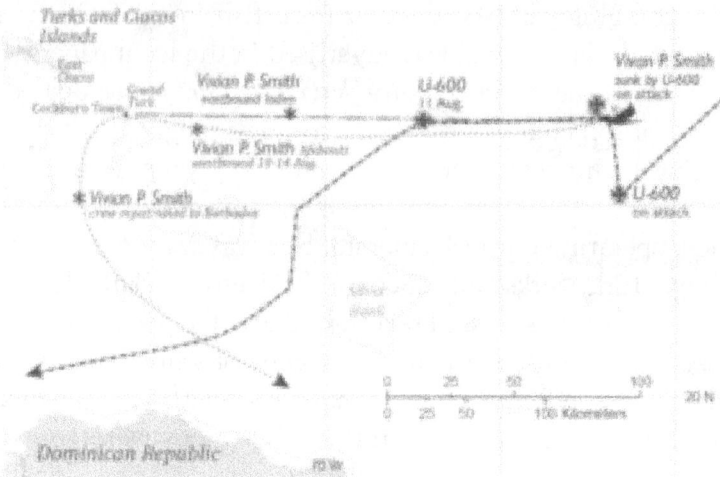

Vivian P. Smith was attacked by U-600 roughly 150 miles northeast of the Turks and Caicos on August 10th, 1942. Since it was Zurmühlen's first successful Allied kill, he was detailed in describing the attack in his KTB, or war diary:

"10:26 am – two masts in view at 155 degrees. Position east, distance ten nautical miles. …View of enemy lost due to rain squall. 11:30 am – cruising at seven knots ahead of him, enemy disappears repeatedly behind rain squalls. 12:30 pm – enemy is in view again, same heading, seems to be a very small vessel, very slow. 2:35 pm – descend, move towards him, to get a look from underwater. 3 pm – It is a two mast gaff schooner with three fore sails, brand new rigging, looks almost like a yacht, no flag, no insignia, no armaments visible, white cabin in the middle. 3:30 pm – emerge 3000 meters behind the schooner, fire a shot in front of the bow, schooner turns, shows no flag. 3:37 pm – fire a second shot in front of bow, now a boat is visible at the stern, still no flag is visible."

"4 pm – waiting 3-4000 meters behind the stopped schooner, until the boat reaches us. Boat is manned with two whites and eight blacks. One of the whites identifies himself, after I ask, as the captain, and confirms that the schooner is of British nationality. Name is "VIVIA," en route from Barbados to Bermuda. Cargo: stones. Answering my question, the captain reports that he's got water, provisions and a sail in his life boat. I order them to move away in a south-westerly direction."

"4:55 pm – distance 100 meters from schooner, wooden sail boat, estimate 150 tonnes, on the stern it says VIVIA P. SMITH, DEMERARA, new vessel, plenty of brass on deck, sinks slowly, first keel level, then the bow. Through an open cargo hatch and upper deck a brown substance is visible. Maybe the "stones" are a type of ore? 5:04 pm – Schooner has sunk! Ammunition used: 139 shots 8.8-cm – at least 25 hits in rigging and 15 in the wooden hull and deck. No smoldering visible. 5:10 pm – Lifeboat has set sail and moves away in south-western direction. Move away at heading 0 degrees until lifeboat is out of sight, then heading 230 degrees, cruising."

Korvettenkapitän Bernhard Zurmühlen, commander of U-600, who circumnavigated Cuba.
Source: uboat.net/men/commanders/1410.html

Vivian P. Smith's crew was last seen setting sail toward Turks and Caicos. They utilized the prevailing winds, currents and seas to land on Grand Turk, a small but busy community of salt harvesters and traders. On Grand Turk the men were put up at the Dora Do Do boarding house, as their predecessor from the Fauna had been. They are not reported to have required medical care. Once in the capital they reported to Lieutenant Thomas of the Royal Naval Reserve. Captain Jones described the submarine as 150' long, light grey and "new" looking. They said that Zurmühlen spoke "perfect English." Thomas added in his report that Captain Jones "had no alternative but to abandon, as 2 shells had struck vessel before crew got away."

One of the *Vivian P. Smith*'s crew was considered quite a musician – given a guitar he loved to sing. According to Carl Coverley, Osvaldo Ariza, and his brother, the sailor became known as "The Song Bird" and would entertain his fellow sailors and islanders at the Dora Do Do, a place known for its "lively social life." At the time the Turks and Caicos were administered from Kingston Jamaica, a situation which changed periodically. Because of regular steamer and schooner traffic between Jamaica and the Turks and Cacios, it is believed that the *Vivian P. Smith* sailors were able to return to Barbados via an initial voyage to Jamaica on another schooner like the one which they had lost. Osvaldo Ariza says that "there was a fleet of sailing vessels in Grand Turk waiting to carry survivors to Jamaica."

The Allies were building up a dossier indicating that the Germans could be raiding inter-island schooners for supplies such as fresh vegetables and information on local merchant movements. Though it did not happen in this instance, the fear was that while the *Vivian P. Smith* crew sailed towards their rescue at the hands of Turks Island fishermen, the German submarine crew were rifling through and pilfering from the guileless schooner.

Meanwhile, Zurmühlen arrived off the mouth of the Windward Passage on the 12th of August. Then U-600 was called to convoy TAW 12 by U-658 under Holtorff. The two subs then attacked the convoy as a wolfpack, in concert with U-598. The following day just inside the Windward Passage, U-600 sank the American passenger ship *Delmundo* and the Latvian freighter *Everleza* in an attack on that convoy. Though the *Everleza* was blown sky-high when her cargo ignited, several of its crew members survived. The master of the *Delmundo* made it to shore, however he later died. During the next week, U-600 began a circumnavigation of the large island of Cuba – the linchpin of the Greater Antilles.

U-600 then cruised up the Old Bahama channel until the 21st of August, at which time it exited the Bahamas area between Key West and Havana. On the 23rd of August, the submarine was sighted by an American Catalina and depth-charged and damaged. Continuing onward, according to Zurmühlen's chart of his patrol, he rounded the western point of the island, cruised south of the Isle of Pines, and then re-entered the Windward Passage between Guantanamo and Jamaica on the 28th of August. U-600 rounded Inagua on the 29th and transited the Crooked Island Passage. On the 30th, the boat emerged from the channels and made northeast for La Pallice. Passing east of Bermuda on the 3rd of September U-600 was refueled again on the way home by U-462 west of the Azores days late. The patrol ended on the 22nd of September.

Zurmühlen's total tonnage sunk amounted to five ships of 28,600 tons and a further three ships damaged of 19,230 tons. He was 32 years of age at the time of this patrol. His highest decoration, the following year was the German Cross in Gold. He was promoted *Korvettenkapitän* three weeks before his death in November 1943. U-600 was sunk near Ponta Delgada, Azores by the British destroyers HMS *Bazley* and HMS *Blackwood* on the 25th of November, 1943. The boat took all 54 officers and crew with it to the bottom, including Bernard Zurmühlen.

The Honduran schooner *Sande* was sunk, allegedly by a submarine off Cuba, but remains just a foot note in the *Lloyd's War Losses* for August 30, 1942. It relates that a 60-ton sailing ship of Honduran registry was sunk between Cuba and Bahamas. *Sande* was reported shelled and sunk by an unknown submarine on the night of 30/31 Aug, 1942. *Sande* was en route from Puerto Rico to Cuba and then onto Honduras. The location of the sinking was about eight miles north of Gibara, Cuba and 40 miles south southwest of Duncan Town, Ragged Island.

However, no U-boat claimed the sinking of this vessel. Furthermore, there were no Axis submarines – either German or Italian, in the immediate area, nor would there be for several days. The U-600 had cleared out of the area several days before. A careful reading of what little evidence remains from the survivors indicates that after being sunk, on their way to Gibara in boats, they thought they saw a submarine's periscope. This would indicate that the *Sande* was not in fact sunk by a submarine, but that her crew merely thought they saw a sub following the ship's loss, presumably by weather or equipment failure. Another possibility – purely conjecture – which might explain why the loss was reported to the insurers, is that the loss was an insurance scam, capitalizing on the fear and uncertainty surrounding numerous attacks on Allied ships at this time.

U-BOAT ACTIVITY 11 AUGUST 1942 TO 6 SEPTEMBER 1944

The period between the loss of the *Vivian P. Smith* on the 10th of August 1942 and the final patrol to the region in September 1944 witnessed the incursion of 29 Axis submarine patrols and the loss of 23 ships in the greater Bahamas region. Despite the fact that Allied defensive measures in terms of convoys and anti-submarine patrols from air bases throughout the area (Bahamas, Cuba, Puerto Rico for example) were in place, several ships were sunk in convoy. However U-boats in the Bahamas region now had to keep a very sharp lookout for aircraft and destroyers, moderate their position and attack radio reports (which could be picked up and deciphered using Enigma decryption at Bletchley Park in the UK), and utilize a number of radar-detection devices such as Metox, or the "Biscay Cross" as early-warning measures against counter-attack.

As U-boat historian Clay Blair put it, the hunters were becoming the hunted. U-boats may still have ruled beneath the waves in the Atlantic, however the Allies maintained uncontested dominance of the air in the region. Furthermore, the implementation of hunter-killer groups based on aircraft carriers in the central Atlantic as well as aggressive air patrols from the UK over the English Channel and Bay of Biscay meant that the U-tankers known as *"milch cows"* that had enabled smaller Type-VII subs to patrol for weeks or even months in the Caribbean and Gulf of Mexico were quickly sunk. All of this made the logistical situation for the Germans much more challenging. It also meant that more and more attack submarines were being attacked and sunk in transit to and from their European bases. A sub destroyed a few hundred miles after departure from France would be one less military craft to menace the Allied trade routes snaking through the Bahamas.

U-511 under Friedrich Steinhoff entered the region south of Bermuda on the 11th of August 1942 and headed straight for the Windward Passage via the Turks and Caicos Passage, which he transited inbound on the 18th. Off Guantanamo Steinhoff dispatched the *San Fabian*, *Esso Aruba* (damaged) and Dutch ship *Rotterdam*, which had earlier rescued the survivors of the *Daytonian* off Abaco in March of the same year. These attacks took place on the 27th of August. U-511 transited the Anegada Passage homebound from the 7th to the 9th. Steinhoff committed suicide at the Charles Street Jail in Boston after surrendering U-873 in New Hampshire in May, 1945. He – and other Axis POWs – are buried at Fort Devens, Massachusetts.

U-164 under Otto Fechner was next to the area, with a straight-forward trajectory from entry south of Bermuda on the 12th of August to an entry into the Caribbean via the Mona Passage on the 15th without having claimed any Allied tonnage during inbound transit. This patrol also originated in Kiel and terminated in Lorient. Karl Thurmann in command of U-553 then entered south of Bermuda on 12 August. Motoring directly for the Windward Passage, it passed south of Turks and Caicos on the 16th and entered the Caribbean on the 18th, on which day it sank three Allied ships of Guantanamo: the British *Empire Bede*, Swedish *Blankaholm* and American *John Hancock*, all in convoy TAW 13 (Trinidad, Aruba, Key West). U-508 under Staats helped vector Thurmann to the spoils but was driven off by aircraft.

U-163 under Kurt-Eduard Engelmann arrived south of Bermuda on the 13th of August 1942 and motored north of Hispaniola and east of the Turks and Caicos, perhaps avoiding anti-submarine flights in that area. The submarine entered the Caribbean via the Windward Passage on the 19th but returned less than a week later, on the 22nd of August. At that point it utilized the Caicos Passage on the 23rd and exited the area midway between Bermuda and Anegada on the 27th without having sunk any ships in the region. Kurt Reichenbach-Klinke brought U-217 into the area for a direct line between south of Bermuda on the 13th of August and exited via the Mona Passage on the 16th. During a 95-day patrol, all U-217 achieved was to shell the inter-island schooner *Sea Gull D.* off Caracas, Venezuela, for which the sub was roundly punished by several Allied aircraft on the 19th of August.

U-558 under Günther Krech returned to the area on the 19th of August, passing close by southern Bermuda. The sub transited the Caicos Passage and entered the Caribbean on the 25th, via the Windward Passage. The same day Krech sank the British *Amakura*.

Unlike his immediate predecessors, U-217 and U-163, this U-boat ace was not one to leave empty-handed. During an 80-day patrol Krech accrued 26,421 tons sunk or damaged, all in convoys in the Caribbean: the Dutch ship *Suriname*, British *Empire Lugard*, damaged Norwegian ship *Vilja* and the American *Commercial Trader*. The *Vilja* was subsequently declared a constructive total loss.

Otto Ites began his final patrol to the region in U-94 by passing south of Bermuda on the 22nd of August. Less than a week later, having just rounded east of Turks and Caicos and entered the Windward Passage, U-94 was detected by aircraft which vectored the Canadian destroyer HMCS *Oakeville* to the submarine. *Oakeville* rammed the U-boat, killing 19 German sailors when the submarine sank, but managing to rescue 26 of them. Imprisoned in North America, Ites lived until age 63, dying in his native Germany in 1982. Walter Schug in U-86 sank the schooner *Wawaloam* under Captain Luis Kenedy northeast of Bermuda on the 6th of August. Kenedy later planted roots in the Bahamas and became known as the last schoonerman (the title of a book written about him). Schug came down from the Hatteras area between Bermuda and Savannah on the 27th of August. U-86 then headed south and east, exiting the region south of Bermuda on the 1st of September, without having sunk anything there.

The next vessel sunk was a schooner, the Canadian 167-ton *Helen Forsey*. Like the *Vivian P. Smith*, the *Forsey* had been built by Smith and Rhuland Shipbuilding Limited of Lunenburg, Nova Scotia. She was dispatched southeast of Bermuda on the 6th of September by U-514 under Hans-Jürgen Auffermann, which did not patrol within the box around the Bahamas. The same can be said of the next two ships sunk south and east of Bermuda: the Swedish *Peiping* sunk by U-66 under Friedrich Markworth on the 9th of September and the American freighter *Patrick J. Hurley*, sunk after a running battle by U-512 under Wolfgang Schultze on the 13th. *Kapitänluetnant* Hans-Heinrich Giessler entered the region just off Savannah on the 20th of September 1942 for a brief three-day incursion into the area after laying mines off Charleston on the 18th. After reaching a point north of Jacksonville he took U-455 due east across the Gulf Stream, then headed east-northeast out of the area roughly midway between the US coast and Bermuda.

U-154 made its third of a record four patrols into the area on the 5th of November, with a short detour to the mouth of the Mona Passage a day later. Following this, the submarine, under the command of *Fregattenkapitän* Heinrich Schuch on the boat's fourth of eight patrols, headed east across the north coasts of Puerto Rico and the Virgin Islands to exit the region off Anegada on the 7th of November. After his transit of a corner of the Bahamas region he sank three ships in less than two weeks; the *D'Entrecasteaux*, on the 8th of November, the *Nurmahal* the next day, and on the *Tower Grange* on the 18th. All were British. En route to the Bahamas area U-154 rendezvoused with a blockade-running supply ship *Tannenfels*.

Günther Reeder opted to utilize the Mona Passage as a means to return to Brest in January of 1943 – the first U-boat to enter the region that year. On the 19th he passed through Mona north-bound and by the 22nd had reached a point roughly midway from Bermuda to Anegada. At that point he turned southeast again to continue U-214's patrol. Reeder refueled from U-118 while southeast of the Azores in mid-February. *Oberleutnant zur Zee* Albert Lauzemis was next, bringing U-68 into the area on the 23rd of February 1943. From midway Bermuda – Anegada, he motored west to a point east of the Bahamas and north of Puerto Rico so that they could repair their Metox device. Metox was a piece of equipment which enabled a U-boat to detect when Allied aircraft had detected the U-boat with centi-metric radar. It gave the submarine a chance to submerge or fight it out on the surface, rather than being surprised at night by an enemy aircraft, which often turned on bright search lights (called Leigh Lights) at the last minute to both illuminate and blind the target. On the 2nd of March, U-68 resumed its course towards the islands, and entered the Mona Passage the following day.

On the 4th of March U-68 exited the area bound for a patrol off Panama. Once inside the Caribbean U-68 attacked and sank two ships – the *Cities Service Missouri* and *Ceres*, both in convoy GAT 49 going from Guantanamo to Trinidad via Aruba, on the 13th of March. On the 31st of March, Lauzemis was to return via the Anegada passage, heading northward on the eastern fringe of the area. Two days later, on the 2nd of April, it was attacked by US Air Force aircraft said to be based in the Bahamas, but more likely based in Puerto Rico. The boat was attacked three times while operating north of Puerto Rico from the 27th of March. The attacks were so fierce that the boat was pinned underwater for 127 hours in six days, which precipitated its return to Europe. It is possible, in light of attacks by four sets of aircraft, that some of them left from Bahamas. On the 4th of April, U-68 turned 90 degrees to the east and exited the area bound northeast for Lorient.

U-155 under the command of Adolf Cornelius Piening both entered and exited the area midway Bermuda-Anegada, spending a total of 19 days in the region. It entered the Windward Passage on the 5th of March. Piening opted to stay close to the northwest coast of Providenciales and the east coasts of both Little Inagua and Great Inagua with no ships sunk. Piening sank the Lysefjord off the Yucatan Channel on the 2nd of April and the Gulfstate east of Key West the following day. From there Piening opted against the Old Bahama Channel in favor or riding the Gulf Stream up the Straits of Florida during the 4th and 5th. On that day he back-tracked briefly towards Grand Bahama, cleared close to Walker's Cay, then passed close to the northeast coasts of Abaco, most likely taking a bearing off the Elbow Cay lighthouse on the 7th of April before taking an easterly course. On the 13th of April, U-155 exited the area south of Bermuda home bound to Lorient.

The next boat into the area was U-185 under Kapitänluetnant August Maus. From west of Bermuda on 3 March 1943 the boat followed a conventional trajectory due south, then southwest for the Caicos Passage between Mayaguana and Caicos, then north of Inagua into the Crooked Island Passage. Turning south on the 9th of March, U-185 entered the Windward Passage and motored west, sinking the American Virginia Sinclair on the 10th of March off Guantanamo. The Sinclair was part of Key-West to Guantanamo Convoy KG 123 and U-185 was counter-attacked and forced to call off a second anticipated attack. Maus also sank the American freighter James Sprunt on the same day. When its cargo of 4,000 tons of explosives were ignited by U-185's torpedo, the ship literally disintegrated, killing all 69 officers and crew and raining debris on the nearby convoy of ships.

Bow of the Virginia Sinclair *floating upper right, US destroyer in foreground, March 10ᵗʰ, 1943.*
Source: National Archives and Record Administration, NARA, College Park, Maryland

Over three weeks later U-185 returned via the Windward Passage and again found success in the area, sinking the *John Sevier* of Convoy GTMO 83 off the very southwestern tip of Inagua on the 6th of April. Maus opted against re-entering the Crooked Island Passage and instead patrolled along the north coast of the Dominican Republic to the Mona Passage. On the 9th of April the boat swung to the northeast and homewards to Bordeaux, exiting the region on the 12th. On the 24th of August 1943, U-185 was caught and sunk in the Central Atlantic by three aircraft from the escort carrier USS *Core*. During the next three years August Maus moved from POW camps in Tennessee to Arizona. He succeeded in escaping in February 1944, only to be captured along with Friedrich Guggenberger in Tucson. Becoming a successful businessman in Hamburg, he lived until 1996 and the age of 81.

U-129 under Hans-Ludwig Witte sank the British *Melbourne Star* of an impressive 12,806 tons on 2 May, 480 miles southeast of Bermuda. There were 119 men on board at the time, and the ship went down in two minutes, taking most of them with it. Four men survived adrift for 38 days before being found by aircraft 250 miles south of Bermuda and were awarded the British Empire Medal. Witte left his patrol area off Hatteras for a 15-day incursion into the area between the Bahamas and Bermuda on the 16th of April 1943. Heading south for four days to a point about 300 miles east of Hope Town Abaco, it doubled back and slowly retraced its route for two days. The sub turned north towards

Bermuda and was rewarded on the 27th with by encountering the *Santa Catalina*, which it sank roughly 300 miles southwest of Bermuda. From there the boat returned to the Cape Hatteras area on the 30th of April and exited the 1st of May. On the way back to France on 21 May, whilst refueling from U-459, two members of U-129's crew were washed overboard by a large wave, and only one of them was recovered.

U-176, a Type IXC under Rainer Dierksen entered the area on the 29th of April 1943 on a trajectory from south of Bermuda. For one week U-176 headed almost due south, ending off the mouth of the Mona Pass on the 8th of May. Dierksen opted to head due west along the coast of Hispaniola, also bypassing the Windward Passage on the 11th in favor of a cruise up the Old Bahama Channel. When the submarine sank the *Mambi* and the ammonia tanker *Nickeliner* (one of the only such ships of its kind) on the 13th of May, the activity did not go unnoticed. In fact, both US and Cuban naval forces picked up on the mayday messages, and began tracking the course of the sub up the channel. By the time U-176 reached the Saint Nicholas Channel a convoy with Cuban escorts was awaiting to attack and destroy the boat on the 15th of May. A small Cuban patrol boat depth-charged the submarine into submission – it sank south of Cay Sal.

A 60-day patrol led by *Kapitänleutnant* Freidrich Markworth in U-66 qualifies as the longest single enemy patrol in the Bahamas area. It began where it ended – one third of the way from Bermuda to Anegada, on the 29th of May 1943 and would last to the 25th of July. U-66 arrived off the Savannah- Jacksonville cruising ground, where it was to remain for the better part of six weeks. On the 10th of June U-66's torpedoes found and sank the large US tanker *Esso Gettysburg*, setting the naval establishment as well as the tanker alight. The loss of life from the inferno (57 men were killed) was sobering to all who were made aware of it. Roughly three weeks later Markworth found the similarly large US tanker *Bloody Marsh* in the same general area and sent her to the bottom on the 2nd of July 1943. Nearing the end of its precious fuel supply, the boat turned slowly homeward, striking off to the southeast and past the exit for the Northeast Providence Channel before encountering the US tanker *Cherry Valley*, which put up a valiant fight on the 22nd of July roughly 300 miles east of San Salvador. The Allied ship managed to escape without being sunk. After this lively battle U-66 turned east and made its way back to Lorient, exiting the area on the 25th of July.

Kapitänleutnant Herbert Uhlig on U-527 opted to utilize the Northeast and Northwest Providence channels when he proceeded inbound south of Bermuda starting June 1st 1943. He arrived off Abaco on the 5th of June and over the following 24 or so hours steamed around Hole in the Wall Light and Great Isaacs Light before breaking into the Straits of Florida and heading south. U-527 motored against the Gulf Stream for two days before exiting the region to prowl in the Gulf of Mexico on the 8th of June. Uhlig was to return on the last day of the month - going up the Straits of Florida, he again passed the colony's capital. U-527's last day in the Bahamas area was the 7th of July. Off the Azores it was sunk by combined Allied efforts. Only 13 men, Uhlig among them, managed to escape and were picked up by the USS *Clemson* and later landed in Casablanca by the USS *Bogue*.

Oberleutnant zur See Heinz Beckman patrolled from just north of Anegada into the eponymous passage between the 4th and the 6th of July, 1943. Just like his two predecessors Beckman was to be sunk after leaving the region. After a patrol to Nicaragua and Costa Rica the sub doubled back and headed for the Anegada Passage. On the 28th of July U-159 was caught on the surface by Allied aircraft – the American Mariner of VP-31 (P-1) commanded by Lt. R. C. Mayo, and sunk south of Santo Domingo, Dominican Republic with the loss of all 53 hands.

U-732 under Claus-Peter Carlsen, began its 24-day patrol into the area on the 5th of July 1943 midway between Bermuda and Anegada. U-732 rounded the northwest tip of Haiti on the 11th of July. The following day, two US OS2U Kingfisher scout aircraft surprised the boat on the surface, damaging it slightly. Carlsen initiated an attack on Convoy ON 376 southbound, only 30 miles west of Great Inagua. The corvette USS *Brisk* depth-charged the sub. No ships were sunk or even damaged during this 83-day patrol. On Saturday the 7th of August 1943 U-732 was witnessed by half a dozen school children from southeast of Clarence Town, Long Island.

Commander Rudolf Schendel would spend an impressive 28 days in the area as he circled the Bahamas en route to other attacks in the US Gulf in July and August 1943. On the 9th of July, the boat turned into the Straits of Florida, where it remained on patrol for the better

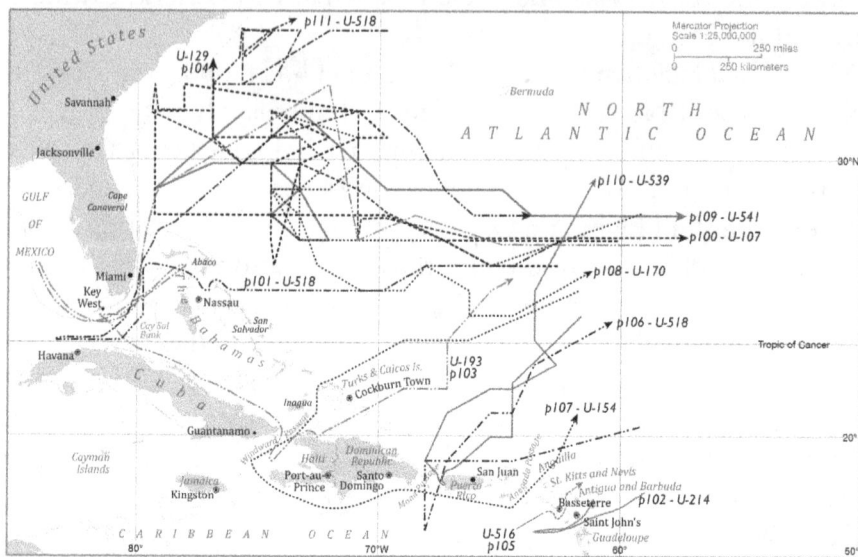

part of a week, until the 16th. Then it resumed its course southwards and motored against the Gulf Stream southwards and around Key West and out of the region on the 19th of July. Schendel opted to take the Old Bahama Channel then crossed the opening of the Windward Passage to a point on the northwest coast of Haiti, where it arrived on the 2nd of August.

On the 4th U-134 rounded the southwest coast of Inagua near Matthew Town and precoded through the Crooked Island and then Caicos passages around Providenciales. After breaking out into the open Atlantic the boat headed northeast for four days until the 9th. On the 10th the boat turned due east and returned, all its torpedoes still in their tubes.

The next skipper into the area, Hans-Günther Brosin, also in command in U-134, opted for a three-week patrol in the Bahamas area by utilizing the Northeast and Northwest Providence channels both for inward and outward passages. The boat was attacked no fewer than four times by Allied forces, the final attack being fatal to the boat. Two days before it entered the area, a Bermuda-based naval aircraft under command of John T. Hitchcock dropped six to eight depth-charges, though the boat was able to survive.

Damage to Lt. John Hitchcock's aircraft after an attack on U-134 south of Bermuda 8 July 1943.
Source: NARA, College Park, Maryland

On the 10th of July Brosin steamed due west for Hole in the Wall Abaco, arriving on the 15th. Two days later, while off the northwest tip of the Cay Sal Bank, the U-boat was spotted and attacked by the US naval airship K-74. Contrary to standing orders, the observation blimp dove in for the attack. Brosin's deck crew was able to shoot down the dirigible, all but one of the crew managing to survive. It was the only such attack by a German submarine on a US blimp during the war.

Harried by both Allied attacks and concomitant technical problems, U-134 was again attacked the following day, this time by US Ventura aircraft piloted by John C. Lawrence. Three depth-charges found their mark, severely damaging the forward battery compartment. After patrolling around Key West, on the 22nd of August the submarine doubled Great Isaacs Light heading east past Nassau, and emerged over the north coast of Eleuthera on the following day. U-134 steamed eastwards and exited the region on the 1st of August at a point south of Bermuda. U-134 was sunk off Vigo, Cape Finisterre, Spain during the same patrol. Whereas a study of a typical patrol in mid-1942 would include roughly four attacks on Allied shipping, by late 1943 patrols like Brosin's were a catalogue of Allied attacks on U-boats, with no effective retribution.

Volker Simmermacher next took U-107 south of Bermuda, steamed west from the 18th to the 20th of August 1943, then swung northwest and exited the region on the border of South Carolina on about the 24th. U-107 exited the area on the 8th of September in the same position as she entered: south of Bermuda, having spent just shy of three weeks in the region. U-107 was one of the boats fitted with an advanced Schnorchel device, enabling it to ventilate and recharge the batteries from under water and reducing the vulnerable surface time required of it.

U-518 next patrolled the region, entering midway Bermuda-Anegada on the 16th of September 1943 and proceeding due west for Abaco and Eleuthera. Transiting the Northeast Providence Channel, it rounded Key West westbound on the 29th. The boat, under Friedrich-Wilhelm Wissman, returned via Key West on the 14th of October. Steaming up the Gulf Stream for the next few days, it rounded West End Grand Bahama on the 16th and was in the open North Atlantic by the following day. It turned due east and exited the area at the same position it had arrived, on the 26th of October. U-518 attacked no ships on this patrol.

U-214 under Rupprecht Stock limited its patrol to two one-day transits of either the Anegada or the Guadeloupe passages. These transits occurred on the 26th of September 1943 and a return voyage on the 18th of October. The third-to-last patrol through the Bahamas was mounted by Hans Pauckstadt in the Type IXC/40 boat U-193 on the 17th of November. Entering south of Bermuda, the boat motored for the Northeast Providence Channel and emerged into the Gulf Stream on the night of 23rd November. Proceeding down the Straits of Florida, it cleared Key West on the 26th. U-193 was attacked twice while in the Caribbean by US Navy aircraft, then re-entered the Bahamas region via the Windward Passage on the 29th of December. South of Inagua Pauckstadt opted to turn east along the north coast of Hispaniola and then turn northeast. The boat exited the area south of Bermuda on 6 January 1944. After it was attacked by Allied aircraft on the 9th of February the boat was forced to duck into El Ferrol, Spain due to urgent repairs.

U-129 under Richard von Harpe entered on the 18th of November 1943 westbound south of Bermuda. The boat headed to a complex patrol area north and east of Grand Bahama and Abaco. On the 25th of November the boat entered the Gulf Stream off Walker's Cay and sailed to a point off Jacksonville. Thereafter, it zig zagged northeast towards Cape Hatteras and exited the area on the 1st of December. During this patrol U-129 was credited with sinking the Cuban freighter *Libertad* off San Salvador on the 4th of December.

However, this is inaccurate, due to an erroneous log entry by von Harpe. The *Libertad* was actually sunk off Hatteras and the rescue of her crew is well documented by photographs. On the way back the boat lost a crewman overboard on the 21st of January.

Next into the region was U-154 under Gerth Gemeiner. U-154 was returning for its fourth mission there during the war, a record tied with U-129. It entered the sector midway Bermuda-Anegada on a southwest course for the Caicos Passage on the 29th of February, 1944. Proceeding inward, it rounded the northwest coast of Inagua and made to the southeast and the Windward Passage. The U-boat made its way back utilizing the Anegada Passage on the 13th of March.

U-539 under Hans-Jurgen Lauterbach-Emden would sink the last ship of the war in this region during a patrol of 15 days, starting on the 1st of June 1944, when the sub entered from south of Bermuda and motored for the Mona Passage. U-539 was attacked by a USN Mariner piloted by Lt. J. G. Tomkins north of Puerto Rico on the 2nd of June but managed to evade damage. On its arrival off Puerto Rico on the 5th of June, Lauterbach-Emden detected a small convoy and several other ships coasting along the shore and moved in for an audacious daytime attack. The Panamanian-flagged, US-manned tanker *Pillory* was the U-boat's first of three victims on this patrol. Though several were killed when the bridge was blown into the sea and the tanks exploded, the US Coast Guard was able to rescue many survivors. The Allies counter-attacked with both surface and air attack, but the damage inflicted was not severe.

U-539 then proceeded through the Mona Passage undetected. On the way back to Germany, Lauterbach-Emden opted to utilize the Mona Passage again, entering on the 17th of July. Hugging the eastern coast of the Dominican Republic, the boat headed northwest east of the Turks and Caicos, and turned east-northeast, exiting the region south of Bermuda on the 26th July, 1944. Given that the Allies were blockading the Bay of Biscay, the route home was uncertain and circuitous. U-539 had to obtain its precious fuel southwest of Iceland. Though bound for Flensburg Germany after a patrol of extraordinary length - nearly five months – U-539 was forced to call instead at Bergen, Norway. By this time, following D-Day, the German baseds in France were either besieged or lost.

The final patrol by a German submarine into the Bahamas area was initiated by U-518 under Hans-Werner Offermann from Hatteras between the 4th and 6th of September 1944. The patrol was notable not only because the boat rode out a hurricane (safer under water than on the surface), but also because it was in the vicinity of the USS *Warrington*, a destroyer which was sunk in a hurricane with the loss of 248 sailors northeast of Abaco on the 14th of September. This boat had new schnorkel equipment, which enabled it to remain underwater, ventilate, and charge the batteries all from beneath the waves – a game-changing modification which arrived too late in the war to make a major difference for the Axis. Offermann was 23 at the time of the patrol and would only live for less than a year and go down as "one of the youngest commanders during WWII." He was killed on 22 April 1945, weeks before the end of the war in Europe.

CONCLUSION

In the final analysis the catalogue of German and Italian submarine attacks in the Bahamas area is a sad chronicle. Thousands of men crossed the waters in fear, and for over 6,000 of them, the fear was realized when they found themselves experiencing sudden and violent attacks by an unseen foe. For the 1,410 men cut down in their youth, most of them serving as civilians and not in military uniform, the region was a scene of tragedy from which they would not drift out.

The 85 German and Italian submarines that attacked Allied shipping in the Bahamas during 112 patrols stalked and struck 130 Allied ships and sank all but a handful of them - several were grounded or limped or were towed to shore and repaired. Four Allied naval craft were lost – a destroyer sunk in a hurricane, a submarine chaser grounded at Fleeming Channel 20 miles from Nassau, a US Navy-converted yacht grounded in Bimini, and the US Navy blimp shot down by U-134.

These attacks occurred over a period of two years and four months, starting with the *Pan Massachusetts* on the February 19th 1942, and ending with the loss of the US tanker *Pillory* off Puerto Rico on June 5th, 1944. This is an average of just under five vessels a month for 28 months. The period of the greatest number of sinkings was the spring of 1942: 25 ships were sunk in June, 23 in May, 21 in March and 14 in April of that year. In addition, a dozen were sunk in August 1942, seven in February, and three in September. The only other spike in activity was the spring and summer of 1943: three ships were sunk in May, and two each in April and July.

There were 15 months when no Allied ships were sunk, as contrasted with the 13 months in which ships were lost. This is consistent with the German strategy of hitting soft targets decisively and swiftly, then moving on to other more vulnerable areas. The Axis submarines also returned at intervals to probe and test and, perhaps, reinstitute Allied defenses, in order to keep the enemy off balance and bleed resources - which were important goals in addition to the actual tonnage sunk. Logically, the period of most intense sinkings of Allied shipping corresponds with the times when Axis submarine activity was highest off the Bahamas. July 1942 saw an average of nine subs patrolling the area on any given day, with a record 12 submarines in the theater on the 1st of July. May 1942 witnessed 230 patrol days, 215 in August, 160 in June and 130 in March, with 110 in April. During the resurgence of patrols in 1943, there were 130 patrol days in July, and 40 each during June and August.

Though the sinkings ended in June of 1944, Axis patrols continued for three more months, until September 1944. In fact there were only two months – October and December 1942 – that there were no German or Italian submarines in the theater at all. As Allied shipping crews were not aware of this, one can state that the islands were effectively and continually under attack or threat of an attack for over two years. This was strictly a tonnage war. The cases of small ships like the *Gertrude* of 16 tons and the schooner *Vivian P. Smith* being sunk were the exception. For the most part the Germans and Italians went after as big a target as they could, including the *O. A. Knudsen* of 11,007 tons.

A composite of the average of an Allied ship, drawn from data on all of the vessels would produce a vessel with the following specifications: it would be a 5,000 steam-driven dry-cargo freighter. It would have been manned by 46 men, and later in the war a handful of naval gunners would be included among them. The registry, or flag, would be that of the United States, and in distant second place that of the United Kingdom. The cargo would have either been general cargo (if a dry cargo freighter), or petroleum products (if a tanker), followed by ballast, ore, and military stores. Once attacked, on the average, the ship would have lost 10 men. However, this data is skewered by the inclusion of the destroyer *Warrington*, lost by hurricane with 248 men, and the *Melbourne Star*, lost with 115 men. In fact, on nearly half the ships, there was only one casualty, and on 44 there were none. Well over half of the sailors would have been American, and 20% British - with those two groups, making up over 70% of the national registries of the ships. Also, Panamanian flagged ships were largely manned by Americans.

Once they abandoned their sinking ships, the majority of the men would have found their own way to shore in the ship's lifeboats. A number of lifeboats from the same ship were rescued in different ways: some by ship and others by making landfall on their own. A number of crews – about 25% - were picked up by other vessels and landed ashore by them. The most likely areas to be landed in the Bahamas region were Abaco, followed by the Turks and Caicos, then San Salvador, Acklins and Nassau. All survivors landed in the Bahamas were taken to Nassau, and all those landed in Turks and Caicos made their way to Grand Turk for further transport.

The average ship would be proceeding independently (without military escort) between Allied ports. Based on an analysis of those ports, New York would be statistically the leading destination as well as departure port. This leads to the inescapable deduction that had all the ships leaving and sailing to New York been given effective military escort, the number of ships sunk in the Bahamas area would have been cut substantially. Most of the ships were sunk in the bulge eastwards of a line between Anegada and Bermuda, or northeast of Anegada and well east of the Bahamas. This was east of the main convoy routes, away from the protection of escorts. These ships are included in this study simply because no other known works treats them as a group. The regions of highest sinkings closest to the Bahamas were the Straits of Florida and the Old Bahama Channel.

If one were to use the rule that a ship sunk closer to the Bahamas than any other country should be considered as having been sunk in the Bahamas theatre, one could include a dozen ships sunk northeast of Abaco, between the Bahamas and Bermuda, which in fact were not sunk very close to the Bahamas at all. But, using this yardstick in the narrow channels, like the Old Bahama Channel and Straits of Florida and Caicos Passage, is more clear-cut. By this method of measurement, there were 15 vessels sunk in close proximity to the Bahamas and two (the *Mariana* and *Vivian P. Smith*) were struck near the Turks and Caicos.

Of the 15 ships sunk in the Bahamas, three were attacked in a single convoy on the same day off Cay Santo Domingo, just south west of Ragged Island - *Standella*, damaged, *Michael Jebson*, and *Empire*

Corporal sunk. *Abgara* and *John Sevier* were both sunk near Inagua, however, the crew did not land in the Bahamas, but were taken to Cuba. There were two vessels sunk near the Cay Sal Bank, though one of them was a blimp (K-74), the other was the *Gulfstate*. The converted schooner, *Sama*, met its end west of Bimini, equidistant from Florida, and the *Nicarao* east of Eleuthera.

Discounting the faraway Cay Sal and the Old Bahama Channel, the large islands of the Bahamas experienced six large-ship attacks. Mayaguana was the closest point of land for the *Vineland* and *Fauna*, but, perhaps since the island is sparsely populated, the survivors of these ships successfully made for the Turks and Caicos. Of the four vessels sunk off the northern Bahamas, three were dispatched by an Italian submarine. The *Enrico Tazzoli* sank the *Cygnet*, *Daytonian* and *Athelqueen*, whilst U-128 sank the *O. A. Knudsen*.

Out of these ship sinkings, 267 merchant sailors and 67 US Navy sailors actually landed in the Bahamas (it is tempting to add the 23 men in the *Hardwicke Grange* lifeboat, who came within one mile of the Turks and Caicos, however, they did not actually land in the Bahamas). Just under two thirds of them, or 165, went directly to Nassau. A further 77 were transported there from San Salvador and Acklins Island, meaning that over 70% of the survivors who landed ashore in the Bahamas and Turks and Caicos were processed through Nassau. The 72 survivors who managed to land in the Turks and Caicos were all processed through the commercial capital of those islands, Grand Turk.

From Grand Turk, the sailors found vessels, to Puerto Rico, Jamaica, Haiti and. From Nassau, the crew typically took steamers (*Ena K.*) or airplanes (US Army Transport) to Miami and from thence a train to New York. Survivors of US Navy casualties (USS *Warrington* for example), were rescued directly by the Navy without being processed through Nassau. Only the *Potlatch* and *Kollskegg* crew were lost far from the Bahamas but landed in the islands. Other ships, like the *Mariana* and *Mamura*, did not have survivors at all. Survivors of the *John Sevier*, *Abgara*, and *Nicarao* as well as *Michael Jebson* and *Empire Corporal*, although they were sunk near the Bahamas, were all picked up shortly after they were sunk and taken to ports outside the Bahamas. This reflects the highly fluid and reactive conditions of rescue.

An aggregate of 690,928 gross tons of Allied shipping was sunk, damaged or attacked in the Bahamas area, or 5,315 tons per ship. Of the 130 merchant ships sunk, roughly 30% were highly valuable tankers, mostly plying the route from Aruba to Halifax and Texas to New York. They were interrupted while bringing their essential cargo to the industrial machines of the US northeast and to the factories, planes, trucks and tanks of Great Britain in her hour of dire need. Sixty percent of the ships were dry cargo freighters, and a further 5% or so were miscellaneous schooners, with a fishing vessel and an abandoned tug accounting for the balance.

Over 5,837 men served on these 130 vessels, or an average of 45 men per ship. Out of these, 1,239 lost their lives in the theater. The 4,605 survivors represent a survival rate of about 80%. Five of the men who survived the shipwreck but subsequently were lost ashore due to landing mishaps, privations of the lifeboat voyage, or injuries, are buried in the Bahamas. Of those buried in the islands, one is located in Abaco – Olaus Johansen from the *O. A. Knudsen* in Cross Harbor. The bodies of three British from the *Athelqueen* were never found off Hope Town. The American David Parson man from the *Potlatch* is buried at Andersons Settlement near Hard Hill, Acklins. At the time of writing there are no markers or memorials on the two graves, thought the *Athelqueen* men are memorialized with a stone monument. Two men, a Brit and an American from the *Daytonian* and *Potlatch*, were buried at sea en route to the Bahamas.

Fifteen of the 130 ships struck in the region were not sunk by German U-boats, but by Italian-built and Italian-manned submarines. This constitutes roughly 12% of the total. Of the five ships sunk squarely in the Bahamas: *O. A. Knudsen*, *Athelqueen*, and *Daytonian* off Abaco, *Nicarao* off Eleuthera, and *Cygnet* off San Salvador, fully three out of five, or 60% of them were sunk by Italians. If one utilized only the German resources, the picture of Axis attacks in the Bahamas would be considerably diminished. This is especially true when you eliminate the 85 survivors of the *Kollskegg* and the *Potlatch*, whose ships were not sunk anywhere near the Bahamas region, but who ended up on the shore of those islands.

It is generally not common knowledge that there was a concerted Axis attack on the Bahamas region and the commercial chokepoints which the colony straddled. Many readers were not aware that there was a submarine war raging around the Bahamas. This in part was due to wartime censorship, the diffuse nature of record keeping (archives in Nassau, Washington, London and Germany), and the chaotic and fluid nature of the rescue operations. These all cover sunken ships of different nationalities whose survivors landed in different countries and at various ports and were rescued by ships under different flags.

Perhaps there is an additional an element - embarrassment. The 112 submarine patrols in the region were answered by the sinking of only four submarines in the Bahamas theatre. There is no doubt, from the statistics and the sad reality of the loss of the entire crews of the ship, *Stangarth*, *Mariana*, *Manaqui* and *Mamura* as well as in the battered men washing ashore, that the entire episode represents a period during which the Allies had their nose badly bloodied. After all, though Britannia may have ruled the waves, as the saying went, Axis submarines ruled beneath the seas. It is telling that several ships' SOS messages were received in Nassau, and the capital was powerless to send out forces to effectively counter-attack. This applied to the Bahamas' nearby ally, the US, for a time as well.

On a sociological level, the arrival of malnourished and all-but-defeated sailors on the colony's shores, as reported in the local press, must have lowered the prestige of the colonial rulers in the eyes of their subjects during these difficult times. Historically maintaining prestige was an important element of the imperial ethos. The process of peeling away the confusion and inaccuracies to get at the hard kernels of truth is rather difficult. One is after all looking for details on incidents which were written in records which were classified and then sealed until recent decades.

To illustrate how opaque the situation was, until this research was initiated 70 years after the fact, it was generally believed and published even in highly reputable books and on websites that the following ships were sunk in the Bahamas: The *Ruth* was said to have been sunk just a few miles east of Acklins, whereas in fact it was lost a thousand miles to the east. The *Albert F. Paul* was said to have been sunk north of the Turks and Caicos and east of Cat Island, Bahamas, however it was in fact sunk off Cape Hatteras. An Italian submarine was said to have sunk the *Stangarth*, when in fact it was a German submarine which sank the ship. The Italian submarine, however, sank the *Manaqui* instead, northeast of Anegada. The Cuban freighter *Libertad* was said to have been sunk a few miles north of San Salvador. However, the *Libertad* in fact never came through that region, and its sinking and the rescue of survivors south of Cape Hatteras, in the Carolinas, is well documented. The schooner *Sande* was said to have been sunk off Gibara, Cuba on the 30th of August. However, there was no submarine which was in position to have delivered the attack at that time.

The *Worden* was said to have been attacked by a submarine off Florida, but, this was a miscommunication by the submarine. When the *Worden* went to the aid of another ship, it called out that it was doing so in the clear on the radio. Hearing the ship's name – *Worden* – over the radio, the German commander assumed that it was the name of the ship he had struck and wrote the name down as such. The error became obvious when examining aerial photographs which show the *Worden*, with its name in bold letters on the side, coming to the aid of another stricken ship. Though the *Worden was* clearly undamaged, even Allied records have been confused on this point since. Uncorrected errors can become amplified and morph into fact.

SS Worden *towing the SS* La Paz *off Florida. Worden was mistakenly named as the victim.*
Photo source: NARA, College Park, Maryland.

To illustrate just how fluid the survivor sagas could be, a number of shipwrecked survivors came across fellow survivors on the vast open spaces of the Atlantic Ocean. For example, the *Koll* and *Kollskegg* were both Norwegian tankers from the same parent company that were sunk within a few hours of each other on the same stretch of water east of Cape Hatteras. Some of the survivors from these boats hailed each other in mid-ocean before being separated by the weather. Likewise survivors of the *Tonsbergsfjord* and the *Montevideo*, both sunk by Italians, met on the high seas. After the group of merged survivors were rescued by the Dutch ship *Telamon*, they were dumped in their lifeboats off the coast of Haiti (the Haitians thought they were Germans invading their island). The Dutch survivors of the sunken *Tysa* came across the survivors of the *Potlatch*, then met survivors of the *Wilimantic* in Saint Martin. The American ship *Nicarao* didn't run into other lifeboats, but her crew claimed to have been virtually surrounded by schooners, who they suspected were sympathetic to the Axis.

There were several instances where Allied ships approached the scene of other wrecks and quickly fled the area, their skippers understandably nervous about falling victim to an attack themselves. In some instances, this flight behavior was witnessed by survivors who were left behind – they tended to attribute such behavior to Axis support vessels. The skipper of the Dutch ship *Rotterdam* bucked that trend by stopping to pick up several lifeboats – all of them – from the *Daytonian*, placing his ship in immediate peril of also being sunk by the *Enrico Tazzoli* lurking nearby.

A number of skippers were made aware of the loss of other Allied ships in the immediate vicinity. Captain Roberts of the *Athelqueen*, for example, first diverted to the aid of the *Charles Racine*, and then learned of the fate of the *Daytonian* sunk nearby before having his own ship sunk by the same submarine. The loss of the *Thomas McKean* was transmitted to the *Sam Houston*, and the loss of the *Anglo-Canadian* to the *Tysa*, and so on. This is particularly true of ships lost south and east of Bermuda, in the vast expanses where rescue was made more crucial due to the sheer distance from the nearest land.

A number of ship's masters were able to meet one another and exchange intelligence and notes on shore. In Nassau, in mid-March 1942, the crews of the *O. A. Knudsen*, *Cygnet*, *Daytonian*, and *Athelqueen* mingled with each other at different times, if only for a day. Captains Egerton of the *Daytonian* and Roberts of the *Athelqueen* are known to have spoken with one another. In Puerto Rico the officers of the *Sam Houston* and *Thomas McKean* compared notes about the level of intelligence obtained by the submarine commanders. In Saint Martin, there were reunions by the crews of a number of ships, including the *Tysa*, *Wilimantic* and *Anglo-Canadian*.

In Guantanamo Bay, Cuba, there were so many hundreds of survivors that, at one time, the officials there claimed that their resources were being drained and the temporary camp for survivors was bursting beyond its capacity. There, the survivors of the *Hanseat* encountered the crew of two other tankers from the same company, which had also been sunk the same week, giving rise to the unsubstantiated rumor that the crew of a single ship had seen to the destruction of three Allied ships. This aspersion was repeated with conviction by the eminent historian Samuel Eliot Morison, showing that even great writers can repeat errors.

There were poignant examples where survivors from one ship were sunk whilst being passengers on another. A Radio Operator from the freighter *Melpomene*, for example, was later sunk east of the Bahamas theatre while a passenger on the *Peder Bogen*. Likewise the captain of the *Thomas McKean*, which was sunk in the east of the theater, was later killed, along with his cabin boy, when the *Onondaga* was sunk between the Bahamas and Cuba. There are also many cases where survivors of ships sunk in the Bahamas theatre were later sunk on ships outside the area. Herb Cox of the *Daytonian* claimed to have been attacked four times, and Alan Heald of the *Athelqueen*, was attacked three times in four months. One of the *Vineland* crew survived several attacks, as did Captain Bringedal of the *O. A. Knudsen* and a number of his crew.

The ship *Robert E. Lee* was carrying survivors of the *Andrea Brovig* and *Stanvac Pelambang* from the Caribbean to New Orleans when she was sunk en route by U-166 which was sunk in the same engagement. There was at least one instance – the *Grenanger* - where survivors in lifeboats refused to board ships which came to their rescue, either because the rescuing ships simply didn't have the resources to provide for the survivors, or they were close to land, or out of fear of being torpedoed twice during a single voyage. In one case, a ship was torpedoed east of Bermuda and the would-be rescuing ship, the *Polyphemus*, was subsequently lost off Nantucket. In the case of the *Frank B. Baird*, the men were rescued by a ship, the Norwegian *Talisman*, which took them to Pointe Noire, French Equatorial Africa, far from their destination of Sydney, Nova Scotia.

Though over 60% of the men managed to rescue themselves by rowing, drifting, or sailing to shore, a percentage of the survivors were rescued by a combination of means – i.e. some lifeboats or rafts made it to shore on their own while other members of the same crew were picked up by ships. About 30% were picked up by rescuing vessels. Of those ships sunk close the Bahamas, the *Cygnet* was only four miles from San Salvador, while the *Abgara* and *John Sevier* were about ten miles from Inagua when lost. As we have seen, four vessels lost their entire crew, representing roughly 4% of the overall total of crew members on vessels lost.

In terms of size, the *Melbourne Star* was the largest ship, with 12,806 tons, followed by the *O. A. Knudsen*, at 11,007 tons. The five vessels closest in size to them were: the *Patrick J. Hurley*, *W. D. Anderson*, *Bloody Marsh*, *Esso Gettysburg*, and *Cherry Valley*, which managed to out-run its pursuers. The *Hardwicke Grange*, *Peder Bogen*, *Eclipse*, *J. A. Moffett Jr.*, *Kollskegg*, *Mobiloil* and *Charles Racine* were all over 9,000 tons. Most of them were tankers. The smallest ship, the *Gertrude*, was a mere 16-ton fishing vessel, and the schooner *Cheerio* was only 35 tons.

Of the ships sunk, including naval vessels, 67 ships or almost exactly half of the Allied ships were American. Twenty-five percent, or 30 ships, were British. Of the three ships flying the Panama flag, two can be considered American and one, the *Vineland*, Canadian. One of the ships, the *Sama*, was owned by the Bahama Shipping Company but flew the flag of Nicaragua. The *Western Head* was owned by the Maritime Navigation Company Limited and registered to Nassau, Bahamas. It was the only 'Bahamian' ship sunk in the theater.

Among other nationalities, the Dutch had nine of their ships sunk, followed by the Norwegians with seven ships. Sweden, Latvia, Honduras, Panama and Cuba each lost three ships in the region - for Latvia, this represented about half of their meager merchant marine fleet which escaped the Soviets and was trading with the Allies. Canada and Uruguay each had two vessels – in the case of the latter both ships were requisitioned from the Italians. Mexico, the Dominican Republic and Brazil each lost a single vessel.

Taking into account ships sunk over 200 miles from the coast, but not in the territorial waters of other countries, Abaco experienced the most sinkings, with 12 off its coast. Next was the Cay Sal Bank in the southwest of the Bahamas, with six sinkings near it. Ragged Island, facing Cuba, experienced six sinkings. The Turks and Caicos, under separate colonial administration, had eight sinkings. Andros and it's off lying Green Cays, Cayo Lobos and Orange Cay, collectively had four ships sunk nearby. Inagua had three; Mayaguana three; Bimini experienced two; Eleuthera one (*Nicarao*); San Salvador one (*Cygnet*); and Grand Bahama also one (*Mamura*).

Casting the net further afield as far east as the bulge eastward of line between Bermuda and Anegada, we find the highest concentration of attacks. The reason that attacks east of the line are included here are twofold: technically the ships are still east of the Bahamas, though they are also northeast of the Caribbean and southeast of Bermuda. The second reason is quite simple - if they were not included in this study they might remain largely lost to history. Unless a book- were to be written about U-boat victims in the nebulous and hard to define Sargasso Sea, these sinkings, as they fall outside of so many other regions, theaters, and areas, they would be truly forgotten. There were 33 ships sunk to the north or east of Anegada, in addition to the five ships attacked southeast of Bermuda. There were numerous sinkings in the Straits of Florida, the Old Bahama Channel, near Cuba, the Dominican Republic, Puerto Rico and in the Windward Passage, but as a general rule they were closer to the US and Cuba than to the Bahamas.

It is unlikely that any of the sunken ships will be found and salvaged in the foreseeable future for two main reasons. First, the average depth of wrecks is thousands of feet. The second reason is that so far as is known, none of the ships were carrying bullion or valuable metals, such as mercury, bronze, tin, or copper. They carried bulk cargoes or military equipment which would have rusted and corroded away by now (except perhaps the *Potlatch* cargo, which is rumored to have included tin valued at $20 million today). In most cases the sheer depth means that it is not economically viable to salvage them. Furthermore, there are many other potentially richer salvage targets in and around the Bahamas, some of which date back to the time of the Spanish galleons.

There were numerous convoys passing through the Bahamas region in World War II. They sailed from Aruba to Halifax via the Windward Passage, from Jamaica to Bermuda at the outset of the war, from Key West to Guantanamo every few days from late 1942 onwards, and from Key West to New York continually from late spring, 1942. Overall, including specialist one-off convoys and military escorts, 60 convoy routes either transited through the Bahamas or connected with those transiting through the islands. Cumulatively, these resulted in many thousands of actual voyages.

There were at least 16,000 merchant ships, which transited through the area during the war, each of them named by historians. A conservative estimate would be that more than 4,000 military ships of all shapes and sizes, passed through, often escorting the merchant ships. So, excluding any independently sailing vessels, there were at least 20,000 vessels transiting the region during this time. A very rough estimate of independent ships going through would be 10,000, for total transit voyages of 30,000 Allied vessels, though this number is highly conjectural. Most likely the number is between 25,000 and 30,000, as ships were not under obligation to report all of their movements to any central authority from the outset of war.

Of the ships known to have transited the area and been attacked in the greater Bahamas theater, 70% were steam-driven bulk or dry-cargo-carrying ships. At least three were Liberty ships. Thirty-three, or about 25% were tankers. Five were described as motor vessels (as opposed to steam), two were passenger ships, one, the *Hagan*, was a chemical tanker. Four were schooners, and the *Sama* was a small freighter converted from a schooner.

The vessels that were sunk carried a wide variety of cargoes. The most commonly carried category of cargo was petroleum, with 22 ships loaded with oil. Eighteen vessels carried general cargo, or dry cargo (which includes ores), and an equal number were empty of cargo and proceeding in ballast. Ten were loaded with military stores including trucks tanks, guns, and equipment for building bases. Six ships were laden with sugar, mostly from the Caribbean; and four with bauxite, mostly from northeast South America. Three carried molasses, and three the highly volatile military cargo - dynamite. Two carried salt, two passengers, and two fruit. The rest transported dry cargoes, except for one tanker, the *Hagan*, which carried ammonia water. Other cargoes include maize, potash, refrigerated food, tinned meat, mahogany, and Welsh coal.

The leading destination port for the sunken vessels was New York with 29 ships due there - 20%. New York was followed by Baltimore, with eight ships destined there, Havana, and Halifax with six each. Trinidad, Philadelphia, and Key West were each the destination of five. San Juan, Puerto Rico; Port Arthur, Texas; Curacao, Dutch West Indies; and Cape Town, South Africa would have posted three ships each as overdue, presumed lost. Other ports of destination for sunken ships were Boston, Tampa, Panama, Valparaiso, Suez, ports in Iran, Melville, Rhode Island, Port Everglades, Rio de Janeiro, Caripito in Venezuela, Grand Turk, Bridgetown, Barbados, and several small ports in Cuba and Florida.

Leading departure ports, or last ports of call of the sunken vessels, are easier to identify. Again, New York leads the list, with twelve ships or 9% of the total. Trinidad comes up second with eleven, primarily because Trinidad was a bunkering (or refueling) and convoy staging area for ships arriving from the South Atlantic and South America before heading towards North American ports and the assembly point for convoys to the UK from Halifax. Key West had six ships leave its port before departing on their doomed voyages, while San Juan and Cape Town had five each. Port Arthur, Texas saw four ships leave forever. Aruba, Curacao, various ports in Florida, Guantanamo, Hampton Roads in Virginia, Havana, Kingston in Jamaica, and Liverpool had three each. The other ports of departure of sunken vessels cover a geographically wide range. The list of ports from which only a single ship was lost is as exotic as it is long: Ascension, in the South Atlantic, Belfast, Bermuda, Cardiff, Demerara, Durban, Guaria in Venezuela, Milford Haven, New Orleans, Recife, Portland, Maine, Santos in Brazil, Barbados, Buenos Aires, Charleston, Saint Lucia, Montevideo, Panama, Philadelphia and numerous smaller ports in Puerto Rico, the Dominican Republic and Cuba.

The men of the *Mariana*, led by Captain Ivan Elroy Hurlstone of the Cayman Islands, were seen floundering in the water by their attackers, but never seen alive again. We can only imagine the unspeakably horrific and lonely, probably slow deaths they experienced far from home and hearth but rather close – only 27 miles – from salvation on nearby Mayaguana. Did the lifeboats and rafts make it to some uninhabited shore in the southern Bahamas only to be dashed to bits on the outlying reefs? Did they, like the *Potlatch* survivors, make it to shore only to find that starvation and thirst threatening to overwhelm them?

    We might know a surprising amount about what the four 4,605 survivors went through to claw their way back into civilization in the remote British colonies of Bahamas and Turks and Caicos, but the voices of those 1,239 lost and drowned have been silenced forever, not only to their friends, colleagues and families, but also to history.

APPENDICES

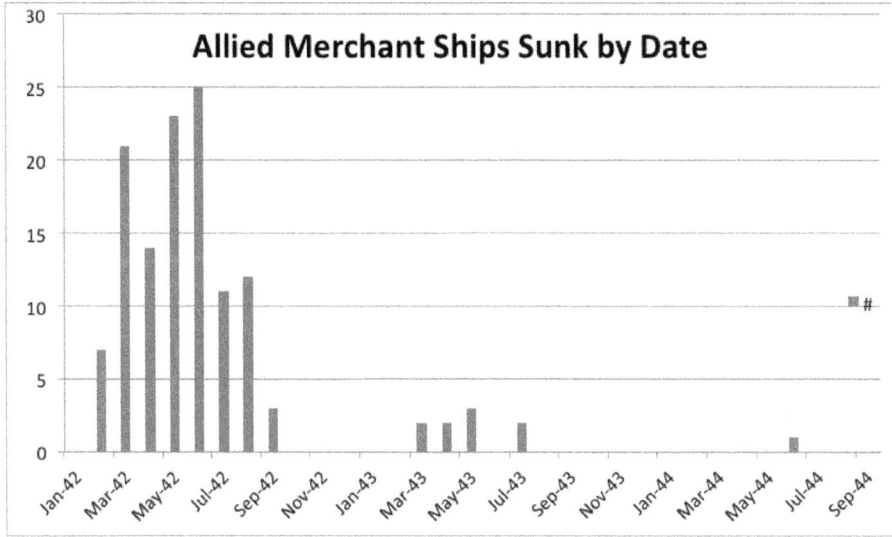

Allied Merchant Ships Sunk by Date

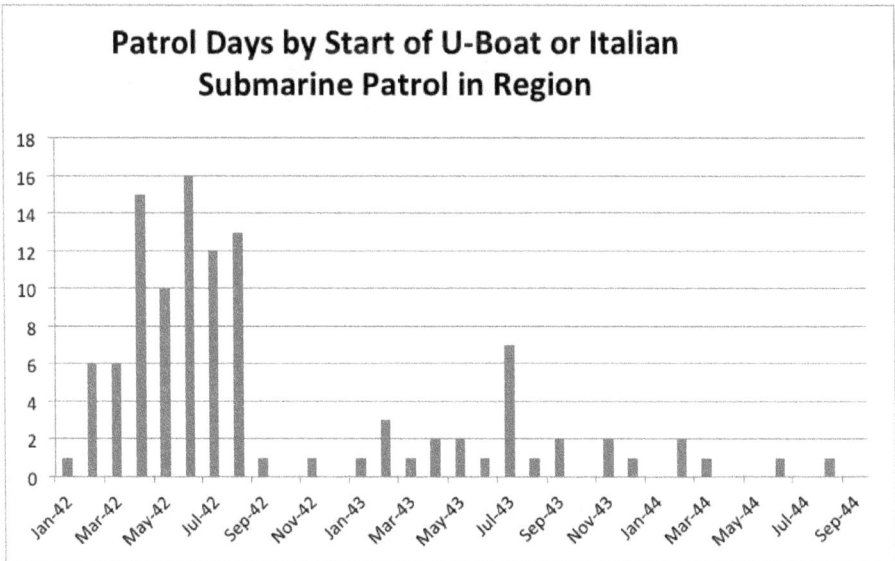

Patrol Days by Start of U-Boat or Italian Submarine Patrol in Region

TOP 20 AXIS SUBMARINE COMMANDERS IN THE BAHAMAS REGION 1942 - 1944

Rank	Ships Attacked	Names of Ships Sunk (Just in Bahamas Region)	Sub.	Sub. Commander	Tons
1	7	Rapana, Astrea, Tonsbergsfjord, Montevideo, Cygnet, Daytonian, Athelqueen	Tazzoli	Carlo Fecia di Cossato	38,959
2	8	Gunny, Mariana, Barbara, Cardonia, Hanseat, Olga, Texan, Colabee U-126	Ernst Bauer		38,468
3	6	L. A. Christiansen, Hardwicke Grange, Millinocket, Onondaga, Melbourne Star, Santa Catalina	U-129	Hans-Ludwig Witt	38,263
4	6	Ocean Venus, Eclipse, Delisle, Ohioan, Lubrafol, Potrero del Llano	U-564	Reinhard Suhren	37,635
5	4	Esso Gettysburg, Bloody Marsh, Peiping, Cherry Valley	U-66	Friedrich Markworth	36,930
6	6	Esso Baton Rouge, Esparta, GulfAmerica, Kortsholm, Leslie, Oklahoma	U-123	Rienhard Hardegen	33,989
7	4	Republic, Mamura, W. D. Anderson, Stangarth	U-504	Hans-Georg Friedrich Poske	29,725
8	3	Pan Massachusetts, Cities Services Empire, O. A. Knudsen	U-128	Ulrich Heyse	27,312
9	4	Manaqui, Oscilla, Peder Bogen, Tysa Morosini Athos Fraternale 24,211			
10	4	Amazone, Halsey, Java Arrow, Clan Skene	U-333	Peter-Erich Cremer	21,923
11	3	Melpomene, Skane, Charles Racine	Finzi	Ugo Giudice	21,226
12	3	James Sprunt, Virginia Sinclair, John Sevier	U-185	August Maus	20,504
13	3	Mobiloil, Abgara, Afoundria	U-108	Klaus Scholtz	19,357
14	3	Anglo-Canadian, Potlatch, Ruth	U-153	Wilfried Reichmann	16,186
15	3	Pedrinhas, Putney Hull, Sam Houston	U-203	Rolf Mützelberg	16,058
16	3	Comol Rico, Catahoula, Vineland	U-154	Walter Kölle	15,651
17	3	Empire Corporal, Michael Jebsen, Standella	U-598	Gottfried Holtorf	15,497
18	3	MacGregor, Oregon, Willimantic	U-156	Werner Hartenstein	14,372
19	3	Darina, Frank B. Baird, Everalda	U-158	Erwin Rostin	13,811
20	3	Vivan P. Smith, Delmundo, Everelza	U-600	Bernhard Zurmühlen	9,682
	82	TOTAL 82 SHIPS SUNK / DAMAGED / ATTACKED		TOTAL TONNAGE:	489,759

ALLIED SHIPS SUNK BY DATE OF ATTACK, SUBMARINE, COMMANDER

#	SHIP NAME	FLAG	DATE	SUBMARINE	SUB. COMMANDER
1	Pan Massachusetts	US	2/19/42	U-128	Ulrich Heyse
2	Cities Service Empire	US	2/22/42	U-128	Ulrich Heyse
3	Republic	US	2/22/42	U-504	Hans-Georg Friedrich Poske
4	Mamura	Dutch	2/26/42	U-504	Hans-Georg Friedrich Poske
5	W. D. Anderson	US	2/26/42	U-504	Hans-Georg Friedrich Poske
6	MacGregor	UK	2/27/42	U-156	Werner Hartenstein
7	Oregon	US	2/28/42	U-156	Werner Hartenstein
8	Gunny	Norway	3/2/42	U-126	Ernst Bauer
9	Rapana	UK	3/3/42	Tazzoli	Carlo Fecia di Cossato
10	Mariana	US	3/5/42	U-126	Ernst Bauer
11	O. A. Knudsen	Norway	3/5/42	U-128	Ulrich Heyse
12	Astrea	Dutch	3/6/42	Tazzoli	Carlo Fecia di Cossato
13	Melpomene	UK	3/6/42	Finzi	Ugo Giudice
14	Skane	Sweden	3/6/42	Finzi	Ugo Giudice
15	Tonsbergsfjord	Norway	3/6/42	Tazzoli	Carlo Fecia di Cossato
16	Barbara	US	3/7/42	U-126	Ernst Bauer
17	Cardonia	US	3/7/42	U-126	Ernst Bauer
18	Montevideo	Uruguay	3/8/42	Tazzoli	Carlo Fecia di Cossato
19	Hanseat	US	3/9/42	U-126	Ernst Bauer
20	Charles Racine	Norway	3/10/42	Finzi	Ugo Giudice
21	Cygnet	Panama	3/10/42	Tazzoli	Carlo Fecia di Cossato
22	Manaqui	UK	3/11/42	Morosini	Athos Fraternale
23	Olga	US	3/11/42	U-126	Ernst Bauer
24	Texan	US	3/11/42	U-126	Ernst Bauer
25	Colabee	US	3/13/42	U-126	Ernst Bauer
26	Daytonian	UK	3/13/42	Tazzoli	Carlo Fecia di Cossato
27	Athelqueen	UK	3/15/42	Tazzoli	Carlo Fecia di Cossato
28	Oscilla	Dutch	3/15/42	Morosini	Athos Fraternale

29	Stangarth	UK	3/16/42	U-504		Hans-Georg Friedrich
Poske						
30	Peder Bogen	UK	3/23/42	Morosini		Athos Fraternale
31	Tredinnick	UK	3/25/42	Calvi		Emilio Olivieri
32	Gulfstate	US	4/3/42	U-155		Adolf Cornelius Piening
33	Comol Rico	US	4/4/42	U-154		Walter Kölle
34	Catahoula	US	4/5/42	U-154		Walter Kölle
35	Kollskegg	Norway	4/6/42	U-754		Hans Oestermann
36	Esso Baton Rouge	US	4/8/42	U-123		Reinhard Hardegen
37	Oklahoma	US	4/8/42	U-123		Rienhard Hardegen
38	Esparta	US	4/9/42	U-123		Reinhard Hardegen
39	Grenanger	Norway	4/11/42	U-130		Ernst Kals
40	Gulfamerica	US	4/11/42	U-123		Reinhard Hardegen
41	Esso Boston	US	4/12/42	U-130		Ernst Kals
42	Korlsholm	Sweden	4/13/42	U-123		Rienhard Hardegen
43	Leslie	US	4/13/42	U-123		Rienhard Hardegen
44	Vineland	Canada	4/20/42	U-154		Walter Kölle
45	Derryheen	UK	4/22/42	U-201	Adalbert Schnee	
46	San Jacinto	US	4/23/42	U-201	Adalbert Schnee	
47	Mobiloil	US	4/29/42	U-108	Klaus Scholtz	
48	Federal	US	4/30/42	U-507	Harro Schacht	
49	La Paz	UK	5/1/42	U-109	Heinrich Bleichrodt	
50	Laertes	Dutch	5/3/42	U-109	Heinrich Bleichrodt	
51	Ocean Venus	UK	5/3/42	U-564	Reinhard Suhren	
52	Sama	Honduras	5/3/42	U-506	Erich Würdemann	
53	Eclipse	UK	5/4/42	U-564	Reinhard Suhren	
54	Abgara	Latvian	5/5/42	U-108	Klaus Scholtz	
55	Afoundria	US	5/5/42	U-108	Klaus Scholtz	
56	Delisle	US	5/5/42	U-564	Reinhard Suhren	
57	Amazone	Dutch	5/6/42	U-333	Peter-Erich Cremer	
58	Halsey	US	5/6/42	U-333	Peter-Erich Cremer	
59	Java Arrow	US	5/6/42	U-333	Peter-Erich Cremer	
60	Ohioan	US	5/8/42	U-564	Reinhard Suhren	
61	Lubrafol	Panama	5/9/42	U-564	Reinhard Suhren	
62	Clan Skene	UK	5/10/42	U-333	Peter-Erich Cremer	
63	Cape of Good Hope	UK	5/11/42	U-502	Jürgen von Rosenstiel	

64	Potrero del Llano	Mexico	5/14/42	U-564	Reinhard Suhren
65	Nicarao	US	5/16/42	U-751	Gerhard Bigalk
66	Fauna	Dutch	5/17/42	U-558	Günther Krech
67	Darina	UK	5/20/42	U-158	Erwin Rostin
68	Frank B. Baird	Canada	5/22/42	U-158	Erwin Rostin
69	Lammot du Pont	US	5/23/42	U-125	Ulrich Folkers
70	Yorkmoor	UK	5/28/42	U-506	Erich Würdemann
71	Western Head	UK	5/29/42	U-107	Harald Gelhaus
72	Fred W. Green	UK	5/31/42	U-506	Erich Würdemann
73	Domino	US	6/2/42	U-753	Alfred Mannhard von Manstein
74	Illinois	US	6/2/42	U-159	Helmut Witte
75	Triton	Dutch	6/2/42	U-558	Günther Krech
76	City of Alma	US	6/3/42	U-172	Carl Emmermann
77	Delfina	US	6/5/42	U-172	Carl Emmermann
78	Letitia Porter	US	6/5/42	U-69	Ulrich Gräf
79	Esso Gettysburg	US	6/10/42	U-66	Friedrich Markworth
80	L. A. Christiansen	Norway	6/10/42	U-129	Hans-Ludwig Witt
81	Hagan	US	6/11/42	U-157	Wolf Henne
82	Hardwicke Grange	UK	6/12/42	U-129	Hans-Ludwig Witt
83	Managua	Nicaragua	6/16/42	U-67	Gunther Müller Stöckheim
84	Millinocket	US	6/17/42	U-129	Hans-Ludwig Witt
85	Cheerio	US	6/19/42	U-107	Harald Gelhaus
86	Willimantic	UK	6/24/42	U-156	Werner Hartenstein
87	Anglo-Canadian	UK	6/25/42	U-153	Wilfried Reichmann
88	Pedrinhas	Brazil	6/26/42	U-203	Rolf Mützelberg
89	Putney Hill	UK	6/26/42	U-203	Rolf Mützelberg
90	Potlatch	US	6/27/42	U-153	Wilfried Reichmann
91	Raphael Semmes	US	6/28/42	U-332	Johannes Liebe
92	Sam Houston	US	6/28/42	U-203	Rolf Mützelberg
93	Sea Thrush	US	6/28/42	U-505	Axel-Olaf Loewe
94	Everalda	Latvian	6/29/42	U-158	Irwin Rostin
95	Onondaga	US	6/29/42	U-129	Hans-Ludwig Witt
96	Thomas McKean	US	6/29/42	U-505	Axel-Olaf Loewe
97	Tysa	Dutch	6/30/42	Morosini	Athos Fraternale
98	Bloody Marsh	US	7/2/42	U-66	Friedrich Markworth
99	Norlandia	US	7/4/42	U-575	Günther Heydemann
100	Umtata	US	7/7/42	U-571	Helmut Möhlmann

101	Jame A. Moffett, Jr.	US	7/8/42	U-571	Helmut Möhlmann
102	Carmen	Dom. Rep.	7/11/42	U-166	Hans-Günther Kuhlmann
103	Oneida	US	7/11/42	U-166	Hans-Günther Kuhlmann
104	Fairport	US	7/16/42	U-161	Albrecht Achilles
105	Gertrude	US	7/16/42	U-166	Hans-Günther Kuhlmann
106	Wm Cullen Bryant	US	7/21/42	U-84	Horst Uphoff
107	Andrew Jackson	US	7/23/42	U-84	Horst Uphoff
108	Ruth	US	7/29/42	U-153	Wilfried Reichmann
109	Maldonado	Uruguay	8/2/42	U-510	Karl Nietzel
110	Vivian P. Smith	UK	8/10/42	U-600	Bernhard Zurmühlen
111	Manzanillo	Cuba	8/12/42	U-508	Georg Staats
112	Medea	Dutch	8/12/42	U-658	Hans Senkel
113	Santiago de Cuba	Cuba	8/12/42	U-508	Georg Staats
114	Delmundo	US	8/13/42	U-600	Bernhard Zurmühlen
115	Empire Corporal	UK	8/13/42	U-598	Gottfried Holtorf
116	Everelza	Latvian	8/13/42	U-600	Bernhard Zurmühlen
117	Michael Jebsen	UK	8/13/42	U-598	Gottfried Holtorf
118	Standella	UK	8/13/42	U-598	Gottfried Holtorf
119	Helen Forsey	UK	9/6/42	U-514	Hans-Jürgen Auffermann
120	Peiping	Sweden	9/9/42	U-66	Friedrich Markworth
121	Patrick J. Hurley	US	9/13/42	U-512	Wolfgang Schultze
122	James Sprunt	US	3/10/43	U-185	August Maus
123	Virginia Sinclair	US	3/10/43	U-185	August Maus
124	Melbourne Star	UK	4/2/43	U-129	Hans-Ludwig Witt
125	Santa Catalina	US	4/24/43	U-129	Hans-Ludwig Witt
126	John Sevier	US	5/6/43	U-185	August Maus
127	Mambi	Cuba	5/13/43	U-176	Rainer Dierksen
128	Nickeliner	Honduras	5/13/43	U-176	Rainer Dierksen
129	Cherry Valley	US	7/22/43	U-66	Friedrich Markworth
130	Pillory	Panama	6/5/44	U-539	Hans-Jürgen Lauterbach-Emden

ALLIED SHIPS SUNK BY TYPE, CARGO CARRIED, DISPOSITION OF CREW

SHIP NAME	TONS	SHIP TYPE	CARGO CARRIED	ABOARD	KIA	LIVED	LANDED
Abgara	4,422	steam freighter	sugar	34	0	34	
Afoundira	5,010	freighter	7,700 tons general cargo: bombs, dynamite, food, lumber and road-building machinery	46	0	46	
Amazone	1,294	steam freighter	926 tons general cargo, mainly coffee and oil	40	14	26	46
Andrew Jackson	5,990	tanker	ballast	49	3	46	
Anglo-Canadian	5,268	motor ship	ballast	50	1	49	
Astrea	3,190	steam freighter	general cargo	30	30	0	
Athelqueen	8,780	tanker	petroleum	49	3	46	
Barbara	4,637	steam freighter	4,015 tons general cargo	85	26	59	
Bloody Marsh	10,195	tanker	102,500 barrels Navy fuel-oil	77	3	74	
Cape of Good Hope	4,963	motor ship	7,500 tons general military cargo	37	0	37	
Cardonia	5,104	steam freighter	81 tons general cargo	38	1	37	
Carmen	84	schooner (two masted)	2000 sacks maize and 476 pieces mahogany and cedar	8	1	7	
Catahoula	5,030	tanker	molasses	45	7	38	
Charles Racine	9,957	tanker	ballast	41	0	41	
Cheerio	35	schooner	mahogany	9	0	9	
Cherry Valley	10,172	freighter	6,000 tons water ballast, 165 tons Army cargo	79	0	79	
Cities Service Empire	8,103	tanker	9,400 barrels crude oil	67	25	42	
City of Alma	5,446	steam freighter	7,400 tons manganese ore	39	29	10	

Clan Skene	5,214	steam freighter	2,006 tons chrome ore	81	9	72	
Colabee	5,518	freighter	38,600 bags sugar	37	23	14	
Comol Rico	5,034	tanker	8,068 tons of bulk molasses	42	3	39	
Cygnet	3,628	freighter	iron ore, rubber	30	0	30	30
Darina	8,113	motor tanker	ballast	56	6	50	
Daytonian	6,434	steam ship	7,500 tons steel, lumber, cotton	58	1	57	57
Delfina	3,480	steam freighter	raw sugar	31	4	27	
Delisle	3,478	steam freighter	2,800 tons general cargo, paint in steel drums on deck	32	2	30	
Delmundo	5,032	steam ship	5,437 tons general cargo	58	8	50	
Derryheen	7,217	steam freighter	11,036 tons general cargo, nitrates, trucks	51	0	51	
Domino	3,170	steam freighter	ballast	30	0	30	
Eclipse	9,767	steam tanker	ballast	47	2	45	
Empire Corporal	7,000	steam tanker	4,532 tons motor spirit, 4,745 tons white spirit	55	6	49	
Esparta	3,365	steam ship	1,450 tons general cargo, bananas, coffee	40	1	39	
Esso Baton Rouge	7,989	tanker	ballast	68	3	65	
Esso Boston	7,699	tanker	105,400 barrels crude oil	37	0	37	
Esso Gettysburg	10,173	tanker	120,120 barrels crude oil	72	57	15	
Everalda	3,950	steam ship	general cargo	36	0	36	
Everelza	4,520	steam ship	manganese ore	37	23	14	
Fairport	6,266	freighter	8,000 tons war material and a deck cargo of tanks	123	0	123	
Fauna	1,254	freighter	general cargo	29	2	27	
Federal	2,881	tanker	water ballast	33	5	28	
Frank B. Baird	1,748	steam ship	2,457 tons bauxite	23	0	23	27

Fred W. Green	2,292	steam ship	725 tons military cargo, trucks	41	5	36	
Gertrude	16	trawler	20 tons of onions	3	0	3	
Grenanger	5,393	motor ship	general cargo, coffee	36	0	36	
Gulfamerica	8,081	steam tanker	101,500 barrels furnace oil	48	19	29	
Gulfstate	6,882	steam tanker	68,417 barrels crude oil	61	43	18	
Gunny	2,362	freighter	3,100 tons manganese ore, mahogany	42	30	12	
Hagan	6,401	tanker	22,676 barrels blackstrap molasses	44	6	38	
Halsey	7,088	tanker	40,000 barrels naphtha, 40,000 barrels heating oil	32	0	32	
Hanseat	8,241	tanker	ballast	40	0	40	
Hardwicke Grange	9,005	steam freighter	700 tons of refrigerated cargo	78	3	75	
Helen Forsey	167	schooner	180 tons molasses & rum	6	2	4	
Illinois	5,447	steam freighter	8,000 tons manganese ore	38	32	6	
James A. Moffett Jr.	9,788	freighter	water ballast	43	1	42	
James Sprunt	7,177	Liberty general cargo ship	4,000 tons explosives	69	0	69	
Java Arrow	8,327	tanker	water ballast, 1,300 drums lube oil	45	2	43	
John Sevier	7,176	Liberty general cargo ship	9,060 tons bauxite ore	57	0	57	
Kollskegg	9,858	tanker	8,000 tons crude oil, 6,300 tons fuel oil	42	4	38	30
Korsholm	2,647	steam freighter	4,593 tons phosphate	26	9	17	
L. A. Christiansen	4,362	steam freighter	ballast	31	0	31	
La Paz	6,548	motor freighter	general cargo, whiskey	57	0	57	
Laertes	5,825	freighter	5,230 tons war material, 3 aircraft, 17 tanks, 20 trucks	66	18	48	
Lammot du Pont	5,102	steam ship	6,812 tons linseed	54	17	37	

Name	Tonnage	Type	Cargo				
Leslie	2,609	steam freighter	3,225 tons raw sugar	32	4	28	
Letitia Porter	15	tugboat	unmanned deck cargo on SS *Koenjit*, sunk by *U-69*	0	0	0	
Lubrafo 1	7,138	tanker	67,000 barrels heating oil	44	13	31	
MacGregor	2,498	steam ship	ballast	31	1	30	
Maldonado	5,285	steam freighter	7,000 tons tinned meat, hides, wool, fats	49	0	49	
Mambi	1,983	coastal freighter	ballast	34	23	11	
Mamura	8,245	tanker	gasoline fully loaded	49	49	0	
Managua	2,220	steam freighter	potash	25	0	25	
Manaqui	2,802	steam ship	general cargo	41	41	0	
Manzanillo	1,025	steam freighter	general cargo	23	0	23	
Mariana	3,110	freighter	sugar	36	36	0	
Medea	1,311	steam freighter	1,636 tons of general cargo, 220 cases of dynamite	28	5	23	
Melbourne Star	12,806	motor ship	8,285 military supplies, general cargo	119	115	4	
Melpomene	7,011	tanker	petroleum	49	0	49	
Michael Jebson	2,300	freighter	2,750 tons sugar	40	1	39	
Millinocket	3,274	freighter	4,300 tons bauxite ore	35	11	24	
Mobiloil	9,925	tanker	water ballast	52	0	52	
Montevideo	5,785	steam ship	6,000 tons wool, meats	49	14	35	
Nicarao	1,445	freighter	500 tons of fruit, bananas, coconuts, charcoal	39	8	31	
Nickeliner	2,249	chemical tanker	3,400 tons ammonia water	31	0	31	
Norlandia	2,689	freighter	ballast	30	9	21	
O. A. Knudsen	11,007	tanker	pool engine spirit, pool vaporising oil (petrol, fuel-oil)	41	2	39	39

Name	Tonnage	Type	Cargo				
Ocean Venus	7,174	steam freighter	9,450 tons lead, lumber, tinned herring, acetone	42	5	37	
Ohioan	6,078	freighter	6,000 tons manganese ore, wool, licorice root	37	15	22	
Oklahoma	9,298	tanker	103,199 barrels gas, kerosene	72	50	22	
Olga	2,496	freighter	ballast	33	1	32	
Oneida	2,309	steam freighter	ballast	29	6	23	
Onondaga	2,309	freighter	magnesium ore	34	20	14	
Oregon	7,017	tanker	78,000 barrels Navy fuel oil	36	6	30	
Oscilla	6,341	motor ship	ballast	55	4	51	
Pan Massachusetts	8,202	tanker	104,000 barrels gasoline, kerosene, diesel oil	38	20	18	
Patrick J. Hurley	10,865	tanker	75,000 barrels gas, 60,000 barrels diesel	62	17	45	
Peder Bogen	9,741	tanker	petroleum	43	0	43	
Pedrinhas	3,666	steam freighter	general cargo, cotton, castor beans	48	0	48	
Peiping	6,390	motor ship	9,950 tons general cargo, wool, hides, dyes, tallow	34	3	31	
Pillory	1,507	freighter	ballast	47	25	22	
Potlatch	6,085	freighter	7,500 tons Army supplies, trucks, tanks, tires	55	9	47	47
Potrero del Llano	4,000	tanker	6,132 tons petroleum	35	14	22	
Putney Hill	5,216	motor freighter	ballast	38	3	35	
Rapana	8,017	tanker	petroleum	35	0	35	
Raphael Semmes	6,027	freighter	7,500 tons manganese ore, tobacco, licorice, wool, rugs	37	19	18	
Republic	5,287	tanker	water ballast	29	5	24	

Ship	Tonnage	Type	Cargo				
Ruch	4,833	bulker	5,000 tons manganese ore	38	34	4	
Sam Houston	7,176	steam / Liberty	10,000 tons army supplies	46	8	38	
Sama	567	motor merchant	bananas	14	0	14	
San Jacinto	6,069	steam passenger ship	3,200 tons cargo, 104 passengers, 32 women/children	183	14	169	
Santa Catalina	6,507	C-2 class steam merchant	6,700 tons tanks, steel, tires, gasoline, small arms	95	0	95	
Santiago de Cuba	1,685	steam freighter	general cargo	29	10	19	
Sea Thrush	5,447	steam freighter	6,800 tons war material, ammunition, aircraft	66	0	66	
Skane	4,258	freight steamer, passengers	freight, passengers	36	0	36	
Standella	6,197	tanker	oil, spirits	58	6	52	
Stangarth	5,966	steam freighter	government stores, general cargo	46	0	46	
Texan	7,005	freighter	10,915 tons general cargo	47	9	38	
Thomas McKean	7,191	steam ship	9,000 tons tanks, aircraft, food	60	5	55	
Tonsbergsfjord	3,156	motor ship	tea, rubber	33	1	32	
Tredinnick	4,589	steam freighter	military stores	30	30	0	
Triton	2,078	steam freighter	3,100 tons bauxite, 60 tons timber	30	6	30	
Tysa	5,327	motor ship	general cargo	43	0	43	
Umtata	8,141	freighter	2,000 tons mineral ore	92	0	92	
Vineland	5,587	steam freighter	ballast	35	1	34	34
Virginia Sinclair	6,151	steam freighter	66,211 barrels aviation gasoline	44	7	37	
Vivian P. Smith	130	schooner (two masted)	260 tons salt, live donkeys	11	0	11	
W. D. Anderson	10,227	tanker	133,360 barrels crude oil	36	35	1	11

Western Head	2,599	steam freighter	3,710 tons sugar	30	24	6
William Cullen Bryant	7,176	steam / Liberty	10,962 tons raw sugar	54	0	54
Willimantic	4,857	steam ship	ballast	38	6	32
Yorkmoor	4,457	freighter	6,700 tons bauxite	46	0	46
TOTAL TONNAGE: 690,928			**TOTAL PERSONS ON BOARD:**	5,844	1,238	4,613 321

#	Type	Sub. #	Entered	Days	Rank	Sub. Commander Name	Age	Died/Status	Flotilla	Departed	Returned / Sunk	Sub. Commander Decorations	# Sank	Tonnag
1	IXB	123	1/23/42	1	Korvettenkapitän	Reinhard Hardegen	28	Alive	2nd	Lorient	Lorient	Knights Cross w/ Oak Leaves,	21	112,447
2	IXC	156	2/4/42	14	Korvettenkapitän	Werner Hartenstein	33	3/8/1943	2nd	Lorient	Lorient	Knights Cross	20	97,504
3	IXC	67	2/10/42	3	Kapitänleutnant	Günther Müller-Stockheim	27	7/16/1943	2nd	Lorient	Lorient	Knights Cross	13	17,138
4	IXC	129	2/11/42	4	Korvettenkapitän	Asmus Nicolai "Nico" Clausen	30	5/16/1943	2nd	Lorient	Lorient	Knights Cross	24	74,807
5	IXC	128	2/14/42	24	Kapitänleutnant	Ulrich Heyse	35	11/19/1970	2nd	Lorient	Lorient	Knights Cross	12	83,639
6	IXC	504	2/14/42	32	Korvettenkapitän	Hans-Georg Friedrich "Fritz" Poske	37	10/1/1944	2nd	Lorient	Lorient	Knights Cross	15	78,123
7	IXC	126	2/28/42	18	Kapitänleutnant	Ernst Bauer	28	3/12/1988	2nd	Lorient	Lorient	Knights Cross	24	111,564
8	CaM	Finzi	3/2/42	11	Capitano di Fregata	Ugo Giudice	N/A	Not known	Betasom	Bordeaux	Bordeaux	Iron Cross	3	21,496
9	CaM	Tazzoli	3/6/42	13	Capitano di Corvetta	Carlo Fecia di Cossato	33	8/27/1944	Betasom	Bordeaux	Bordeaux	Iron Cross	16	86,535
10	IXC	161	3/15/42	8	Kapitänleutnant	Albrecht Achilles	28	9/27/1943	2nd	Lorient	Lorient	Iron Cross	12	60,107
11	Marcello	Morosini	3/15/42	16	Capitano di Corvetta	Athos Fraternale	33	7/30/1963	Betasom	Bordeaux	Bordeaux	Silver Medal of Military valor "Sul Campo"	5	35,600
12	IXB	124	3/20/42	1	Kapitänleutnant	Johann Mohr	25	4/2/1943	2nd	Lorient	Lorient	Knights Cross w/ Oak Leaves	27	129,976
13	CaM	CaM	3/25/42	3	Capitano di Corvetta	Emilio Oliveri	N/A	Not known	Betasom	Bordeaux	Sunk - Biscay	Iron Cross	1	5,162
14	IXC	154	4/3/42	13	Fregattenkapitän	Walther Kölle	34	1/10/1992	2nd	Lorient	Lorient	Iron Cross	7	31,352
15	IXB	123	4/5/42	10	Korvettenkapitän	Reinhard Hardegen	29	Alive	2nd	Lorient	Lorient	Knights Cross w/ Oak Leaves,	21	112,447
16	IXC	130	4/14/42	16	Korvettenkapitän	Ernst Kals	36	11/2/1979	2nd	Lorient	Lorient	U-Boat War Badge w/ Diamonds	17	111,249
17	VIIC	201	4/21/42	3	Kapitänleutnant	Adalbert Schnee	28	11/4/1982	1st	Brest	Brest	Knights Cross w/ Oak Leaves	21	90,189
18	VIIC	654	4/24/42	5	Oberleutnant zur See	Ludwig Forster	26	8/22/1942	1st	Brest	Brest	Iron Cross 2nd Class	3	17,755
19	VIIC	402	4/25/42	4	Korvettenkapitän	Siegfried von Forstner	31	10/13/1943	3rd	St. Nazaire	St. Nazaire	Knights Cross	15	71,036
20	IXB	109	4/26/42	18	Kapitänleutnant	Heinrich Bleichrodt	32	1/9/1977	2nd	Lorient	Lorient	Knights Cross	24	151,260
21	IXC	125	4/26/42	13	Kapitänleutnant	Ulrich Folkers	27	5/6/1943	2nd	Lorient	Lorient	Knights Cross	17	82,873
22	IXC	507	4/26/42	14	Kapitänleutnant	Harro Schacht	34	1/13/1943	2nd	Lorient	Lorient	Knights Cross	19	77,143
23	IXB	108	4/27/42	22	Korvettenkapitän	Klaus Scholtz	34	5/1/1987	2nd	Lorient	Lorient	Knights Cross w/ Oak Leaves	24	111,546
24	VIIC	98	4/28/42	20	Korvettenkapitän	Herbert Schultze	32	Alive	7th	St. Nazaire	St. Nazaire	Knights Cross w/ Oak Leaves	0	0
25	VIIC	333	4/28/42	13	Kapitänleutnant	Peter Erich "Ali" Cremer	31	7/5/1992	3rd	La Pallice	La Pallice	Knights Cross w/ Wounded Badge in Silver and U-Boat Front Clasp	6	26,873
26	IXC	506	4/28/42	15	Kapitänleutnant	Erich Würdemann	28	7/12/1943	10th	Lorient	Lorient	Knights Cross	14	69,893
27	VIIC	582	4/28/42	1	Korvettenkapitän	Werner Schulte	29	10/5/1942	1st	Brest	Brest	Knights Cross	7	38,872
28	VIIC	564	4/30/42	23	Kapitänleutnant	Reinhard "Teddy" Suhren	26	8/25/1984	1st	Brest	Brest	Knights Cross w/ Oak Leaves & Crossed Swords,	18	95,544
29	VIIC	69	5/3/42	14	Kapitänleutnant	Ulrich Graf	26	2/17/1943	7th	St. Nazaire	St. Nazaire	War Merit Cross 2nd Class w/ Swords	6	16,627
30	VIIC	594	5/5/42	27	Korvettenkapitän	Dietrich Hoffmann	29	Alive	7th	St. Nazaire	St. Nazaire		0	0
31	IXB	103	5/8/42	13	Kapitänleutnant	Werner Winter	30	9/9/1972	2nd	Lorient	Lorient	Knights Cross	15	79,302
32	IXB	106	5/13/42	16	Kapitänleutnant	Hermann Rasch	27	6/10/1974	2nd	Lorient	Lorient	Knights Cross	12	78,553
33	IXC	502	5/13/42	2	Kapitänleutnant	Jürgen von Rosenstiel	29	7/5/1942	2nd	Lorient	Sunk - Biscay	Knights Cross	14	78,843
34	VIIC	751	5/14/42	8	Kapitänleutnant	Gerhard Bigalk	33	7/17/1942	7th	St. Nazaire	St. Nazaire	U-Boat War Badge 1939	5	21,412
35	VIIC	558	5/15/42	10	Kapitänleutnant	Günther Krech	27	6/3/2000	1st	Brest	Brest	Knights Cross	17	93,186
36	VIIC	753	5/15/42	14	Kapitänleutnant	Alfred Manhardt von Mannstein	34	5/13/1943	3rd	La Pallice	La Pallice	Knights Cross	3	23,117
37	IXB	107	5/22/42	13	Kapitänleutnant	Harald Gelhaus	26	12/2/1997	2nd	Lorient	Lorient	Knights Cross U-Boat Front Clasp	19	10,068
38	IXC	504	5/22/42	9	Korvettenkapitän	Hans-Georg Friedrich "Fritz" Poske	37	10/1/1944	2nd	Lorient	Lorient	Knights Cross	15	78,123
39	IXC	158	5/24/42	10	Kapitänleutnant	Erwin Rostin	34	6/30/1942	10th	Lorient	Sunk - Bermuda	Knights Cross and U-Boat War Badge 1939	17	101,321
40	IXC	172	6/2/42	8	Kapitänleutnant	Carl Emmermann	27	3/25/1990	10th	Lorient	Lorient	Knights Cross w/ Swords, U-Boat Merit Cross 2nd Class w/ Swords, U-Boat Front Clasp	26	152,080

#	Type	Sub. #	Entered	Days	Rank	Sub. Commander Name	Age	Died/Status	Flotilla	Departed	Returned / Sunk	Sub. Commander Decorations	# Sank	Tonnage
41	IXC	68	6/3/42	4	Kapitän zur See	Karl-Friedrich Merten	26	5/2/1993	2nd	Lorient	Lorient	Knights Cross w/ Oak Leaves,	27	170,151
42	IXC	159	6/3/42	6	Kapitänleutnant	Helmut Witte	27	10/3/2005	10th	Lorient	Lorient	U-Boat War Badge w/ Diamonds	23	119,554
43	IXC	157	6/6/42	8	Korvettenkapitän	Wolf Henne	36	6/13/1942	2nd	Lorient	Sunk - Key West	Knights Cross	1	6,401
44	IXC	129	6/9/42	21	Kapitänleutnant	Hans-Ludwig Witt	27	2/13/1980	2nd	Lorient	Lorient	Knights Cross, U-Boat Front Clasp	19	100,773
45	IXC	67	6/10/42	15	Kapitänleutnant	Gunther Müller-Stöckheim	27	7/16/1943	2nd	Lorient	Lorient	Knights Cross	13	17,138
46	VIIC	584	6/15/42	6	Kapitänleutnant	Joachim Deecke	29	10/31/1943	1st	Brest	Brest	German Cross in Gold	4	18,684
47	CaM	Finzi	6/20/42	38	Capitano di Fregata	Ugo Giudice	N/A	Not known	Betasom	Bordeaux	Bordeaux	Not known	5	29,031
48	IXC	154	6/25/42	8	Fregattenkapitän	Walther Kölle	34	1/10/1992	Betasom	Lorient	Lorient	Not known	7	31,352
49	VIIC	203	6/25/42	8	Kapitänleutnant	Rolf Mützelburg	29	9/11/1942	1st	Lorient	Lorient	Knights Cross w/ Oak Leaves	19	81,961
50	VIIC	332	6/27/42	6	Kapitänleutnant	Johannes Liebe	29	10/18/1982	3rd	La Pallice	La Pallice	Iron Cross First Class	8	46,729
51	IXC	153	6/28/42	8	Fregattenkapitän	Wilfried Reichmann	36	7/3/1942	2nd	Lorient	Sunk - Panama		3	16,186
52	Marcello	Morcello	6/28/42	30	Tenente di Vascello	Francesco D'Alessandro	N/A	Not known	Betasom	Bordeaux	Sunk - Biscay	Not known	1	5,327
53	IXC	505	6/30/42	5	Korvettenkapitän	Axel-Olaf Loewe	33	12/18/1984	2nd	Lorient	Lorient		7	37,832
54	VIIC	571	6/30/42	19	Kapitänleutnant	Helmut Möhlmann	29	4/17/1977	3rd	La Pallice	La Pallice	Knights Cross U-Boat Front Clasp	5	33,511
55	VIIC	575	6/30/42	7	Kapitänleutnant	Günther Heydemann	28	1/2/1986	7th	St Nazaire	St Nazaire	Knights Cross	8	36,010
56	VIIB	84	7/1/42	29	Kapitänleutnant	Horst Uphoff	25	8/7/1943	1st	Brest	Brest	German Cross in Gold	6	29,905
57	VIIC	134	7/1/42	33	Korvettenkapitän	Rudolf Schendel	28	4/12/1970	3rd	La Pallice	La Pallice		3	12,147
58	VIIC	437	7/1/42	13	Korvettenkapitän	Werner-Karl Schulz	31	11/20/1960	6th	St Nazaire	St Nazaire		0	0
59	IXC	166	7/7/42	9	Oberleutnant zur See	Hans-Günther Kuhlmann	28	7/30/1942	10th	Lorient	Sunk - New Orleans		4	7,593
60	IXC	161	7/11/42	8	Kapitänleutnant	Albrecht Achilles	28	9/27/1943	2nd	Lorient	Lorient	Knights Cross	12	60,107
61	IXC	171	7/13/42	15	Kapitänleutnant	Günther Pfeffer	27	4/25/1966	10th	Kiel	Sunk - Biscay	U-Boat War Badge 1939	2	22,304
62	IXC	173	7/16/42	10	Kapitän zur See	Heinz-Ehler Beucke	38	5/23/1979	2nd	Lorient	Lorient		0	0
63	Oceanico	Giuliani	7/16/42	10	Capitano di Fregata	Giovanni Bruno	N/A	Not known	Betasom	Bordeaux	Santander	Not known	3	16,103
64	IXC	509	7/21/42	5	Fregattenkapitän	Karl-Heinz Wolff	32	6/11/1970	10th	Lorient	Lorient		0	0
65	IXC	508	7/26/42	19	Kapitänleutnant	Georg Staats	26	11/12/1943	10th	Kiel	Lorient	Knights Cross	14	74,087
66	VIIC	658	7/29/42	30	Kapitänleutnant	Hans Senkel	32	10/30/1942	6th	Kiel	St Nazaire		3	12,146
67	IXC	510	7/30/42	7	Korvettenkapitän	Karl Neitzel	39	11/13/1966	10th	Lorient	St Nazaire	Knights Cross	3	14,128
68	VIIC	564	8/3/42	6	Kapitänleutnant	Reinhard "Teddy" Suhren	26	8/25/1984	1st	Brest	Brest	Knights Cross w/ Oak Leaves 2nd Class & Crossed Swords. War Merit Cross 2nd Class w/ Swords	18	95,544
69	VIIC	98	8/5/42	7	Korvettenkapitän	Wilhelm Schütze	33	Alive	7th	St Nazaire	St Nazaire		3	
70	VIIC	654	8/6/42	7	Oberleutnant zur See	Ludwig Forster	26	8/22/1942	1st	Lorient	Sunk - Panama	Iron Cross 2nd Class	3	17,755
71	VIIC	598	8/7/42	21	Korvettenkapitän	Gottfried Holtorf	30	7/23/1943	6th	St Nazaire	St Nazaire		2	9,295
72	VIIC	600	8/8/42	17	Kapitänleutnant	Bernard Zurmühlen	33	11/25/1943	10th	Kiel	La Pallice		5	28,600
73	IXC	511	8/11/42	13	Kapitänleutnant	Friedrich Steinhoff	33	5/19/1945	10th	Kiel	Lorient	U-Boat War Badge 1939	2	21,999
74	IXC	164	8/12/42	4	Korvettenkapitän	Otto Fechner	36	1/6/1943	10th	Kiel	St Nazaire	U-Boat War Badge 1939	3	8,133
75	VIIC	553	8/12/42	9	Fregattenkapitän	Karl Thurmann	32	1/20/1943	3rd	St Nazaire	Lorient	Knights Cross	12	61,390
76	VIIC	163	8/13/42	12	Fregattenkapitän	Kurt-Eduard Engelmann	29	3/13/1943	10th	Kiel	St Nazaire	U-Boat War Badge 1939	3	15,011
77	VIID	217	8/13/42	4	Kapitänleutnant	Kurt Reichenbach-Künke	25	6/5/1943	9th	Kiel	Brest		3	10,651
78	VIIC	558	8/19/42	7	Kapitänleutnant	Günther Krech	27	6/3/2000	1st	Brest	Brest	Knights Cross	17	93,186
79	VIIC	94	8/22/42	6	Oberleutnant zur See	Otto Ites	24	2/21/1982	7th	St Nazaire	Sunk - Haiti	Knights Cross	15	76,882
80	VIIB	86	8/27/42	6	Kapitänleutnant	Walter Schug	31	11/23/1943	1st	Brest	Brest	Knights Cross	3	9,614

#	Type	Sub. #	Entered	Days	Rank	Sub. Commander Name	Age	Died/Status	Flotilla	Departed	Returned / Sunk	Sub. Commander Decorations	# Sank	Tonnag
81	VIIC	455	9/21/42	5	Korvettenkapitän	Hans-Heinrich Giessler	31	Alive	7th	St Nazaire	St Nazaire	Iron Cross 1st Class	2	13,908
82	IXC	154	11/5/42	3	Fregattenkapitän	Heinrich Schuch	36	1/21/1968	2nd	Lorient	Lorient		6	37,641
83	VIID	214	1/19/43	4	Kapitänleutnant	Günther Reeder	27	Alive	9th	Brest	Brest	German Cross in Gold	3	18,266
84	IXC	68	2/23/43	13	Oberleutnant zur See	Albert Lauzemis	24	4/10/1944	2nd	Lorient	Lorient	German Cross in Gold	5	27,302
85	IXC/40	183	2/24/43	10	Fregattenkapitän	Heinrich Schäfer	36	1/8/1944	2nd	Lorient	Lorient		2	8,582
86	IXC	155	2/27/43	19	Korvettenkapitän	Adolf Cornelius Piening	32	5/15/1984	10th	Lorient	Lorient	Knights Cross	25	126,664
87	IXC/40	185	3/3/43	18	Kapitänleutnant	August Maus	28	9/28/1996	10th	Lorient	Lorient	Knights Cross	9	62,761
88	IXC	129	4/16/43	15	Kapitänleutnant	Hans-Ludwig Witt	33	2/13/1980	2nd	Lorient	Lorient	Knights Cross, U-Boat Front Clasp	19	100,773
89	IXC	176	4/29/43	17	Korvettenkapitän	Rainer Dierksen	35	5/14/1943	10th	Lorient	Sunk - Cuba	German Cross in Gold	11	53,307
90	IXC	66	5/27/43	60	Kapitänleutnant	Friedrich Markworth	28	Alive	2nd	Lorient	Lorient	Knights Cross	13	74,067
91	IXC/40	527	5/28/43	16	Kapitänleutnant	Herbert Uhlig	27	10/20/1997	10th	Lorient	Sunk - Azores		1	5,242
92	VIIC	759	6/29/43	7	Kapitänleutnant	Rudolf Friedrich	28	7/15/1943	9th	Brest	Sunk - Haiti		2	12,764
93	IXC	159	7/4/43	3	Oberleutnant zur See	Heinz Beckman	30	7/28/1943	10th	Lorient	Sunk - Haiti	Iron Cross 1st Class	0	0
94	VIIC	732	7/5/43	24	Oberleutnant zur See	Klaus-Peter Carlsen	23	Alive	1st	Lorient	Brest	Iron Cross 1st Class	0	0
95	VIIB	84	7/6/43	15	Kapitänleutnant	Horst Uphoff	26	8/7/1943	1st	Brest	Sunk - Bermuda	German Cross in Gold	6	29,905
96	VIIC	615	7/9/43	2	Kapitänleutnant	Ralph Kapitsky	26	8/7/1943	3rd	La Pallice	Sunk - Caribbean		4	27,231
97	VIIC	134	7/10/43	21	Kapitänleutnant	Hans-Günther Brosin	26	8/24/1943	3rd	La Pallice	Sunk - Biscay	U-Boat War Badge 1939	0	0
98	VIIC	634	7/13/43	19	Oberleutnant zur See	Eberhard Dahlhaus	22	8/30/1943	9th	Brest	Sunk - Azores	Iron Cross 1st Class	1	7,176
99	IXC/40	190	7/19/43	6	Kapitänleutnant	Max Wintermeyer	29	Alive	2nd	Lorient	Lorient	U-Boat War Badge 1939	1	7,015
100	IXB	107	8/18/43	22	Oberleutnant zur See	Volker Simmermacher	24	8/27/1999	2nd	Lorient	Lorient		2	7,324
101	IXC	518	9/16/43	25	Kapitänleutnant	Friedrich-Wilhelm Wissmann	28	Alive	2nd	Lorient	Lorient		8	52,346
102	VIID	214	9/26/43	4	Oberleutnant zur See	Rupprecht Stock	27	Alive	9th	Brest	Lorient		1	200
103	IXC/40	193	11/17/43	19	Fregattenkapitän	Hans Pauckstadt	27	8/14/1984	2nd	La Pallice	El Ferrol		1	10,172
104	IXC	129	11/18/43	27	Oberleutnant zur See	Richard von Harpe	26	3/2/1945	2nd	St Nazaire	Lorient	German Cross in Gold	3	17,362
105	IXC	516	12/25/43	2	Kapitänleutnant	Hans-Rutger Tillesen	29	6/1/1986	10th	Brest	Lorient	German Cross in Gold	7	34,632
106	IXC	518	2/28/44	9	Kapitänleutnant	Friedrich-Wilhelm Wissmann	28	Alive	2nd	Lorient	Lorient		8	52,346
107	IXC	154	2/29/44	11	Oberleutnant zur See	Gerth Gemeiner	25	7/3/1944	2nd	Lorient	Lorient		0	0
108	IXC/40	170	3/17/44	33	Kapitänleutnant	Günther Pfeffer	29	12/25/1966	10th	Lorient	Lorient		4	22,304
109	VIID	218	3/30/44	7	Kapitänleutnant	Richard Becker	33	Alive	9th	Brest	Brest	U-Boat Front Clasp	1	146
110	VIIC	541	4/6/44	30	Kapitänleutnant	Kurt Petersen	25	Alive	10th	Lorient	Lorient	German Cross in Gold	1	2.14
111	IXC/40	539	6/1/44	15	Kapitänleutnant	Hans-Jürgen Lauterbach-Emden	24	Alive	10th	St Nazaire	Flensburg	German Cross in Gold	1	1,517
112	IXC	518	8/28/44	3	Oberleutnant zur See	Hans-Werner Offermann	23	4/22/1945	2nd	Kristiansand	Flensburg	German Cross in Gold	1	3,401

TOTAL DAYS: 1453   **AVERAGE AGE DURING PATROL: 28**   **15 ALIVE**

ILLUSTRATION CREDITS

11 Kelshall, Gaylord, *U-Boot Krieg in der Karibik*, Verlag E.S. Mittler & Sohn, Hamburg, 1999, Archive of Peter Tamn

12 wikipedia.org/wiki/German_Type_VII_submarine

13 Kevin James photograph, with permission of Mr. Pratt

15 home.comcast.net/~srweiss/bahamas05/roadtrip.html

16 uboat.net/men/commanders/163.html

22 Kelshall, Gaylord, *U-Boot Krieg in der Karibik*, Verlag E.S. Mittler & Sohn, Hamburg, 1999, U-Boat Museum, Cuxhaven

24 U-Boat Museum, Cuxhaven, from Kelshall, Gaylord, *U-Boot Krieg in der Karibik*

27 Samuel Eliot Morison, *History of the United States Navy in World War II*

35 William Gordonson, "U-Boat Tactics of World War II"

40 Helgason, Gudmundur, uboat.net

46 Kristian Olav Bringedal, originally from Knutsen OAS of Haugesund

47 Kristian Olav Bringedal, Uskedalposten, Side 18, Krigsseglarane frå Uskedalen, 2011

48 Kristian O. Bringedal, nephew of Capt. Bringedal

49 Rebecca Mason, great-grand daughter of Olaus Johansen, UK

63 Bentsen family members, Larvik, Norway, c/o Sten Kittelsen, Oslo and Larvik

64 marinas.com/view/lighthouse/355_Hole_in_the_Wall_Lighthouse_AB_Bahamas

65 uboat.net/allies/merchants/ships/1692.html

68 Author's collection, courtesy of Orjan Lindroth for diverting his airplane.

68 Rosenfeld Collection, Mystic Seaport Museum, Mystic Connecticut, USA

72 Dr. Harold Munnings, the Centre for Digestive Health, Nassau
75 The Rumelier Collection, therumelier.com
76 Ronald Lightbourn, "Nostalgic Nassau, Picture Postcards 1900-1940"
77 Ronald Lightbourn, c/o Captain Paul Aranha
78 Courtesy of the Masonic Lodge, Nassau, Bahamas.
79 Rebecca Mason, UK, great-grand daughter of Olaus Johansen
79 Author's collection
80 Rebecca Mason, UK, great-grand daughter of Olaus Johansen
82 "The Harbour Island Story," Anne & Jim Lawlor, page 134
87
  seawolfproductions.com/shipwreck%20museum/Florida%20Wrecks/
  pan%20mass/
  Aubrey%20Withee/AubreyWithee.htm
92 guardian.co.uk/culture/2010/nov/13/william-boyd-any-human-heart-
  murder
93   e-reading-lib.org/bookreader.php/1007828/Sebba_-
  _That_Woman.html
94 yachtserenity.com/storyserenity.html
99   piombino-storia.blogspot.com/2010/09/capitano-carlo-fecia-di-
  cossato.html
101 Antonio Maronari, "The Submarine Which Didn't Return"
103 wrecksite.eu/wreck.aspx?194990
105 homeaway.com/vacation-rental/p161215
109 Survivors Statements, National Archives and Record Administration
  (NARA)
111 John Bowen, Model Shipwright, Number 90, December 1994, p. 58
115 Kelshall, Gaylord, U-Boot Krieg in der Karibik, VerlagsArchiv,
  Hamburg, 1999
117 Linda Ryan, daughter of Henry Mapplebeck, Third Officer of
  Daytonian 1941-1942
124 Linda Ryan, daughter of Henry Mapplebeck, Third Officer of
  Daytonian 1941-1942
125 Linda Ryan, daughter of Henry Mapplebeck, Third Officer of
  Daytonian 1941-1942
127 Linda Ryan, Mapplebeck's daughter, taken by his great-
  granddaughter Alexandra

129
  freepages.family.rootsweb.ancestry.com/~treevecwll/athelqueen.htm
131 Courtesy of Alan B. Heald.
136 SuperSkyline89, flickr.com/photos/28583390@N07/4691821775/
139
  freepages.family.rootsweb.ancestry.com/~treevecwll/athelqueen2.ht
  m
141 piombino-storia.blogspot.com/2010/09/capitano-carlo-fecia-di-cossato.html
146 Gale, David, *Below Another Sky, A Bahama Memoir*, 2011, author
  interview with Vernon Malone
147 Earl McMillen, McMillen Yachts, woodenyachts.com
148 Courtesy of Captain Paul Aranha, from various sources.
151 Wyannie Malone Historical Museum, Hope Town.
156 Siri Holm Lawson, warsailors.com/singleships/kollskegg, Bjørn
  Pedersen's collection
160 "Survivors Meet Royalty – Survivors of Sunken Ships Keep Duchess
  Busy," dated 23 April 1942, by the *San Antonio Express-News*, Texas
163 Chris Voorhees, Riverton Utah, USA, BuyandSellWWII.com
166 Radall, Thomas H., *The Mersey Story*, Liverpool, Nova Scotia
  Canada, 1979
167 Edna Greenwood, daughter of Capt. Ralph Williams
169 Erlin Conrad c/o Rev. Karen Ohrt, daughter.
172 Dr. Edward Harris, Bermuda Maritime Museum, and Georgia Dunn
  Belk,   descendant   of   the   Harriotts,
  royalgazette.com/apps/pbcs.dll/article?AID=/20130323/ISLAND09/
  703239983 &template=printart
174 Sherlin Williams, Turks and Caicos historian
175 Erling Conrad's papers, c/o his daughter Rev. Karen Ohrt
176 Erlin Conrad c/o Rev. Karen Ohrt, daughter.
179 Kelshall, Gaylord, *U-Boot Krieg in der Karibik*, U-Boat Museum,
  Cuxhaven
184 National Archives and Records Administration (NARA) College
  Park, Maryland.
185 National Archives and Records Administration (NARA) College
  Park, Maryland.
187 wrecksite.eu/imgBrowser.aspx?3883

189 Helgason, Gudmundur, uboat.net/men/krech.htm
192 Sherlin Williams, Turks and Caicos historian.
194 Sherlin Williams, Turks and Caicos historian.
198 National Archives and Records Administration (NARA) College Park, Maryland.
203   mille-sabords.com/forum/index.php?showtopic=40300&pid=356130&st=175&#entry356130   and   u-historia.com/uhistoria/historia/huboots/u100-u199/u0153/u153.htm
206 mille-sabords.com/forum/index.php?showtopic=40300&st=175
209 Steamship Historical Society of America archives, sshsa.org
210 Liberty Magazine 1943
211 Jake Jatho
212 National Archives and Records Administration (NARA) College Park, Maryland.
215 *San Francisco Examiner*, July 1943
216 *Liberty Magazine*, June 19, 1943, page 22
218 Kelshall, Gaylord, *U-Boot Krieg im der Karibik*, VerlagsArchiv,
219 *Liberty Magazine*, June 19, 1943, page 22
222 *Liberty Magazine*, June 19, 1943, page 22
223 *Liberty Magazine*, June 19, 1943, page 22
231 Knoblock, Glenn A., *African American World War II Casualties and Decorations in the Navy, Coast Guard and Merchant Marine: A Comprehensive Record*, McFarland, 2009
233 Mari Anderson and Fritz Damler
234 Mari Anderson and Fritz Damler
235 Mari Anderson and Fritz Damler
236 Mari Anderson and Fritz Damler
239 Courtesy of Capt. Paul and Kim Aranha.
241 Courtesy of Capt. Paul and Kim Aranha.
242 Courtesy of Capt. Paul and Kim Aranha, from the United States Library of Congress.
243 Courtesy of Capt. Paul and Kim Aranha.
244 Hugo Vickers, *Behind Closed Doors*, from the Associated Press.
245 *Aiken Standard*, South Carolina, August 19, 1942
246 Jake Jatho
247 kpbs.org/photos/galleries/extraordinary-women-wallis-simpson/

248 Courtesy of Capt. Paul Aranha
251 oldbahamas.com/id11.html
253 Becky Jatho, daughter of Jake Jatho
254 National Maritime Union *Pilot*, August 1942
266 Courtesy of Will Johnson, Bridgetown Barbados
269 Helgason, Gudmundur, uboat.net/men/commanders/1410.html
277 National Archives and Record Administration (NARA), College Park, Maryland.
281 National Archives and Record Administration (NARA), College Park, Maryland.
291 National Archives and Record Administration (NARA), College Park, Maryland.
321 Author's collection
362 Sara Signorelli

CHART INDEX

All original maps by Robert Eller Pratt

CHAPTER NOTES

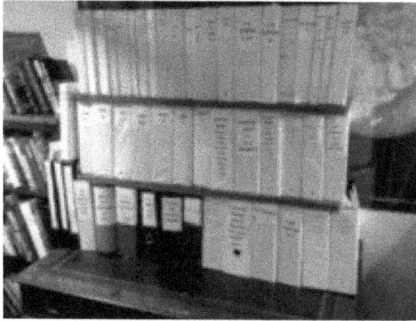

Fifty three-ring binders of research, 2009-2015.

In order to identify every ship sunk in the greater Bahamas area, a number of resources have been combed, page by page. This includes the *Eastern Sea Frontier's Enemy Action Diary* onwww.uboatarchive.net, *Axis Submarine Success of World War Two* by Jürgen Rohwer, Samuel Eliot Morison's *History of United States Naval Operations in World War II*, and *U-Boat Operations of the Second World War*, by Wynn. Rohwer's *Chronology of the War at Sea* was also covered, as was Clay Blair's two-volume history, *Hitler's U-Boat War*. The series *Nortaships Flate*, or Norwegian Ship Fleet, was consulted, as were Captain Arthur Moore's *A Careless Word, a Needless Sinking*. One of the most useful resources was Roger W. Jordan's *The World's Merchant Fleets, 1939*, which provides thumbnail sketches of each of the casualties. It is possible vessels which were attacked in the Bahamas area have been missed in this research, in which case either the ship was not destroyed, or it was mistakenly attributed to another region. It is hoped that this research will lead to revelations of new incidents.

Without the first-hand accounts of each loss, called Survivors Statements, such a book could not be written credibly. Since I relied heavily on them for most ship chapters, and often for the details in the bridge chapters about Allied losses, it will suffice to list the exact citation here, and hereinafter refer to them simply as Survivors Statements. After many years of searching in person and on line and via correspondence, it was Michael J. Contandy of Westmoreland Research (westmorealandresearch.org) who finally found them. The citation is as follows:

Survivor's Statements (1941-1942) Series: Papers of Vice Admiral Homer N. Wallin, compiled 1941 - 1974. Record Group 38: Records of the Office of the Chief of Naval Operations, 1875 - 2006 Entry P-13. National Archives at College Park - Textual Reference (Military) 8601 Adelphi Road, College Park, MD, USA 20740.

PREFACE, U-732, CARL-PETER CARLSEN AND ANCIL PRATT

Kevin James of Nassau and Long Island introduced me to Ancil Pratt. I interviewed Mr. Pratt via phone in June 2013. Kevin James then took and sent the photos. The KTB of U-732 was sent by Jerry Mason or Uboararchive.net. He also sent a site which converts German graph positions into estimated Lat/Long coordinates. The translation from German to English was done by Mason and Prof. Stephen Aranha.

SUMMARY OF AXIS ACTIVITY

Gudmundur Helgason, Rainer Kolbicz, www.uboat.net, 2011, Kenneth Wynn, *U-boat Operations of the Second World War*, Clay Blair, *Hitler's U-boat War*, Franz Kurowski, *Knight's Cross Holders of the U-Boat Service*, Axel Niestlé, *German U-Boat Losses*, Kenneth Wynn, *U-Boat Operations of the Second World War*, Rainer Busch and Hans-Joachim Röll, *German U-Boat Commanders of World War II*.
JANUARY 21 TO MARCH 5, 1942 – same as for "Summary of Axis Activity" at top.

ULRICH HEYSE AND U-128

The primary sources for this chapter were the ONI interrogation report of U-128 survivors from 1943, "Op-16-Z, O.N.I. 250 – G/Serial 13, Report on the Interrogation of Survivors from U-128 Sunk on May 17, 1943," dated 9 July, 1943, published by the Navy Department, Office of the Chief of Naval Operations, Washington. Thanks also to input from Peter Monte at the UBoat Museum in Cuxhaven, and Uboat.net.

The details of the sub, its armament, history, crew, and Heyse were mostly drawn from the ONI report, which was quoted where appropriate. Map and description of the attack on the *O. A. Knudsen* and KTB of the attack on U-128 by Allied aircraft supplied by Mason. The forum at Mille-Sabords.com provided several images of Ulrich Heyse and U-128.

O. A. KNUDSEN

Too many sources were referenced over nearly five years to cover every individual article and contact for this chapter. I travelled to Abaco three times looking for Johansen's grave and interviewed a number of locals in Sandy Point, Marsh Harbour, and Crossing Rocks, many of them informally. Most of the biographical information on Knut O. Bringedal was supplied by his relative Kristian O. Bringedal, whom I contacted through Linkedin.com.

Most of the information on *O. A Knudsen* and the history of the ship and crew came from Dame Siri Holm Lawson of warsailors.com and the books she cited, which I purchased. Also the National Archives of Norway (Rasmus Austad Christensen and Anne B. Hagstrom), were extremely helpful and generous with information both on Bringedal and Johansen. Oivind Lauritzen III introduced me to his father, whose father was a leader of the Norwegian Shipping and Trade Mission (Nortraship) in New York during the war.

A list of some of the many articles turned up in the Bahamas National Archives, The National Archives at Kew, London, and the National Archives and Records Administration (NARA) outside Washington as well as sites such as newspaperarchives.com include the following: the main source of information was ONI "Survivor Statements" and crew lists. Sjohistorie.no for an article on the *O. A. Knudsen*, the publication "Nortrashipsflatens Skyttere 1941-1946," for an entry on Waldemar Lund and the Knudsen, my friend Sten Kittelsen for photos of and information on Leif Bentsen. Information on *Nueva Andalucia* was from Warsailors.com, the Eastern Sea Frontier (ESF) Enemy Action Reports, which is from Uboatarchive.net (Capt. Jerry Mason) as well as fold3.com.

Petter Syse graciously gave of his time to find the (empty) grave of Olaus Johansen in Norway. For photos and backstory to Johansen provided by Kari Elisabeth Myhre and Rebecca Mason, Johansen's great-granddaughter, as did her aunt, Doreen Johansen, his granddaughter. Wrecksite.eu had some information and images of the Knudsen company flags and funnel markings. Shipindex.org cited three articles on the ship. Jane Haase of the Liverpool UK Echo put a free ad in the paper which turned up Johansen's granddaughter. The John H. Marsh Maritime Research Center had a photo of the Knudsen. James Allen Knechtmann at the Washington Navy Yard Navy Department Library was most helpful.

Ms. L. Delaney of the Bahamas National Archives turned up the death certificate of Johansen in Nassau, sent from Abaco in 1942. Mike Constandy located hard-to-find documents at the State Department Archives relating to the repatriation of *Knudsen* survivors from Nassau to Miami. Jim Lawlor's article "History of Trinity Methodist Church Nassau" was helpful in determining leadership in the church in 1942, as was Rev. Carl Campbell. Alan Murray and Michele Robinson of St. Andrews School were highly encouraging.

Articles included "4 More Vessels Sunk in Atlantic," *New York Times*, 13 March 1942, "Sailors United Nations Defy Axis U-boats," Cumberland Maryland *Evening Times*, "38 Rescued as Vessel Sinks," Port Arthur (Texas) *News*, "Windsors Greet Sub Survivors at Nassau," Charleston (South Carolina) *Gazette*, Fri. 13 March 1942, "Sea Captain Visits Here," Rowland (Iowa), 13 April 1943, "How to Abandon Ship," Chapter 3, Hypwerwar, ibiblio.org/ hyperwar, Tor Christian Bringedal, email to author April 2013, introduced me to Kristian O. Bringedal, a font of information on the captain., "Krigsselarane fra Uskedalen," by Kristian Olav Bringedal, *Uskedalposten*, Easter 2011, page 18 –, and "Axis Subs Sink Four More Ships."

On Abaco David Ralph, David Bethel, Debbie Patterson, Lucille Bethel, and Vernon Malone, Jeanie Russell, Orjan Lindroth, Dale Hill, Floyd Lowe, Larry Smith, Ray Brown, Sherwin Archer's daughter were all very helpful. Haziel Albury's *Man-O-War, My Island Home*, and Ruth Rodriguez's *Out Island Portraits* were helpful regarding the *Content S.* and *Arena*, as was *Islanders in the Stream* by Saunders and Craton. I spoke with Dan Thompson regarding lumber camps in 2011. Paul Bethel told me about his father salvaging the lifeboat re-named *Beluga*. The website Abaconian.com has a good timeline of history of the island with geographic locations of saw mills. David Knowles, Chief Park Warden of Abaco National Parks and his team were helpful.

I spoke with J. W. Roberts' son in Grand Bahama. Historian Darius Williams taught me a lot about Cornwall and the railways of Abaco. Lennard Rambusch, a New York attorney shared the 16 April 1940 message from the Norwegian government in exile appointing Haight Griffin and Gardner to organize Norwegian shipping in the Americas. Captain Andrew D. Melick, a historian of the Port of Miami told me about Captain Henry Warren. John O. Mozolak's "New York Ships to Foreign Ports" was helpful in tracking the *Knudsen's* movements.

DUCHESS OF WINDSOR

The primary texts for the Duchess of Windsor were published articles and books, but also two unpublished manuscripts which I was able to unearth dealing with her years in the Bahamas. Bloch, Michael, "The Duke of Windsor's War," Weidenfeld & Nicolson, London, UK, 1982 which is the ultimate resource for all things Windsor during their stay in the Bahamas. It is a virtual play-by-play of their daily activities, backed by personal diaries, letters, official correspondence and their social and travel calendars. An indispensable resource. This lead to the Duchess' personal memoir, "The Heart Has its Reasons," David McKay, Inc., 1956, however on the topic of U-boat victims landed in Bahamas Bloch had already covered the issue well.

Hugo Vickers' "Behind Closed Doors: The Tragic, Untold Story of the Duchess of Windsor," Hutchinson, London, UK, 2011 does not cover the Bahamas extensively, but is a good study of the Windsors. Mr. Vickers kindly corresponded with me on matters of mutual interest, and published an extraordinary article retracing the Windsor's imprint on the Bahamas entitled "Banished to the Bahamas: Holidaying in the lap of luxury on Edward and Mrs Simpson' island of love," in the *Daily Mail* of London, 2 February, 2012. Based less on original materials is "The Royal Governor.....and The Duchess: The Duke and Duchess of Windsor in The Bahamas 1940-1945," by Owen Platt (iUniverse, 2003) which brings considerably less new material to the table.

The first unpublished memoir I found is the typescript of "The Windsors I Knew, An American Private Secretary's Personal Account,

Nassau, Bahamas, 1940 – 1943," by Jean D. (nee Drewes) Harcastle-Taylor, written in the 1950s and graciously shared (in relevant part) by her son, Michael and his wife Gloria Hardcastle-Taylor of San Diego, California. The produced "There were numerous sinkings and the surviving crews of allied merchant ships, under the able and personal direction of the Duchess, were lodged in a Bay Street hostelry, cared for, and given adequate food and clothing by the British Red Cross Society." There is an article with photo about Miss Drewes' appointment to become the social secretary to the Duchess in the *Gettysburg Times*, 3 December, 1940, page 2. Another article announcing her wedding to RAF officer Brian W. Hardcastle-Taylor was published in *The Herald Statesman*, Yonkers, NY 31 December 1943.

        The second unpublished manuscript about the Duchess is from the "The Nassau Years, 1940-45"of an unpublished book by Maxine Sandberg in 1965 entitled "Wallis Warfield Biography, 1942-1985" from the Maryland Historical Society, Damon Talbot, Special Collections Archivist. The document is located in the Special Collections Reading Room, Call # MS 2901 and Item # Q200060329, "Gift of Maxine Sandberg on March 12, 1985." The website is mdhs.org. Of particular relevance were Sandberg's interviews in 1965 with Alice Hill Jones, E. Bryn Jones, P. M. Lightbourn, Lady Solomon, F. A. Wanklyn, and Sam Whyms. A sample from Lady Solomon's interview reads "Both the Duchess and the Duke came down to see the men [from *O. A. Knudsen*], and received a rousing cheer. Again Lady Solomon remarked that she had always found the Duchess extremely helpful and enthusiastic about helping with the war effort and did everything she could."

        Mark Gaulding, head of the Duke & Duchess of Windsor Historical Society in San Diego at the time, very kindly shared a number of highly illustrated and informative articles from their quarterly, *Duke & Duchess of Windsor Historical Society Quarterly*, Mark Gaulding (Publisher, Palm Desert, CA) particularly Issue 4 – 2009, Issue 1- 2010, and Issue 2 – 2010. These include a three-part serialization of Jean D. Hardcastle-Taylor's memoir entitled "The Windsors I Knew" prepared by her son Michael Hardcastle-Taylor, who also presented to the DDWHS on the topic of "Getting to Know WE," in October, 2009.

        I was able to find frustratingly little about the Duke & Duchess' tenure in Nassau during WWII in the British archives at The National

Archives Kew, or the collections of Churchill papers at Cambridge University, or at the Royal Archive at Windsor, mostly because of the widely held belief that royal minions "scrubbed" the records of anything that could be compromising to the Duke, the Royal family or the British government at the time. This despite enlisting the expertise of a number of professional readers, or researchers on the ground in the UK who all report the same thing – there is virtually nothing there. I went myself for two days without result, fortunate to have come away with a chart showing the locations and relative strengths of various radio towers around the Bahamas and Caribbean.

Tidbits which were unearthed included a memo from the War Diary dated 4 March 1942 about the risk of the Duke being captured by the crew of a U-boat and the dispatch of "one company of 4th Bn. Cameron H. now at Fort Slocum Long Island New York to Nassau....... (J.S.M. Washington, 1933Q/4 to Govr. Bahamas)." This was not a well-kept secret, as on the 11th of March 1942 the AP was publishing a report entitled "British Send Force to Protect Bahamas, Landing of Detachment at Nassau Believed on Duke's Appeal." Another published report, from 24 April 1942 reads "Duke of Windsor May Ask U.S Aid for Colony," appearing in the Hattiesburg (Miss.) *American*. Two other possible sources of information are "Colonial Office memorandum on security and defense in the Bahamas, relating to protection of the Duke of Windsor." Churchill Archives Center, CHAR 20/63," and "Governor (H.R.H. the Duke of Windsor) to Secretary of State for the Colonies, 6 June, 1942. Colonial Office Records, CO 23.731," however the former does not relate to any actual U-boat raid on Nassau, and the latter deals primarily with the labor/race riots of 1942.

Another, more detailed example found at The National Archives in the UK is entitled "Report by Major E. H. Baume, G. (Ops & Plans), On a Visit to Nassau, New Providence, from 13th to 18th August, 1942." This report is highly disparaging of the local populace, citing their "intense apathy and lethargy." A typical paragraph reads "Although a number of these idle young men have put their names down as volunteers for coast watching, practically none have ever actually done coast watching, and all say they are too busy when asked to take a turn."

Before the submarine attacks on the Bahamas began this typical piece was carried: "Windsor May Be On Yacht Stranded Off Nassau, Bahamas," in the Dunkirk New York *Evening Observer*, April 3, 1941. This follows an article about the Sloan yacht, with the Windsors aboard, getting into trouble off Abaco ("The Windsors' Yacht Runs Aground on Island" is a typical headline of the incident). There is a photo of the Sloan yacht *Rene* in the Pusey & Jones Photograph Collection and another of the interior entitled "Yacht '*Rene*,' owned by Alfred P. Sloane, Jr. Library fireplace" at popartmacine.com. The *Kingston Gleaner* of Jamaica wrote about the Bahamas as a place of "Sunshine and no Income Tax to Pay," April 4, 1938. Another piece in the *Morning Avalanche*, of Lubbock, Texas on August 14, 1942 decries that "Once Liberal Nassau Has Stricter Rules," banning swim wear from downtown.

On September 23, 1941 the AP wrote about "Flying Start – Windsors Reach Miami on Start of Journey in U.S. and Canada," in the Winnipeg, Canada *Free Press*, September 23, 1941 – this underscores what a fortunate twist of fate it was that despite their heavy social and business travel schedule, the Duke and Duchess were able to welcome and interact with all of the survivors of ships sunk in the area that landed in Nassau. Given the Windsor's peripatetic travels, these encounters could easily have been missed.

Since the Windsor's yacht *Gemini* is allegedly still afloat, there are numerous articles about it, one of them in the *Lebanon Daily News*, September 4, 1976 entitled "Restoration of Old Boats Growing Hobby," by Lillian O'Connell, UPI Life-Style Editor about David Fuller, they yacht's owner, from Cleveland Ohio. Another article identifying "restaurant chain executive Vernon B. Stouffer" as the owner is entitled "Steering Cable Breaks – Yacht Continues Trip After Repairs in the City," published in Lorain, between Detroit and Cleveland (date unknown). The *Palm Beach Daily News* of August 26, 1984 features an article and photo of *Gemini* under "Way to Cruise," by Wendy Keeler. By that time Chuck Spinella owned her. The best resource on this yacht is the "Story of *Serenity*" at yachtserenity.com/storyserenity.html, which is a sister ship to the *Gemini*.

There are numerous articles written about the Duchess of Windsor during WWII, fewer though providing new intelligence about her life in the Bahamas. One article published in the *Oakland Tribune* in California on 24 April 1942 is entitled "Duchess Endears Herself to Bahamians." Another is the *Lethbridge Alberta Herald* of Canada, appearing 23 April 1942 under the title 'Duchess of Windsor is Busy and Popular in Bahama Capital." Another from Burlington, North Carolina on April 23 1942 declares "Duchess of Windsor Proves Active in Life in the Bahamas," by Fred L. Strozier in the *Daily Times-News*. It reads in part "during three weeks of March, 17 survivors [more like 170] from four allied vessels reached Nassau. Under the personal direction of the duchess each seaman was provided with clothing, food and shelter and with such essentials a shaving kits, all of which they had lost before reaching shore. The duke and duchess were on the dock to greet each group and talked with them at great length."

A photo of the Duke and Duchess, he wearing Scottish kilt and she in Red Cross garb, appears in the April 15, 1942 edition of the local paper in Mirror Lake, Kalispell, Montana. The AP on 23 April 1942 put out a story entitled "Duchess of Windsor Active Welfare Worker." More relevant is an article from 16 June, 1943 entitled "Duke to Look After Seamen," when in fact they had already been doing so for over a year. The short article states that "....the Duke and Duchess of Windsor had agreed to look after the interests of American seamen in hospital at Nassau... the Duchess will visit the men in hospital and offer to relay messages to their homes."

MARCH 6 TO 10, 1942 – same as for "Summary of Axis Activity" at top.

CARLO FECIA DI COSSATO AND R.SMG. *ENRICO TAZZOLI*

Cristiano D'Adamo, www.regiamarina.net, Sir Holm Lawson, www.warsailors.com, Platon Alexiades, "Un Sommergibile non e Rientrato Alla Base," or "the submarine which did not return to base," published by SB Saggi, Milan, in 1999 – it is a first-hand memoir of crewman Antonio Maronari, in Italian. Translation provided by Google translate as well as historian Platon Alexiades of Montreal. Mr. Alexiades very generously shared the actual War Diary of the *Enrico Tazzoli*, as well as translations, and advice on utilizing them CYGNET

The Survivor Statements and crew list are from NARA in DC. Mike Constandy also discovered detailed US Immigration telegrams from US Consul John Dye to the State Department regarding repatriation (First Officer Antonios Falangas essentially emigrated to the US on 21 March, moving to Massachusetts, where his family remains). Extensive details of the wartime and postwar movement of Capt. Mamais, Falangas, Third Officer William Forest Dods, Demetreos Vlachakis, and John (Yoannis, or Johny) Aiginitis (Eginitis) appear in ancestry.com. There is a useful board discussion there called "Falangas Family."

The interview of Mrs. Ypapanti Alexiou in Nassau was kindly done by local historian Pericles Maillis on 30 March 2011. Dr. Thomas A. Rothfus, Executive Director of the Gerace Research Station on San Salvador interviewed the (unnamed) local man who was witness to *Cygnet* survivors as a child. The background about the one-legged American comes from Survivor Statements and was corroborated by Dr. Rothfus' witness. Details of Thomas Williams who "lost a foot in a boating accident and died about the same time that the U.S. military came to the use the island as a missile-tracking base in the 50's." appears at islands.thebahamian.com/ sansalvador.html.

The primary resource for di Cossato's patrol in *Enrico Tazzoli* was "Un Sommergibile non e Rientrato Alla Base," by Maronari, in Italian. Translation provided by Google Translate as well as historian Platon Alexiades. Mr. Alexiades shared the actual War Diary of the *Enrico Tazzoli*, as well as translations, and advice on utilizing them for the *Cygnet*, *Daytonian* and *Athelqueen* casualties. The Greek Consul to the Bahamas, Gus Constantakis was very helpful in looking through old records for me. He believed the nurse in the foreground and side of the photo of *Potlatch* survivors was a Mrs. Tiliacos.

There were two articles in the local Nassau papers about the *Cygnet*: "Thanks So Very Much," a letter from Captain Mamais, in the "Nassau Tribune," March 14, 1942 (page 1, lower right), and "Men from Torpedoed Freighter Land at Nassau," also Nassau *Tribune*, March 15, 1942. An article in the Charleston, South Carolina *Daily Mail*, of 21 March 1942 is about the *Cygnet* and reads "U-Boat Blasts Greek Vessel."

I found a brief citation from "Schip en Werf, Mei 1939, RDM collective Johan Journee" giving technical details of the Mirach which became the *Cygnet*. A history of RDM, or Rotterdamsche Droogdok Maatschappij (Rotterdam Drydock Company) is provided at Wikipedia.org. This cites a book named "Schip en Werf," by Piet de Heer, TU Delft as well as wivonet.nl/nicopag2.htm. The history of the *Mirach* in the format standardized by the Dutch government records can be found at marhisdata.nl/printschip.php?id=4325.

Wrecksite.eu also has a detailed page with photos. A lovely photo and technical details of the *Mirach* appears at shipmotiions.nl/RDM/RDM/RDM-061.html. My brother John and his wife Sofia Wiberg provided phone contacts for locals in San Salvador. On Newspaper archive.com I found several articles including "Survivors of Sub Attack are Landed," based on Associated Press wires on March 14, 1942 as well as "Unidentified Freighter is Sunk Near Bahamas," also by the AP. A short blurb in another paper, also from the AP, simply states "Sub Sinks Freighter," and yet another appears under the title "Enemy Subs Cruises Brazenly on Surface, Showing Lights." The *Lima News* of Ohio reported on 15 March 1942 about the *Cygnet* (unnamed) under "Axis U-Boats Renew Raids in U.S. Waters."

The search for details on the SS *Monarch of Nassau* took almost as much work as the *Cygnet*. It started with a legal citation in "Carl Sawyer, Inc. v. Poor Et. Al., the *Monarch of Nassau*, 180 F.2d 962 (5th Cir. 1950)" found on federalcircuits.vlex.com. Kendal Butler, historian, provided details of some of the Bahamian officers and crew. *Monarch of Nassau* appears in Fold3.com on March 20, 1944 being escorted with the Richard Campbell from Miami to Nassau and on 9 February 1945 going from Port au Prince to Miami. A plan for the ship under its original name *Sir Charles Orr* was featured on the site modelboatmayhem.co.uk – on the forums, October 2010. From that lead I was able to order, from the UK, Model Shipwright Magazine, December 1994 issue. This was the Holy Grail as it had an image of the vessel in the builder's dock as well as detailed specifications for modelers to work from, down to the gig, or boat.

The Jamaican *Kingston Gleaner* of June 13, 1941 has an article on Rear Admiral John Scaife, OBE, entitled "Naval Intelligence Officer Known Here Raised to Flag Rank." A list of Governors of the Bahamas at Wikipedia provides details of the tenure of Sir Charles William James Orr. Vesselindex.com provides the official number, as does crewlist.org.uk. The Singapore *Straits Times* of 2 October 1930 offers in "An Epic of the Atlantic – Crossed in 19 Days by a 90-ton Model Vessel," an account of Captain E. R. Westmore's crossing to the Bahamas. The *Joplin Globe* of Missouri on 14 April 1940 tells of pilgrims being plucked from Inagua by the *Monarch of Nassau* after a failed settlement bid from California ("Group Disillusioned by Life on Island").

There were numerous references to the *Sir Charles Orr* and *Monarch of Nassau* in the shipping news columns of Miami newspapers, all found on newspaperarchive.com. An August 13, 194 example is entitled "New Boat Sails on its Maiden Trip Late Today." Rusty Bethel of Cherokee Sound wrote a memoir kindly shared by his daughter in which he cites early training on the *Monarch of Nassau* between Nassau and Miami as Radio Operator. (He later went on to help found ZNS, the national radio and TV station, in 1944 – information provided by Capt. Paul Aranha). Finally, a Texas newspaper featured an ad for the sale of the *Monarch of Nassau* by name in the 1950s, listing Carl Sawyer Steamship Agency in Miami as the seller.

MARCH 11 TO 15, 1942 – same as for "Summary of Axis Activity" at top.

DAYTONIAN

Researching the *Daytonian* casualty posed a challenge at first because it was sunk by an Italians submarine, not a German, and thus did not appear on Uboat.net and similar sites. This was made up for by the highly detailed site regiamarina.net run by Cristiano d'Adamo. One early source was the Tower Hill Memorial in London, accessed via findagrave.com and lost-at-sea-memorials.com, also the Commonwealth War Graves Commission, cwgc.org/find-a-cemetery. Platon Alexiades shared the actual War Diary of the *Enrico Tazzoli*, as well as translations.

The Survivors Statements could not be found at The National Archives at Kew, London, but were located by Contstandy/Westmoreland. This includes telegrams about the *Daytonian* and illustrations as well as crew lists. At NARA I was assisted by Mr. Nenninger, Chief, Textual Records Reference Staff in June, 2011. The primary resource for di Cossato's patrol in *Enrico Tazzoli* was "*Un*

Sommergibile non e Rientrato Alla Base," or "the submarine which did not return to base," published by SB Saggi, Milan, in 1999 – it is a first-hand memoir of crewman Antonio Maronari, in Italian. Translation provided by Google Translate as well as Mr. Alexiades.

Historian Dr. Billy McGee was helpful in trying to find the Survivors Statements. Anthony "Herb" Cox posted a message about his having been sunk aboard other ships (*British Councillor, Carsbreck North* on June 19, 2005 on a forum at warsailors.com entitled "Attack on Unknown Norwegian Ship." The clydesite.co.uk/clydebuilt/ships/1922/DAYTONIAN webpage has a very detailed entry with illustrations under the column "Shipping Times".

The French website lemairesoft.sytes.net:1944 has a detailed history of the *Daytonian's* convoy activities in WWII under "LemaireSoft, *Daytonian.*" Uboat.net has a good site about the *Rotterdam*, which rescued survivors, and its demise. The website oldbahamas.com has photos of historic hotels where the survivors stayed (oldbahamas.com/ id12.html). Michael Constandy dug up the immigration documents for the *Daytonian* crew which provides specifics of their movements, particularly vessels involved and the crew who stayed behind in hospital. These documents were found in the State Department Archives and most are to or from US Consul John Dye.

Starting in May, 2013 Linda Byrne, daughter of Henry Mappleback, Third Officer of the *Daytonian*, provided invaluable background information, photographs, diaries and log books of her father's service aboard the ship. She also provided a letter of recommendation from Captain Egerton to her father, as well as his "sign on" and discharge papers from the *Daytonian* and the SS *Daghestan* on 9 May 1942. Her granddaughter also submitted photographs of the shell which was deeded to Mr. Mappleback from the Bahamas to England after the Nassau "sheller's" death.

There were numerous short articles about the loss of the ship in various papers, the provenance of each not always being clear. An example is an undated piece in the *Gazette* of Indiana, Pennsylvania quoting Capt. J. J. Egerton. Another was entitled "Captain Thinks Sub was Italian," found on newspaperarchive.com. A paper called the *Daily News* of 7 April 1942 is entitled "British Vessel Sunk off U.S. by Italian Sub," and is posted at regiamarina.net as well as Linda Byrne's ancestry.com page for Mr. Mapplebeck. Another blurb reads "Fifty-seven survivors Landed," and is attributed to "CP" wire services and dated March 18, 1942. On fold3.com there is a 715am entry in the *Eastern Sea Frontier Enemy Action Diary*, most likely on the 15th or 16th of March reporting that the Captain reported the sub which sank them was Italian. The *World* of Lawrence, Kansas of March 17 1942 is entitled "Survivors Reach Nassau," and the subtitle is "Third Group to Reach City in Eight Days," (at newspaperarchive.com).

ATHELQUEEN

This chapter would lack its personal resonance without the contributions of Alan Heald, Third Assistant Radio Operator of the Athelqueen, who is alive at the time of writing and supplied numerous email accounts of his experience to the author, as well as phone interviews in England between 2011 and 2013. I owe a great debt of gratitude to Tony Bennett, supporter of the Wyanie Malone Historical Museum, Hope Town, Elbow Cay, Bahamas, for sharing his early research, photographs and the Survivor Statements provided by Tony Cooper in the UK, as well as introducing me to Mr. Heald and local historians in Hope Town, which I visited in 2012. Tony Bennett also was instrumental in erecting an impressive plinth on Elbow Cay to the survivors and dead from the *Athelqueen*, the only known monument to merchant mariners in the Bahamas in World War II. (I met with Tony in Vancouver in 2012). The monument is memorialized on the website "Athel Line Ships, Part of the Acorn Archive, Hearts of Oak," at freepages.family.rootsweb.ancestry.com/~treevecwll/athelqueen2.htm.

Platon Alexiades of Montreal shared the actual War Diary of the *Enrico Tazzoli*, as well as translations, and advice. The primary resource for di Cossato's patrol in *Enrico Tazzoli* was "Un Sommergibile non e Rientrato Alla Base," or "the submarine which did not return to base," published by SB Saggi, Milan, in 1999 – it is a first-hand memoir of crewman Antonio Maronari, in Italian. Translation provided by Google Translate as well as historian Mr. Alexiades. The Survivors Statements were provided by Constandy/Westmoreland. An early source was the Tower Hill Memorial in London, accessed via findagrave.com and lost-at-sea-memorials.com, also the Commonwealth War Graves Commission, cwgc.org/find-a-cemetery.

Constandy dug up the immigration documents for the *Athelqueen* crew which provides specifics of their movements, particularly vessels involved and the crew who stayed behind in hospital. These documents were found in the State Department Archives and most are to or from US Consul John Dye. Dick Coulson and Peter Christie of Nassau, who attended Belmont School during the war as day boys, contributed information regarding the English pupils who braved the U-boat menace to spend the war in Nassau. There were several tangents in this research: The Belmont School students in Nassau whose teachers the *Athelqueen* survivors mingled with (the story was too dense for ultimate inclusion in this narrative), the *Orduna* which carried the students to Nassau, and the mistaken assumption that the Royal Yacht *Albert and Victoria* not the *Content S.* rescued survivors from Abaco. Also there was a lot of research done into Trinity Church as well as the Farrington family who Alan Heald felt were both so helpful to the sailor's convalescence.

There is a commendable image of a model of the Athelqueen under the title "'Athelqueen' Tanker – England – 1928" on flickr.com a flickr.com/photos/28583390@ N07/4691821775/ taken by "SuperSkyline89." There are various articles about the casualty, one of them found in the Charleston, South Carolina *Daily Mail*, of 21 March 1942 subtitled "46 Safe in Bahamas" (the headline is about the Cygnet and reads "U-Boat Blasts Greek Vessel.") The *New York Times* ran an article on March 21, 1942 entitled "U-Boat Sinks Ship as Plane Passes," the second paragraph of which covers the *Athelqueen* loss, as well as the second-to-last paragraph.

The Nassau papers were quite loquacious about the *Athelqueen*, and clearly the survivors endeared themselves to many locals during their sojourn on the island. On March 19th the Nassau *Guardian* declared on page two that "Forty-Six More Survivors Arrive in Nassau," with a sub-title of "Three Drowned While Swimming Ashore from Reef." There is below that a related article about the "IODE Canteen." On March 26, 1942 the Nassau *Guardian* carried a thank-you letter from Captain Roberts under the heading "Acknowledgements." On the 21st of March the same paper thanked an anonymous donor of money for the Athelqueen crew to call home, under the heading "Generosity," both articles appearing on the lower right and partially garbled. Before the first submarine victims landed in March 1942, but well after Tapscott and Widdicombe, victims of a German raider arrived in 1940, the Nassau *Daily Tribune* carried an "Appeal for Sailors Fund," dated February 25th, 1942.

MARCH 16 TO APRIL 6, 1942 – same as for "Summary of Axis Activity" at top.

KOLLSKEGG AND BUSHRANGER

The primary source for this chapter was warsailors.com and the excellent thorough research by Dame Sir Holm Lawson on all Norwegian ships lost in WWII. I am particularly indebted to her for this and the chapter on the *O. A. Knudsen*. The Survivors Statements of the *Koll* and *Kollskegg* detail the rescue by the *Bushranger*, landing in Nassau on 11 April 1942 and subsequent transport to Miami aboard the *Ena K.* on 23 April. Reference to the sinking of the *Koll* is provided at history.navy.mil/fags//fa97-1.htm. Info on the rescue ship *St. Cergue* is provided at swiss-ships.ch/schiffe/st-cergue_005/ Dame Holm Lawson kindly shared her survivor report, from Tony Cooper in the UK, with me in 2009 or so.

The *New York Times* carried an article entitled "Nine-Day Lighter" about a nine-day voyage by Norwegians, saying the culprit was an Italian, not German submarine. The interviewee was Karsten Idzal and the date was 24 April, 1942. The Tower Hill Memorial in the UK has the names of Norman Hunter, Assistant Steward, aged 17, featured from the *Kollskegg*.

The Nassau *Guardian* scooped the story on 11 April, the same day the *Kollskegg* survivors arrived, with a front-page blurb at bottom right entitled "More Survivors Arrive This Afternoon," identifying the Windsor and Lucerne hotels as their domiciles. There is a rare photo of both the Duke and Duchess of Windsor greeting survivors of the *Kollskegg* at the Rozelda Hotel in April, 1942 – the only known photo of the two of them greeting submarine victims in WWII. It is entitled "Survivors Meet Royalty – Survivors of Sunken Ships Keep Duchess Busy," and is dated 23 April 1942, by the *San Antonio Express-News*, Texas, on newspaperarchive.com.

Another article found on newspaperarchive.net is entitled "Norwegian Ship Hit by Torpedo" and is dated April 4th, 1942. A Salt

Lake City Utah paper on 14 April 1942 carried the article "Subs of Axis Sink Nine Allied Vessels" on page 1. The sub-article dated 13 April talks about *Kollskegg* survivors landing in Nassau and begins "NASSAU, Bahamas." A short article unknown paper, date unknown, is entitled "Ship Survivors Land At Nassau" and was put out by the Associated Press on the 13th of April 1942.

In the files of the US State Department Constandy found the immigration papers for the *Kollskegg* officers and crew dated April 14 1942 and signed by the US Consul, John Dye. It includes a detailed crew list of those arrived Nassau, missing in the other lifeboat, and killed. As late as July 15th 1942 there remained in Nassau a crew member from the *Kollskegg*, Harald Haugvik, who left via the *Betty K.* on 17 July 1942, right before the men of the *Potlatch* arrived. Two others are detailed leaving Nassau on 1st July 1942 by a letter from Dye to Francis J. H. Dever, Inspector in charge of Immigration at Miami.

APRIL 7 TO 20, 1942 – same as for "Summary of Axis Activity" at top.
VINELAND

Initial research was greatly aided by a detailed article and matrix entitled "Canadian Merchant Ship Losses of the Second World War, 1939-1945," by Robert C. Fisher, Social Archivist at the National Archives of Canada, revised June 2001 (familyheritage.ca/Articles/ merchant1.html). *Vineland* is cited on pages 5 and 18. Fisher also kindly faxed me a letter from Furness, Withy & Company, Ltd. and the Markland Shipping Company, Ltd. of April 29, 1942 informing the Department of Transport in Ottawa about the loss of the *Vineland*. He also faxed a notice from the British Admiralty reporting the loss of the *Vineland* to Ottawa, Washington DC, Kingston and London on April 28, 1942. Early in the research a site named seawaves.com provided a short history of the *Vineland* and U-154.

The Ellis Island, New York website ellisisland.org provides some passenger history for the *Sapiniero*, *Vineland*'s previous name, in 1922. Uboat.net and wrecksite.eu also provide helpful background details of her loss and location, builders and owners. John Mozolak Jr.'s "New York Ships to Foreign Ports 9.1939 thru 8.1945 cites the *Vineland* four times from 1941 to 1942. Ann Bridges of the University of New Brunswick Libraries, Canada, kindly faxed "The *Vineland* Story," by Captain

Charles W. Copelin, from *The Mersey Quarterly*, pp. 6-7 (date unknown, in the 1980s I believe).

Another source was the book "Running the Gauntlet: Oral History of Canadian Seamen in World War II," by Mike Parker, 1994 (page 122: "Ralph Kelly"). Parker was very helpful to me, particularly as regards Ralph Kelly of the *Vineland*. Bob Emery of the Submariners Association of Canada, West, was helpful with introductions. Commander Fraser M. McKee of the Canadian Nautical Research Society and co-author with Captain Robert A. Darlington of "The Canadian Naval Chronicle, 1939-45: The Successes and Losses of the Canadian Navy in World War Sink All the Shipping There: The Wartime Loss of Canada's Merchant Ships and Fishing Schooners" on his own (Vanwell Publishing Ltd., 2004) was very helpful. He introduced me to the family of Captain Charles Copelin of the Mersey Paper Company. I also reached out to the Maritime Museum of the Atlantic in Nova Scotia. David Smith, who served authors at the New York Public Library on Bryant Park from 1975 to about 2011, helped me to research the *Vineland*.

Correspondence and interviews with John Leefe (interviewed via phone June 8, 2013), Erlin Conrad, Edna Greenwood (nee Williams, daughter of Capt. Ralph Williams) (called June 6, 2013). I interviewed Erlin Conrad on June 16, 2013). From Ms. Greenwood and the family of Erlin Conrad (his daughter Rev. Karen Ohrt), I received a trove of information, including a photograph of the crew on their arrival in Halifax, the exact publisher and date not clear but believed to be from the *Chronicle* in May of 1942. They also sent a letter of protest attesting to the death of Lawrence Hanson and their rescue by the *Emily F. Convey*, notarized by Stanley Jones in Grand Turk. John Leefe provided a sheath of papers between survivors of the *Vineland*, including Hector MacLean and Capt. Williams, and members of the Canadian government, including Colonel H. R. Winters, Member of Parliament, in Ottawa in the mid-late 1940s regarding compensation. Hector A. MacLean also wrote "Markland Shipping Co. Ltd." for the *Mersey Quarterly* which is lavishly illustrated (date unknown). Erlin Conrad and his daughter kindly provided news clippings, photos, and images of his seamen's book. Ms. Greenwood provided several original photographs from her father's and her uncles' collections.

An excellent, detailed article was "The Last Days of the *Vineland*," by A. H. MacLean, (Hector), former Radio Operator of the *Vineland*. It was shared by John Leefe and appeared on pages 19 to 21 of the Summer issue of a *Mersey Quarterly*, date unknown. It has great line drawings as well as photographs. Another article is entitled "Most Survived When Liverpool Ship Was Torpedoed", by Armand F. Wigglesworth in his column "Off the Cuff." John Leefe is a renowned community leader and past politician in the Halifax area, and he shared his article on the loss of the Vineland from the local perspective. It is entitled "A Moment in Time – Surviving the U-154."

In Turks and Caicos my primary sources with Mr. Osvaldo Ariza (interviewed Nov. 9, 2012) and local historian Sherlin Williams, who provided details of the locals' reception of and aid to *Vineland* survivors. Also instrumental in this regards was Georgia Dunn, of the Herriott family whose family provided a home to the *Vineland* officers at their stately home The White House. She kindly cited "Grits, Grunts and Gravy and the Caribbean Sea… Childhood Remembrances of an Island Home, Its History, Our Family, Our Lives," by Barbara Durham Armstrong, 2007. She also cites an interview she had with her cousin Rosalie Harriott in 2011, as well as a thesis by Anthony Gregory in 1970 entitled "The Turks Island Salt Trade and Industry: An Historical Economic Geography," for the University of California at Berkeley. A wonderful article on the family history is "Raking for Heritage in the Salt Islands," with illustrations, by Dr. Edward Harris, Director of the National Museum at Dockyard, Bermuda. This was published by the *Royal Gazette* in Bermuda on 23 March 2013. There was a good aerial photo of Balfour Town and the White House, Salt Cay at visittci.com/salt-cay/about.

APRIL 21 – 30, 1942– same as for "Summary of Axis Activity" at top.

FEDERAL AND IVAL

For this short chapter only a few resources were utilized. Primarily the Survivor Statements. Also the Nassau *Tribune* article on page one of the 14 May 1942 edition. And for the Cuban perspective, Maximino Gomez' thorough blog, u-boatsenelmarcaribe.blogspot.com. He is also the author of the book "U-boats del III Reich en Cuba" (Edit.

Entrelíneas, Madrid 2009). KTB or attack report provided by Jerry Mason, uboatarchive.net. Maps provided by Robert Pratt.
MAY 1 TO 17, 1942 – same as for "Summary of Axis Activity" at top.
FAUNA

Much biographical detail about Capt. Jacob den Heyer (Jacobus den Heijer) as well as his wife, height, weight, other ships he worked on and addresses before during and after the war, were found at ancestry.com. Dr. A. P. van Vliet at the Dutch Ministry of Defense provided useful information on both the *Fauna* and Capt. Den Heyer. Volkert van Reesema and Lukas Kolff were very helpful providing introductions at Het Scheepvaartsmueum, or the Ship History Museum in Amsterdam. Among those who assisted me there were Marja Goud, Dr. Willem Bijleveld and Dr. Henk Dessens. The museum has a databank of thousands of ships, with history, loss, and even sometimes photographs.

Other resources about the loss of the *Fauna* generally were found at uboat.ne (Krech), wrecksite.eu (location), and the Survivors Statements and crew list. Capt. Jerry Mason of uboatarchive.net provided the sub attack report, or KTB. John Mozolak Jr.'s massive compendium verified that on 6 May the *Fauna* left New York. Marianne Kaajan of the Dutch National Archives was helpful.

Alain Wattiez in Turks and Caicos was helpful with local questions. Kendal Butler verified information on the schooner *Firefly*. Sherlin Williams provided an extensive report on first hand witnesses to the landing of *Fauna* survivors. Georgia Dunn also provided family lore about survivors, particularly of the *Vineland*, who stayed with her relatives at the White House. Ms. Dunn very kindly shared excerpts from her relative's book "Grits, Grunts and Gravy and the Caribbean Sea…. Childhood Remembrances of an Island Home, Its History, Our Family, Our Lives," by Barbara Durham Armstrong, 2007.

An article entitled "I Remember When" by Andre Garneau and Embry Rucker in "The Times of the Islands," in the summer of 2007 is a biopic of patriarch Hilly Ewing going back to the war days (timespub.tc/2007/06/362). Sherlin Williams unearthed in the Turks and Caicos National Archives the letter from the Secretary of the Dutch Central Transport Workers Union in New York to the Commissioner of the Turks Islands, dated 24 July 1942, as well as identifying who the commissioner was.

In newspaperarchive.com a news article in the *Morning Herald* entitled "Freighter *Fauna* Sunk" clarified that it was the *Fauna*, not the *Flora* sunk off the Bahamas (from an AP story May 28 1942). The *Joplin Globe* of Missouri ran a piece from the AP on 28 May 1942 entitled "Dutch Freighter Sunk by Submarine" misnaming the ship the *Flora*. The Ellis Island website has the *Fauna* listed among the emigrant vessels on its site claiming that five passengers were carried on two voyages, in 1915 and 1920 respectively (ellisisland.org). On November 9, 2012 I interviewed Mr. Osvaldo Ariza, aged 79 at the time. Though not on the islands at the time he was a font of background information and was very generous with introductions, explaining who was who and who was on the islands at the time. Arendnet.com provides a photo of the Fauna in wartime gray as well as useful technical details in Dutch.

MAY 18 TO JUNE 27, 1942 – same as for "Summary of Axis Activity" at top.

WILFRIED REICHMANN AND U-153

Fort the emblem of U-153 see "Unknown Emblems," *U-Boot im Focus*, Edition 6/2010, "U-153 – Into Combat with a Battleaxe Emblem on its Conning Tower," learned about from u-historia.com, originally the image was found mille-sabords.com. Details of Osterwein, where Reichmann hailed from, are from freepages.genealogy.rootsweb.ancestry.com. Information on the Ruth, also sunk by U-153 was drawn from uboat.net as well as the form at warsailors.com. Relevant pages from the *Eastern Sea Frontier Diary* were accessed from uboatarchive.net, as was the reconstructed KTB or war diary of the submarine. Crew lists and ranks and dates of birth were found on ubootwaffe.net/crews.

Extensive details about Wilfried Reichmann's early career were graciously provided by Peter E. Monte of the U-Boat Museum in Cuxhaven, Germany, also known as the Deutsches U-Boot Museum-Archiv. Juergen Haak of the Bundeswehr, an *Oberstabbootsmann* in the German Navy assisted, as did the Deutsche Dienstelle (WASt) in Berlin. Biographical details on Reichmann also came from u-boote.fr/Reichmann.htm, a French site. Clay Blair's Chapter "The U-Boat War Against the Americas" in "The Hunters" was instrumental in determining how U-153 met its end (p.632), as well as summarizing its patrol (p.631).

POTLATCH

This research covers three three-ring binders and involved travel to NARA in DC, all of the relevant collections in the Virginia and DC area (by Mike Constandy of Westmoreland Research), digging in the Bahamas National Archives by the author and Capt. Paul Aranha and the Archivist, personal visit to survivor Jake Jatho outside St. Louis, Missouri, and an extensive tour of witnesses in Pinefield and Hard Hill Acklins by Mari Anderson and her husband Fritz Damler. Authors of the book "Plunge" and residents of Crooked Island for 15 years, this couple went above and beyond by providing interviews and photos of first-hand witnesses to the landing of *Potlatch* survivors on Acklins, as well as photos of the gravesite where Parson was buried.

The material on the Duchess' reception came from two unpublished memoirs – one in the Maryland Historical Society and the other from family of the Hardcastle-Taylors in San Diego, California. In no particular order, resources included: "SS *Potlatch*," a diary of Voyage #6 by Capt. John J. Lapoint, 10 pages single spaced: the ultimate first-hand narrative of adventure, filled with individual names such as Commissioner H. V. Wiley, Lt. Bilgore, and Capt. Collie as well as references to the Prince George Hotel. Written by Capt. Lapoint probably in late 1942 for the Weyerhaeuser Archives, and used by them in their selective/censored account for employees in wartime entitled "Nothing Sighted Today." Donated by Tristan Rhys "Russ" Hayden of Gig Harbor Washington State, whose father, a long-serving mariner with Weyerhaeuser, was given it by Capt. John D. Knox, Operations Manager in order to prompt him to provide his own memories of wartime service on Dec. 11, 1953. Also provided with "Duchess Greets Survivors" photo (Associated Press) and "Live Adrift is Related by Sailor," unattributed.

Photos of historic hotels and old buildings in Nassau from oldbahamas.com and an article entitled "I'se a Man – Political Awakening and the 1942 Riot in the Bahamas," by Nona Martin and Virgil Henry Storr, 2006. Henry Jensen's family Sara Jensen and Rich and Eileen Hansen provided his story and photographs via email. I learned that Jensen and Earl Schenck wrote a manuscript about Jensen's ordeal on the *Potlatch*, and I was given the contract for the book, which apparently was never completed. "Survivor of Torpedoed Ship, Navy Adviser Slate Talks." National Maritime Union's NMU "Pilot": "Survivors of the *Potlatch* present beefs and greetings...." page 14, 21 Aug. 1942, from Jensen as well as SUNY Maritime College and Kheel collections.

Other articles researched include "Merchant Marine Sailors Cited Following Enemy Attacks on Their Vessels," "Forty-Seven Men Survive 32 Days of Sailing in Lifeboat," Lubbock, TX, Thurs., Aug. 6, 1942, "Too Late for One: Saga of 32 Days Adrift on Lifeboat Told by 47 Men," "47 Survivors Tell Stirring Sea Tale," *Waterloo Daily*, Aug. 6, 1942, "Seamen Finally Reach Port After Given False Report," (AP), "Two July Sinkings Disclosed by Navy," *New York Times*, Aug. 6, 1942, *Potlatch* overdue notice, 30 June 1942, from S.O.I. Jamaica 1121R/30 to Admty. C. in C. A.W.I. N.S.H.Q. B.A.D., fold3.com, in NARA, *Potlatch* sunk notice in *ESF Enemy Action and Distress Diary*, Aug. 5, 1942, Serial #913, fold3.com, NARA, War Diary details of shield on U-153 in Admiralty report, fold3.com/image/#302122196, 18 Aug. 1942, report that Marine Corps Air Station at St. Thomas reported *Potlatch* survivors landed at St. Kitts, July 26, 1942, fold3.com/image/#267813920, details of "Special Assignment" convoy including *Potlatch, Empire Sydney, PL Esterd, Michigan* and *Empire March* left Cape Henry escorted by plane from NAS (NOB) dated 21 June 1942 from HQ Fifth Naval District at fold3.com/image/#267941099.

Contact with grandchildren of Capt. Lapoint (John M., Charles E. and Michael B. Lapoint) was established through Ancestry.com (his wife Adaline M.) and various search sites such as whitepages.com and the *Baltimore Sun* archive. April 25, 1942 letter from US Department of State authorizing Lt. (jg) Aaron L. Bilgore USNR to serve as US Naval Liaison Officer at Nassau, April 25, 1942, FA 740.00118 European War 1939/1276, from NARA/Constandy. Letter discontinuing appointment from Navy Department to Nassau, Serial 3794616 dated Nov. 18, 1942, signed H. C. Train, NARA/Constandy. Another letter on 27 Oct. 1942 confirms Bilgore's transfer to O.N.I, in the US. A letter dated 7 Nov. 1942 cites Boatswain John E.

Montgomery, USNR, Serial 4062516, dated 7 Nov., 1942, NARA/Constandy.

Lapoint's death in June 1966 in Richmond, Staten Island, and birth date of 29 Feb. 1896 in Havestraw, both in New York State, are verified at Ancestry.com. Likewise his service on the *Pomona*, *Potlatch*, *Port Paix*, and *Oregonian*. His census reports as well as Registration Card and evidence that in April, 1916 he was married to Marion (nee Huntley) of Southampton, England and signed his name "Lapointe" with an "e" are also on Ancestry.com, "Certificate of Registration of American Citizen," 68406, with letter of support from his aunt Adelaide of Fall River, Massachusetts. His occupation was listed as "seafaring carpenter," address 16 Liverpool Street, Newport, Monmouthshire, no children. He was 19 years old.

Several articles about Lapoint appear in the online archives of the *Baltimore Sun*, namely: "Merchant Seamen Have no Picnic, Either," "Baltimore Skipper Pilots Crew 32 Days in Open Boat," "Baltimore Skipper Loses Ship to Sub," "Captain Describes Suffering During 32 Days in Lifeboat," "Hero Given Double Honor." Other articles citing the *Potlatch* in the general press include "Four More Ships Bagged by Subs: Sinkings to 412," "Duchess Greets U. S. Ship Survivors," *The Gettysburg Times*, 11 Aug. 1942. Costandy unearthed first-had witness reports of the sinking by US Merchant Marine Academy Cadets Nathan J. Kaplan and Michael James Carbotti, both entitled "Torpedoing of S/S *Potlatch*" dated on or after 28 August 1942.

C. "Bud" Shortridge researched a very good illustrated article about *Potlatch* and other Weyerhaeuser ships on his site. Ms. Toni Horodysky of the US Merchant Marine Academy Museum provided leads from the Capt. Arthur Moore collection about the booklet "Nothing Sighted Today," published by Weyerhaeuser. The Bahamas Red Cross Society kindly allowed me access to their archives. The log of the *Tysa* is from Survivor Statements.

An immense trove of original articles (including the "Ripley's *Believe it or Not*" piece and "Nothing Sighted Today" was provided by Ms. Megan Moholt, Weyerhaueser Archives. These are cited under RG#5 Weyerhaeuser Steamship Company, Box 1 Oversize Scrapbook 1942-1945. For information on the *Anglo-Canadian*, also sunk by U-153 see "The Nitrate Boats," by David Burrell, information provided by Ted

Finch of the Mariners Archives on archiver.rootsweb.ancestry.com and also the CWGC Tower Hill Memorial. The text of the Merchant Mariners Medal citation for Capt. Lapoint is listed at www.archive.is/ookw.

Original sources include a letter from Jake Jatho, Naval Gunner, to the author dated 10 November 2012, as well as phone interviews with Estil Dempsey Ruggles and his wife, on 26 April, 2011, October 9th, 2012 and other dates. Pamela Carbotti Watters, daughter, and Robin Watters, son-in-law to Michael James Carbotti spoke, met and emailed with me several times, starting March 28, 2012 up to October 2013, as did Carbotti's sons Michael and Martin. Arnette Chisholm, The Rev. Dr. Hervis Bain, designer of the Bahamian Coat of Arms, and the Honorable A. Loftus Roker and Bernard Ferguson connected me with sources on Acklins Island. A detailed article by Deck Engineer Alfonso Delatorre entitled "The Crew That Wouldn't Die," appeared in *Action for Men* magazine, September, 1964, Vol. 8, Number 5, pages 28-29 and 63-65. Henry Jensen dictated a two-part article entitled "Torpedoed," to US Navy publicist Earl Schenck which was published in *Liberty* magazine, the second installment appearing in the June 12 (page 17) and 19, 1943 editions, pages 22-24 and page 40.

Voyage movement cards, including one erroneously saying that the survivors were landed in Anguilla then St. Kitts and taken by SS *Nitro Pollux* to Norfolk, later corrected, were provided by Constandy. These documents include a chart and routing instructions as well as the cargo manifest for previous voyages. They were in RG or Record Group 38, stack area 370, row 46, compartment 34, Ship Movement Cards Box 410, A1 348. The Summary of Statements by Survivors were dated 14 August 1942 and received by the Commander in Chief, US Fleet on 17 August 1942.

Regarding the *Potlatch's* previous voyages under the identity *Narcissus* there some 100 citations from the 1920s and 1930s in the database newspaperarchive.com. An example are the "Marine Reports" under "Shipping News" in the *New York Tribune*, dated 20 February 1922. In the *Galveston Daily News* of Texas there are numerous citations and advertisements for the *Narcissus* under the heading Sgitcovich Lines, an example being November 21, 1922. The official Ellis Island website says that *Narcissus* made an immigrant run from Libau (Liepaja,

Latvia) to New York in 1922. Mike Holdoway and Tony Cooper of
convoyweb.co.uk were helpful in determining what convoy, if any,
Potlatch sailed from New York in company with (it was a small convoy
escorted from the air only as far as the Delaware Capes). Uboat.net was,
as always, the primary resource for learning the essential facts about the
ship loss and earlier name/s.

Information on the Weyerhaeuser Corporation and the Potlatch
Corporation came in part from fundinguniverse.com. John Mozolak,
who created a massive and accurate database of tens of thousands of ship
movements out of New York in WWII was very helpful in tracking the
beginnings of *Potlatch's* final voyage. *Potlatch's* cargo of "2,000 tons of
Tin   plate"   was   valued   at   "$27,600,000"   at
treasurenet.com/forums/shipwrecks/142141-list-treasure-wrecks.html.
The definition of a potlatch comes from searchdictionaries.com.
wrecksite.eu/wreck.aspx?170411 provides details of the location of the
Potlatch as well as a ship image and the history of the ship and its
builders. A memo in the *Eastern Sea Frontier War Diary* of 29 July 1942
cites the "POTLASH …survivors ashore at St. Kitts."

There were dozens of articles on newspaperarchive.com detailing
human interest stories and bio-data on individual survivors of the
Potlatch. The most detailed of these appeared as a serialization and
derived from "Nothing Sighted Today" by Captain Lapoint. It is entitled
"The Sinking of the S.S. *Potlatch*," in five parts, by Dorothy McDowell,
starting May 11, 1973. It was published in the *Aiken Standard* of South
Carolina under the column "Yesteryear." There are photographs of Lt.
Dorcey Lybrand in the *Aiken Standard* of Sept. 8, 1970 ("Lybrand to
Direct Council Campaign") as well as in the *Aiken Standard Review* of
August 28, 1942, under "Lieut. Lybrand Tells of Experiences When His
Boat Was Torpedoed," when Lybrand was able to return home briefly
following his ordeal. There was an earlier story entitled "Aiken Torpedo
Victim Tells of Harrowing Lifeboat Trip" in the same paper on August
12, 1942. An obituary on Lybrand appears in the *Aiken Standard* of July
21, 1977.

The *Rocky Mount Sunday Telegram* of Oct. 9, 1955 relates the
experiences, with a photograph, of Thomas Marion King under the
heading "Local Resident Recounts Hectic Month in Lifeboat," by King
as told to James Pike. A biopic of gunner Sol Goodman appears in the

Petersburg Index of Virginia on the 22nd of June 1958 under the title "Thirsty Jackasses Helped 'Save' Hopewell Politician." Journalist G. Sam Piatt wrote an illuminating piece about gunner Estil Dempsey Ruggles in the *Portsmouth Daily Times* (Kentucky), on January 29, 2011. It is entitled "Ruggles Adrift 32 Days after Ship Torpedoed." Another resource for Cadets Carbotti and Kaplan was the book "In Peace and War: A History of the US Merchant Marine Academy at Kings Point," by Jeffrey L. Cruikshank and Chloe G. Kline, pages 101-102.

The US Merchant Marine Academy also published an article during the war by Cadet-Midshipman D. W. Heiney entitled "A Lifeboat, Adventure, The Bahamas, the Duchess" with an etching of both cadets. Kaplan's son, Nathan Stark, helped verify biographical details about his father. The University of Pittsburgh Medical School published a detailed obituary of Nathan J. Stark (formerly Kaplan) in December, 2002. Without access to a single complete list of the crew, finding details of Potlatch was sailors was difficult, however a biography of the US merchant marine was helpful, as was a letter sent from Terese Straton, Commandant of the Bahamas Red Cross, to Michael J. Carbotti in the 1960's. In it she lists the names of the survivors from her notes, bringing the list to more than 30 individuals out of 47.

A map in "Inagua – An Island Sojourn," by Gilbert Klingel, Lyons and Burford, 1940 / 1997, identifies the peninsula where the Potlatch survivors landed as Christophe Point (inaguabook.com/photo-galleries/color-slides). Amanda Graham, a genealogist from Nassau and Connecticut, helped trace the family history of Terese Straton, Commandant of the Red Cross in WWII. Telegrams between US Consul John Dye and the Secretary of State were kindly shared by Dr. Robert Browning, USCG Historian, and later accessed at NARA by Constandy. An article about Lapoint's medal appears in the *New York World Telegram*, 20 March 1943 under the title "Merchant marine Officer Awarded Posthumous Medal, Honor Three Others for Heroic Acts in Ship Sinkings."

The Bahamas Department of Archives' Ms. T. A. Delaney provided detailed information on the Lucerne and Rozelda hotels, where the officers, gunners, and men of the Potlatch stayed, and "Reminiscing – Memories of Old Nassau" but Valeria Mosely Moss as well as "Reminiscing II – Photographs of Old Nassau," by Ronald G.

Lightbourn, provide exemplary photographs of the hotels and buildings of Nassau during and before WWII. Mrs. Straton's letter tells of the Victoria Hotel Annex and Capt. Lapoint's detailed log of "Voyage #6" tells of his staying with Lybrand at the Prince George Hotel.

Although reporting that "the press in Nassau is severely restricted as to what it may publish about survivors arriving in this island," the Nassau *Daily Tribune* and the Nassau *Guardian* did manage to publish a few articles about the *Potlatch* survivors, including an August 6, 1942 piece in the *Tribune* from the *Miami Herald* under "Nassau News via Miami." On August 1, 1942 the Nassau *Guardian* carried a blub under the title "Forty-Seven Survivors Arrive Here" on page 4. In the Nassau *Tribune* of July 10, 1968, an article by Nancy Savage entitled "Torpedoed Michael Searches for Lost Weekend" details Cadet Michael Carbotti's quest for news about he and his compatriots 26 years before, when he returned with his wife as a tourist to Nassau.

Jake Jatho sent articles entitled "Survivors tell of Starving 15 Days at Sea," "Jake L. Jathos Hear from Son, J. L. Jr.," and "Jake Jatho, Waif of the Seas, Home to Tell Story." An entry in the *Eastern Sea Frontier War Diary* for 24 July 1942 notes the arrival of *Tysa* men in St. Kitts on 9th July 1942 (fold3.com). Patrizia Sione of the Kheel Center for Labor Management Documentation and Archives at Cornell University kindly printed the article on *Potlatch* survivors arriving in New York, originally published in the National Maritime Union *Pilot*.

Ambassador Charles Freeman kindly provided great detail about the Royal Victoria Hotel under his parents' ownership in the post-war years, as well as his father's management roles before purchasing the hotel. Barbara Nico (nee Aranha) assisted with queries as to the Lucerne Hotel, Savoy Theater, etc., as was author Ronald G. Lightbourn, whose relatives owned the Lucerne. Information on Joan Straton and her brother was available from the "Old Scholars of Queen's College Who Have Served in the Forces," published by the Nassau *Guardian*. The background of the Rozelda Hotel was provided by the founder's son, Craig Symonette. The author flew to St. Louis, Missouri to interview Jake Jatho on April 20, 2013. This visit was greatly facilitated by his wife Velma and daughters Becky and Nancy.

There are numerous news articles in August 1942 referring vaguely due to censorship to the *Potlatch*. These can be found at newspaperarchive.com and include titles "Sinkings of Four Vessels Revealed," "Survivors Reach Nassau," and "Four Sinkings are Announced, Total Losses Climb to 412." A more detailed account was published in *The Lowell Sun* of Massachusetts on Dec. 21st, 1942 as "Merchant Marine Heroes: 32 Homeric Days in Life boat – Most of Them Without Food, Water," by Inez Robb. Her source at the National Maritime Union offices in New York was a crewman named "Matte." An articles about Ruggles' war bond drive is entitled "Alaskan Addresses Rally: Greer Garson Due Friday," in the *Charleston Daily Mail*, West Virginia, 3 Sept. 1942. The Mason City Iowa *Globe Gazette* of 12 Sept. 1942 had an article about Curtiss Liscomb returning home from the *Potlatch*. Another about James A. Acton of Moxham, Pennsylvania appears in the *Lock Haven Express* of 13 August, 1942, as "Cheats Death Twice: Escaping Axis Sub Torpedoeings at Sea." A similar story was carried by the *Indiana Evening Gazette* on 18 Aug. 1942.

The *Bismark Tribune* of North Dakota on 6 August 1942 published an article citing David Parson entitled "Too Late for One: Saga of 32 Days Adrift in Lifeboat Told by 47 Men," quoting Allen Holmes Jackson. Another article in the same vein (circulated by the International News Service) was entitled "Saved After Being Adrift 32 Days," and another 'Sinkings of Four Vessels Revealed." On August 16, 1942 a paper called the *Times Sunday Bulletin* ran a piece from the Associated Press entitled "Wild Jackasses Lead to Water." The *Sheboygan (Wis.) Press* of August 6 1942 wrote of "Survivors of Attack Adrift for 32 Days," also from the AP. A typical story from the *Globe* was titled "47 Men Spend 32 Days in Lifeboat," from the AP on August 5, 1942.

The *New York Times* on August 4, 1942 carried a citation to the *Potlatch* under "4 More Ships Lost in U-Boat Raids." They also carried a piece about Lapoint's Merchant Mariner's Medal under "Merchant Marine Decorates Heroes" on March 21, 1943. On the same day the *New York Herald Tribune* carried an article entitled "Seamen Heroes in Nazi Attacks Receive Medals." Another article is entitled "Two July Sinkings Disclosed by Navy" on August 6, 1942.

MARION CARSTAIRS AND *VERGEMERE IV*

The best resource on the life of Marion Carstairs generally is "The Queen of Whale Cay," by Kate Summerscale, Viking New York, 1998. There is a review entitled "No Ordinary Joe" by Carolyn T. Hughes on May 17, 1998 in the *New York Times Book Review*. There is a detailed summary of her life on Wikipedia.org. Betty Carstairs appears in the press during her tenure in the Bahamas in WWII mostly for her nautical exploits in rescuing people by boat.

A well-illustrated biopic appears as "New Adventure for Astonishing 'Queen Betty'" in *The American Weekly*, published 30 December 1945 (it also appeared in the *San Antonio Light* of Texas on the same date). A good piece about her visit to New York in 1941 appears under "New York Day by Day," by Charles Driscoll in the *Painesville Telegraph* of October 23, 1941 on page 4 as well as The *Burlington Daily Times News* of October 23, 1941.

Another is entitled "Carstairs Helps 47 Who Drifted Months," on newspaperarchive.com. On January 21, 1938 the Jamaican *Kingston Gleaner* featured a derisive article entitled "Betty Carstairs Subjects Desert Her – Raid Island Empire." In the *San Antonio Light* of July 13, 1940 appears a parody of both Carstairs and the Duke of Windsor under the heading "Brighter Side," By Damon Runyon.

The Odgen Standard Examiner of January 16, 1938 has a very detailed well illustrated multi-page article about Carstairs entitled "The 'Paradise' the Heiress Crusoe Found." The subtitle is "Even way off on an Island, Betty Carstairs Can't Help Being Spectacular." There are images of Carstairs "inspecting her Whale Cay army" at allposters.com. *The Gazette* of Montreal on 6 August 1942 has a piece on page 16 headlined "47 Sail 32 days in a Lifeboat," in which they devote a paragraph to Carstairs. *The Schenectady Gazette*, on the same day carried the AP story under "Adrift 32 Days, U-Boat Victims Reach Safety." *The Gettysburg Times* of 11 August 1942 has the photo entitled "Duchess Greets U.S. Ship Survivors" of the *Potlatch* men with Carstairs in the background, but her niece Kim Aranha does not believe it is actually Carstairs.

Capt. Paul and Mrs. Kim Aranha, niece of Ms. Carstairs, were instrumental in providing images and biographical detail on her, as well as correcting errors in the manuscript. Capt. Aranha also shared an excerpt from page 45 of "The Ultimate Guide to Motor Boats" about Carstairs. He also shared and article from the Nassau *Tribune* of January 21, 1943 entitled "Miss Carstairs Puts Yacht in War Service," about the yacht *Sonia*. The *Abeline Reporter* of June 4, 1944 details Carstair's deployment of a four-vessel cargo fleet under the title "Ex-Speedboat Queen Uses Luxurious Yacht as Fleet Flagship," by E. V. W. Jones, Miami Beach, Florida.

JUNE 28 TO AUGUST 10, 1942 – same as for "Summary of Axis Activity" at top.

VIVIAN P. SMITH

The main source of information on the ownership and Caribbean history of the *Vivian P. Smith* was Mr. Will Johnson, patriarch and historian of Saba. He wrote three pieces of great interest: "Memories of a Father 'The Sailor's Sailor,'" Special Saba Features, sabatourism.com/ scenes_wj45.html+schooner+albert+f.+paul, "Saban Lore: Tales From My Grandmother's Pipe" CaribSeek Books, 1989 and "Saban Lore: Seeking fame and fortune on other shores." On Uboat.net and indeed in Mr. Johnson's book the owners of the *Vivian P. Smith* were listed as Uldaric Hassell of Bridgetown, Barbados, however the ownership at the time of her loss has devolved to Kenneth Johnsons of the same port. Ms. Erica Luke Hassell, head of a shipping firm in Barbados, was instrumental in both clarifying her family's ownership stake in various vessels such as the sister ship *Frances W. Smith*, as well as introducing me to Will Johnson, who provided photos of the vessels. David Williams, Chief Archivist of the Barbados Department of Archives was helpful in pointing me to various publications.

Robert C. Fisher, Archivist in the Social Archives of the Library of Archives, Canada, very kindly provided the original Certificate of Registration of the *Vivian P. Smith* as well as details of her early, Canadian ownership from 1915 up until 1927. The A&C Society, or Archives & Collections Society of Picton, Ontario, provides a detailed history of vessels build by Smith and Rhuland Limited at aandc.org. Ted Finch provided some help with the World Ship Society's Starke / Schell Registers (worldshiposociety.org/5565.html).

Attempts to obtain information from governmental sources and the national museum in the Turks and Caicos were complicated first by damaging hurricanes and secondly by budget cuts as the islands experienced political upheaval in the 2009-2012 time-frame. I was able to place advertisements seeking information on the *Vivian P. Smith* in both Turks & Caicos as well as Barbados newspapers, however neither ad led to direct leads. It was not until I enlisted the help of local historian Sherlin Williams that substantial progress was made in the Turks and Caicos. The Survivors Statements were very useful as was the KTB or attack report shared kindly by Capt. Jerry Mason of uboatarchive.net and translated by Prof. Stephen. The reference to donkeys being exported from the islands is from "Turks Island Landfall" by H. E. Sadler, thanks to Sherlin Williams for making the connection to the *Vivian P. Smith*, which is the only vessel which left the Turks and Caicos laden and was subsequently sunk by a German submarine in the region. The reference to the crew nicknamed "Song Bird" is also from Sherlin Williams' research on the ground, which I commissioned, including inter-island travel and interviews.

AUGUST 11, 1942 TO SEPTEMBER 6, 1944 – same as for "Summary of Axis Activity" at top.

CONCLUSION: SUMMARY OF ALLIED ACTIVITY
Gudmundur Helgason and Rainer Kolbicz, www.uboat.net, 2011, Kenneth Wynn, *U-boat Operations of the Second World War*, Clay Blair, *Hitler's U-boat War*, *Eastern Sea Frontier's Enemy Action Diary* on uboatarchive.net, *Axis Submarine Success of World War Two* by Jürgen Rohwer, *U-Boat Operations of the Second World War*, by Wynn. Rohwer's *Chronology of the War at Sea*. The series *Nortaships Flate*, or Norwegian Ship Fleet, Captain Arthur Moore's *A Careless Word, a Needless Sinking*, and Roger W. Jordan's *The World's Merchant Fleets, 1939*

SELECT BIBLIOGRAPHY

Over 300 books were consulted. For other titles see chapter notes.

Bloch, Michael, "The Duke of Windsor's War," Weidenfeld & Nicolson, London, UK, 1982

Blair, Clay, "Hitler's U-Boat War: The Hunted, 1942-1945," Random House, New York, 1998

Busch, Rainer, Roll, Hans-Joachim Röll and Brooks, Geoffrey, "German U-Boat Commanders of World War II: A Biographical Dictionary," Naval Institute Press, Annapolis, MD, 1999

Craton, Michael, "A History of the Bahamas," San Salvador Press, Waterloo, Ontario, 1987

Cressman, Robert J., "The Official Chronology of the U.S. Navy in World War II," Naval Historical Center, Contemporary History Branch, Washington DC, 1999

Deans, Ralph, Managing Editor, "Bahamas Handbook," Etienne DePuch Jr. Publications, Ltd., Nassau, Bahamas 2007, 2008 (various years, cited specifically)

Gannon, Michael, "Operation Drumbeat," Harper Perennial, New York, NY, 1991

HarperCollins, "Atlas of the Second World War," Borders Press, Ann Arbor, MI, 1999

Hickam, Hiram H., Jr., "Torpedo Junction: The U-boat War off America's East Coast, 1942" Naval Institute Press, Annapolis 1996

Högel, Georg, "U-Boat Emblems of World War II 1939 – 1945," Schiffer Military History, Atlglen, PA, 1999

Jordan, Roger W., "The World's Merchant Fleets 1939," Naval Institute Press, Annapolis, MD, 1999

Kelshall, Gaylord, "The U-boat War in the Caribbean," Naval Institute Press, Annapolis, MD, 1988, 1994 (Kelshall has corresponded with this author)

Kurowski, Franz, "Knight's Cross Holders of the U-Boat Service," Schiffer Military/Aviation History, Atglen, PA, 1995

Lindbaek, Lise and Solum, Nora O., "Norway's New Saga of the Sea," Exposition Press, new York, NY, 1969

Morison, Samuel Eliot

- "History of United States Naval Operations in World War II, vol. 1,

- "The Battle of the Atlantic, September 1939-May 1943," Boston, 1948,

- "History of United States Naval Operations in World War II, vol. 1, The Atlantic Battle Won, September 1943-May 1945," Boston, 1948,

- "The Two Ocean War," Little, Brown & Co., Boston, 1963

Miller, Nathan, "The War at Sea," Scribner, New York, 1995

Niestlé, Axel, "German U-Boat Losses During World War II," Frontline Books, London, 2014

Noli, Jean, "The Admiral's Wolf Pack," Doubleday& Co., Garden City NY 1974

Office of Naval Intelligence, Post-Mortem Reports, http://www.uboatarchive.net/U-527PostMortem.htm

Platt, Owen, "The Royal Governor.....and The Duchess: The Duke and Duchess of Windsor in The Bahamas 1940-1945," iUniverse, 2003

Rohwer, Jürgen, "Axis Submarine Successes of World War Two: German, Italian and Japanese Submarine Successes, 1939-1945" Naval Institute Press, Annapolis, 1999

Roskill, Capt. Stephen Wentworth, "The War at Sea," Three Volumes, 1954-1961

Russell, Joe, "The Last Schoonerman – The Remarkable Life of Captain Lou Kenedy," The Nautical Publishing Company, Far Horizons Media Co., NetPV, Inc. Rockledge Florida, 2006

Spector, Ronald H., "At War At Sea," Scribner, NY, 1995

Saunders, Gail D. (Ph.D), Editor, "Journal of the Bahamas Historical Society," Nassau, Bahamas, October 2006

Simpson, Wallis, Duchess of Windsor, "The Heart Has its Reasons," David McKay, Inc., 1956

Stigloe, John R., "Lifeboat," University of Charlottesville Press, 2003

Stern, Robert C., "U-Boats in Action," illustrated by Don Greer, Squadron/signal publications, Inc. 1977, Carrollton, Texas

Suhren, Teddy, with Brustat-Naval, "Ace of Aces, Memoirs of a U-Boat Rebel," Chatham Publishing, London, 2006

Summerscale, Kate, "The Queen of Whale Cay," Penguin Books, London, UK, 1997

Vause, Jordan, "Wolf, U-Boat Commanders in World War II," Naval Institute Press, Annapolis, MD, 1990

Werner, Herbert A., "Iron Coffins – A Personal Account of the German U-Boat Battles of World War II," DeCapo Press, Cambridge, MA, 1969

ACKNOWLEDGEMENTS

There are half a dozen stellar researchers and friends who went above and beyond in providing assistance. Among the professionals are Mike Constandy of Westmoreland Research, US Coast Guard Historian Dr. Robert Browning, Sherlin Williams in the Turks and Caicos, and the staff of the Norwegian National Archives. On a more personal level my work has had three overriding mentors: Capt. Jerry Mason of uboatarchive.net has never failed to immediately send KTBs via email, Dame Siri Holm Lawson (warsailors.com) for Norwegian ships, Rainer Kolbicz (uboat.net) for U-boats, Captain Paul Aranha in Nassau, Peter Monte at the U-boat Archive in Germany, Platon Alexiades in Montreal for Italian submarines, and Roman Hruby, a volunteer editor, proof-reader and an amateur historian in Ottawa who put in hundreds of hours on this manuscript to help bring the original 1,500 pages of it under control.

Thanks to my Agent, Alan Morell, who sold my book to Brick Tower Press and Publisher John Colby Jr., without whom this book would not exist in its present form. Thanks to J. Revell Carr for generously sharing his time on the foreword. I am afraid that the hundreds of others who volunteered their time can only be listed by name, Gudmundur Helgason, Dr. Axel Niestlé, Christiano D'Adamo, Patricial O'Neal, and Amanda Graham included. Fellow authors Michael Gannon, Nathaniel Philbrick, Mike Parker, Farley Mowat, Michael C. Bernette, Fraser McKee, Bob Darlington, Matt McCleery, Robert Kurson, James P. Duffy, and many more have been highly encouraging and supportive. Others include Jim and Anne Lawlor of the Bahamas Historical Society, Basil Goulandris, Pericles Maillis, Roger Jones, Bill Bardelmier, Dr. Gail Saunders in Nassau.

Many of the following individuals are cited in the chapter notes. Dr. Howard at the State University of New York Maritime College, Andy Chase at Eaglebrook, Dr. George Billy at the US Merchant

Marine Academy, Captain Ivan Elroy Hurlstone's son and namesake Ivan Hurlstone , Rebecca Hatton, David Stark, Megan Moholt, Archivists at the Weyerhauser Company and Martin, Michael and Pam Carbotti and Rear Admiral Robin Watters.

Thanks to Tony Bennett, Alan Heald, G. Sam Piatt, Estil Dempsey Ruggles, Dr. Tom Ruthfus, and Jack Gray, Esq. My employers at the Connecticut Maritime Association, Marine Money, TradeWinds, and McAllister Towing have been extremely understanding and supportive of this project. In particular, I would like to thank Lorraine Parsons, Jim Lawrence, Lee Denslow, and Capt. Brian McAllister. Joe Cheung assisted with layout. In Norway, Bård Tiegland and Kristian O. Bringedal were helpful at background research. Sten Kittelsen and his father were a huge help in Larvik, Norway. Oivind Lorentzen took an active interest in this. Petter Syse was kind enough to photograph and research Olaus Johansen's grave on a visit to Tromso. Ken Dunn, Marcus Mitchell, Ray D'Arville of Overseas Salvage Northern Bahamas, Michael Holdoway and Robert Fisher of the Canadian National Archives. In New England Kevin Rea, Rich Schlegel, and Landfall Navigation.

On Abaco David Ralphs, Patrick J. Bethel, Dale Hill, David Bethel and the staff of the Abaco National Park were very helpful as was Rev. Carl Campbell. Bradley Roberts of the *Abaconian* published excerpts of this research, as did Orjan Lindroth of the Schooner Bay development, for which I owe them both a debt of thanks. Larry A. Smith and Neil E. Sealey at Media Enterprises Bahamas, Ralph Deans, Paul Thayer and Etienne Dupuch Jr. at Dupuch Publications and the *Bahamas Handbook* were highly supportive. Their copy editor Paola Alvino did a superb and thorough job.

Persons who have contributed invaluable subject-matter expertise include the Hon. John Leefe, Jordan Haughn, David Knowles, Becky Jatho, Dr. Ralph of the Abaco Forum, Nancy Albury, Fernando Ruben Pontilillo Benitez, Sandy Eastabrook, Tammie Chisholm, Capt. Alex and Dominique Koutsakis, Andrew Lewis, Andrew Ridall, Craig Symonette, Neil Cobbett at The National Archives, UK, Athena Gray, Capt./Prof. Austin Becker, Graham Weatherford, Barry W. Plunkett, Elizabeth Berilla and Shafeek Fazal at SUNY Maritime College Library, Marja Goud, Henk Dessens, and Willem Bijeveld of Het

Scheepvaartmuseum, Billy McGee, Capt. Billy Black, Allison Ball, Bonnie Schubert, Ambassador Charles Clifton Freeman, Arnette and Julius Chisholm, Rev. Dr. Hervis Bain, Chris Voorhees, C. A. Lloyd, Susan Brook, Brian McDermott, Brandon Russell, Brian and Lisa Blank, Dominic Corbin, Dr. Carlton Mills, Dr. Maarten van Bourgondiën, Charles Bash, Cindy Falgoust, Cindy Szabo, Claire Cabot, Kelly Kimpton, John Rousmaniere, Joan Lightbourn, Kari Elisabeth Myhre, Capt. Justin Sands, Kendal Butler, Kelly Gibson, Linda Byrne, and Lisa Thompson.

Also helpful were Vanessa Cameron, Lindsay Totino and Rae Derke of the New York Yacht Club, Scott C. Steward of the New England Historic Genealogical Society, Margarita Aguilar, granddaughter of a crew member of the Manzanillo, Maria Govan, Nicola Hepburn, Mark Gaulding, Maximino Gomez Alvarez, Irina Meyman, Mike Lightbourn, Mike Niemi, Michael and Gloria Hardcastle-Taylor, Joe Radigan, Nigel Pope, Norma Bulman, Norman Reiach, Norm Byers, Olav Vaagen, Geir Forde, Patricia Weatherford, Paul Campbell, Paul Harmon, Mrs. Ypapanti Alexiou, Peter Swanson, Scott Price, Edward Malone, Kimberly King-Burns, R. W. "Bob' O'Hara, Roger E. Nixon, Rolf Voss, Ron Lightbourn, Sara Elizabeth Jensen, Charles and Daniel Thompson, Dr. Simon Fowler, Hilde Schistad of the Knutsen OAS Shipping AS and *Haugesund Sjømanns- og Skipperforening* (ship's officers association) in Haugesund.

Prof. Stephen B. Aranha for translations from German, Stephen Roberts, Terrill and John McDermid, archivists at the Taminment Library and Robert F. Wagner Labor Archives, New York, Teresa Kaufman, Bill Keefe, Troy Cooper, Patrina Moore, *Turks and Caicos Sun*, Tore Strømøy, Will Johnson in Barbados, Wickes Helmboldt, Capt. Warren Brown, Volkert and Nickel van Reesema, Lukas Kolff, Vincent O'Hara, Tim Colton, Dr. Theron P. Snell, Ray Merriam, Rebekah Bethel, Kenneth T. Wilhite, Jr., Kent and Petra Post, Karl Koeningsbauer, Johny Clarke, Jordan P. Biscardo of the Seafarers International Union, John Mozolak, John and Sofia Wiberg and James and Lynette Wiberg, John Palmieri at the Herreshoff Museum, Jack Dillon at *Woodenboat*, Joan Thompson, and Mrs. Delaney at the Bahamas National Archives.

Other suppliers of critical information of varying sizes include Barbara Nico, Alain Wattiez, Harvard University Archives, Pusey Library, Barbara Merdith, Edna (nee Williams) Greenwood, Betty (nee Williams) Kennedy, Linda Rafuse, Barbara Cooke Meredith, Bonnie Phillips, Jan-Einar Bringedal, C. Peter Chen, Chris Preovolos, Damon Talbot, Dave Gale in Abaco, Hans Dirk Steffen, Don Humphreys, Doreen Johansen, Earl McMillen III of woodenyachts.com, Susan L. Goraczkowski, Maureen Houston, Hjørdis Bondevik, The Norwegian Maritime Museum, Sharon Jacker, Jackie McKenna, James Lightbourn, Jerome Lee, John Knowles of R. H. Curry agency in Nassau, Jeorg Friese, Joni McRae, Jostein Hauge, Kendall Williamson, Patrizia Sione at the Kheel Center for Labor Management, Cornell, Kristian Olav Bringedal, Kurt C. Haselbalch of the Francis Russel Hart Collection, MIT, Leandra Esfakis, Irene Miramontes, Linda Dianto, of the National Lighthouse Museum, Louisa Watrous, Mystic Seaport, Magnus Heimvik, and Ivar Vaage.

Others include Michele Robinson, Alan Murray, Gillian Watson, Michelle Badger, Ned Roseberry, Per-Åge Nygård, Peter Formanek, Richard du Moulin, Peter and James Drakos, Rita Cramer Giovannini, Scott Heywood, Tor Christian Bringedal, Tracy Minsky, Wanda Christensen, Mari Anderson and Fritz Damler, Mathew Schulte, Jim Pennypecker and Astrid M. Drew of the Steamship Historical Society of America, Alneka Russell and Ana Lord at the Nassau *Guardian*, Eileen Dupuch Carron and Martin Biddle at the Nassau *Tribune*, Andrea P. Major of the Bahamas Minitry of Antiquities, Andrew Melick at the Port of Miami, Capt. Andrew Sinclair in Bermuda, Ann Bridges, T. K. Nenninger at NARA, Arne Eide, Norway, Bill Barker, Bill Fentress, Patrick M. Bickers, Bob Price, David L. Boutros, Bradley Albury, Michel Brideau, National Library and Archives Canada, Bud Shortridge, Candace Clifford, Cari Koellmer, Cathrine Astad, Charles E. Murphy, Esq., John Rosseland, Chris Maxey, Christopher McNally, Claas Gräfe, Clark Davenport of GeoForensics, Laura Cody, Anne Crowne, N. McEachan of the UK Hydrographic Office, Darius Williams, Dave and Martha Dings, David Reade.

I am grateful for their input to David Walker, Don Bresnan, Doug Camp, Clarissa J. Dean, Deirdre O'Regan, Dennis Fanucchi, Diane DeWitt, Ambassador John W. Dinkelman, Don MacDonald, Don

Horton, Donovan Hohn, Derek Donovan, Doug Sulipa, Elena
Emanuela Prandoni, Elena Sokolova of RTR TV, Russia, Curt Lawson,
NMNA, NAS Pensacola, FL, Emma Alexander, Emma Penick, Eric
Charbit, Patsy Bolling (nee Kenedy), Dr. Bob Arnot for introducing me
to Alan Morell, Erica Luke (nee Hassell), Eric Hassell & Son Ltd.
Barbados, Ernst Garmann, Sean and Sarah Farrington, Fina Johnson,
Jean-Michel Forsas, Frederick Assar, George Cruickshank, Gordon
Lomer, Grace Friary, Consul Gus Constantakis, Gustaf Wachtmeister,
Esq., Halvard Olafsen, Norsk Maritimt Museums Venner, Han van
Blanken, Dr. John B. Hattendorf, US Naval War College, Liv Asta
Ødegaard, Herdis Lien, and Terje Carlsen, Archives and Government
of Svalbard Norway, Karin Hill, National Museum of the United States
Navy, James Allen Knechtmann, Naval History and Heritage
Command, Kevin Leonard, The Leonard Group, Inc., Scott Hoge, Ivar
S.A. Isaksen, Jack Burgess, Jad Davenport, Curt Curtiss, Jane Haase,
Trinity Mirror PLC, Janis Blower, Shields Gazette, Jay Picotte of the
International Yacht Restoration School, Jeanie Russell, Prof. Jean-Paul
Rodrigue, Jennifer O'Neill of Dupuch Publications, Jim Kerr, journalist,
Nassau, Janis Jorgensen, Josef Hermanns, Ketherine Flyne, Ike Taylor,
Ken Atherton, Sharon Cummings, Kim Aranha, Roger Kreiger, Laura
Bugden, Dr. Mitch Leventhal.

For help with the maps, Robert Pratt, Tim Lewis, and Dr. Adrian
Webb, United Kingdom Hydrographic Office. Also Rebecca L. Litton,
Louis Cuevas Hall, Mackenzie Gregory, Lynda Silver, Nova Scotia
Museum Library, Manfredi of Harbour Island, Eleuthera, Maribeth
Bielinski, Mystic Museum Collections, Mark McShane, Jürgen Haak,
German Navy, Merdith and John Gray, Michael Laurie, Michelle
Bullard, Michael A. Klonaris, Robert and Lisa Myers, Nancy Albury,
Dr. William H. Thiesen, Nathaniel Patch of NARA for his patience
and persistence, Jerry Osterberg, Pablo Achurra, Panama, Patricia Leigh-
Wood, Patricia Watkins, Patrick Osborn, Paul Hurlston, Paul Schue,
Peter J. Roberts, Capt. Peter Squicciarini, Judy Randall, Raymond J.
Burke, Esq., Renee Holden, Richard (Rick) Lowe, Richard Farrington,
Richard Klattenberg, Richard Miller, Rik F. van Hemmen, Schuyler
Bogel, Rasmus A. Christensen, National Archives of Norway, Alan
Shard, Vancouver, Simon Trewin, and Mark Waldie.

I would also like to thank Trevor Bevens and Jessie Hurwitz of FleetWeather, Reuben Goossens, Stan Norcom, Stacey Bobo, Dr. Steven Smith, Tanya McDonald, Memorial University, Sant John's, Newfoundland, Ted Finch, Thomas J. Hawley, Tina Fenimore, Turks & Caicos, Tito "Froggy" Baldwin, Tom Hawkins, Dr. Thomas Hedberg, Tore Bjerkek, Bernard Collie, Robert Hurlstone, Dani Janer Åkerberg, Valerio Giannini, Toni Horodysky, Wes Wheeler, Willa France, Geoffrey Minsky, Capt. William Shephard, Greg and Michelle Sweeney, Sean and Emily Meehan, Patrick Cosgrove and Larry Stein, David and Ashley Skatoff and Zachary Cutler. Mari Anderson and her husband Fritz Damler performed yoeman's duty – and miracles – by trekking to and around Hard Hill Acklins for a day to gather, photograph, record and document the arrival of *Potlatch* survivors there from first-hand witnesses.

Winifred Gray was kind enough to tolerate many hours of work during holidays at her home. My parents ensured an abiding interest in books by replacing our TV with them when I was six. My wife Alexandra deserves more credit than anyone for tolerating the increasing reams of papers and books which stacked up in the basement and office, the frequent all-nighters, the quirky working relationships struck up by this topic, and the visits to the Archives in Nassau, London and DC when we were supposed to be on holiday. I must thank our son Felix, owner of at least one toy submarine, for his help with my research – his sketches and drawings of the routes of several U-boat patrols were, as the children's books say, just like Daddy's.

ABOUT THE AUTHOR

Eric Wiberg grew up in the Bahamas, the son of the Swedish Consul-General there. A licensed maritime lawyer, his thesis for a Master's Degree in Marine Affairs was published as *Tanker Disasters*. For three years he commercially operated tankers in Singapore. Over 25 years he has sailed on 100 vessels, most of them sailboats, for 75,000 miles, including voyages across the Atlantic and Pacific and over 30 ocean passages to or from Bermuda. He has published four books, the latest being *Round the World in the Wrong Season*. A graduate of Boston College, he studied at Harris Manchester College, Oxford, and in Lisbon. Employed in the shipping industry in New York City, he lives with his wife and son in Westport, Connecticut.

Sonia 241, 242, 351

Southbound 197, 258, 264, 279

Sparrow 186

Stakesby 158

Standella 264, 287, 300, 304, 310

Stangarth 116, 154, 290, 300, 302, 310

Stanvac Pelambang 293

Stede Bonnett 146

Sumatra 152

Suriname 158, 274

Talisman 293

Telamon 101, 292

Texan 115, 300, 301, 310

The Queen 146, 350, 355

The Sisters 191

Theodor Riedel 41

Thomas McKean 219, 221, 257, 262, 292, 293, 303, 310

Tillie Lykes 176

Titania Tonsberg 84

Tonsbergsfjord 95, 101, 292, 300, 301, 310

Torny 182

Tower Grange 275

Tredinnick 154, 302, 310

Triton 196, 201, 303, 310

Troisdoc 196

Tysa 219, 220, 221, 254, 255, 257, 292, 293, 300, 303, 310, 320, 344, 348

U-103 183

U-106 183

U-107 197, 201, 281, 303

U-108 12, 178, 185, 300, 302

U-109 178, 184, 302

U-117 28

U-1228 36

U-123 22, 31, 155, 162, 300, 302

U-124 24, 154

U-125 34, 178, 201, 303

U-126 22, 33, 95, 115, 300, 301

U-128 7, 21, 31, 34, 35, 37, 38, 39, 40, 41, 42, 43, 44, 51, 52, 53, 54, 55, 57, 58, 59, 60, 61, 62, 64, 86, 87, 133, 288, 300, 301, 320, 322, 323

U-129 12, 13, 22, 31, 165, 199, 200, 262, 277, 278, 282, 283, 300, 303, 304

U-130 162, 302

U-134 21, 259, 280, 281, 285

U-153 8, 21, 200, 203, 204, 205, 206, 207, 211, 212, 215, 216, 255, 256, 300, 303, 304, 320, 341, 342, 343, 344

U-154 21, 22, 154, 165, 169, 170, 175, 176, 201, 275, 283, 300, 302, 320, 337, 339

U-155 276, 302

U-156 32, 200, 202, 300, 301, 303

U-157 199, 264, 303

U-158 198, 206, 257, 263, 300, 303

U-159 199, 279, 303

U-161 34, 258, 260, 304

U-163 273, 274

U-164 273

U-166 259, 260, 293, 304

U-171 34, 260

U-172 22, 199, 303

U-173 261

U-176 264, 278, 304

U-185 12, 276, 277, 300, 304

U-193 282

U-201 177, 302

U-203 21, 201, 257, 300, 303

U-214 275, 282

U-217 273, 274

U-25 36, 206

U-30 204

150, 159, 233, 238, 247, 249, 251, 252,
330, 333, 335, 337, 347
Edmondson, Leslie 123, 126
Egerton, John James, Capt. 118, 119, 120,
124, 127, 292, 333, 334
Eide, Arne 57, 60
Emmermann, Carl 22, 199, 303
Engelmann, Kurt-Eduard 273
Ericksons, W. 247
Esfakis, Christopher 111, 113
Eve, Ben 43, 188, 195
Ewing, Arthur 191, 340
Ewing, Doris 191
Ewing, Ralph A., Capt. 191
Ewing, William, Capt. 191
Falangas, Antonios 105, 113, 330
Fechner, Otto 273
Felsch, Wolfgang 203, 217
Fickling, J. G., USN Ensign 61
Firth, David W. 130
Flagler, Henry 249
Folkers, Ulrich 178, 201, 303
Forbest, Constable 178, 263
Forster, Ludwig 21, 178, 263
Foster, John 21, 65, 66, 67, 88, 130
Fraternale, Athos 116, 132, 154, 257, 300,
301, 302, 303
Freshwater, Phillip Roland 130
Friedrich, Rudolf 21, 24, 29, 128, 199, 206,
272, 274, 277, 282, 300, 301, 302, 303,
304
Friestad, Andreas 56
Furst, Walter, Capt. 180
Gale, David 146, 317
Gelhaus, Harald 161, 197, 201, 303
Gemeiner, Gerth 283

George V, King 90, 113
George, VI, King 90
Gibbs, H. E. Lieutenant 87
Giessler, Hans-Heinrich 29, 274
Gill, William George 50
Gillies, Bill 146
Giudice, Ugo 21, 300, 301
Goodman, Solomon 249, 347
Gräf, Ulrich 102, 175, 183, 202, 303, 365
Grand, Felicia 31, 44, 67, 86, 134, 171, 172,
173, 174, 178, 179, 182, 183, 188, 192,
193, 194, 195, 198, 200, 249, 257, 259,
267, 269, 270, 276, 282, 287, 288, 295,
297, 315, 316, 325, 338
Greenwood, Edna 167, 317, 338, 339
Grønning, Einar 159, 160
Guggenberger, Friedrich 277
Gundersen, Arthur 158
Hance, Percy L. 68
Hanson, J. Lawrence 169, 170, 338
Hardegen, Reinhard 29, 31, 155, 162, 300,
302
Harris, Edward, PhD. 172, 317, 339
Hårstad, Barleif å 48
Hart, Robert W., Capt. 177
Hartenstein, Werner 32, 200, 202, 300,
301, 303
Hassell, Eric 266, 351
Hassell, Frank, Capt.
Haugvik, Harald 159, 160, 337
Hawes, John, "Father Jerome" 110
Heald, Alan B. 93, 130, 131, 144, 146, 148,
149, 151, 293, 317, 334, 335
Heape, W. L. 71
Hearse, James Read 130
Henderson, E. D., USN Ensign 117, 252

For sales, editorial information, subsidiary rights information
or a catalog, please write or phone or e-mail
Brick Tower Press
Manhanset House
Shelter Island Hts., NY, 11965-0342 US
Sales: 1-800-68-BRICK
Tel: 212-427-7139
www.BrickTowerPress.com
email: bricktower@aol.com

www.IngramContent.com

For sales in the UK and Europe please contact our distributor,
Gazelle Book Services
Falcon House, Queens Square
Lancaster, LA1 1RN, UK
Tel: (01524) 68765 Fax: (01524) 63232
stef@gazellebooks.co.uk